You may be reading the WRONG WAY!!

IT'S TRUE: In keeping with the original Japanese comic format, this book reads from right to left—so action, sound effects and word balloons are completely reversed. This preserves the orientation of the original artwork—plus, it's fun! Check out the diagram shown here to get the hang of things, and then turn to the other side of the book to get started!

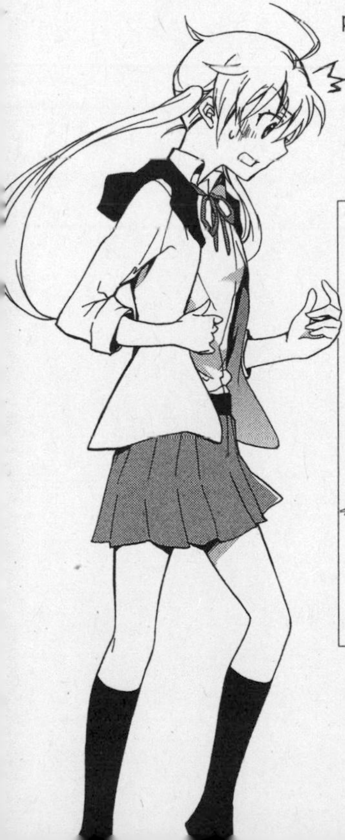

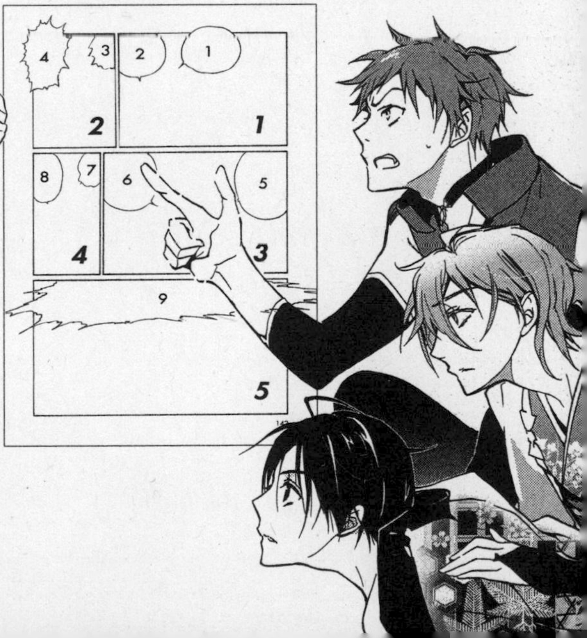

1
2
3
4
1
2
5
6
7
8
3
4
9
5

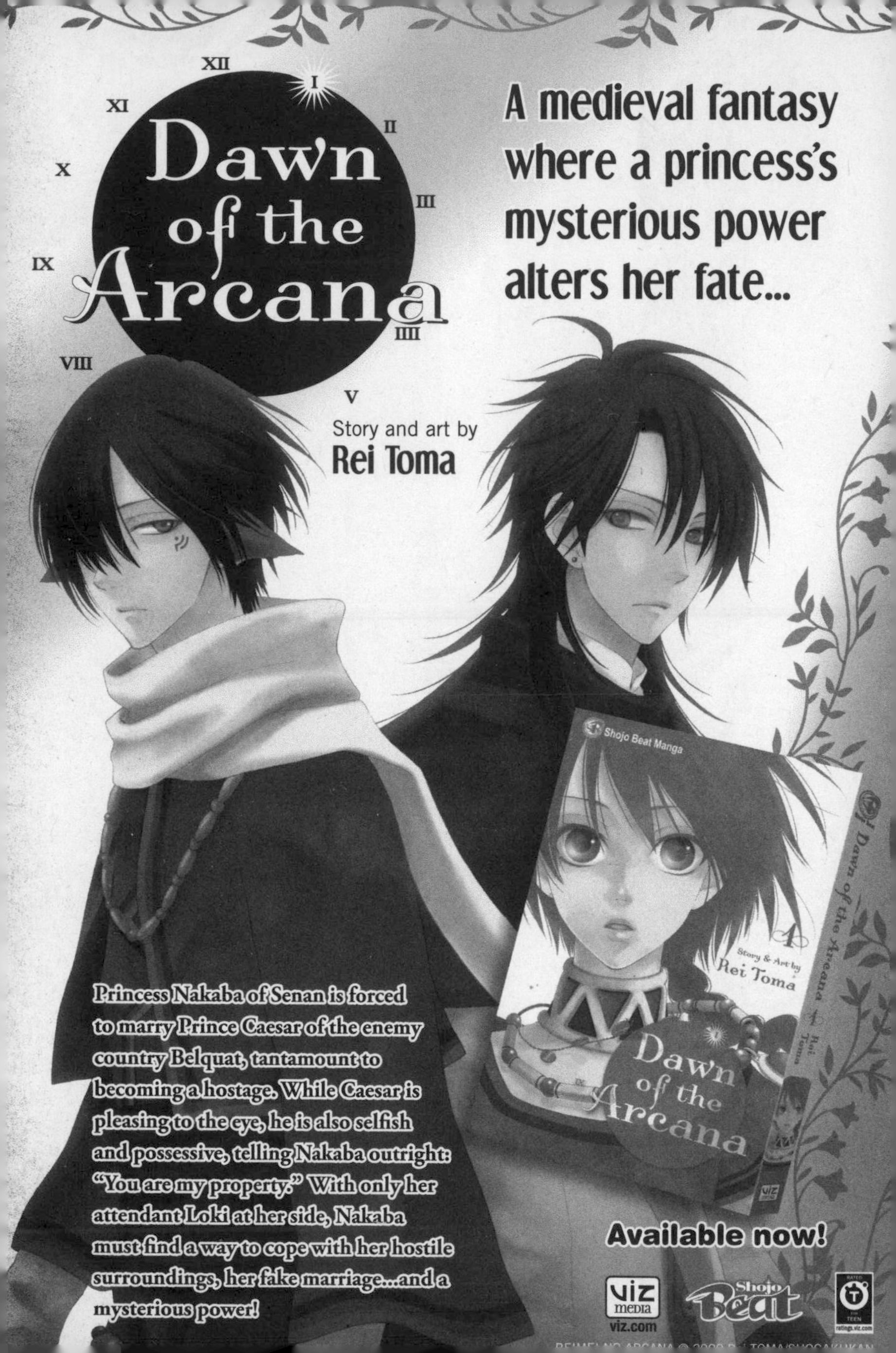
Dawn of the Arcana
A medieval fantasy where a princess's mysterious power alters her fate...
Story and art by
Rei Toma
Shojo Beat Manga
Dawn of the Arcana
1
Story & Art by
Rei Toma
Princess Nakaba of Senan is forced to marry Prince Caesar of the enemy country Belquat, tantamount to becoming a hostage. While Caesar is pleasing to the eye, he is also selfish and possessive, telling Nakaba outright: "You are my property." With only her attendant Loki at her side, Nakaba must find a way to cope with her hostile surroundings, her fake marriage...and a mysterious power!
Available now!
viz media
viz.com
Shojo Beat
RATED T TEEN
ratings.viz.com

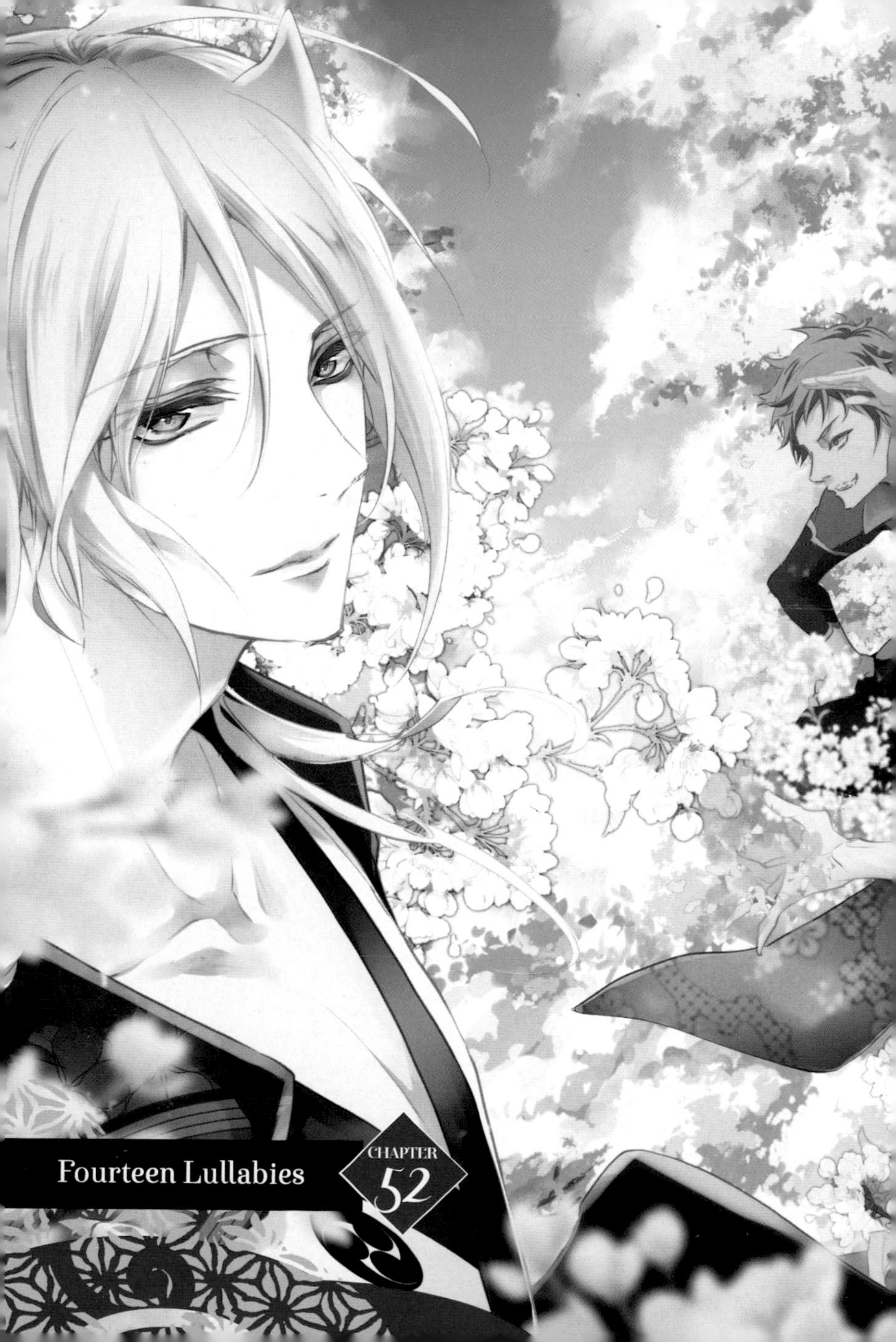
Fourteen Lullabies
CHAPTER
52

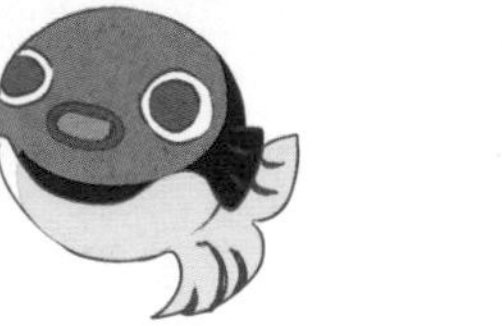

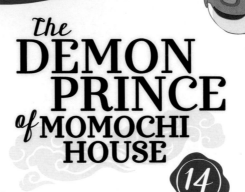

The DEMON PRINCE of MOMOCHI HOUSE

14

Contents

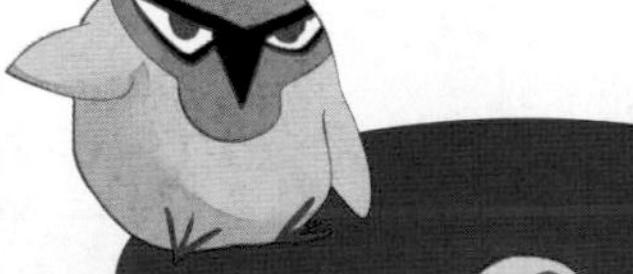

The Mysterious Residents of Momochi House

Aoi Nanamori

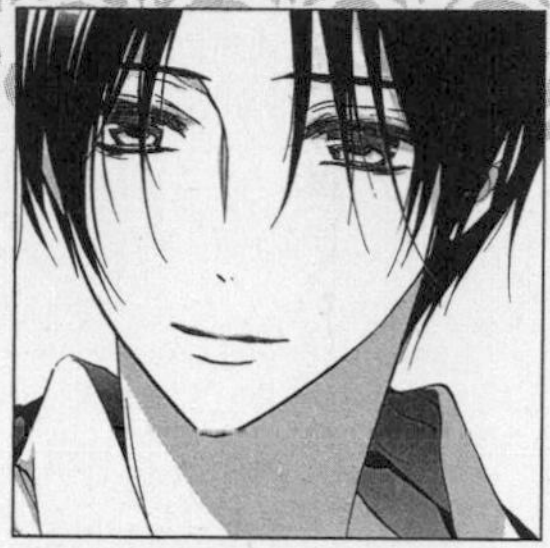

When he was 7 years old, he wandered into Momochi House and was chosen as the Omamori-sama. He transforms into a nue to perform his duties, but it seems this role was meant for Himari.

Omamori-sama (Nue)

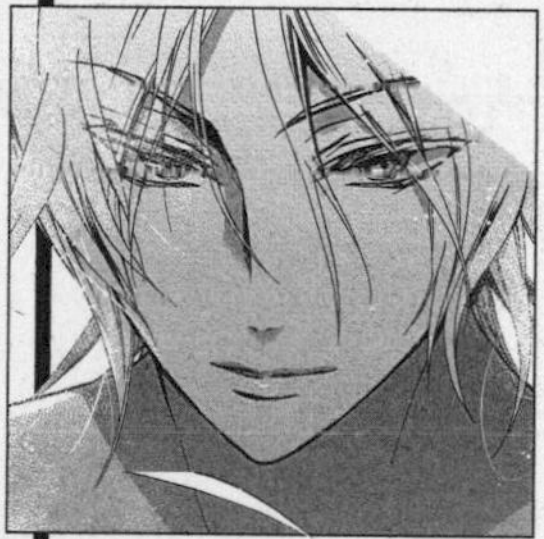

An ayakashi, or demon, with the ears of a cat, the wings of a bird, and the tail of a fox. As the Omamori-sama, the nue protects Momochi House and eliminates demons who make their way in from the spiritual realm.

Ise

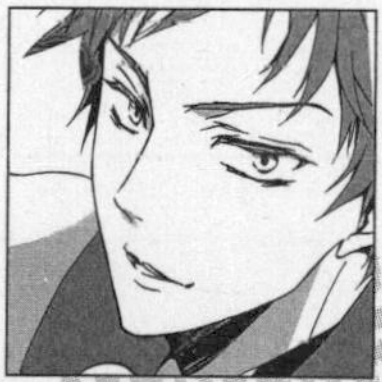

One of Omamori-sama's shikigami. He's an orangutan.

Yukari

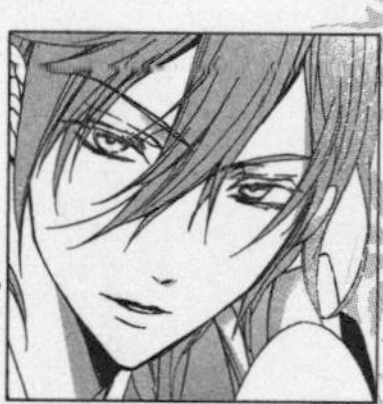

One of Omamori-sama's shikigami. He's a water serpent.

Lesser Yokai

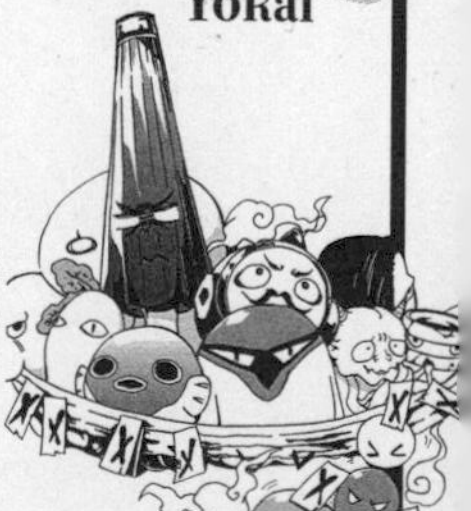

Himari Momochi

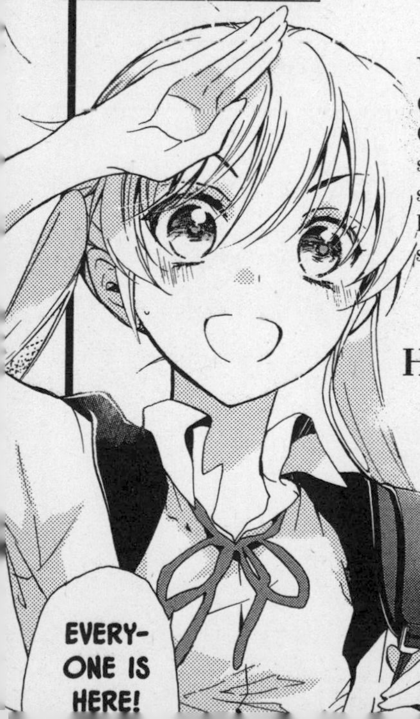
EVERY-ONE IS HERE!

A 16-year-old orphan who, according to a certain will, has inherited Momochi House. As rightful owner, she has the ability to expel beings from the house.

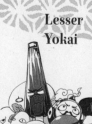

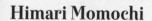

Momochi House: Story Thus Far

After being removed from her body by one of Kasha's pranks, Himari's soul is forced out of Momochi House, but she is able to make it back with the help of Mr. Nachi. Unfortunately there isn't much time to celebrate: Kasha reveals himself and kidnaps Aoi right before her eyes. Himari tries to get Yukari and Ise to help her, but Kasha's spell has placed everyone in the house into a deep sleep. Hakka, however, has avoided the spell because he was in a pot. Himari manages to coax him into helping her break into Kasha's mansion in the spiritual realm. The two of them retrieve Aoi's stolen soul, and Aoi answers Himari's desperate plea to divulge his past with Kasha. Meanwhile, the staff of Kasha's mansion are making preparations for a wedding, but just who is getting married?!

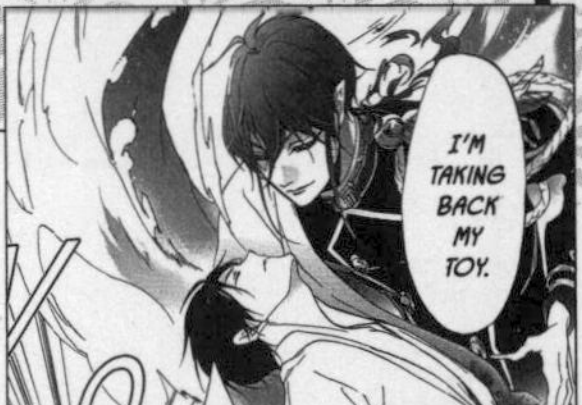
I'M TAKING BACK MY TOY.
AOI!

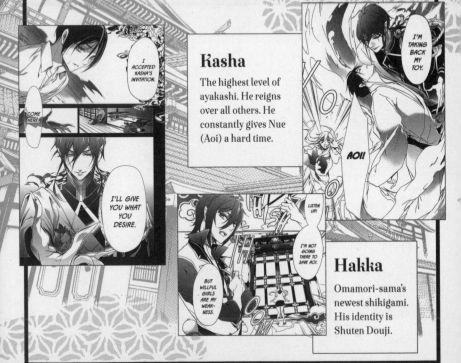

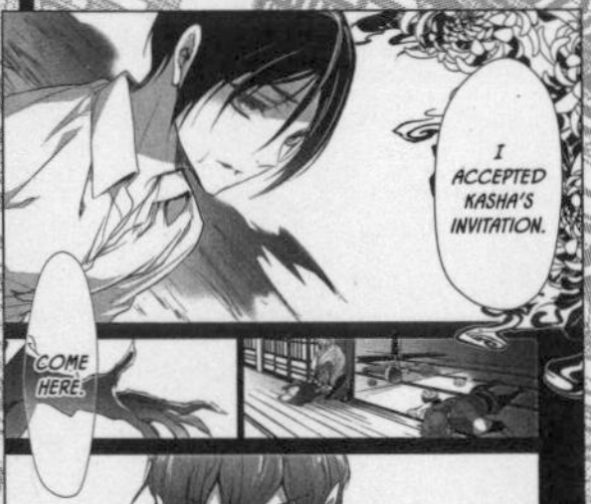
I ACCEPTED KASHA'S INVITATION.
COME HERE.
I'LL GIVE YOU WHAT YOU DESIRE.

Kasha

The highest level of ayakashi. He reigns over all others. He constantly gives Nue (Aoi) a hard time.

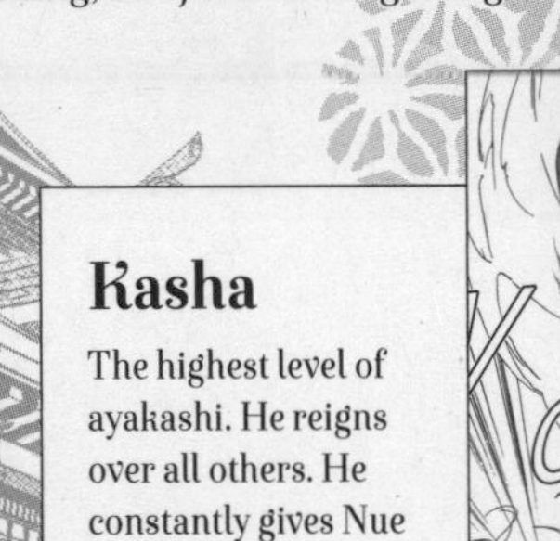
LISTEN UP!
I'M NOT GOING THERE TO SAVE AOI.
BUT WILLFUL GIRLS ARE MY WEAK-NESS.

Hakka

Omamori-sama's newest shikigami. His identity is Shuten Douji.

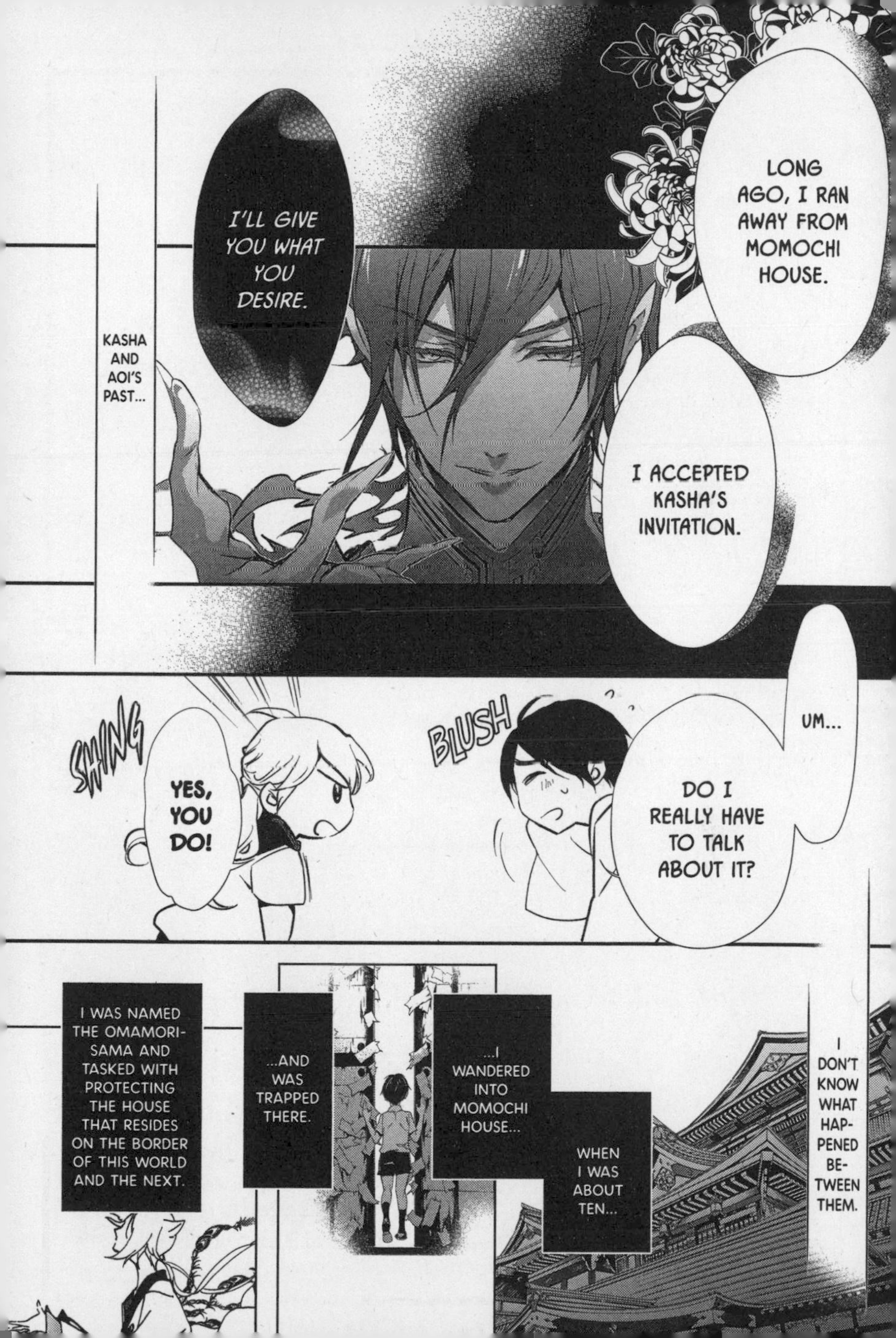
LONG AGO, I RAN AWAY FROM MOMOCHI HOUSE.
I'LL GIVE YOU WHAT YOU DESIRE.
I ACCEPTED KASHA'S INVITATION.
KASHA AND AOI'S PAST...
UM...
DO I REALLY HAVE TO TALK ABOUT IT?
BLUSH
SHING
YES, YOU DO!
I DON'T KNOW WHAT HAP-PENED BE-TWEEN THEM.
WHEN I WAS ABOUT TEN...
...I WANDERED INTO MOMOCHI HOUSE...
...AND WAS TRAPPED THERE.
I WAS NAMED THE OMAMORI-SAMA AND TASKED WITH PROTECTING THE HOUSE THAT RESIDES ON THE BORDER OF THIS WORLD AND THE NEXT.

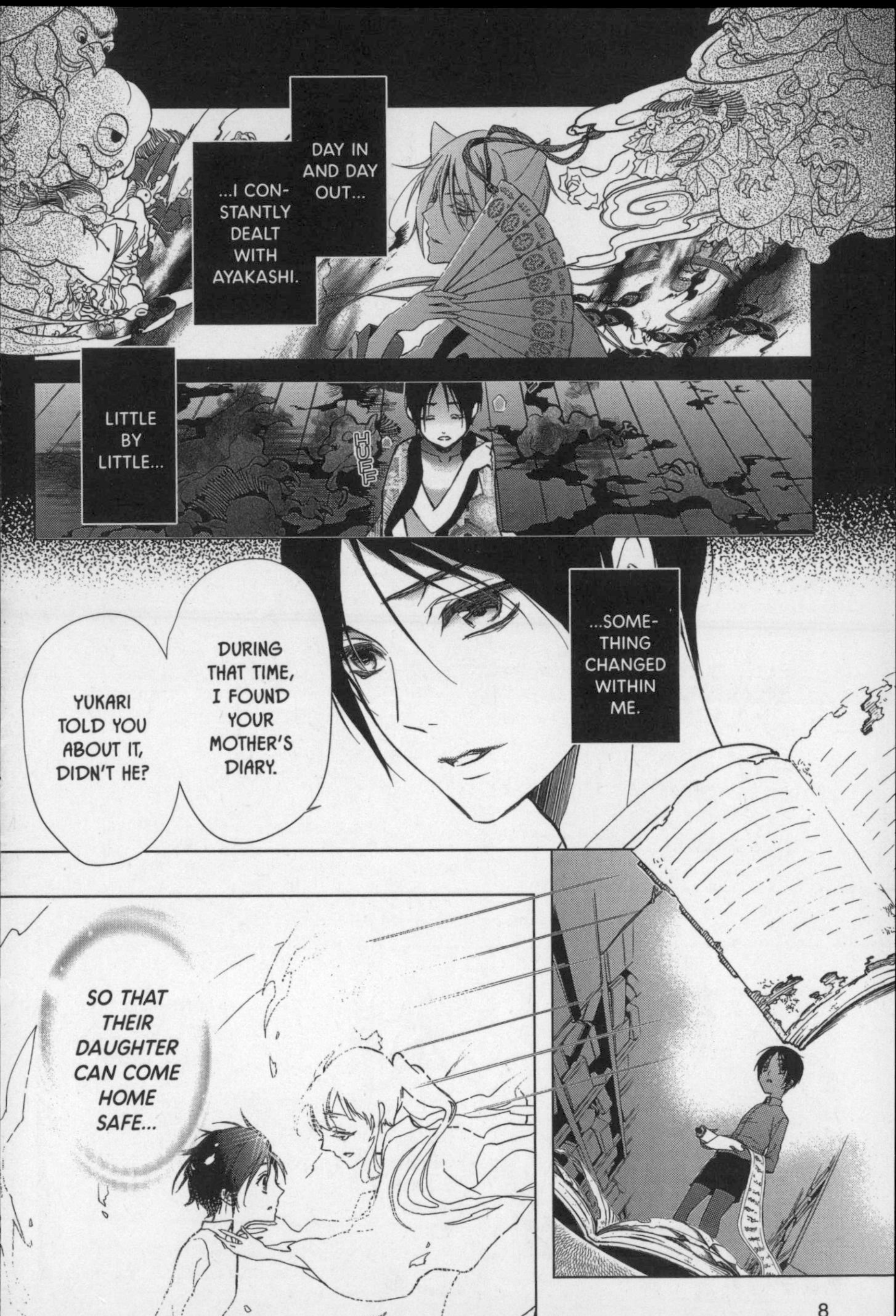

DAY IN AND DAY OUT...
...I CON-STANTLY DEALT WITH AYAKASHI.
LITTLE BY LITTLE...
HUFF
...SOME-THING CHANGED WITHIN ME.
DURING THAT TIME, I FOUND YOUR MOTHER'S DIARY.
YUKARI TOLD YOU ABOUT IT, DIDN'T HE?
SO THAT THEIR DAUGHTER CAN COME HOME SAFE...

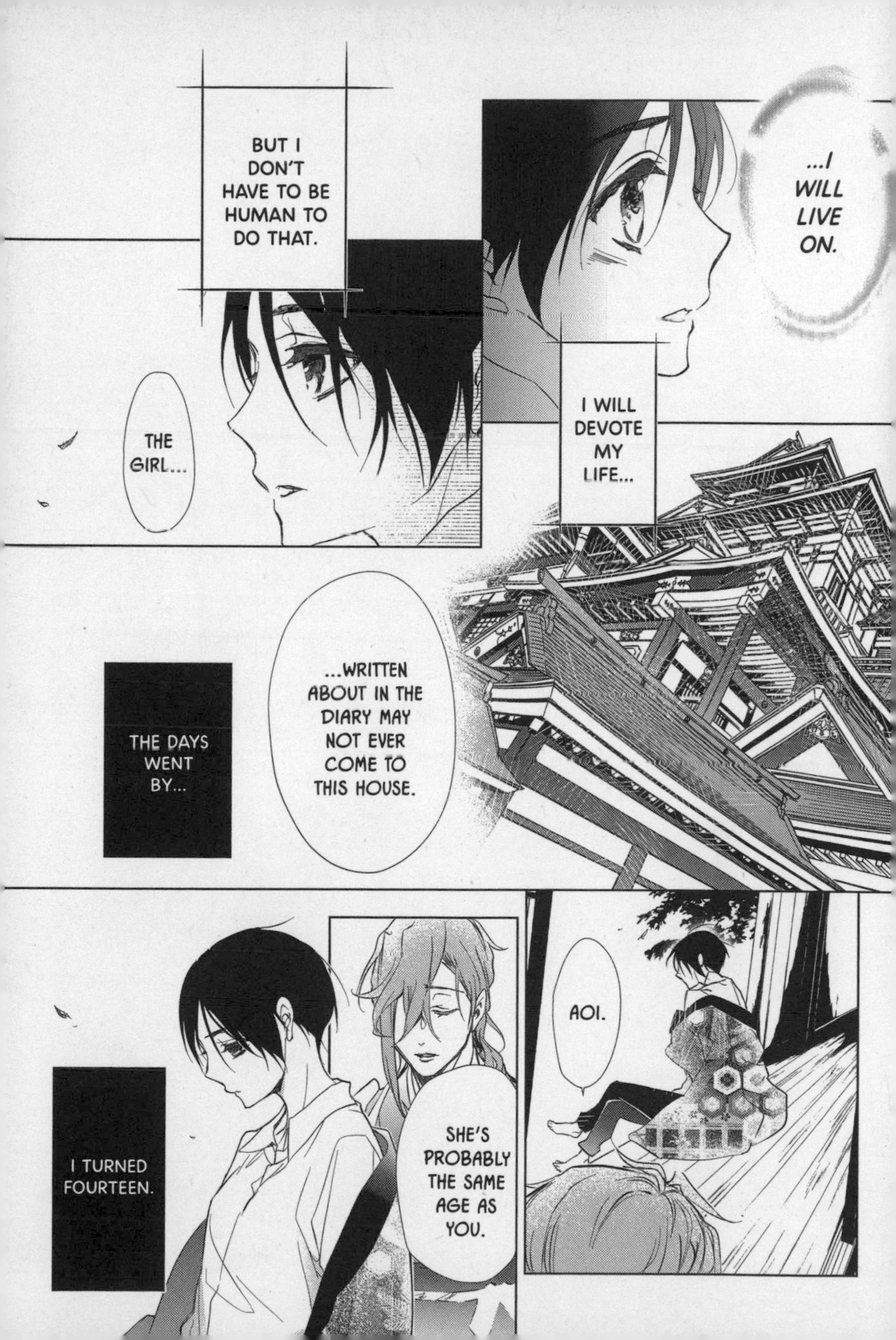

...I WILL LIVE ON.
I WILL DEVOTE MY LIFE...
BUT I DON'T HAVE TO BE HUMAN TO DO THAT.
THE GIRL...
...WRITTEN ABOUT IN THE DIARY MAY NOT EVER COME TO THIS HOUSE.
THE DAYS WENT BY...
AOI.
SHE'S PROBABLY THE SAME AGE AS YOU.
I TURNED FOURTEEN.

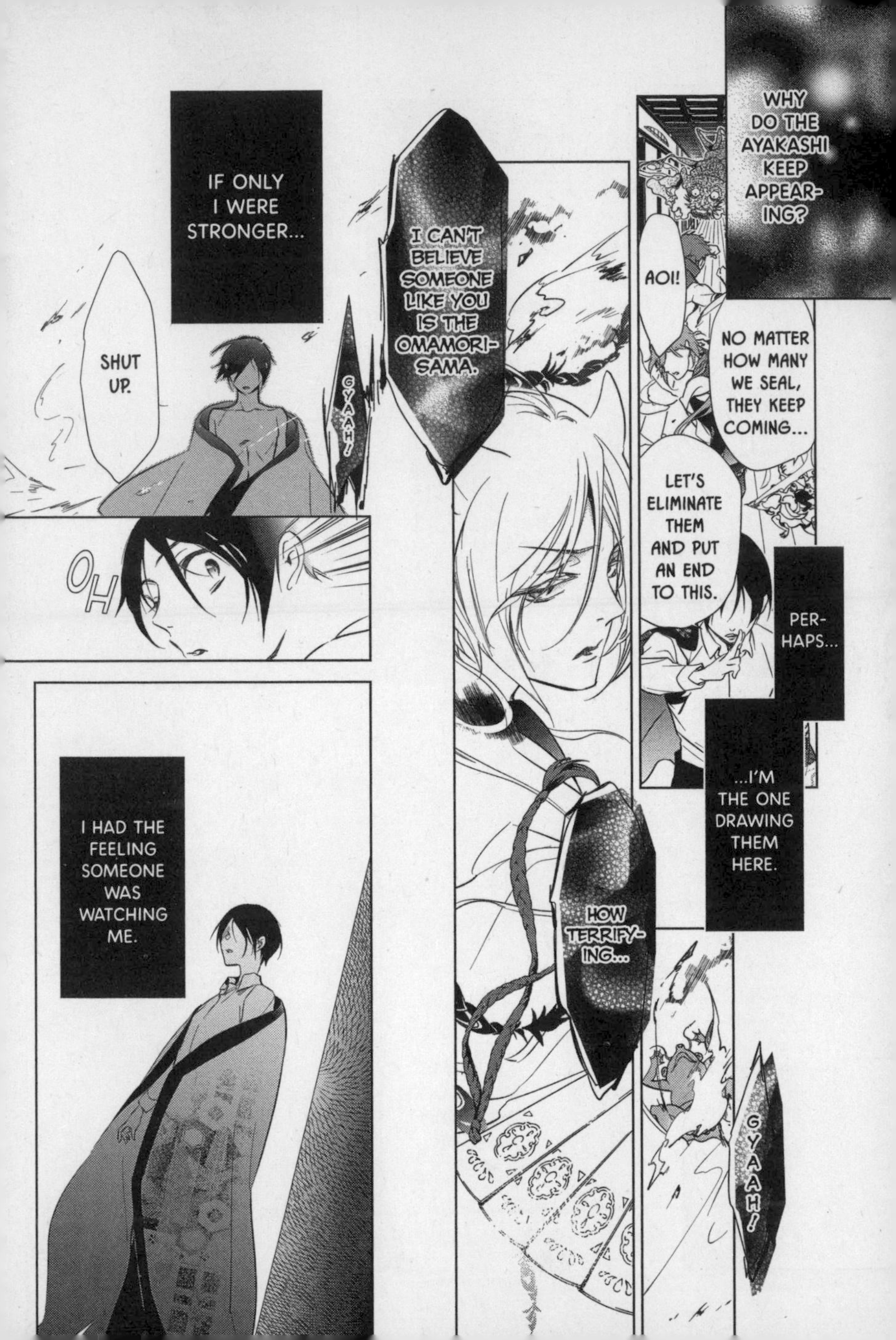
WHY DO THE AYAKASHI KEEP APPEARING?
AOI!
NO MATTER HOW MANY WE SEAL, THEY KEEP COMING...
LET'S ELIMINATE THEM AND PUT AN END TO THIS.
PERHAPS...
...I'M THE ONE DRAWING THEM HERE.
GYAAH!
HOW TERRIFYING...
I CAN'T BELIEVE SOMEONE LIKE YOU IS THE OMAMORI-SAMA.
IF ONLY I WERE STRONGER...
GYAAH!
SHUT UP.
OH
I HAD THE FEELING SOMEONE WAS WATCHING ME.

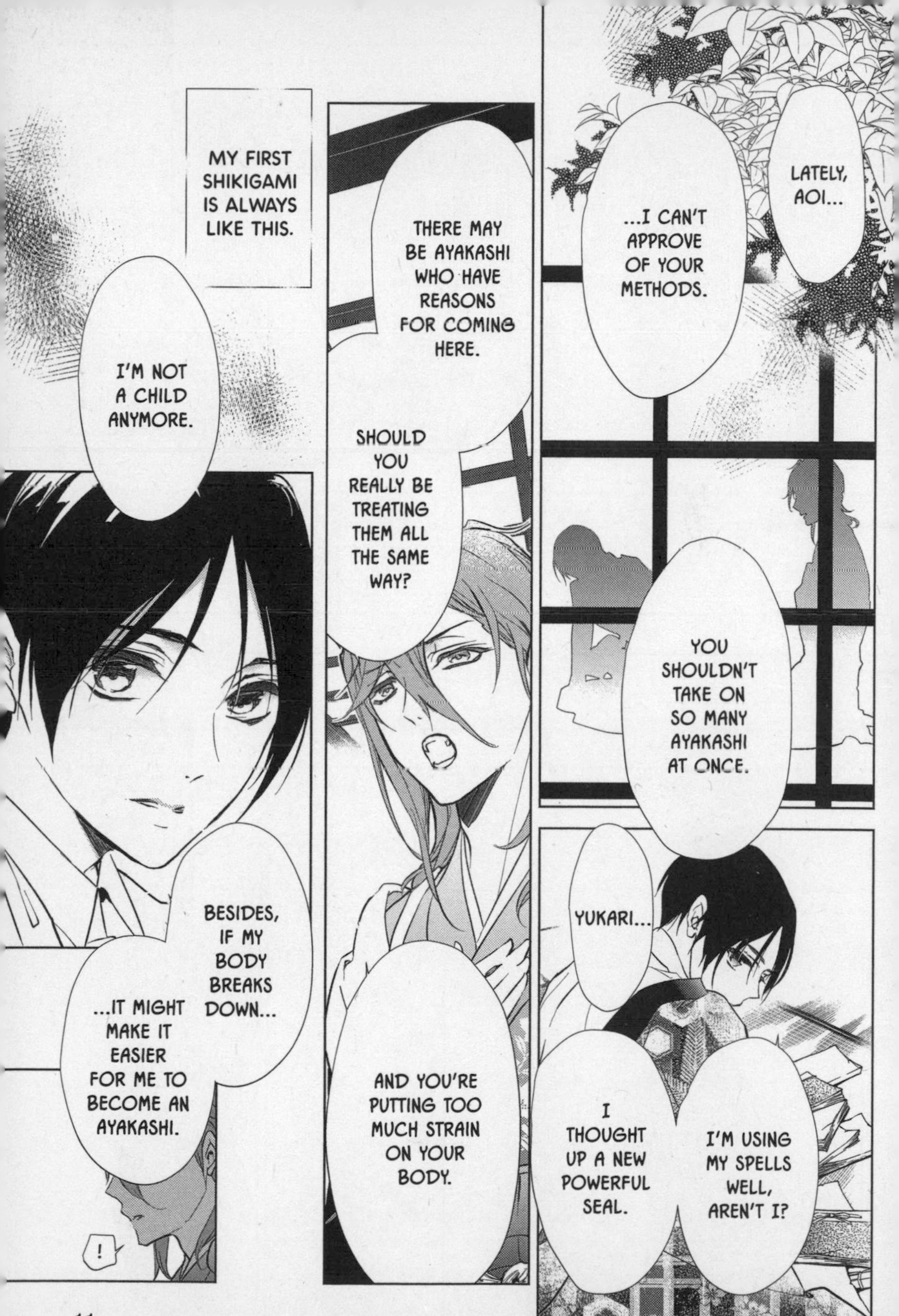
LATELY, AOI...
...I CAN'T APPROVE OF YOUR METHODS.
YOU SHOULDN'T TAKE ON SO MANY AYAKASHI AT ONCE.
YUKARI...
I'M USING MY SPELLS WELL, AREN'T I?
I THOUGHT UP A NEW POWERFUL SEAL.
THERE MAY BE AYAKASHI WHO HAVE REASONS FOR COMING HERE.
SHOULD YOU REALLY BE TREATING THEM ALL THE SAME WAY?
AND YOU'RE PUTTING TOO MUCH STRAIN ON YOUR BODY.
MY FIRST SHIKIGAMI IS ALWAYS LIKE THIS.
I'M NOT A CHILD ANYMORE.
BESIDES, IF MY BODY BREAKS DOWN...
...IT MIGHT MAKE IT EASIER FOR ME TO BECOME AN AYAKASHI.
!

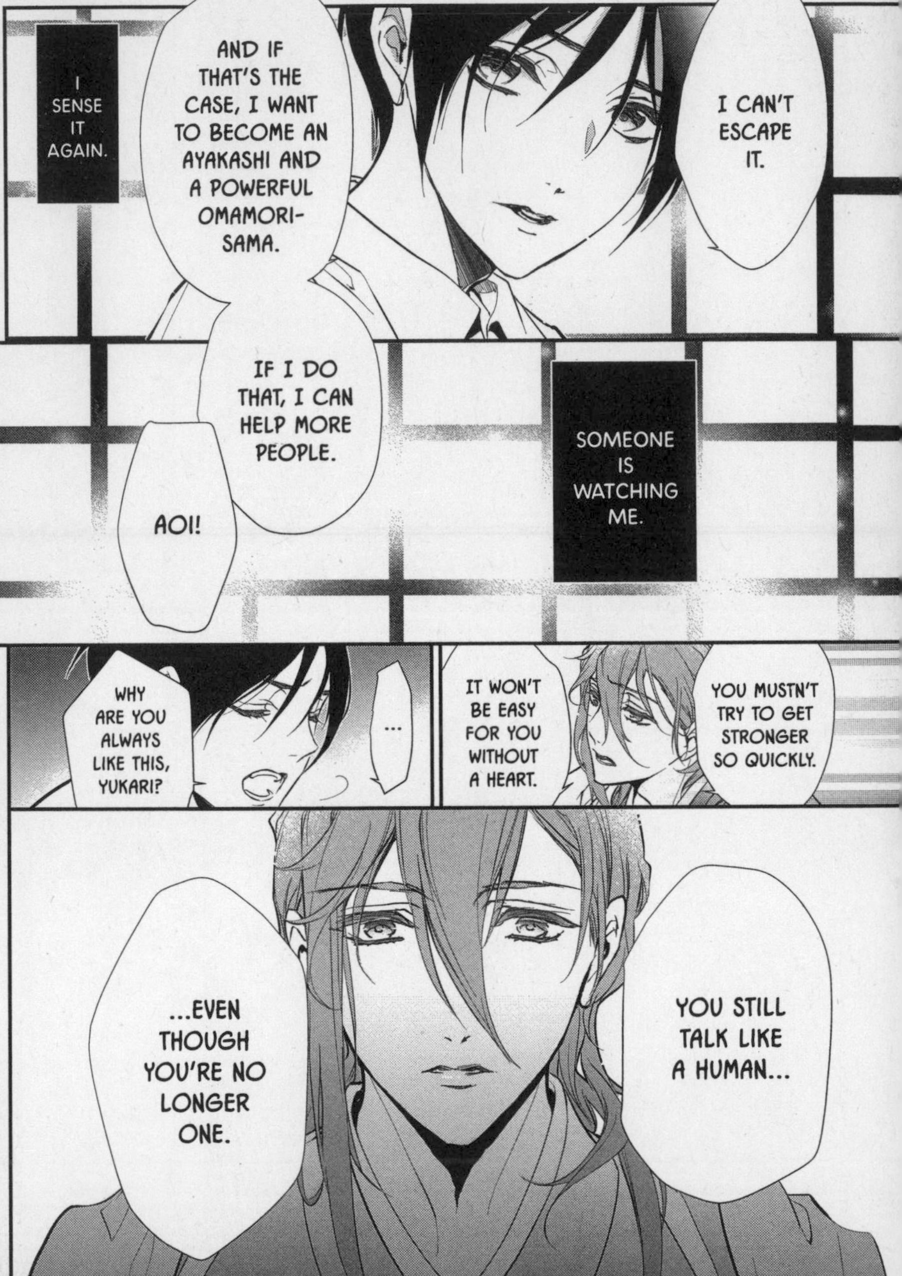
I CAN'T ESCAPE IT.
AND IF THAT'S THE CASE, I WANT TO BECOME AN AYAKASHI AND A POWERFUL OMAMORI-SAMA.
I SENSE IT AGAIN.
SOMEONE IS WATCHING ME.
IF I DO THAT, I CAN HELP MORE PEOPLE.
AOI!
YOU MUSTN'T TRY TO GET STRONGER SO QUICKLY.
IT WON'T BE EASY FOR YOU WITHOUT A HEART.
...
WHY ARE YOU ALWAYS LIKE THIS, YUKARI?
YOU STILL TALK LIKE A HUMAN...
...EVEN THOUGH YOU'RE NO LONGER ONE.

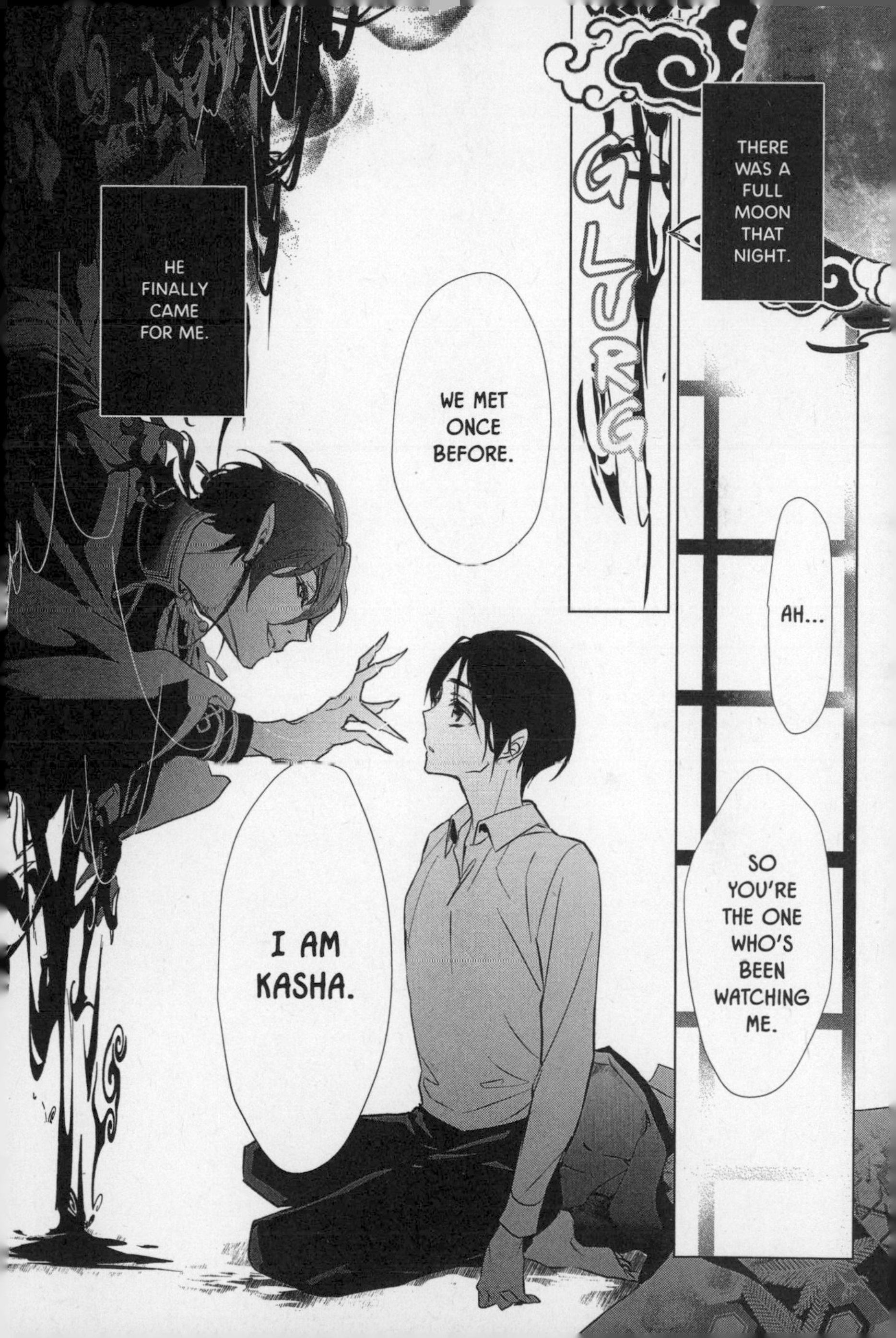
THERE WAS A FULL MOON THAT NIGHT.
GLURG
WE MET ONCE BEFORE.
HE FINALLY CAME FOR ME.
AH...
SO YOU'RE THE ONE WHO'S BEEN WATCHING ME.
I AM KASHA.

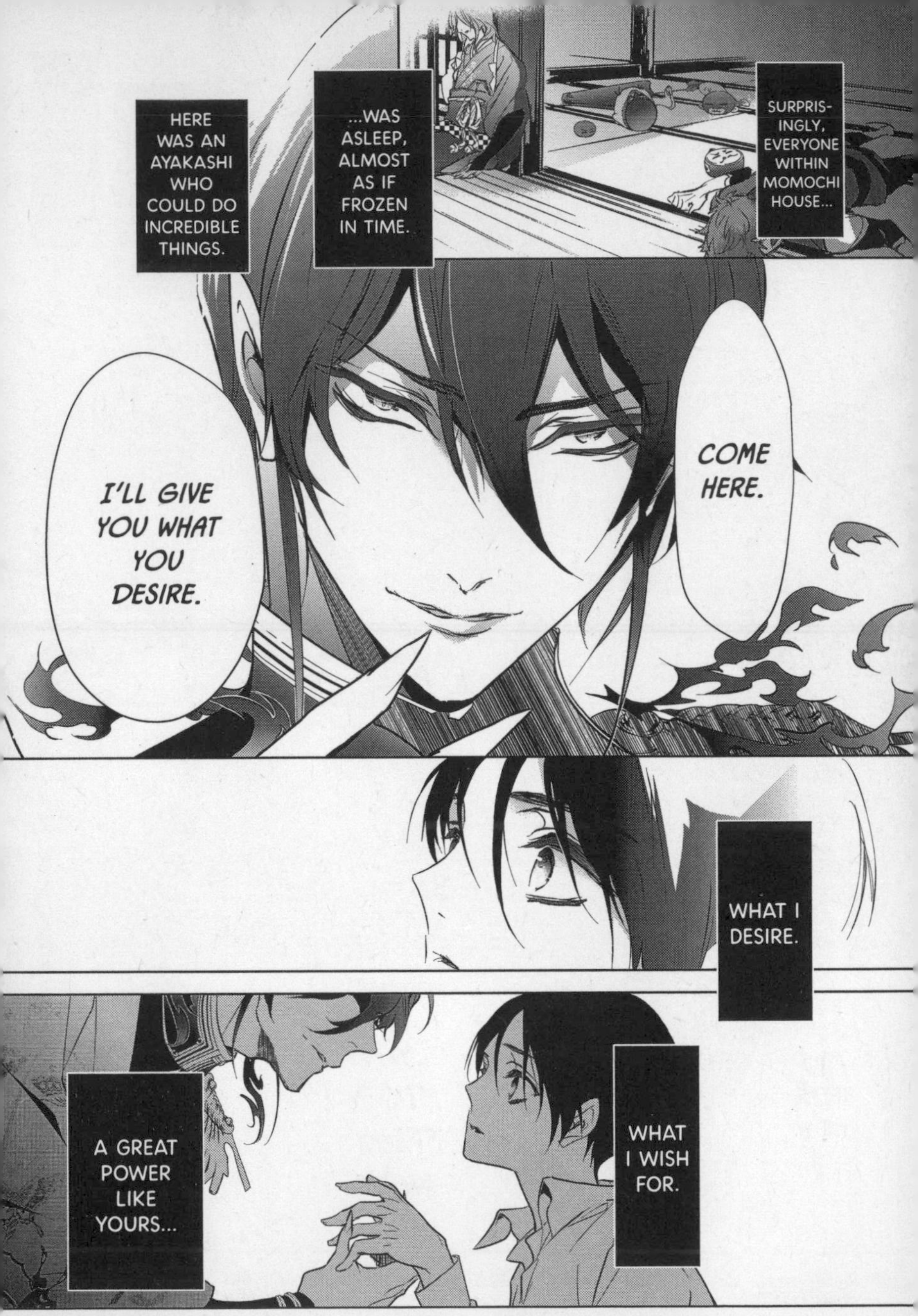
SURPRIS-INGLY, EVERYONE WITHIN MOMOCHI HOUSE...
...WAS ASLEEP, ALMOST AS IF FROZEN IN TIME.
HERE WAS AN AYAKASHI WHO COULD DO INCREDIBLE THINGS.
COME HERE.
I'LL GIVE YOU WHAT YOU DESIRE.
WHAT I DESIRE.
WHAT I WISH FOR.
A GREAT POWER LIKE YOURS...

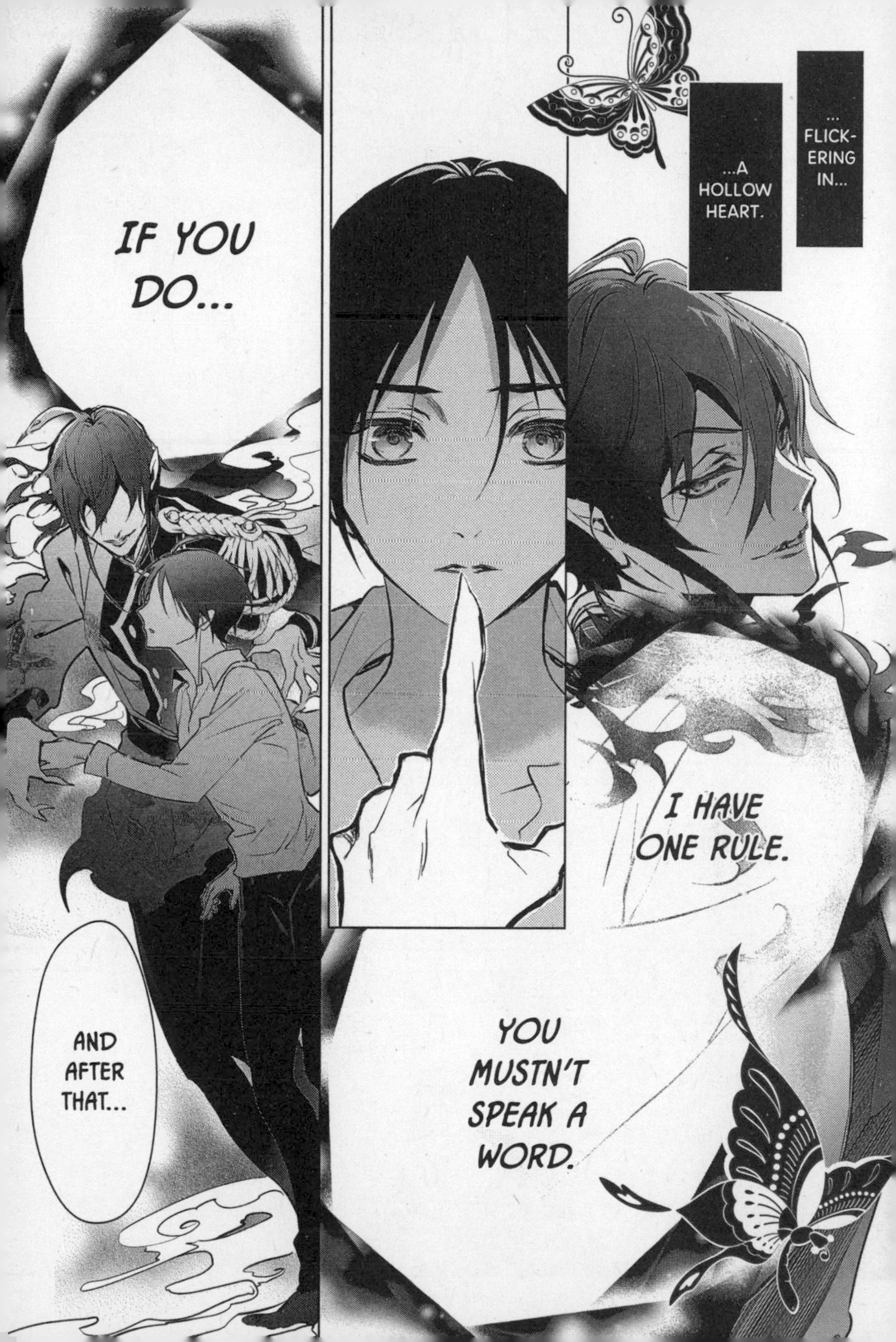
...FLICK-ERING IN...
...A HOLLOW HEART.
I HAVE ONE RULE.
YOU MUSTN'T SPEAK A WORD.
IF YOU DO...
AND AFTER THAT...

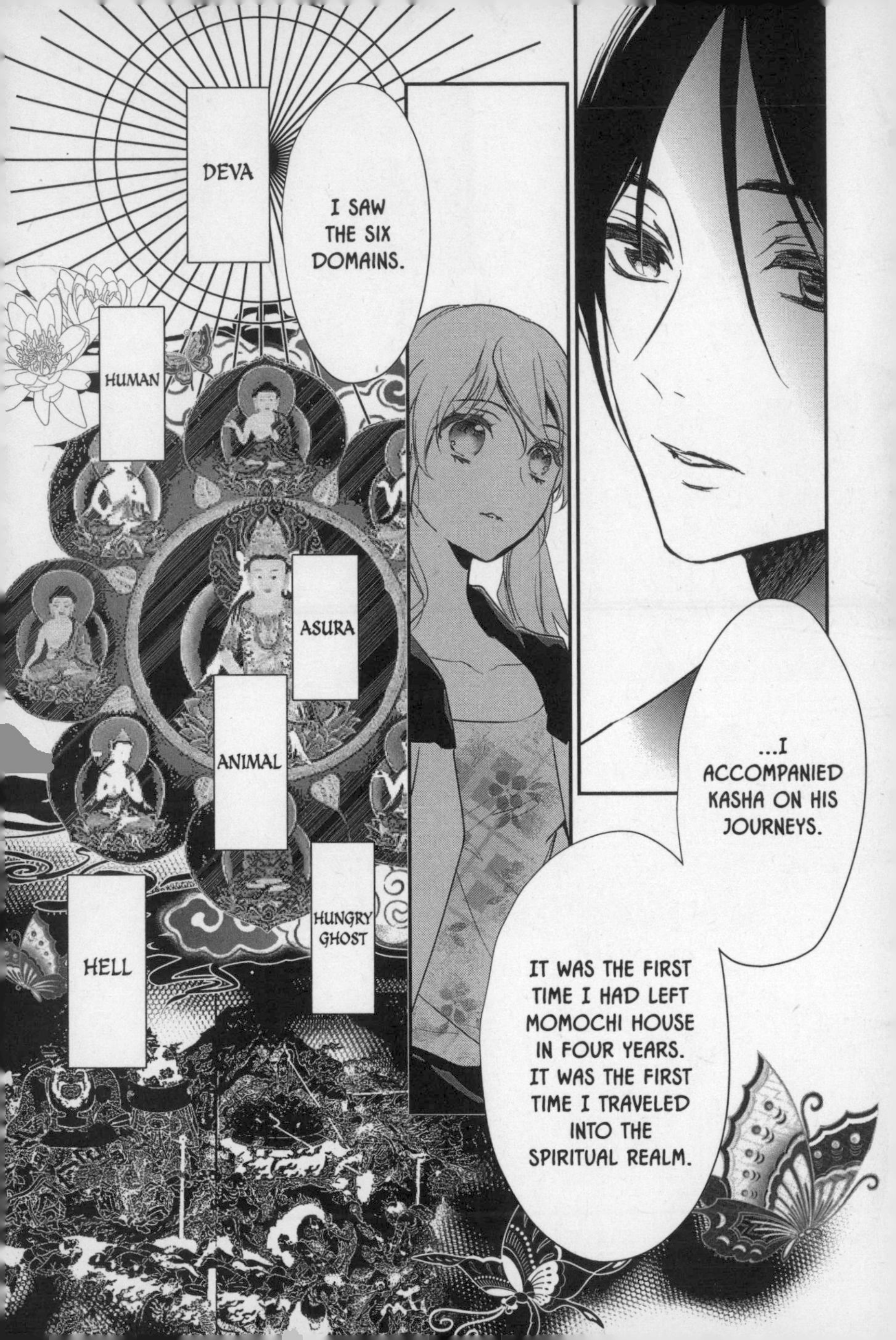
...I ACCOMPANIED KASHA ON HIS JOURNEYS.
IT WAS THE FIRST TIME I HAD LEFT MOMOCHI HOUSE IN FOUR YEARS. IT WAS THE FIRST TIME I TRAVELED INTO THE SPIRITUAL REALM.
I SAW THE SIX DOMAINS.
DEVA
HUMAN
ASURA
ANIMAL
HUNGRY GHOST
HELL

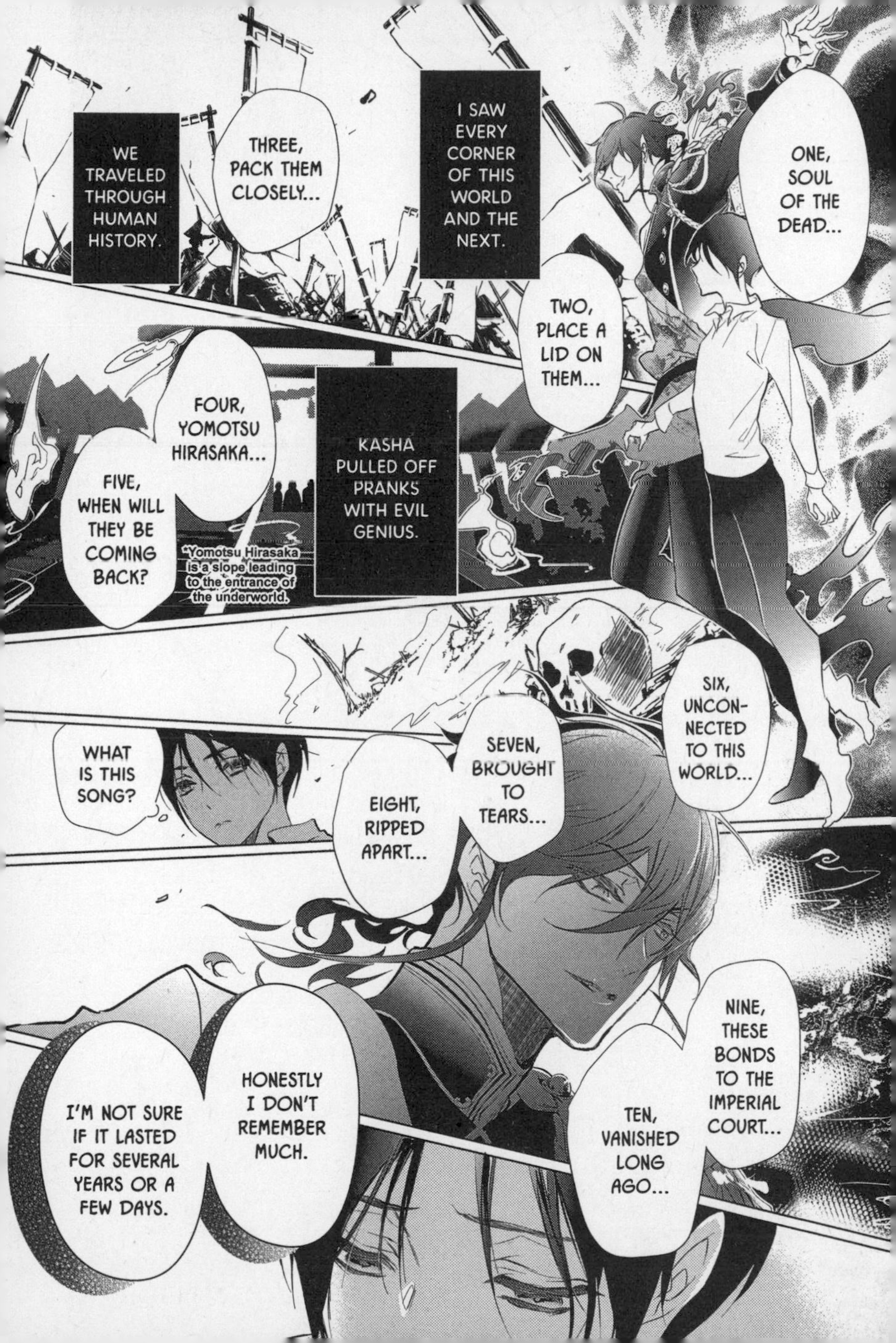
ONE, SOUL OF THE DEAD...
TWO, PLACE A LID ON THEM...
I SAW EVERY CORNER OF THIS WORLD AND THE NEXT.
THREE, PACK THEM CLOSELY...
WE TRAVELED THROUGH HUMAN HISTORY.
KASHA PULLED OFF PRANKS WITH EVIL GENIUS.
FOUR, YOMOTSU HIRASAKA...
FIVE, WHEN WILL THEY BE COMING BACK?
*Yomotsu Hirasaka is a slope leading to the entrance of the underworld.
SIX, UNCONNECTED TO THIS WORLD...
SEVEN, BROUGHT TO TEARS...
EIGHT, RIPPED APART...
WHAT IS THIS SONG?
NINE, THESE BONDS TO THE IMPERIAL COURT...
TEN, VANISHED LONG AGO...
HONESTLY I DON'T REMEMBER MUCH.
I'M NOT SURE IF IT LASTED FOR SEVERAL YEARS OR A FEW DAYS.

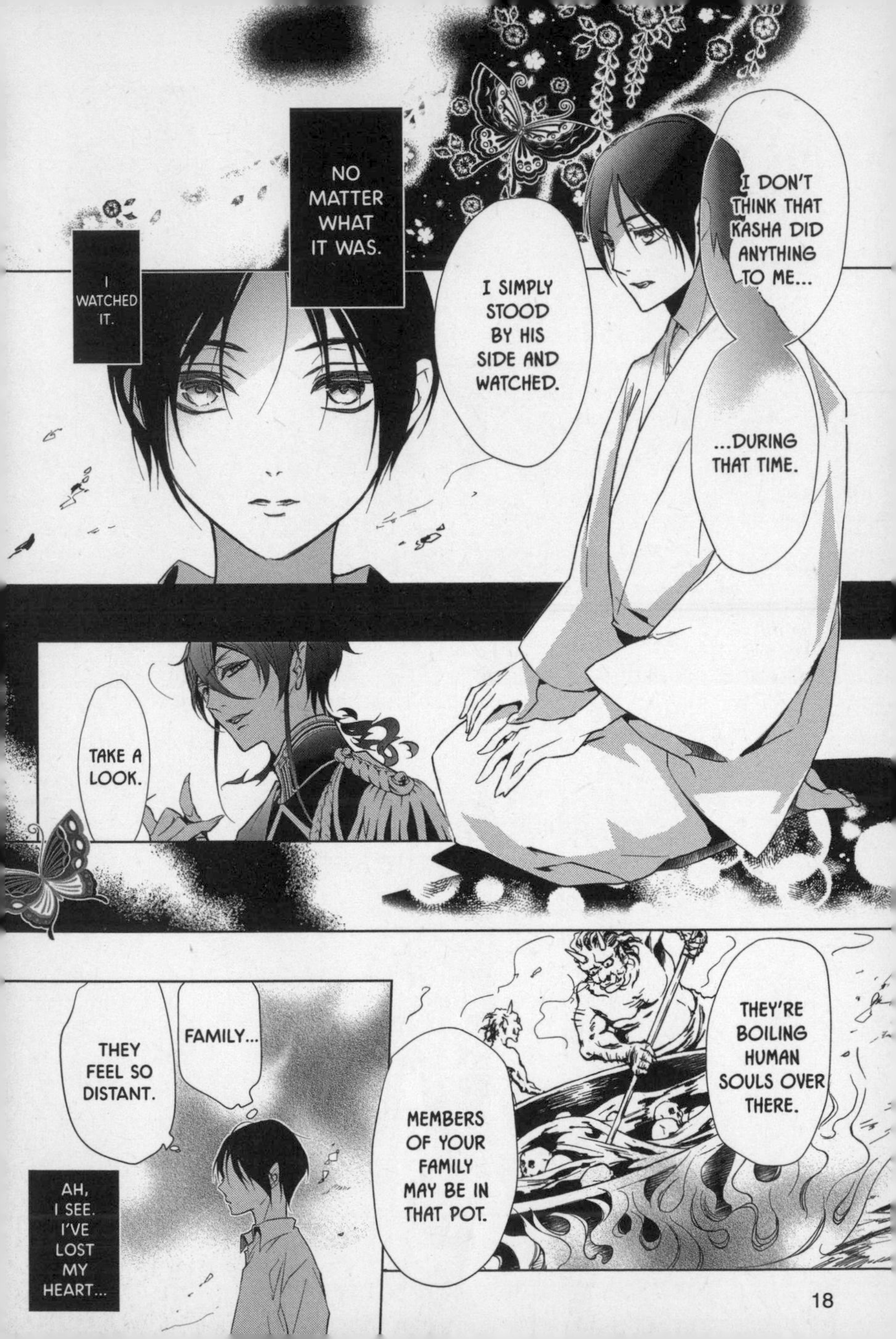

I DON'T THINK THAT KASHA DID ANYTHING TO ME...
...DURING THAT TIME.
I SIMPLY STOOD BY HIS SIDE AND WATCHED.
NO MATTER WHAT IT WAS.
I WATCHED IT.
TAKE A LOOK.
THEY'RE BOILING HUMAN SOULS OVER THERE.
MEMBERS OF YOUR FAMILY MAY BE IN THAT POT.
FAMILY...
THEY FEEL SO DISTANT.
AH, I SEE. I'VE LOST MY HEART...

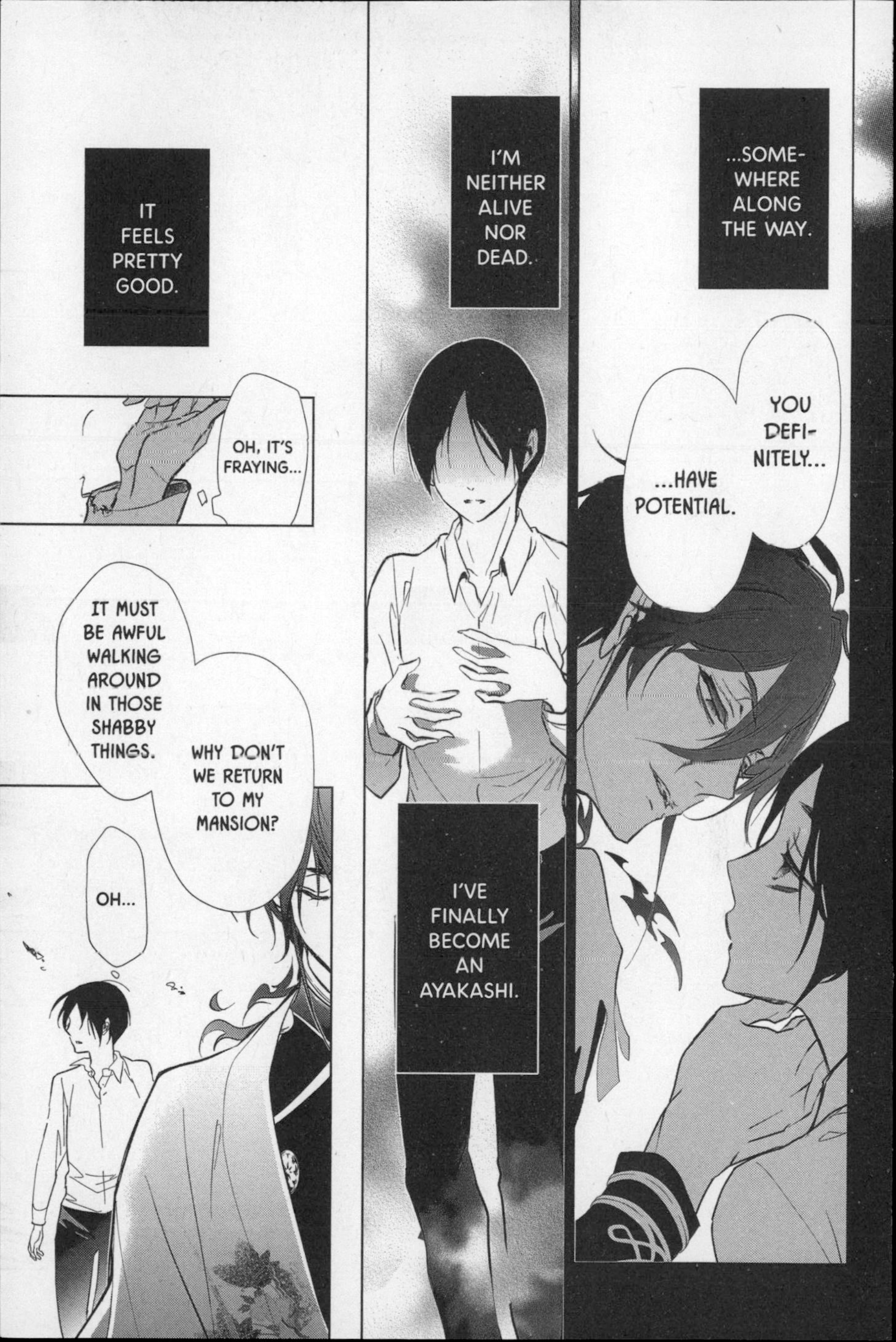
...SOME-WHERE ALONG THE WAY.
YOU DEFI-NITELY...
...HAVE POTENTIAL.
I'M NEITHER ALIVE NOR DEAD.
I'VE FINALLY BECOME AN AYAKASHI.
IT FEELS PRETTY GOOD.
OH, IT'S FRAYING...
IT MUST BE AWFUL WALKING AROUND IN THOSE SHABBY THINGS.
WHY DON'T WE RETURN TO MY MANSION?
OH...

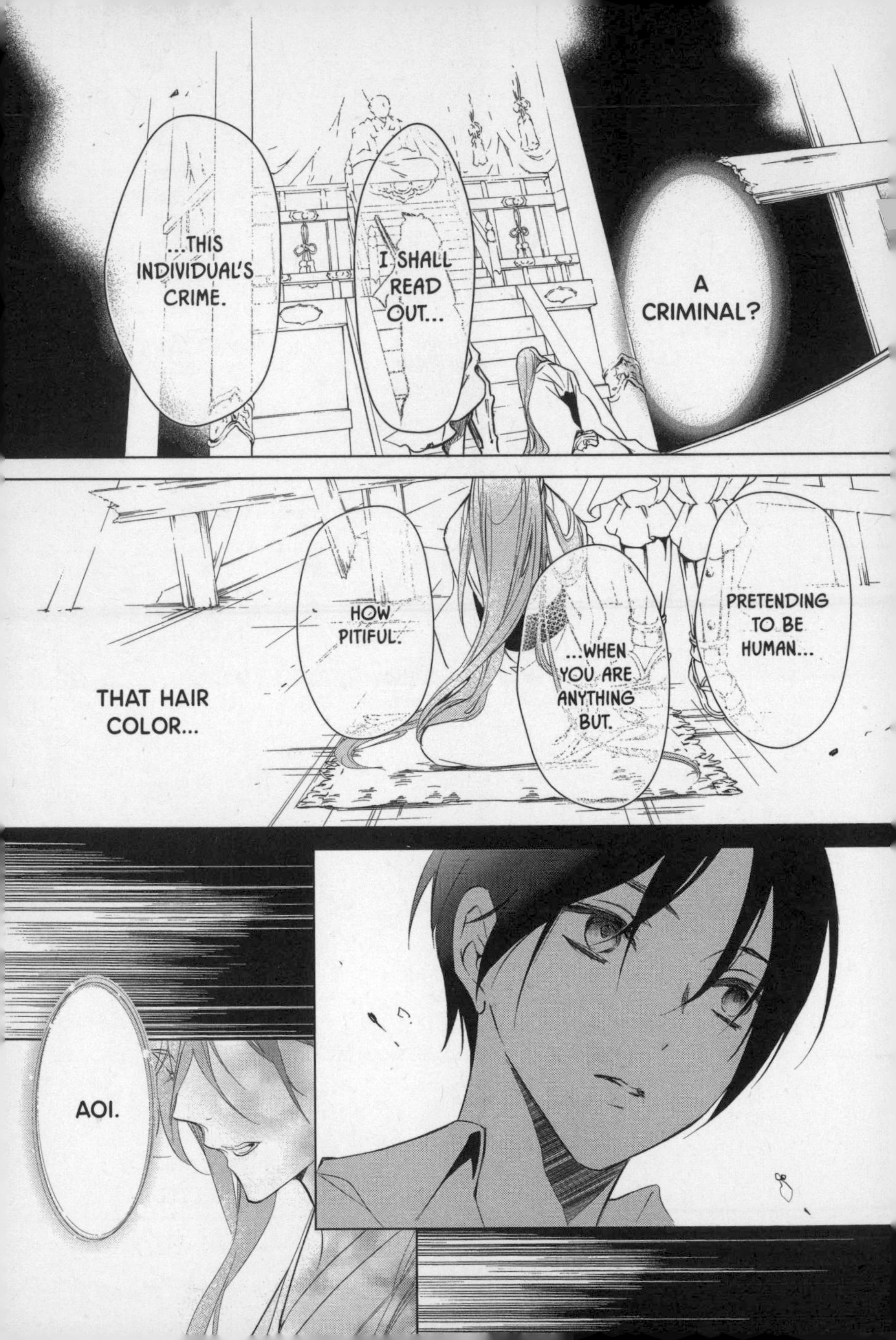
A CRIMINAL?
I SHALL READ OUT...
...THIS INDIVIDUAL'S CRIME.
PRETENDING TO BE HUMAN...
...WHEN YOU ARE ANYTHING BUT.
HOW PITIFUL.
THAT HAIR COLOR...
AOI.

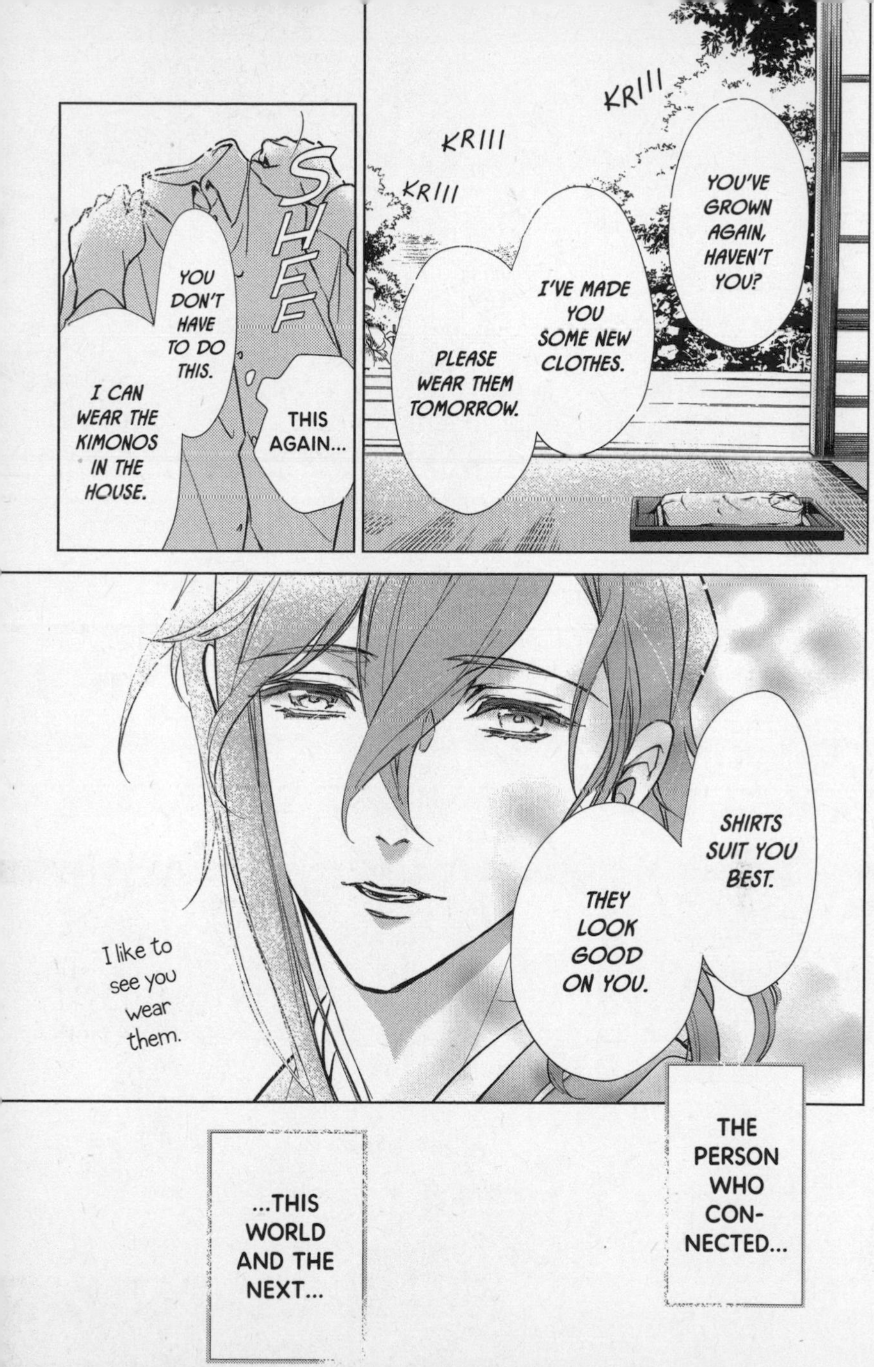
KRIII
KRIII
KRIII
YOU'VE GROWN AGAIN, HAVEN'T YOU?
I'VE MADE YOU SOME NEW CLOTHES.
PLEASE WEAR THEM TOMORROW.
SHFF
YOU DON'T HAVE TO DO THIS.
THIS AGAIN...
I CAN WEAR THE KIMONOS IN THE HOUSE.
SHIRTS SUIT YOU BEST.
THEY LOOK GOOD ON YOU.
I like to see you wear them.
THE PERSON WHO CON-NECTED...
...THIS WORLD AND THE NEXT...

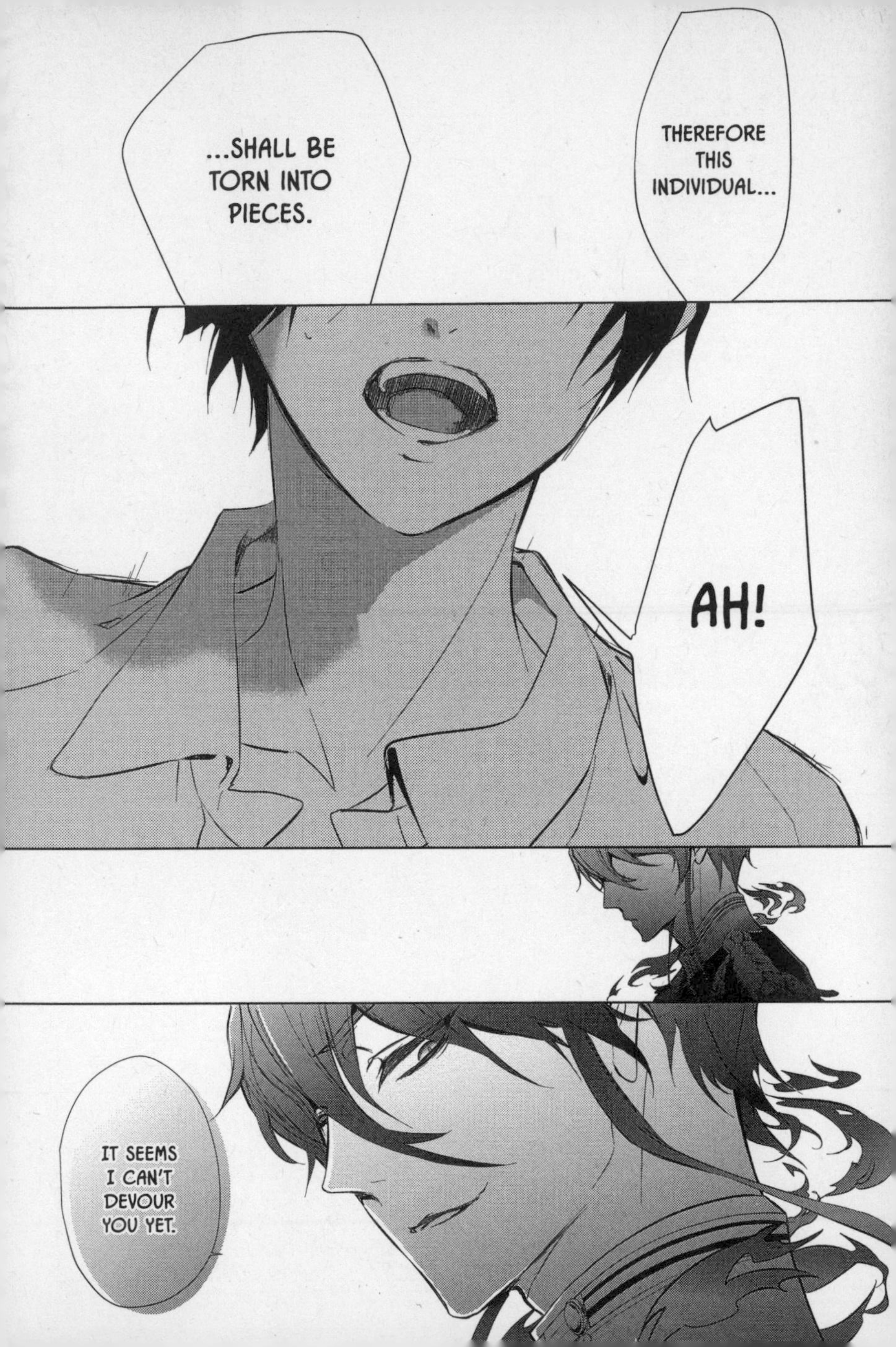
THEREFORE THIS INDIVIDUAL...
...SHALL BE TORN INTO PIECES.
AH!
IT SEEMS I CAN'T DEVOUR YOU YET.

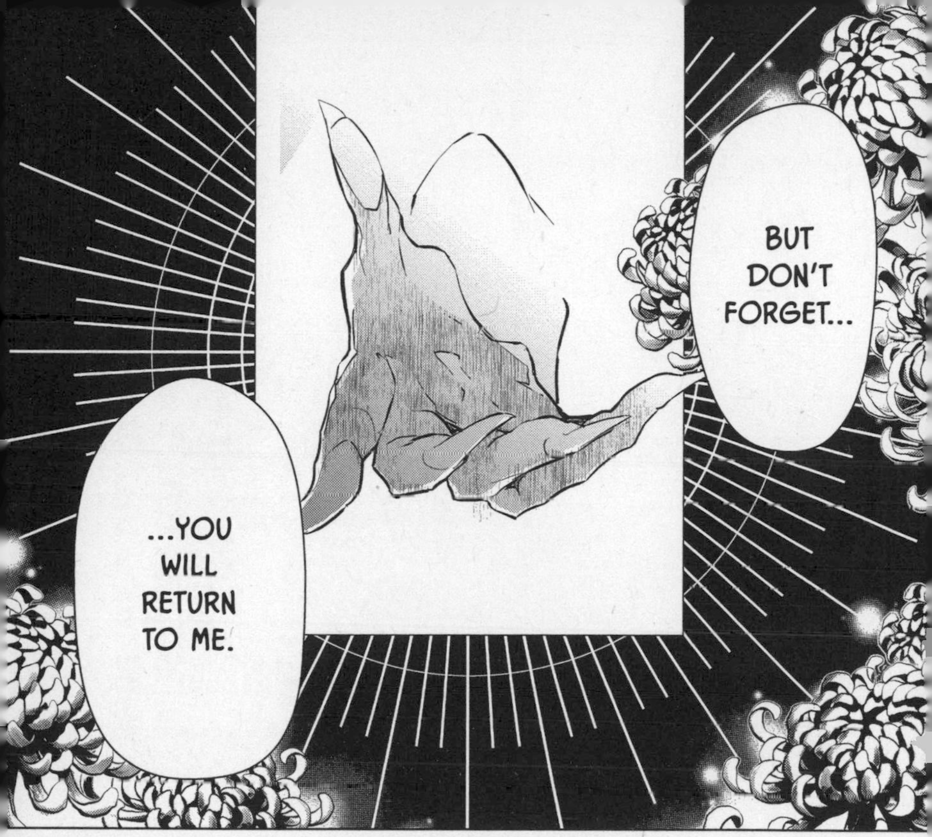
BUT DON'T FORGET...
...YOU WILL RETURN TO ME.
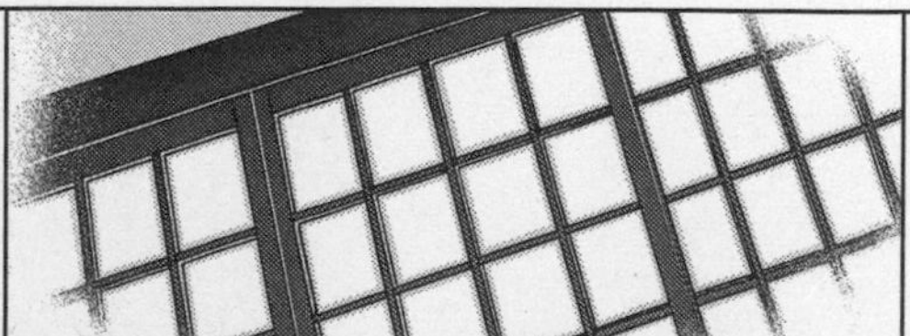
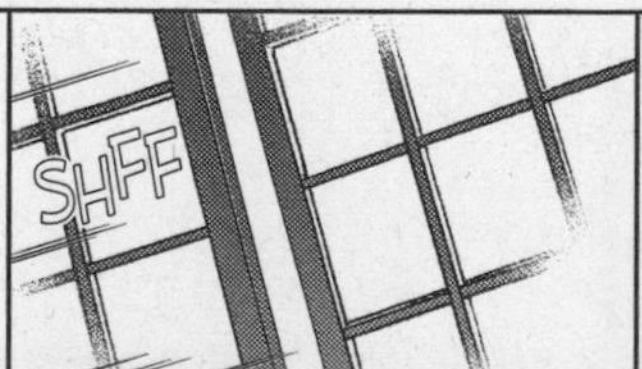
SHFF

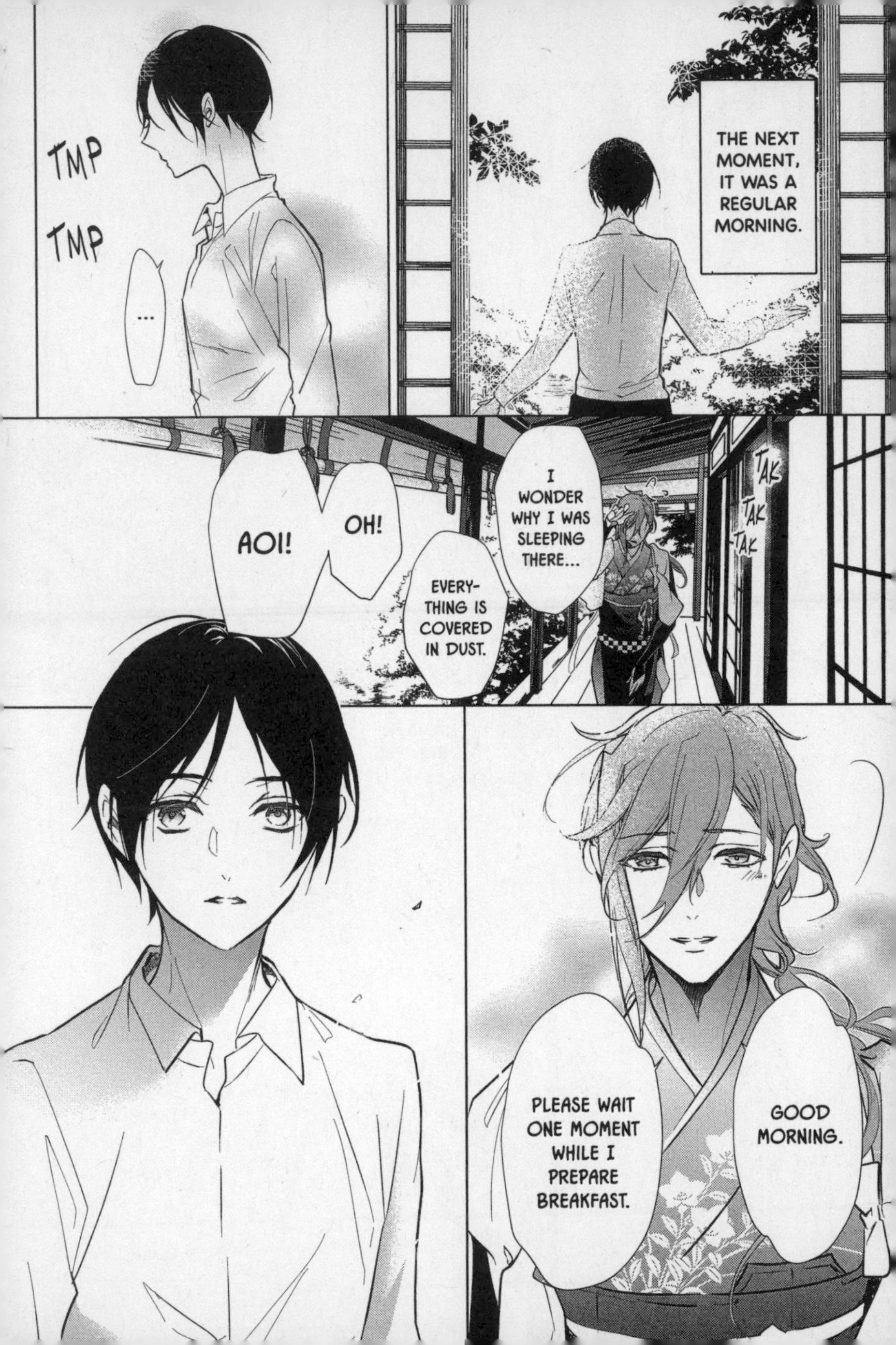
THE NEXT MOMENT, IT WAS A REGULAR MORNING.
TMP
TMP
...
TAK
TAK
TAK
I WONDER WHY I WAS SLEEPING THERE...
EVERY-THING IS COVERED IN DUST.
OH!
AOI!
GOOD MORNING.
PLEASE WAIT ONE MOMENT WHILE I PREPARE BREAKFAST.

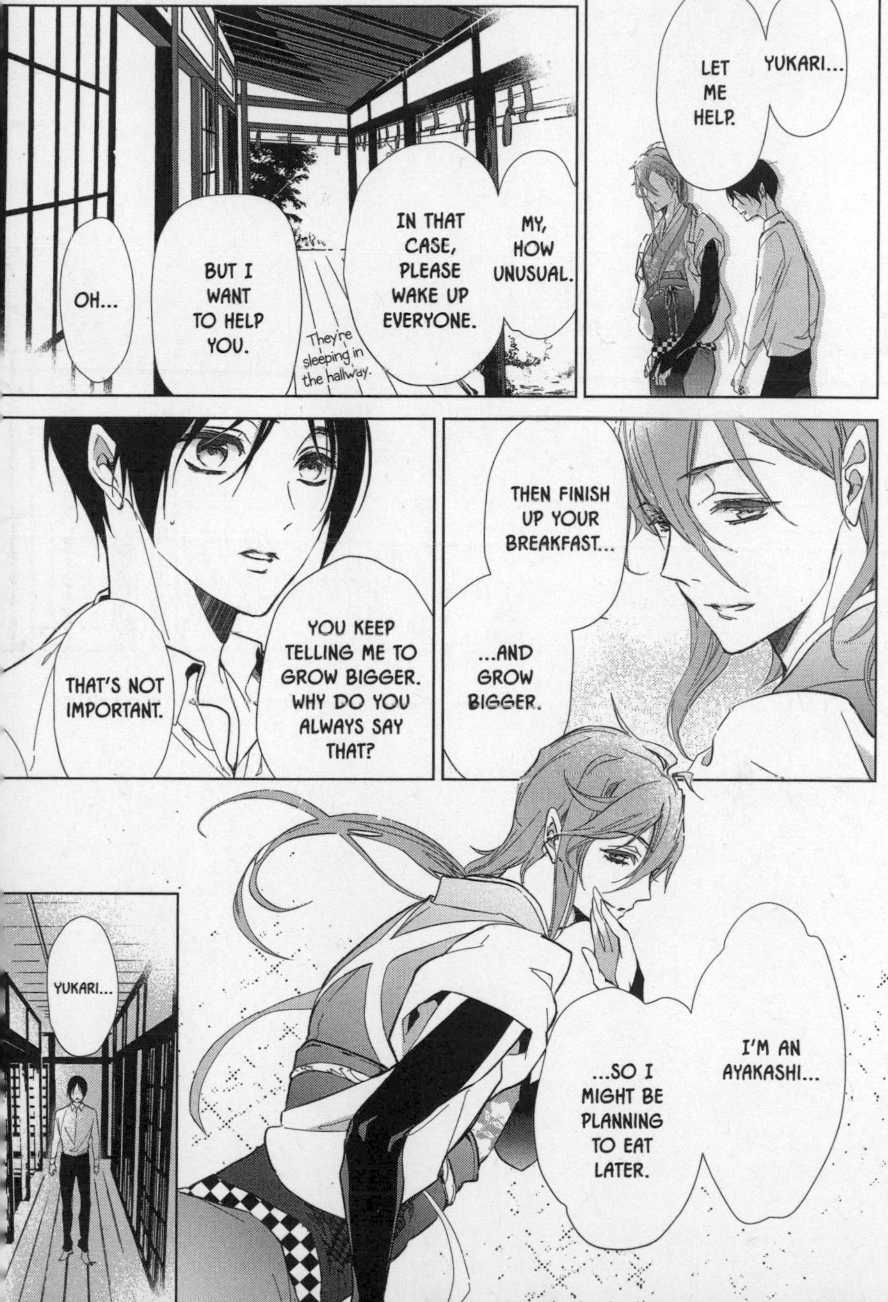
YUKARI...
LET ME HELP.
MY, HOW UNUSUAL.
IN THAT CASE, PLEASE WAKE UP EVERYONE.
They're sleeping in the hallway.
BUT I WANT TO HELP YOU.
OH...
THEN FINISH UP YOUR BREAKFAST...
...AND GROW BIGGER.
YOU KEEP TELLING ME TO GROW BIGGER. WHY DO YOU ALWAYS SAY THAT?
THAT'S NOT IMPORTANT.
I'M AN AYAKASHI...
...SO I MIGHT BE PLANNING TO EAT LATER.
YUKARI...

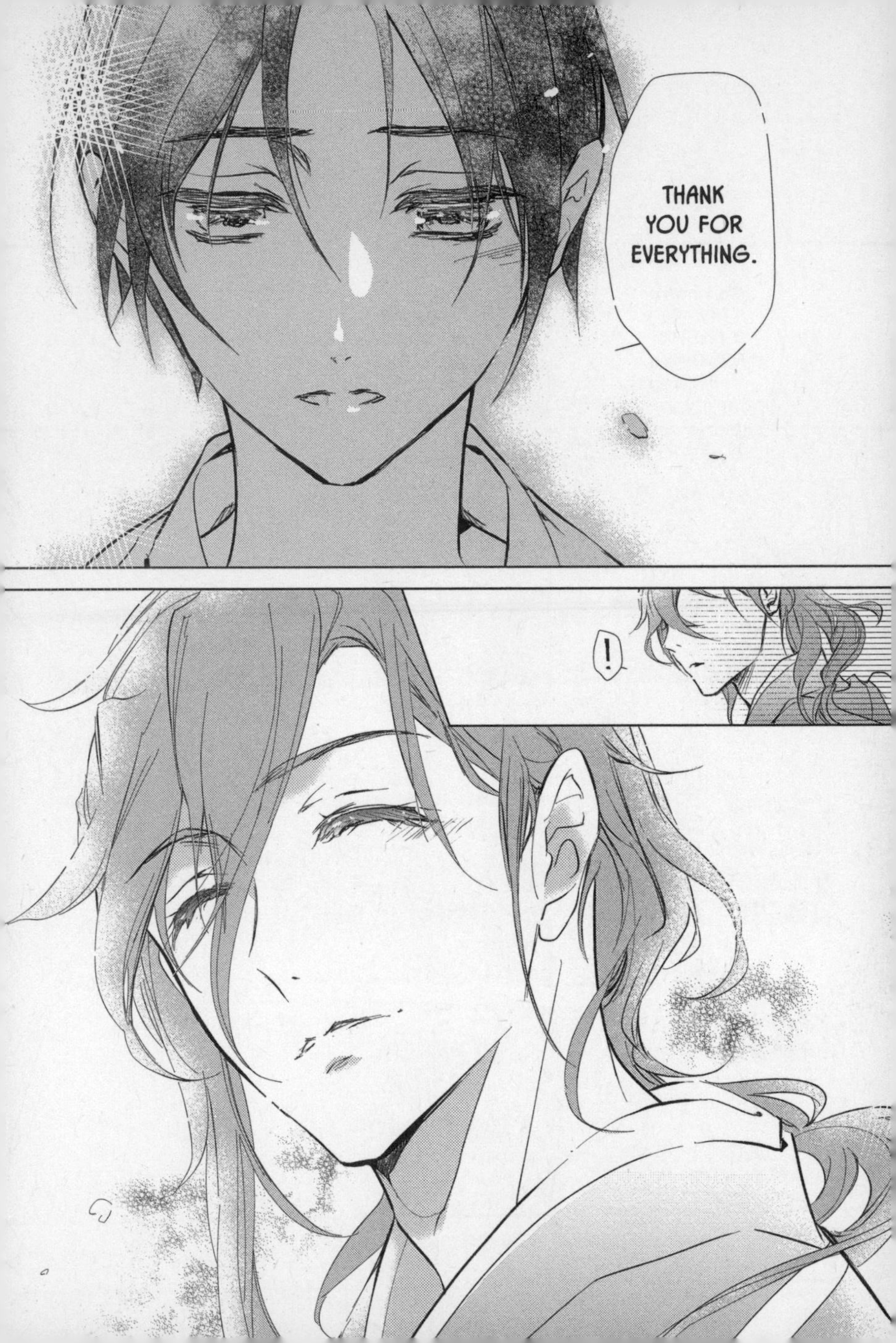
THANK YOU FOR EVERYTHING.
!

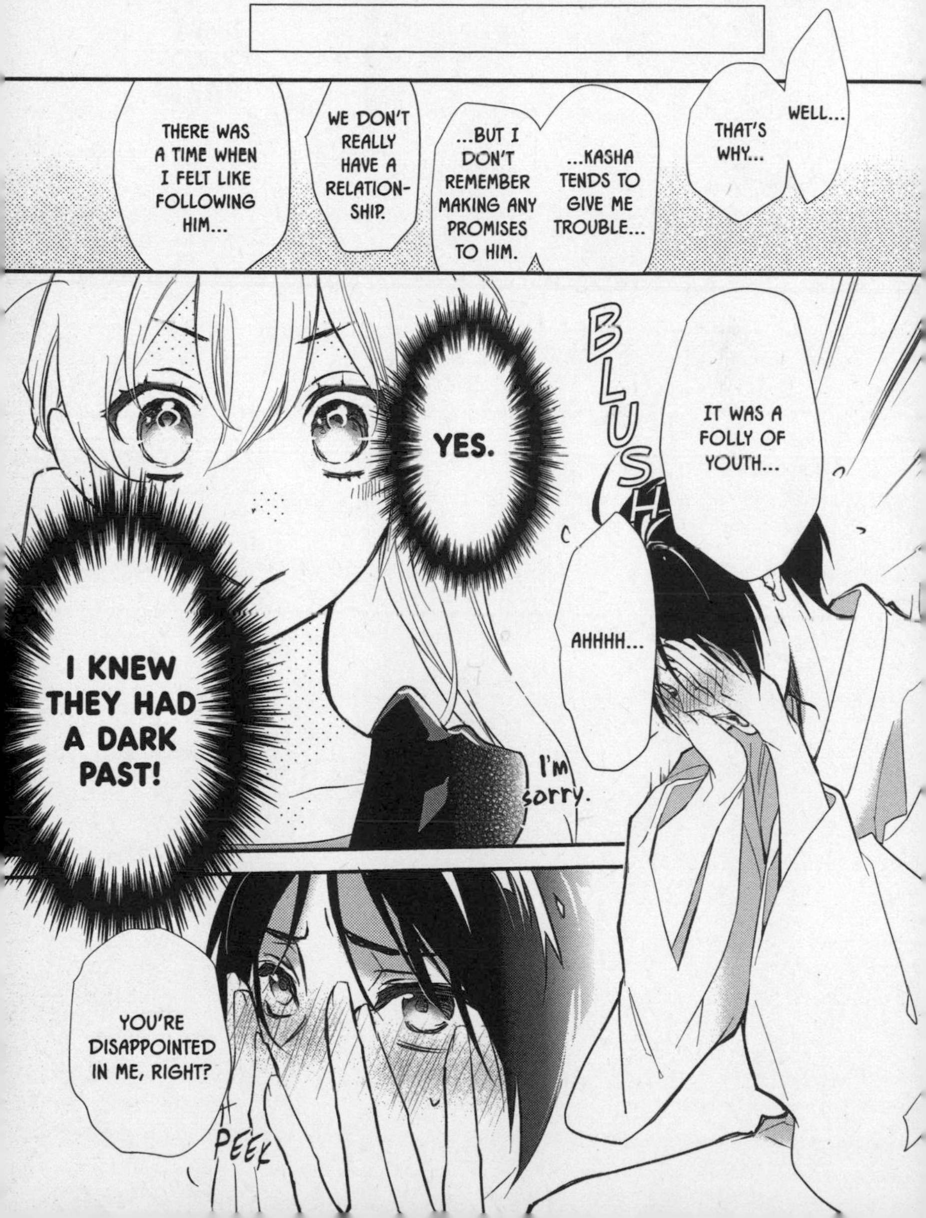
WELL...
THAT'S WHY...
...KASHA TENDS TO GIVE ME TROUBLE...
...BUT I DON'T REMEMBER MAKING ANY PROMISES TO HIM.
WE DON'T REALLY HAVE A RELATIONSHIP.
THERE WAS A TIME WHEN I FELT LIKE FOLLOWING HIM...
BLUSH
IT WAS A FOLLY OF YOUTH...
AHHHH...
I'm sorry.
YES.
I KNEW THEY HAD A DARK PAST!
YOU'RE DISAPPOINTED IN ME, RIGHT?
PEEK

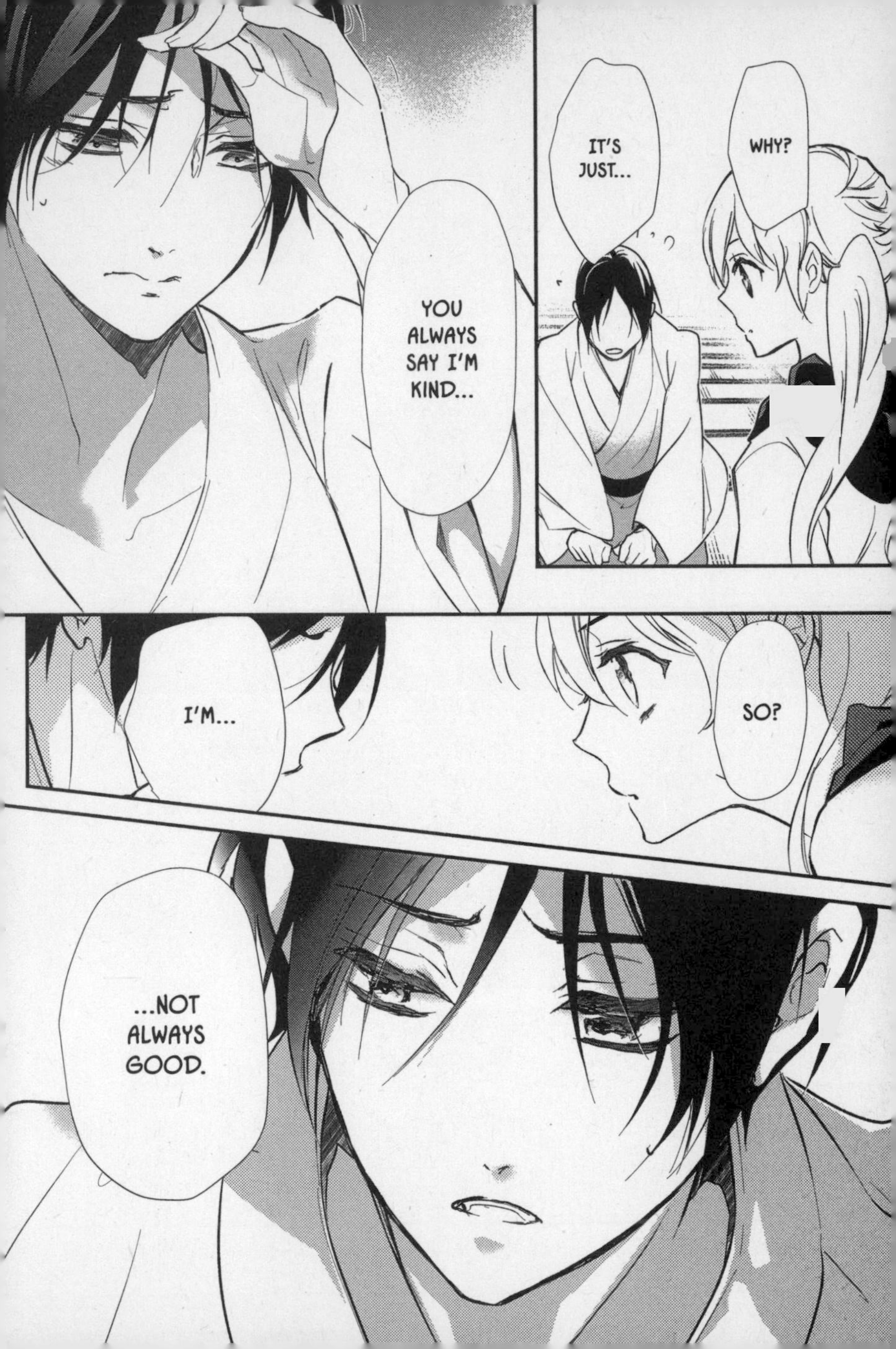
WHY?
IT'S JUST...
YOU ALWAYS SAY I'M KIND...
SO?
I'M...
...NOT ALWAYS GOOD.

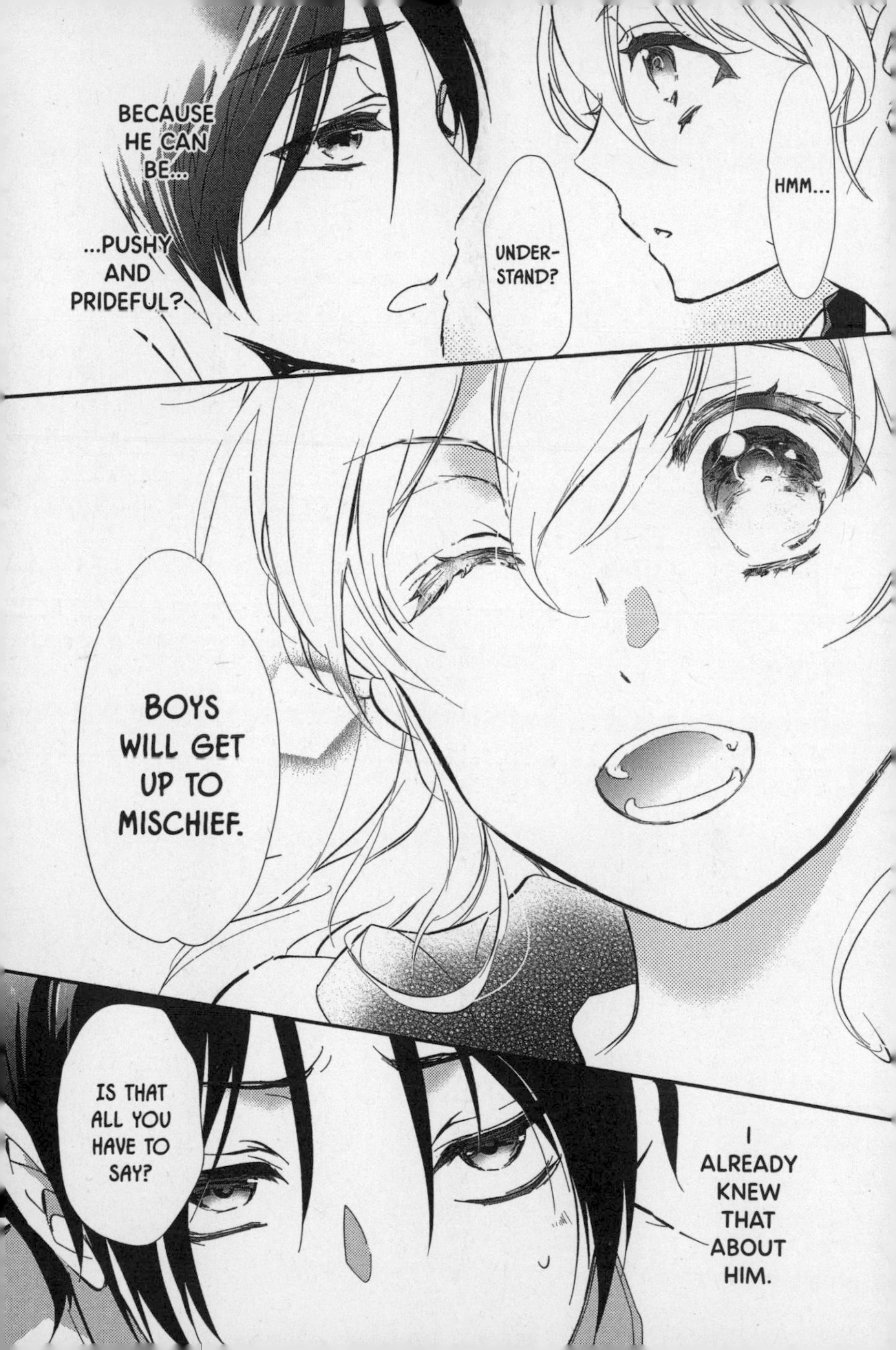
HMM...
UNDER-STAND?
BECAUSE HE CAN BE...
...PUSHY AND PRIDEFUL?
BOYS WILL GET UP TO MISCHIEF.
I ALREADY KNEW THAT ABOUT HIM.
IS THAT ALL YOU HAVE TO SAY?

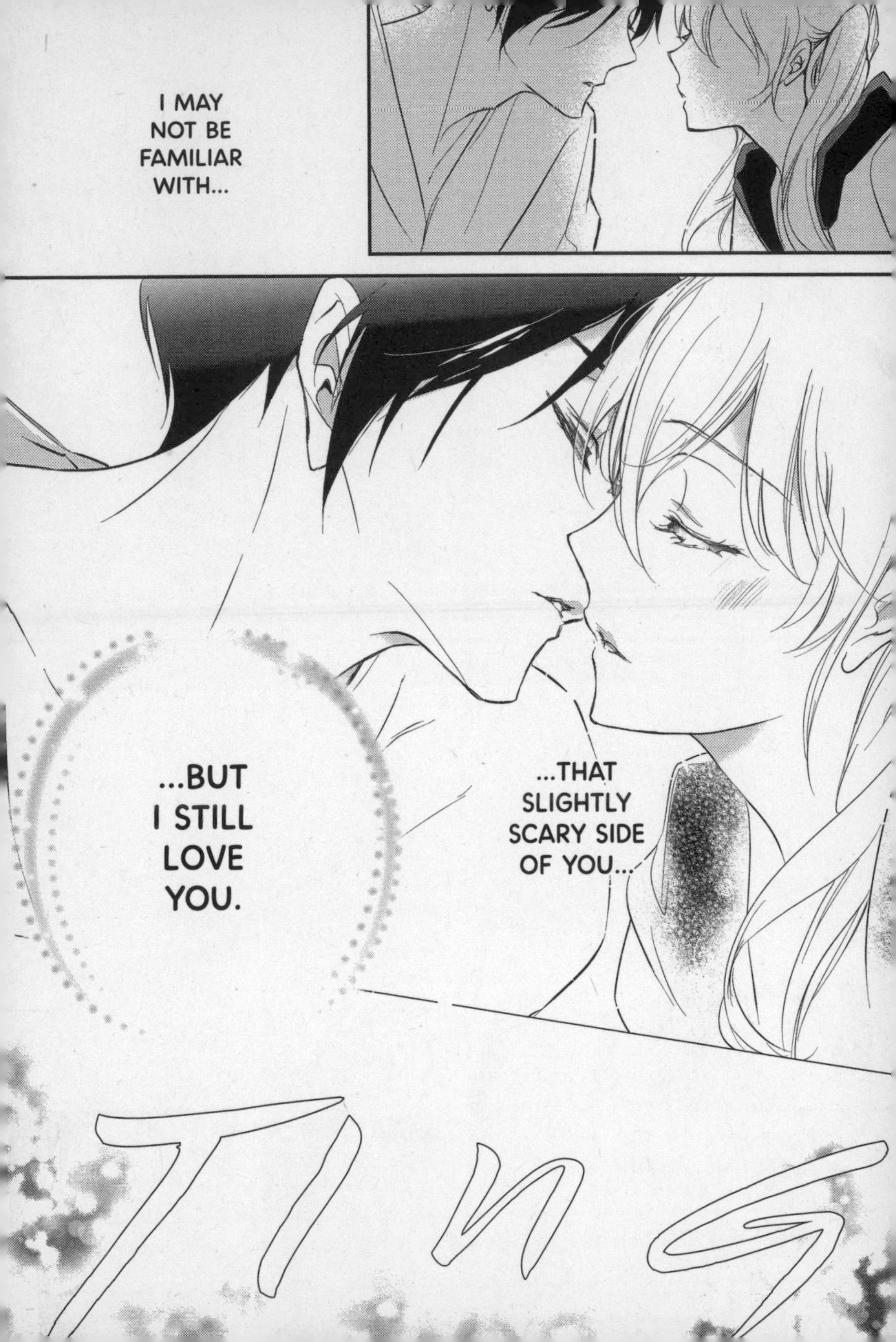
I MAY NOT BE FAMILIAR WITH...
...THAT SLIGHTLY SCARY SIDE OF YOU...
...BUT I STILL LOVE YOU.

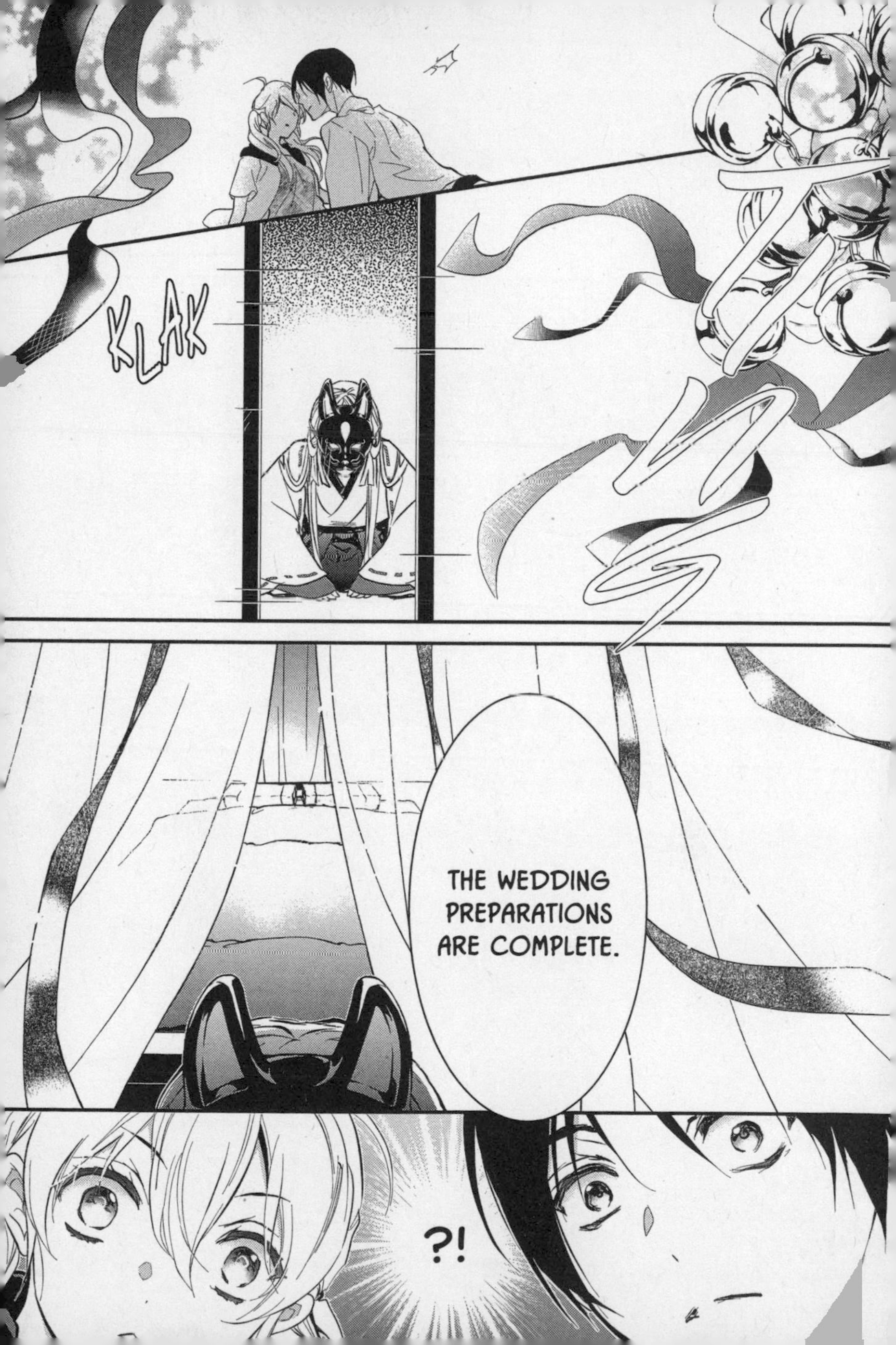
KLAK
THE WEDDING PREPARATIONS ARE COMPLETE.
?!

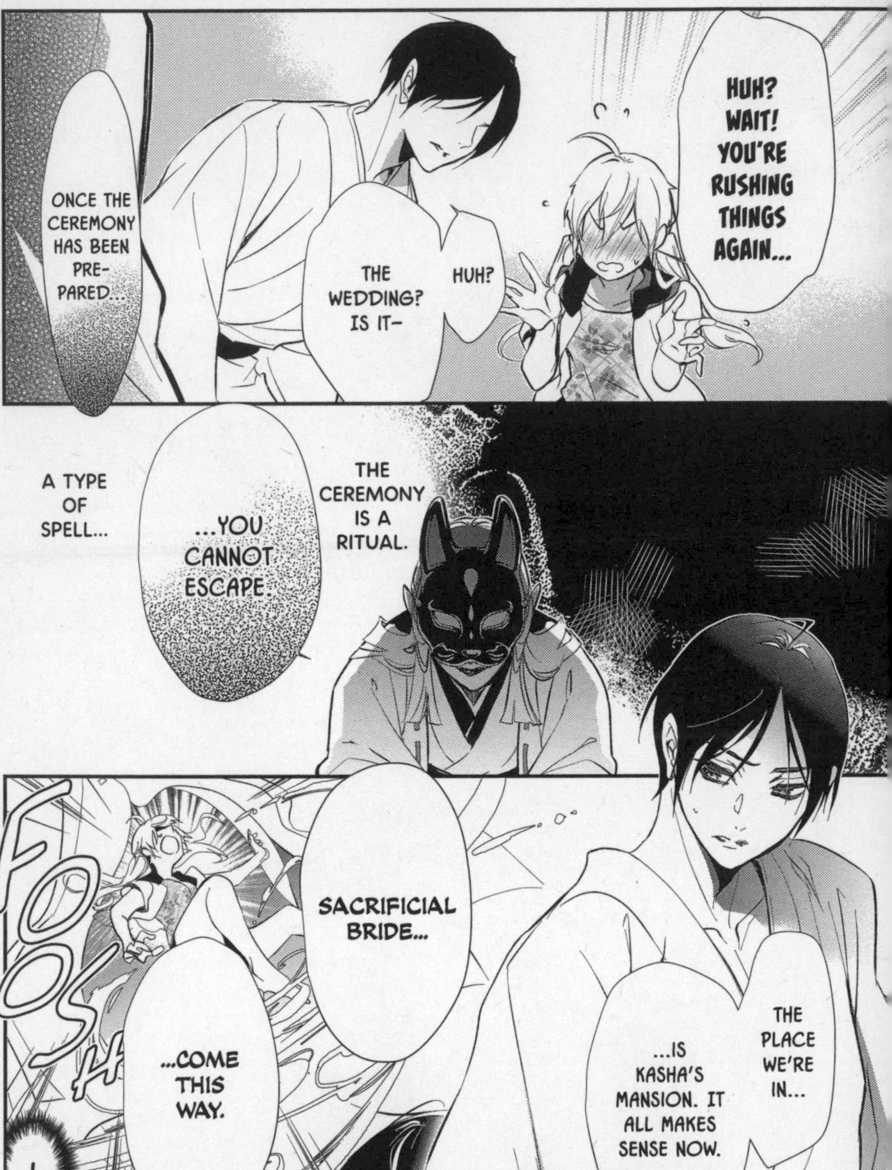
HUH? WAIT! YOU'RE RUSHING THINGS AGAIN...
HUH?
THE WEDDING? IS IT–
ONCE THE CEREMONY HAS BEEN PRE-PARED...
THE CEREMONY IS A RITUAL.
A TYPE OF SPELL...
...YOU CANNOT ESCAPE.
THE PLACE WE'RE IN...
...IS KASHA'S MANSION. IT ALL MAKES SENSE NOW.
SACRIFICIAL BRIDE...
...COME THIS WAY.
FOOSH
!

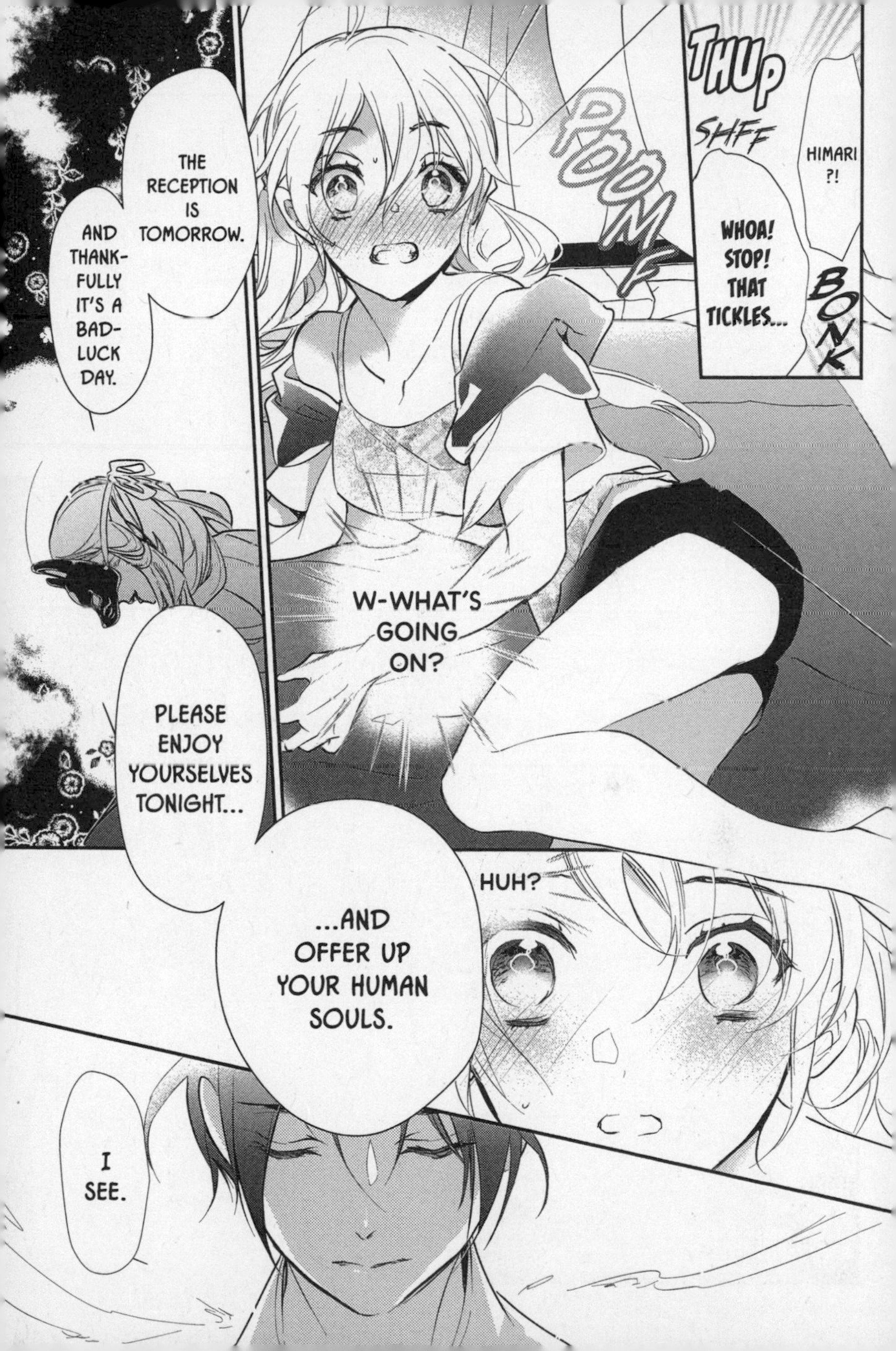
THUP
HIMARI?!
SHFF
WHOA! STOP! THAT TICKLES...
BONK
POOMF
W-WHAT'S GOING ON?
THE RECEPTION IS TOMORROW.
AND THANKFULLY IT'S A BAD-LUCK DAY.
PLEASE ENJOY YOURSELVES TONIGHT...
HUH?
...AND OFFER UP YOUR HUMAN SOULS.
I SEE.

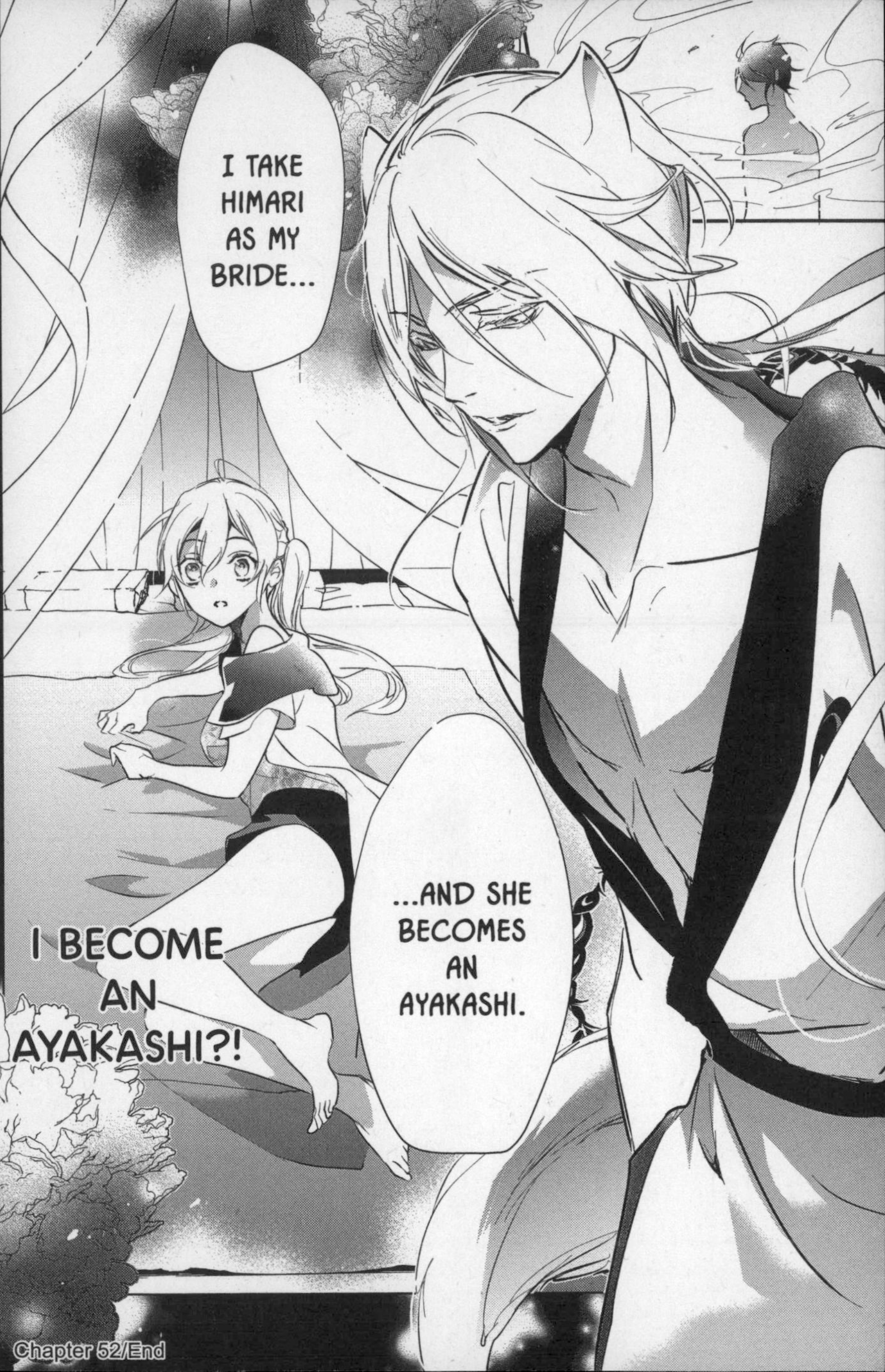
I TAKE HIMARI AS MY BRIDE...
...AND SHE BECOMES AN AYAKASHI.
I BECOME AN AYAKASHI?!

Chapter 52/End

The
DEMON
PRINCE
of MOMOCHI
HOUSE

The
DEMON
PRINCE
of MOMOCHI
HOUSE

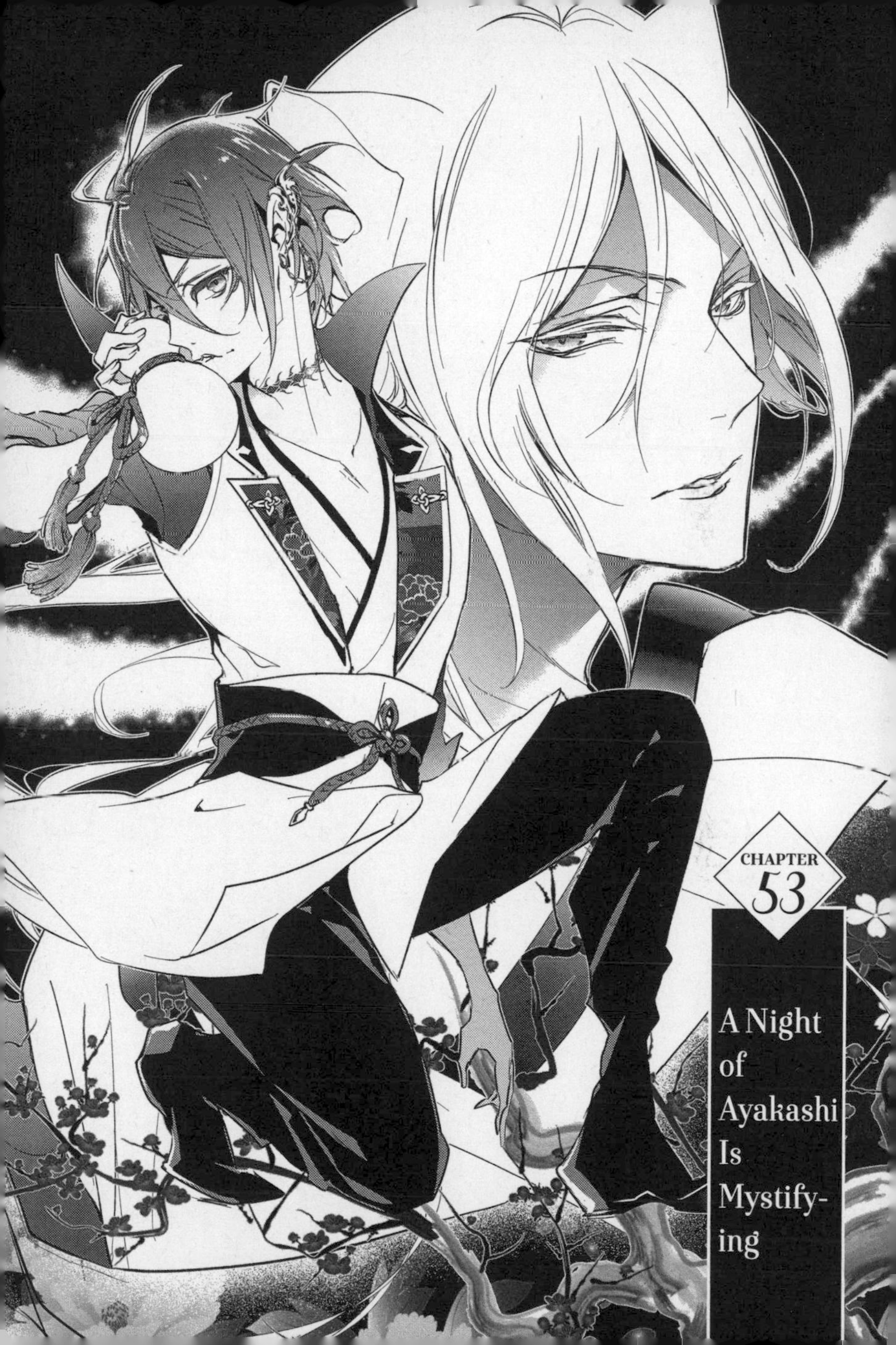
CHAPTER
53
A Night of Ayakashi Is Mystify-ing

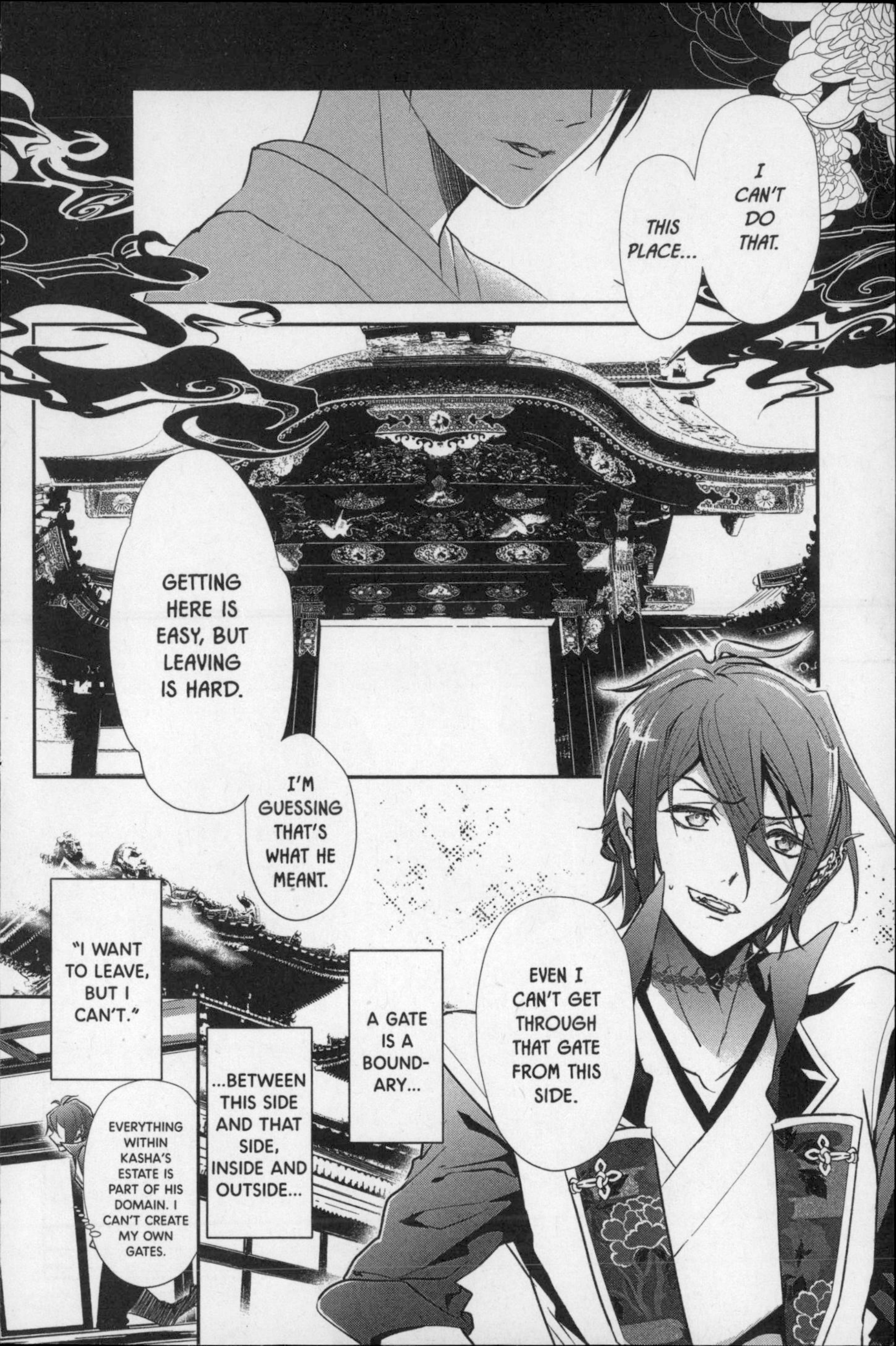
I CAN'T DO THAT.
THIS PLACE...
GETTING HERE IS EASY, BUT LEAVING IS HARD.
I'M GUESSING THAT'S WHAT HE MEANT.
EVEN I CAN'T GET THROUGH THAT GATE FROM THIS SIDE.
A GATE IS A BOUNDARY...
...BETWEEN THIS SIDE AND THAT SIDE, INSIDE AND OUTSIDE...
"I WANT TO LEAVE, BUT I CAN'T."
EVERYTHING WITHIN KASHA'S ESTATE IS PART OF HIS DOMAIN. I CAN'T CREATE MY OWN GATES.

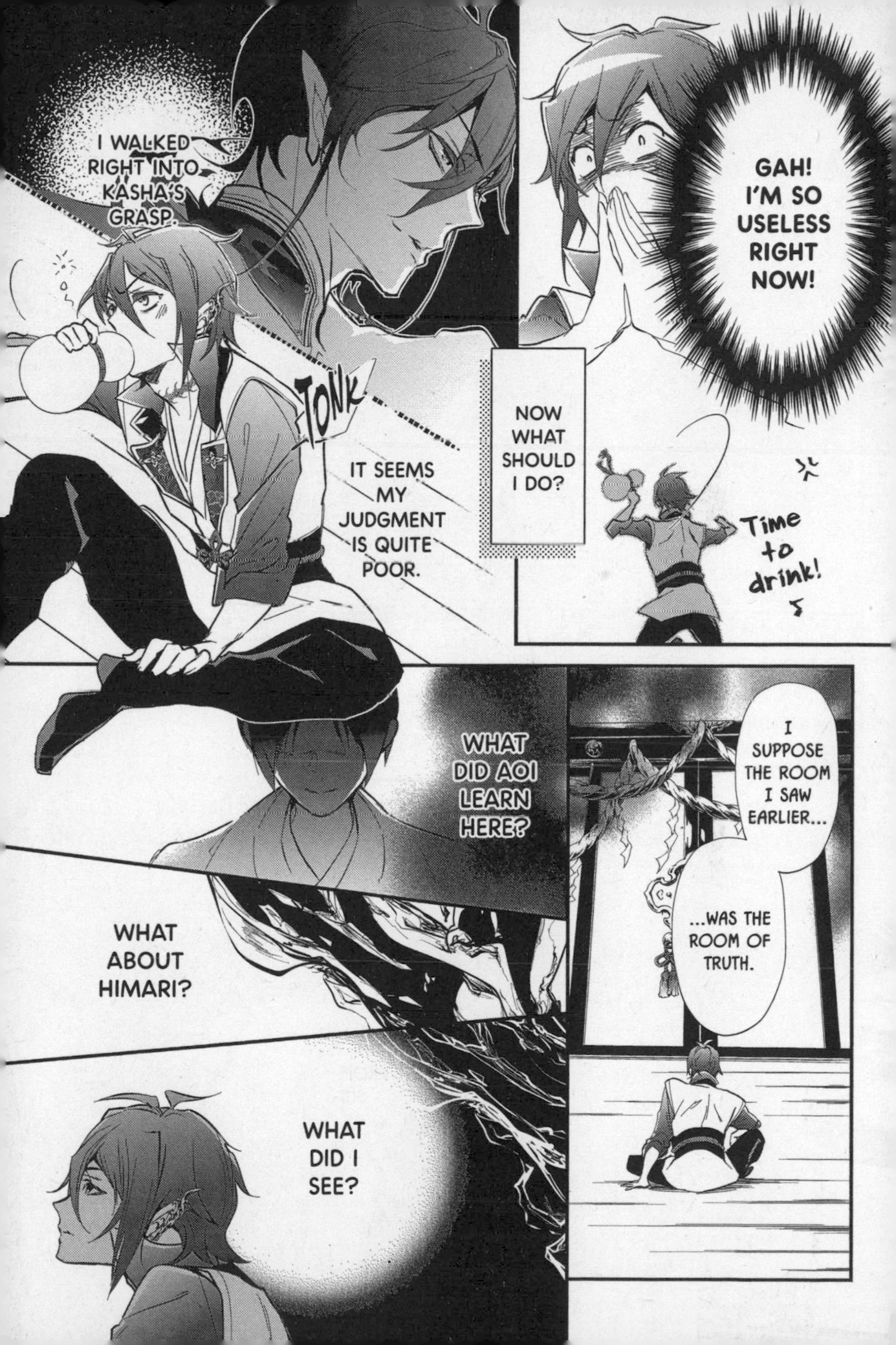
GAH! I'M SO USELESS RIGHT NOW!
NOW WHAT SHOULD I DO?
Time to drink!
I WALKED RIGHT INTO KASHA'S GRASP.
TONK
IT SEEMS MY JUDGMENT IS QUITE POOR.
I SUPPOSE THE ROOM I SAW EARLIER...
...WAS THE ROOM OF TRUTH.
WHAT DID AOI LEARN HERE?
WHAT ABOUT HIMARI?
WHAT DID I SEE?

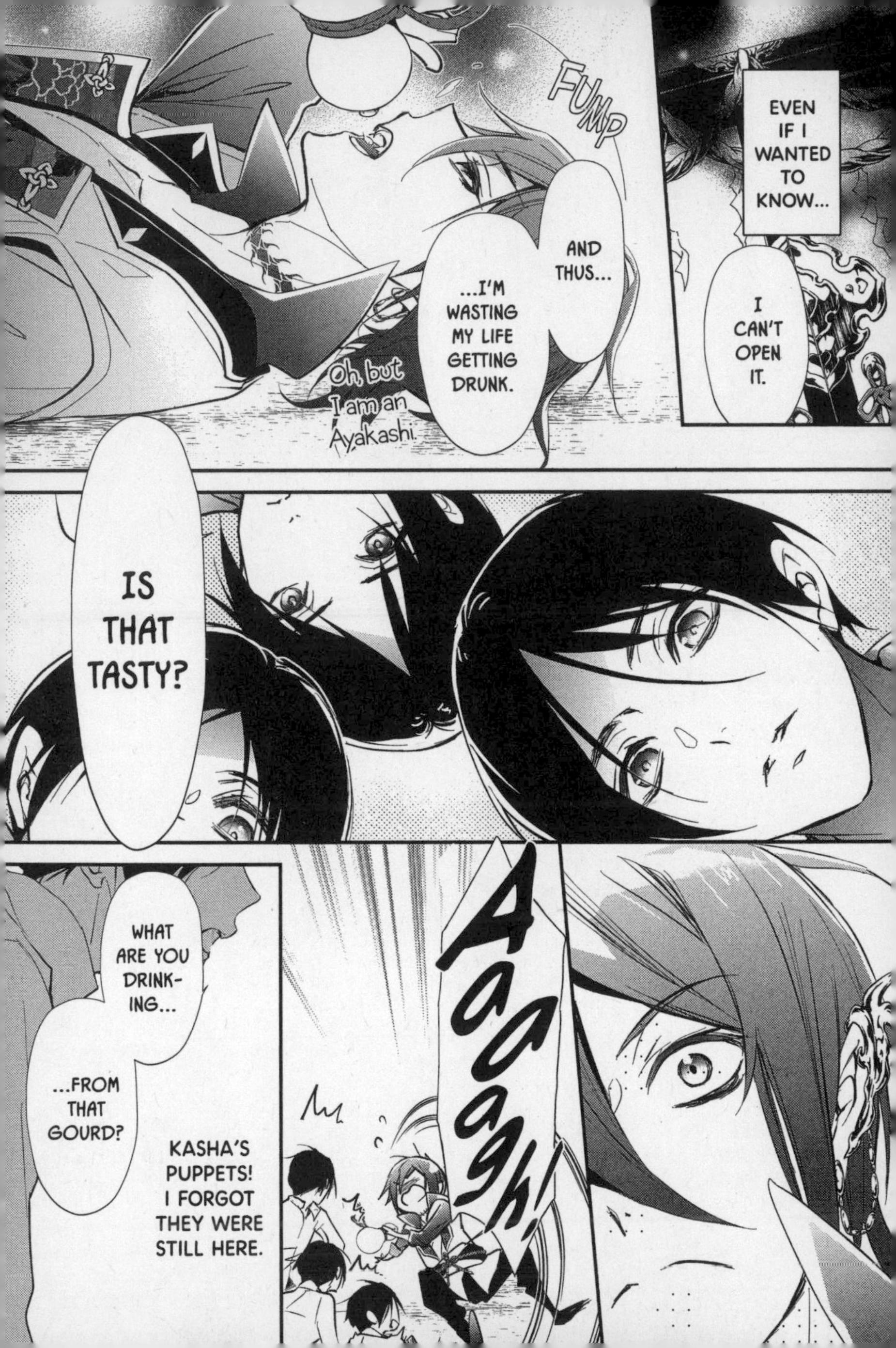
EVEN IF I WANTED TO KNOW...
I CAN'T OPEN IT.
FUMP
AND THUS...
...I'M WASTING MY LIFE GETTING DRUNK.
Oh, but I am an Ayakashi.
IS THAT TASTY?
Aaaagh!
WHAT ARE YOU DRINK-ING...
...FROM THAT GOURD?
KASHA'S PUPPETS! I FORGOT THEY WERE STILL HERE.

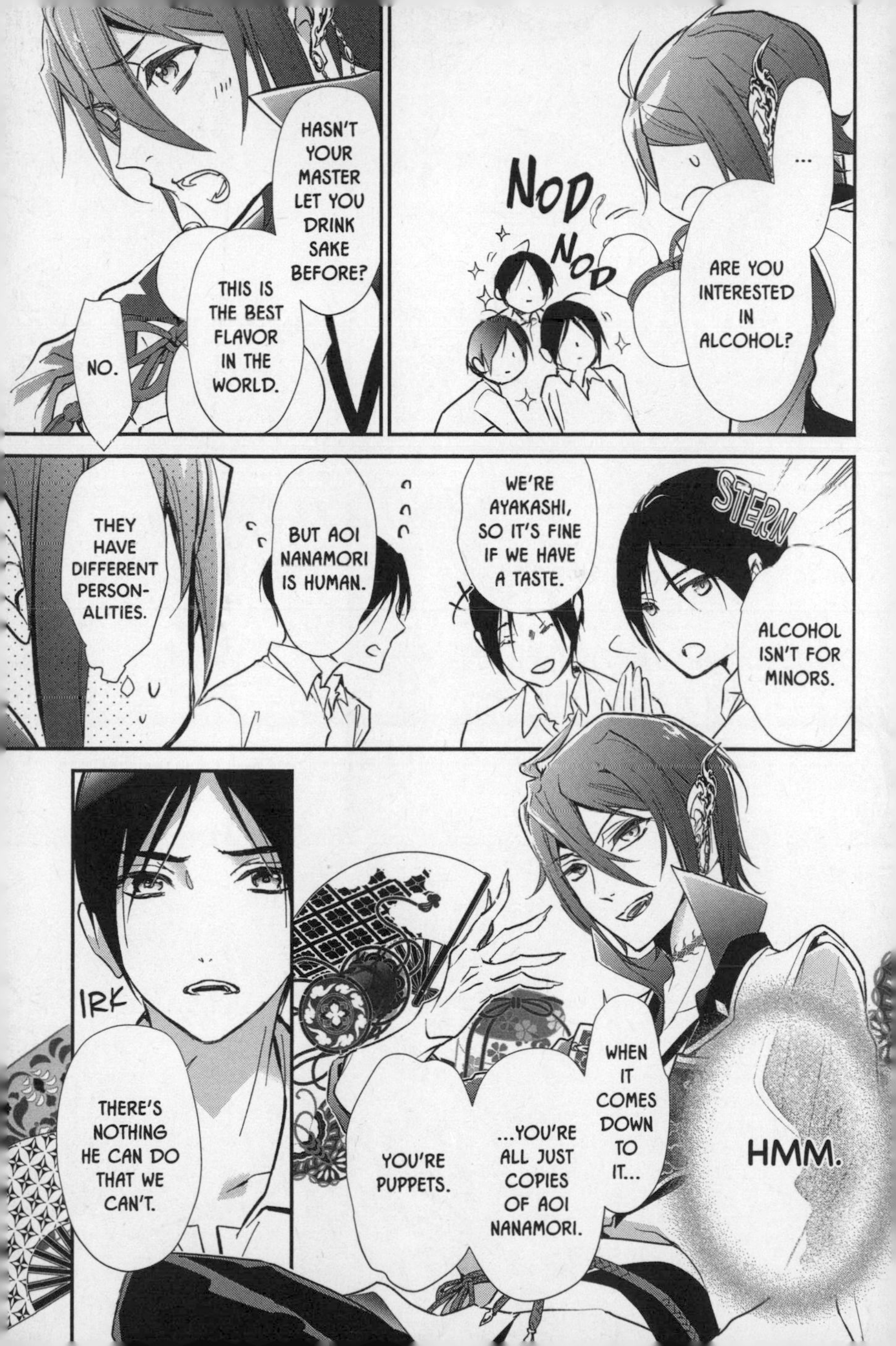
...
ARE YOU INTERESTED IN ALCOHOL?
NOD NOD
HASN'T YOUR MASTER LET YOU DRINK SAKE BEFORE?
THIS IS THE BEST FLAVOR IN THE WORLD.
NO.
ALCOHOL ISN'T FOR MINORS.
STERN
WE'RE AYAKASHI, SO IT'S FINE IF WE HAVE A TASTE.
BUT AOI NANAMORI IS HUMAN.
THEY HAVE DIFFERENT PERSONALITIES.
HMM.
WHEN IT COMES DOWN TO IT...
...YOU'RE ALL JUST COPIES OF AOI NANAMORI.
YOU'RE PUPPETS.
IRK
THERE'S NOTHING HE CAN DO THAT WE CAN'T.

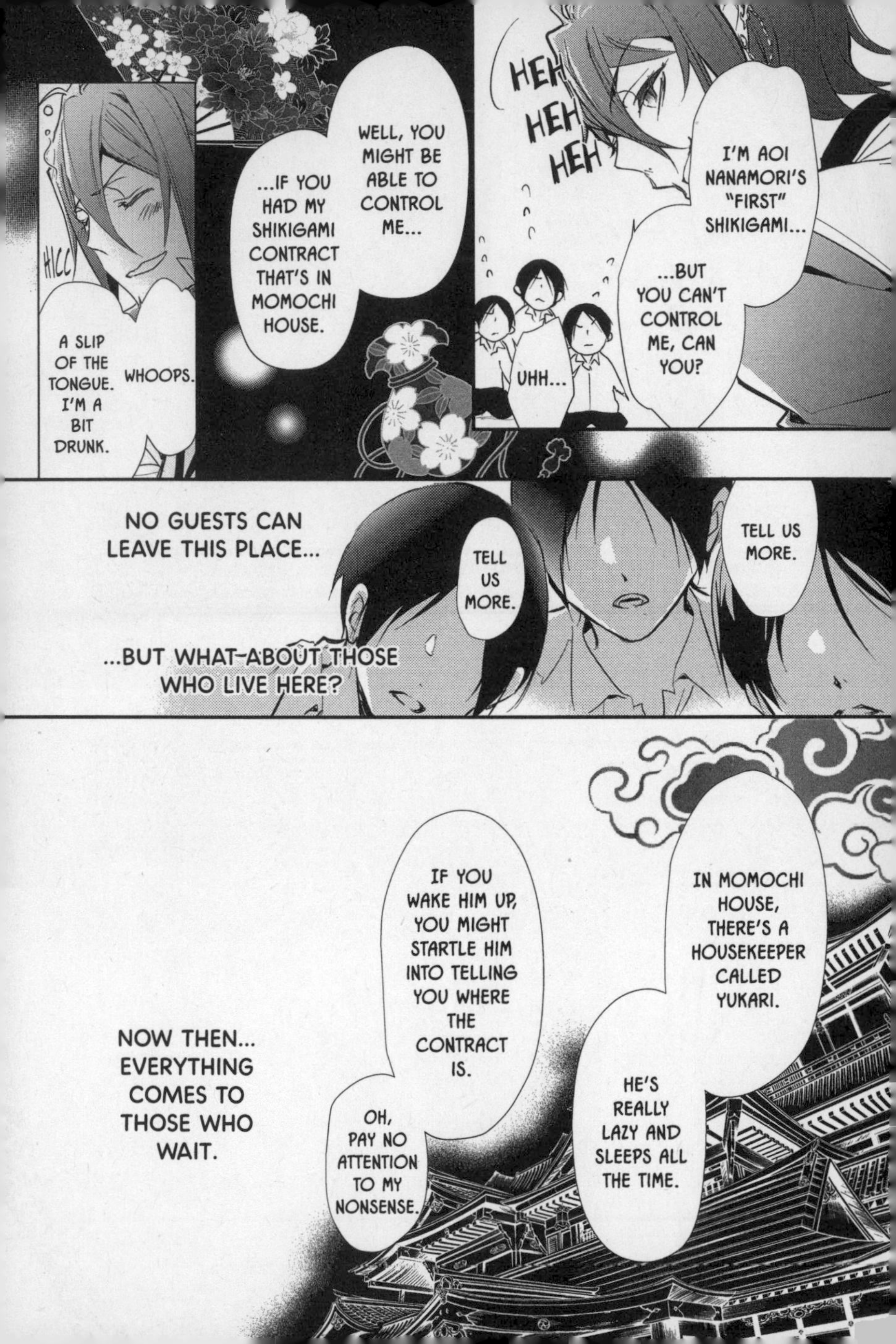
HEH HEH HEH
I'M AOI NANAMORI'S "FIRST" SHIKIGAMI...
...BUT YOU CAN'T CONTROL ME, CAN YOU?
UHH...
WELL, YOU MIGHT BE ABLE TO CONTROL ME...
...IF YOU HAD MY SHIKIGAMI CONTRACT THAT'S IN MOMOCHI HOUSE.
HICC
WHOOPS.
A SLIP OF THE TONGUE. I'M A BIT DRUNK.
TELL US MORE.
TELL US MORE.
NO GUESTS CAN LEAVE THIS PLACE...
...BUT WHAT ABOUT THOSE WHO LIVE HERE?
IN MOMOCHI HOUSE, THERE'S A HOUSEKEEPER CALLED YUKARI.
HE'S REALLY LAZY AND SLEEPS ALL THE TIME.
IF YOU WAKE HIM UP, YOU MIGHT STARTLE HIM INTO TELLING YOU WHERE THE CONTRACT IS.
OH, PAY NO ATTENTION TO MY NONSENSE.
NOW THEN... EVERYTHING COMES TO THOSE WHO WAIT.

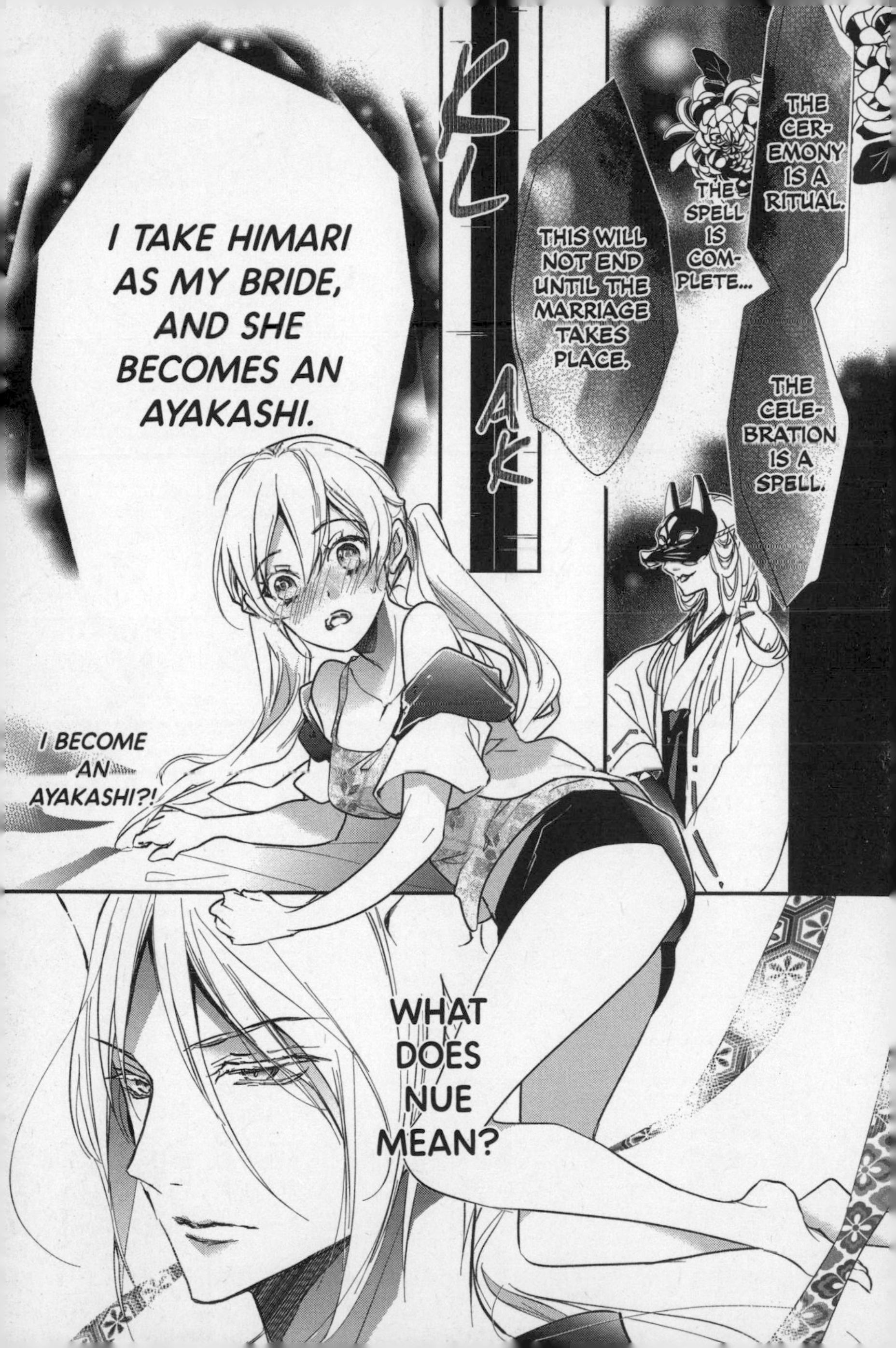
THE CEREMONY IS A RITUAL.
THE CELEBRATION IS A SPELL.
THE SPELL IS COMPLETE...
THIS WILL NOT END UNTIL THE MARRIAGE TAKES PLACE.
I TAKE HIMARI AS MY BRIDE, AND SHE BECOMES AN AYAKASHI.
I BECOME AN AYAKASHI?!
WHAT DOES NUE MEAN?

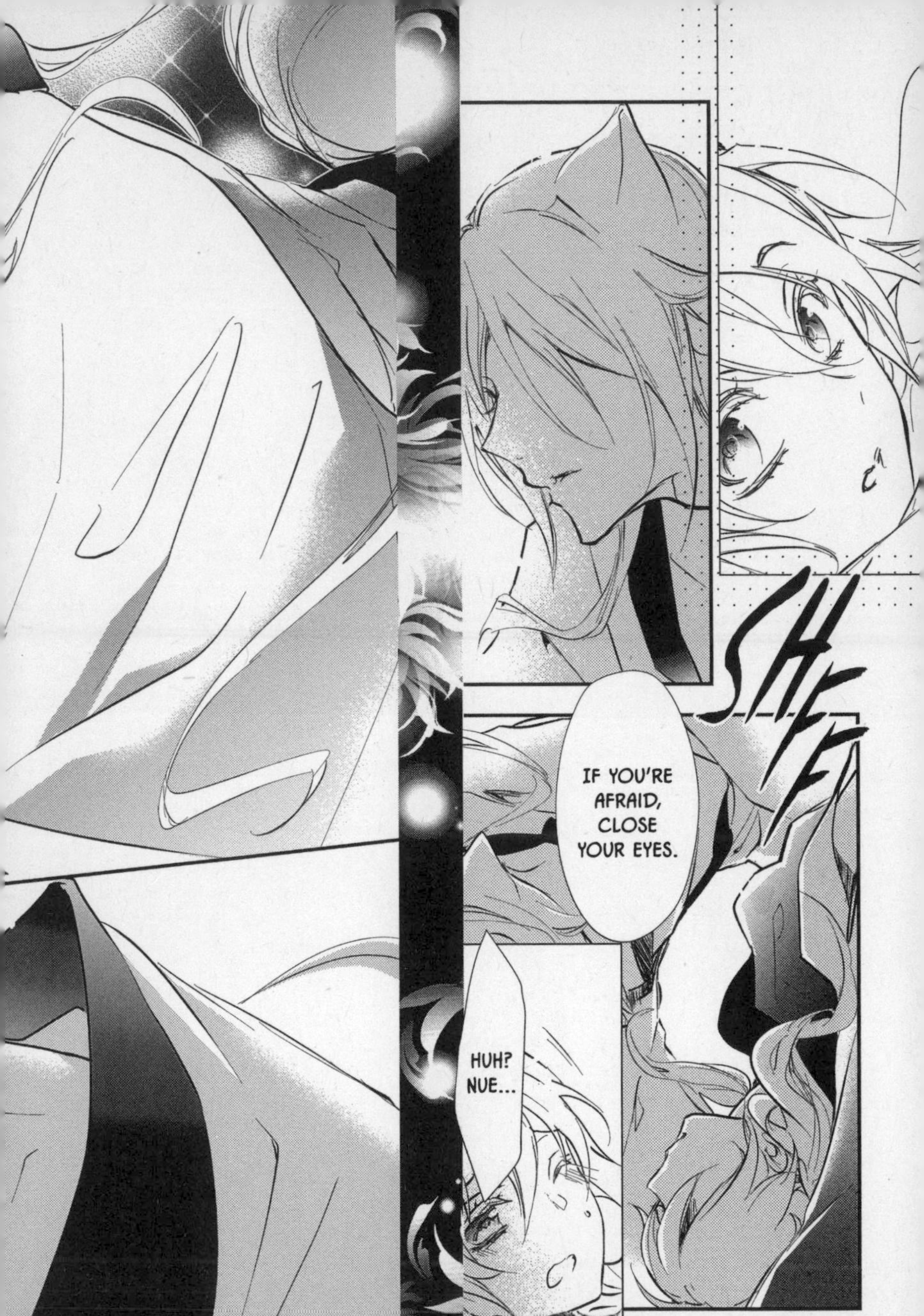
SHFF
IF YOU'RE AFRAID, CLOSE YOUR EYES.
HUH? NUE...

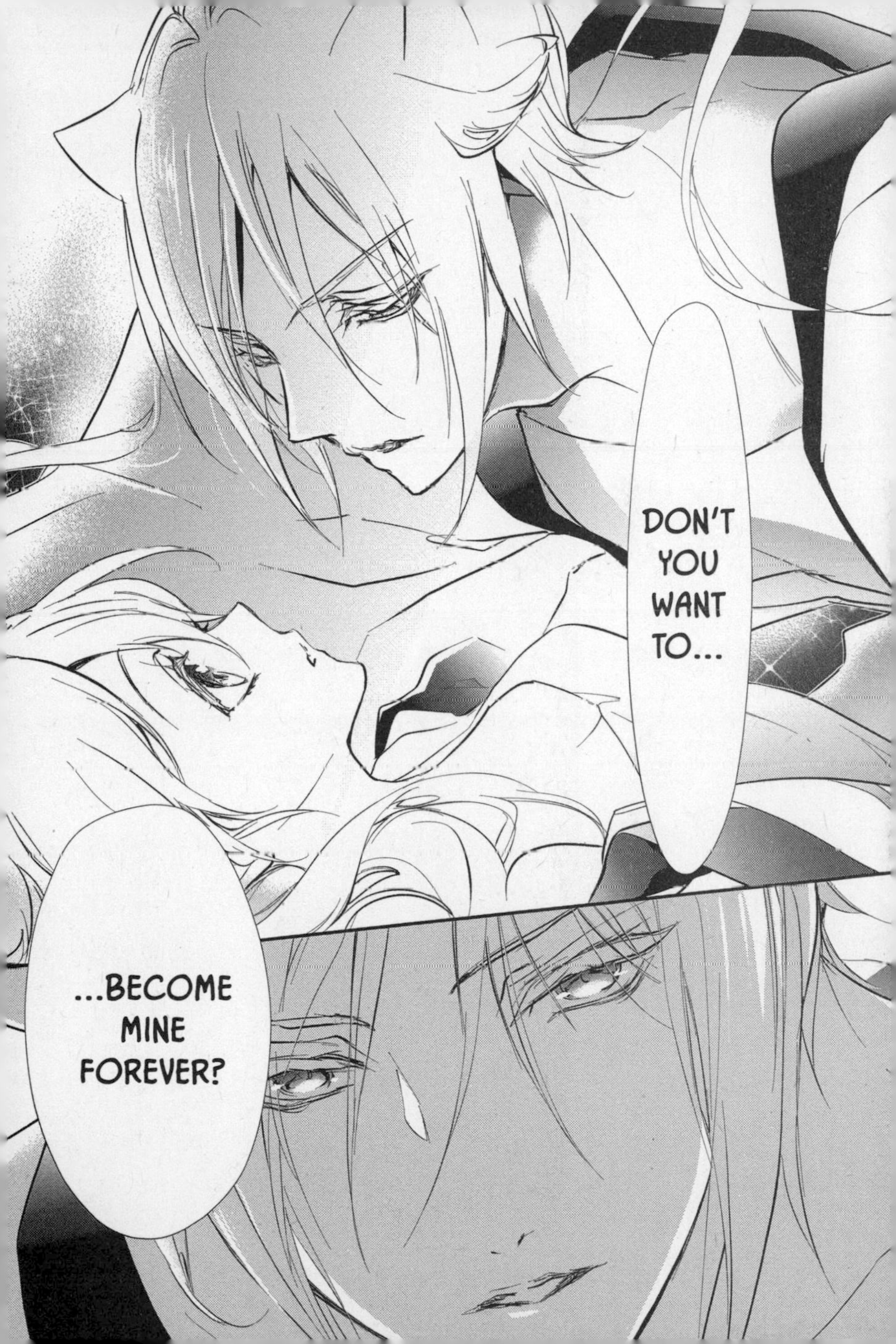
DON'T YOU WANT TO...
...BECOME MINE FOREVER?

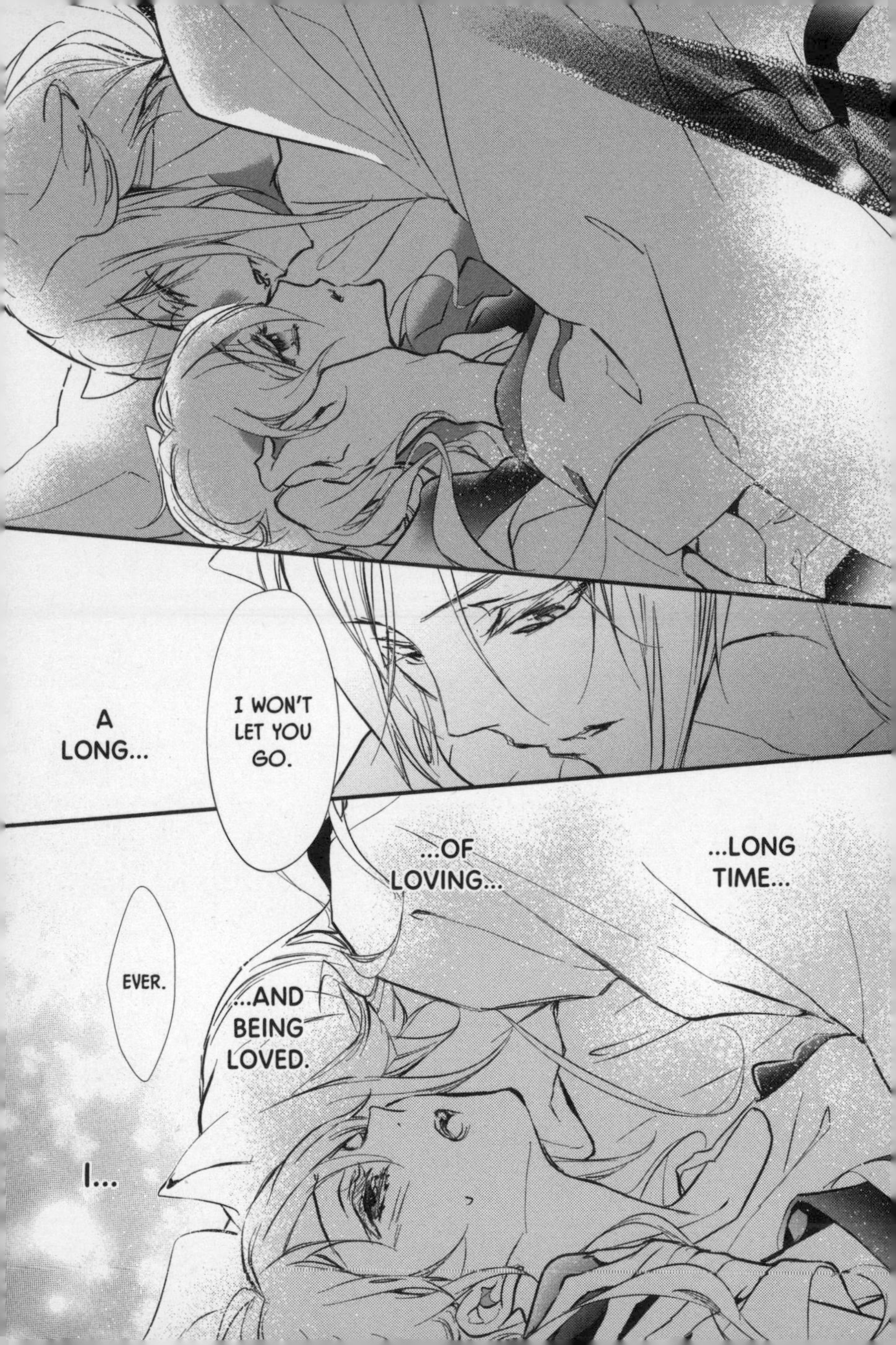
I WON'T LET YOU GO.
A LONG...
...LONG TIME...
...OF LOVING...
EVER.
...AND BEING LOVED.
I...

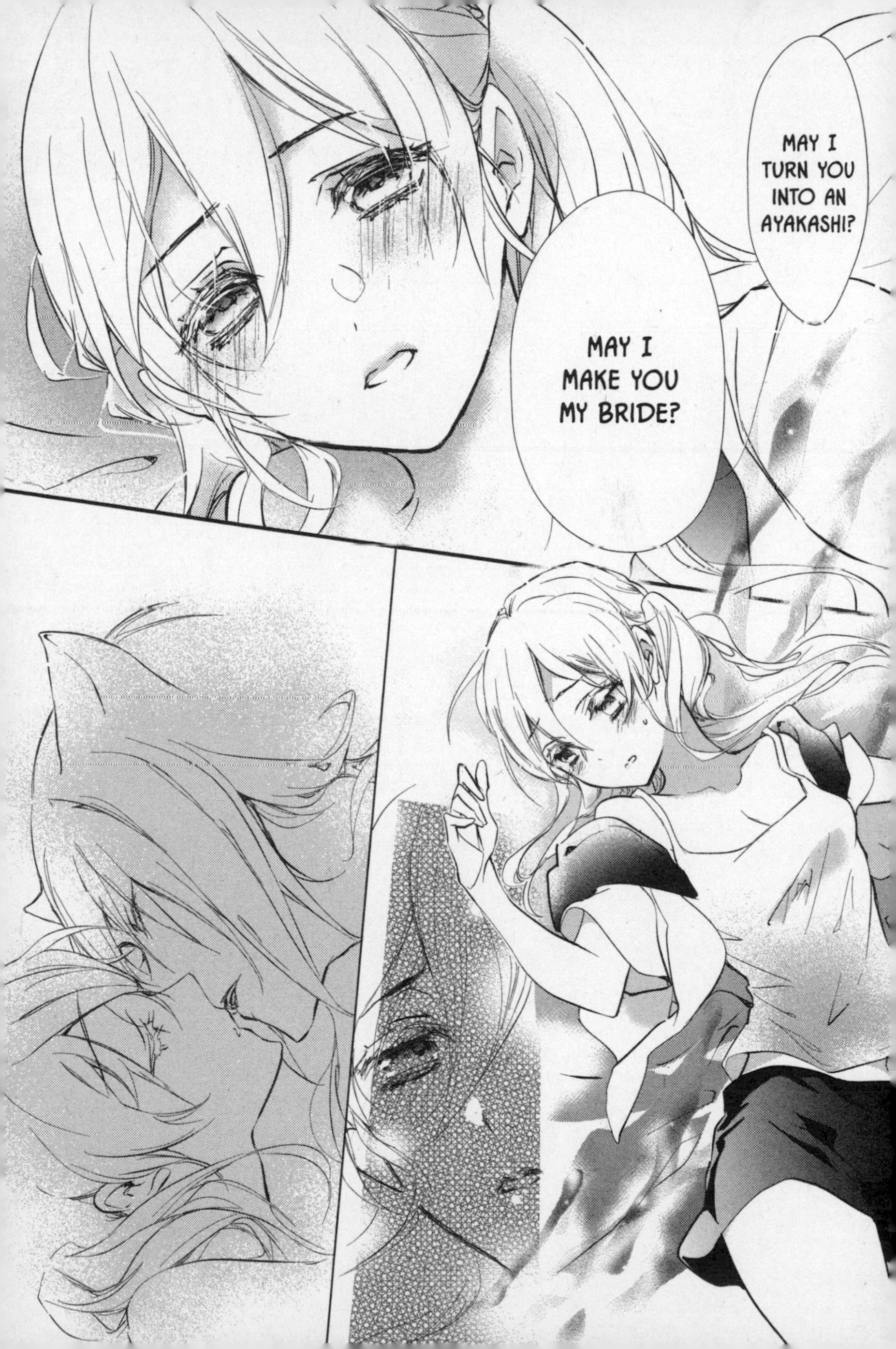
MAY I TURN YOU INTO AN AYAKASHI?
MAY I MAKE YOU MY BRIDE?

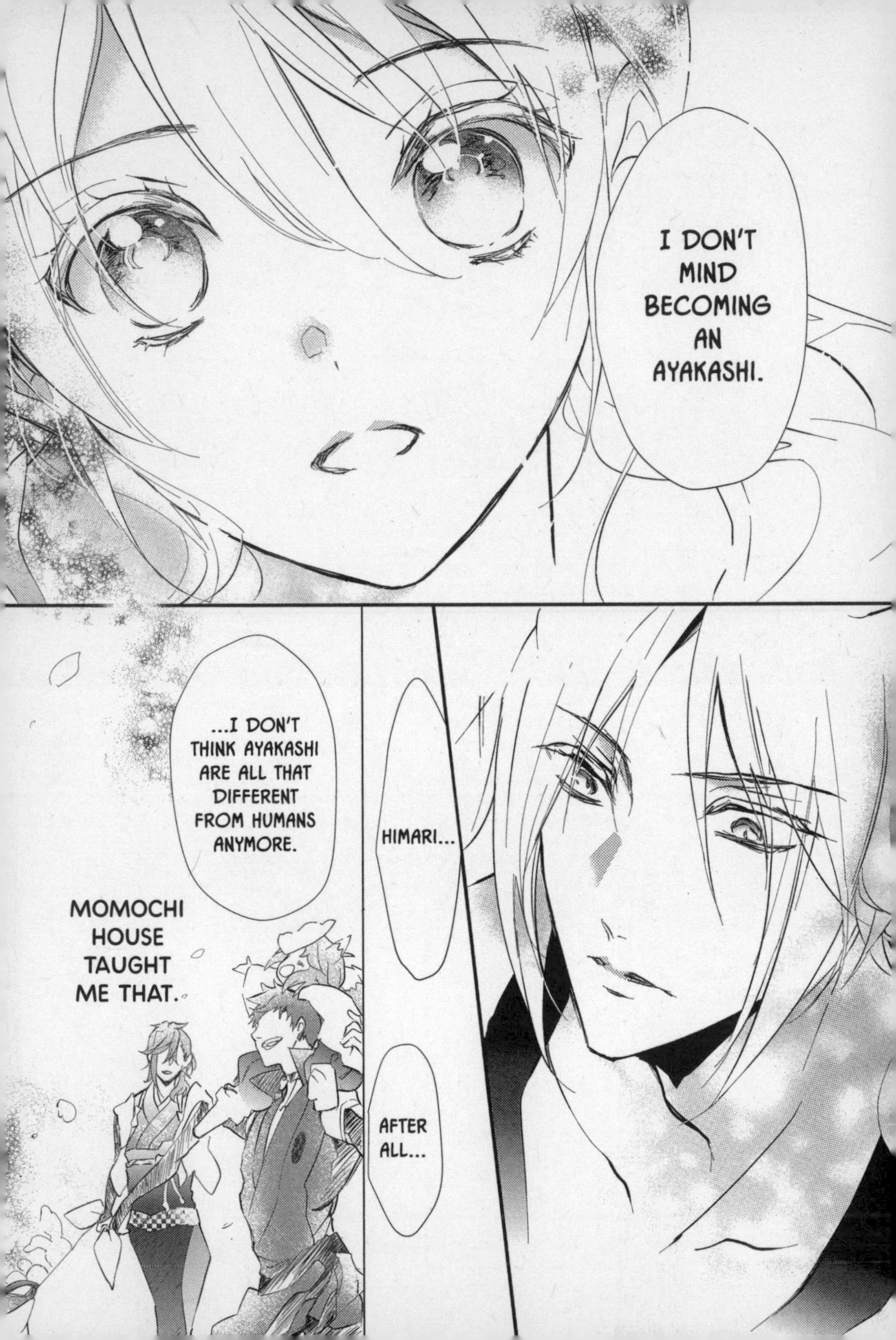
I DON'T MIND BECOMING AN AYAKASHI.
HIMARI...
AFTER ALL...
...I DON'T THINK AYAKASHI ARE ALL THAT DIFFERENT FROM HUMANS ANYMORE.
MOMOCHI HOUSE TAUGHT ME THAT.

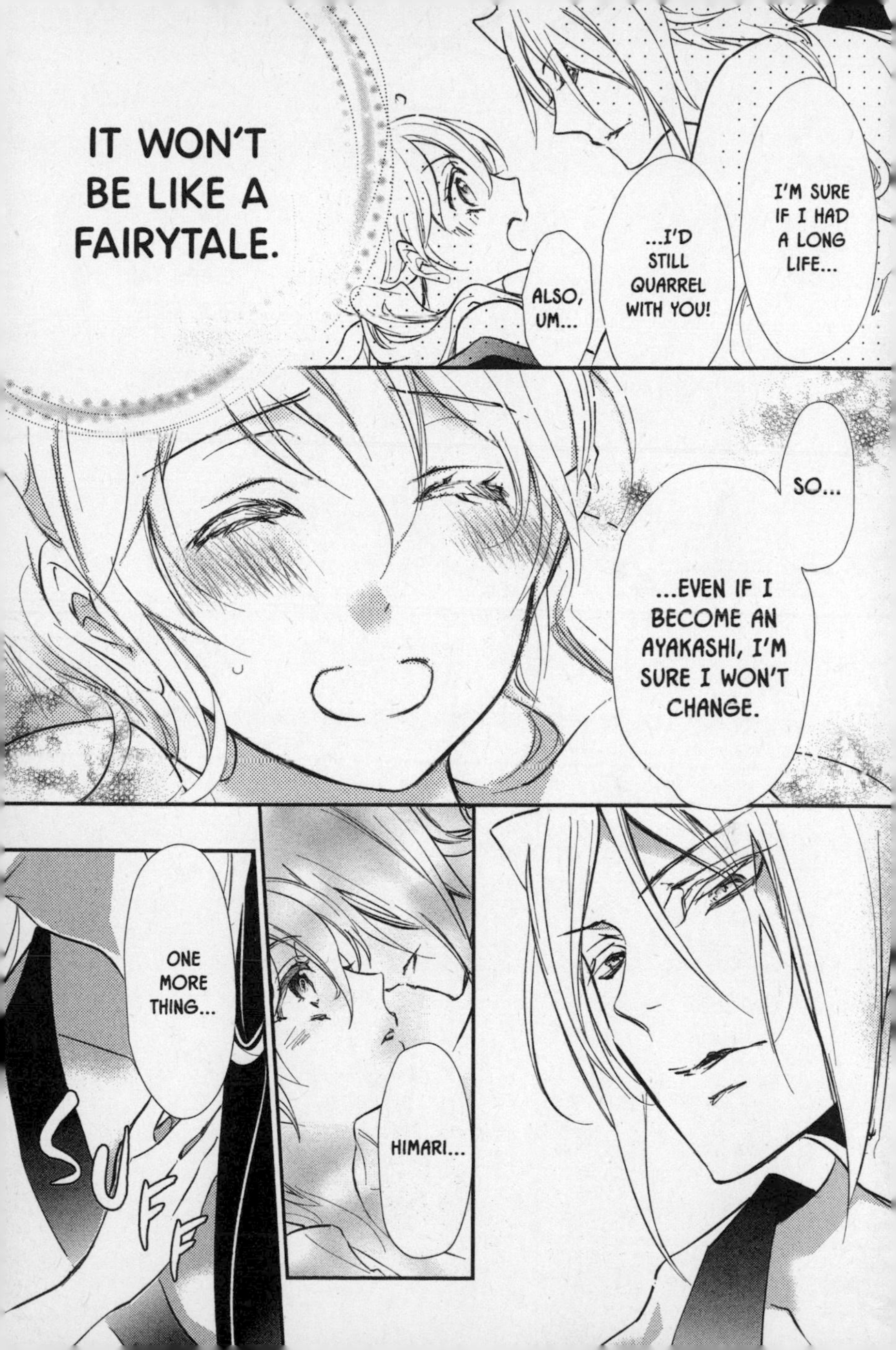
I'M SURE IF I HAD A LONG LIFE...
...I'D STILL QUARREL WITH YOU!
ALSO, UM...
IT WON'T BE LIKE A FAIRYTALE.
SO...
...EVEN IF I BECOME AN AYAKASHI, I'M SURE I WON'T CHANGE.
HIMARI...
ONE MORE THING...
SUFF

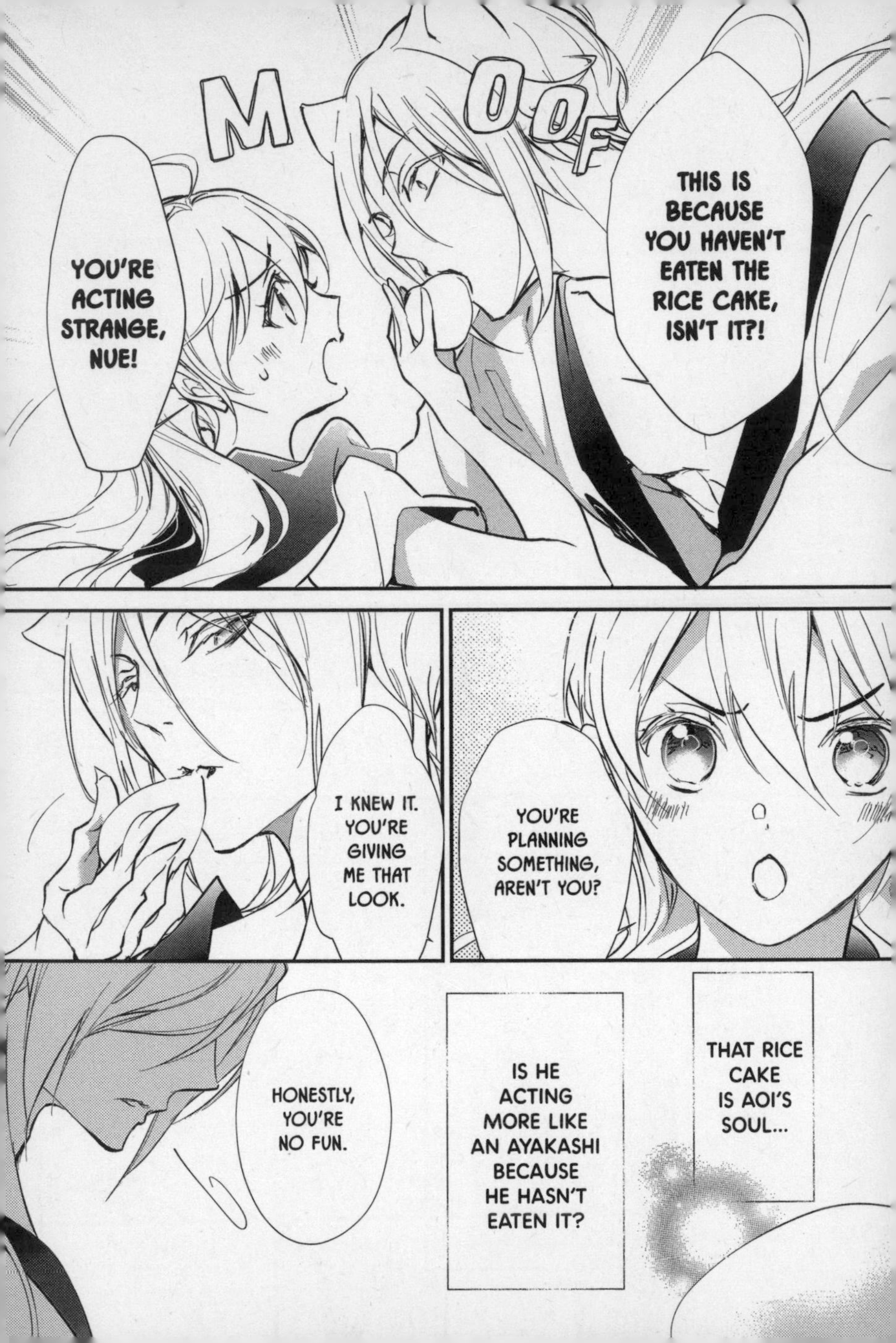
MOOF
THIS IS BECAUSE YOU HAVEN'T EATEN THE RICE CAKE, ISN'T IT?!
YOU'RE ACTING STRANGE, NUE!
YOU'RE PLANNING SOMETHING, AREN'T YOU?
I KNEW IT. YOU'RE GIVING ME THAT LOOK.
THAT RICE CAKE IS AOI'S SOUL...
IS HE ACTING MORE LIKE AN AYAKASHI BECAUSE HE HASN'T EATEN IT?
HONESTLY, YOU'RE NO FUN.

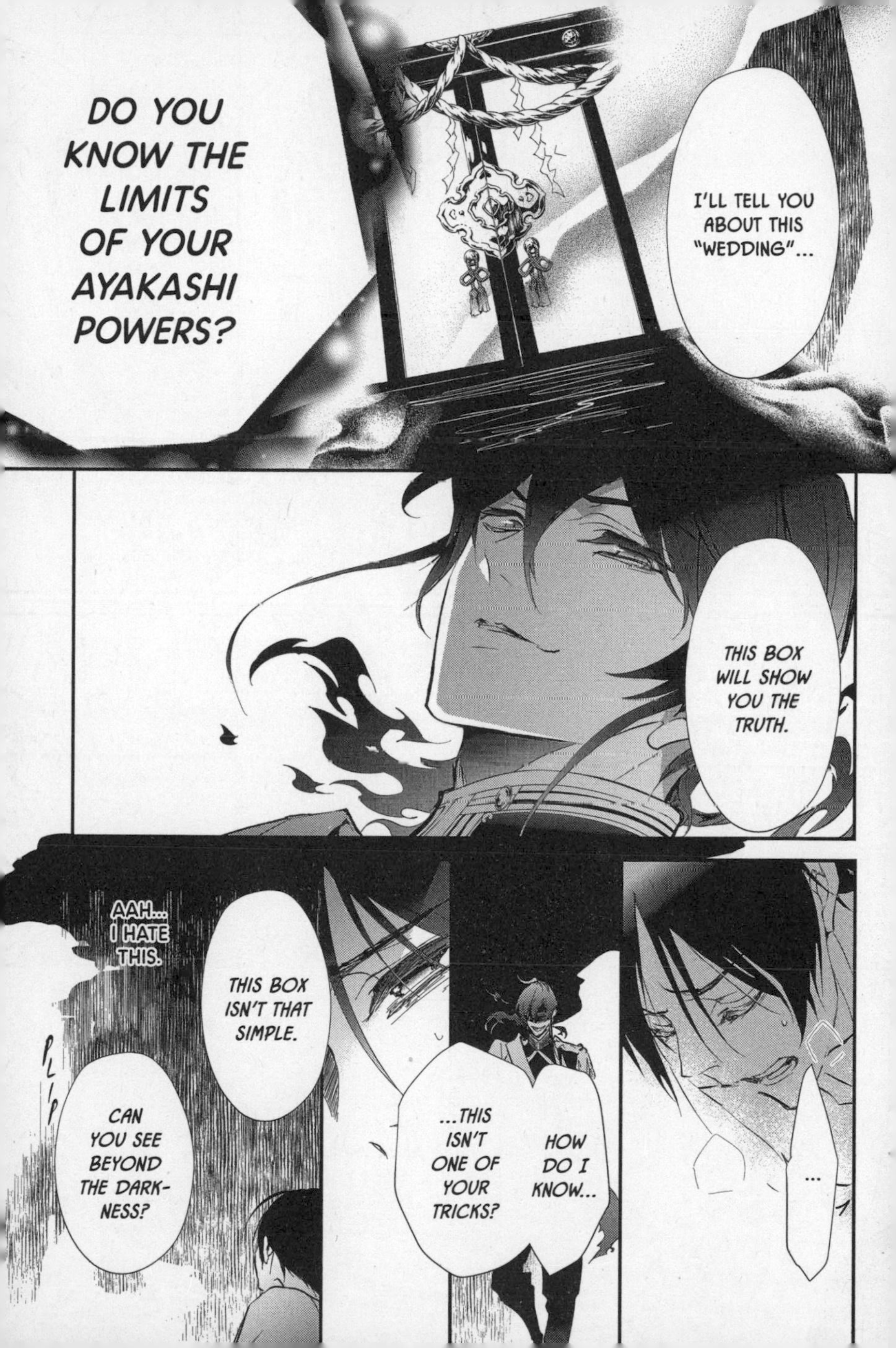
I'LL TELL YOU ABOUT THIS "WEDDING"...
DO YOU KNOW THE LIMITS OF YOUR AYAKASHI POWERS?
THIS BOX WILL SHOW YOU THE TRUTH.
...
HOW DO I KNOW...
...THIS ISN'T ONE OF YOUR TRICKS?
THIS BOX ISN'T THAT SIMPLE.
AAH... I HATE THIS.
CAN YOU SEE BEYOND THE DARK-NESS?
PLIP

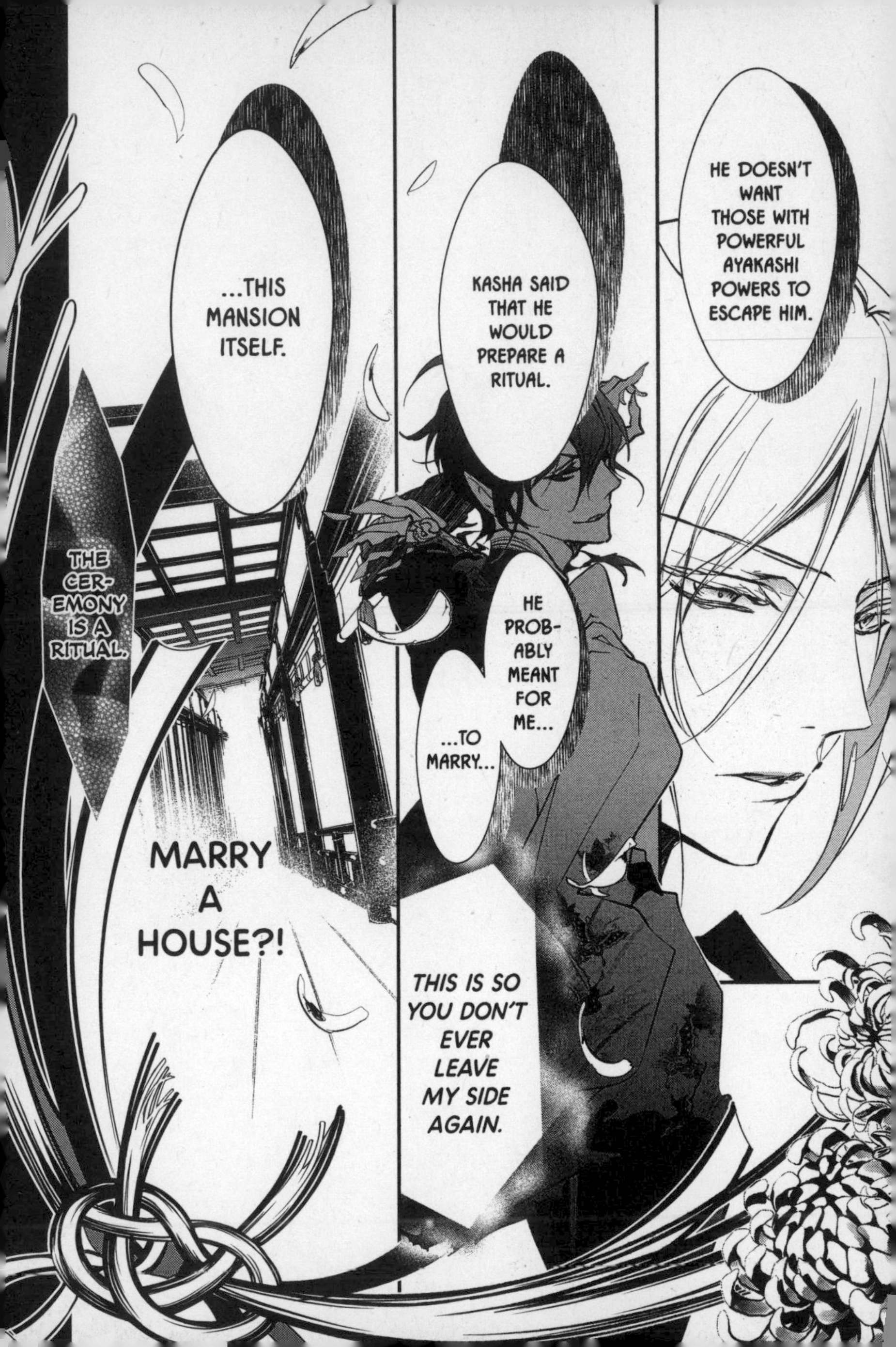
HE DOESN'T WANT THOSE WITH POWERFUL AYAKASHI POWERS TO ESCAPE HIM.
KASHA SAID THAT HE WOULD PREPARE A RITUAL.
HE PROB-ABLY MEANT FOR ME...
...TO MARRY...
THIS IS SO YOU DON'T EVER LEAVE MY SIDE AGAIN.
...THIS MANSION ITSELF.
THE CER-EMONY IS A RITUAL.
MARRY A HOUSE?!

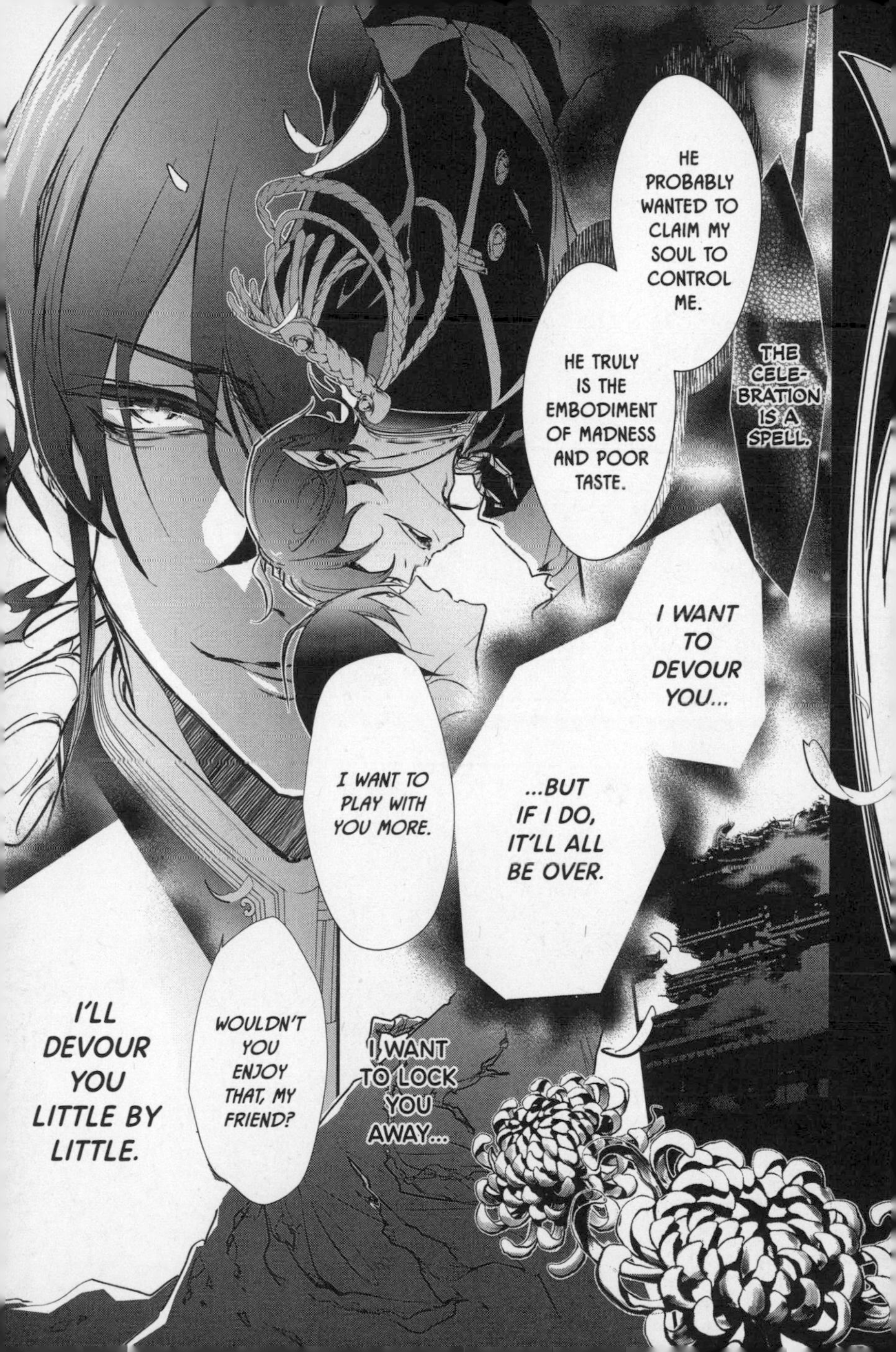
HE PROBABLY WANTED TO CLAIM MY SOUL TO CONTROL ME.
HE TRULY IS THE EMBODIMENT OF MADNESS AND POOR TASTE.
THE CELE-BRATION IS A SPELL.
I WANT TO DEVOUR YOU...
...BUT IF I DO, IT'LL ALL BE OVER.
I WANT TO PLAY WITH YOU MORE.
I WANT TO LOCK YOU AWAY...
WOULDN'T YOU ENJOY THAT, MY FRIEND?
I'LL DEVOUR YOU LITTLE BY LITTLE.

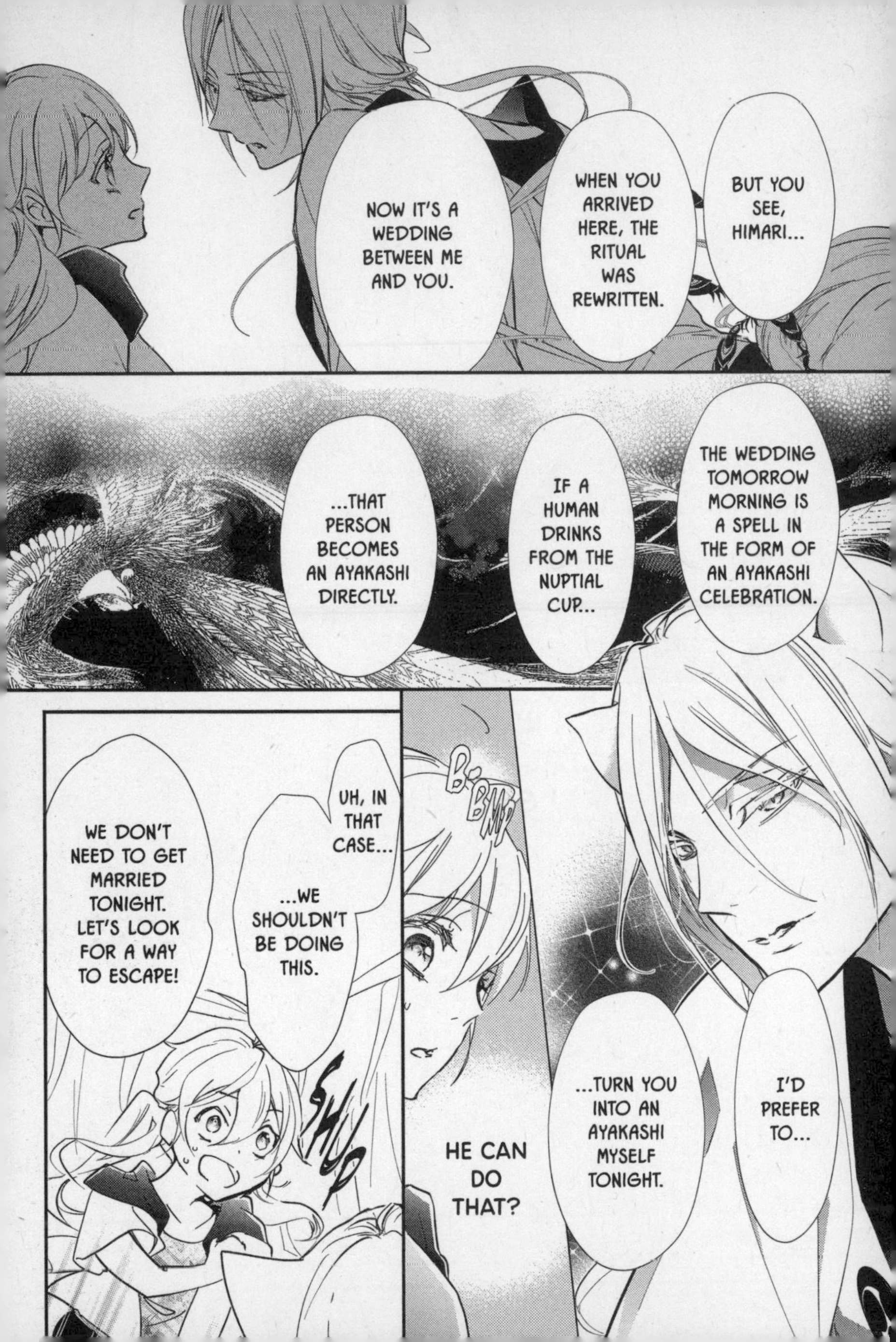
BUT YOU SEE, HIMARI...
WHEN YOU ARRIVED HERE, THE RITUAL WAS REWRITTEN.
NOW IT'S A WEDDING BETWEEN ME AND YOU.
THE WEDDING TOMORROW MORNING IS A SPELL IN THE FORM OF AN AYAKASHI CELEBRATION.
IF A HUMAN DRINKS FROM THE NUPTIAL CUP...
...THAT PERSON BECOMES AN AYAKASHI DIRECTLY.
I'D PREFER TO...
...TURN YOU INTO AN AYAKASHI MYSELF TONIGHT.
B-BMP
HE CAN DO THAT?
UH, IN THAT CASE...
...WE SHOULDN'T BE DOING THIS.
WE DON'T NEED TO GET MARRIED TONIGHT. LET'S LOOK FOR A WAY TO ESCAPE!

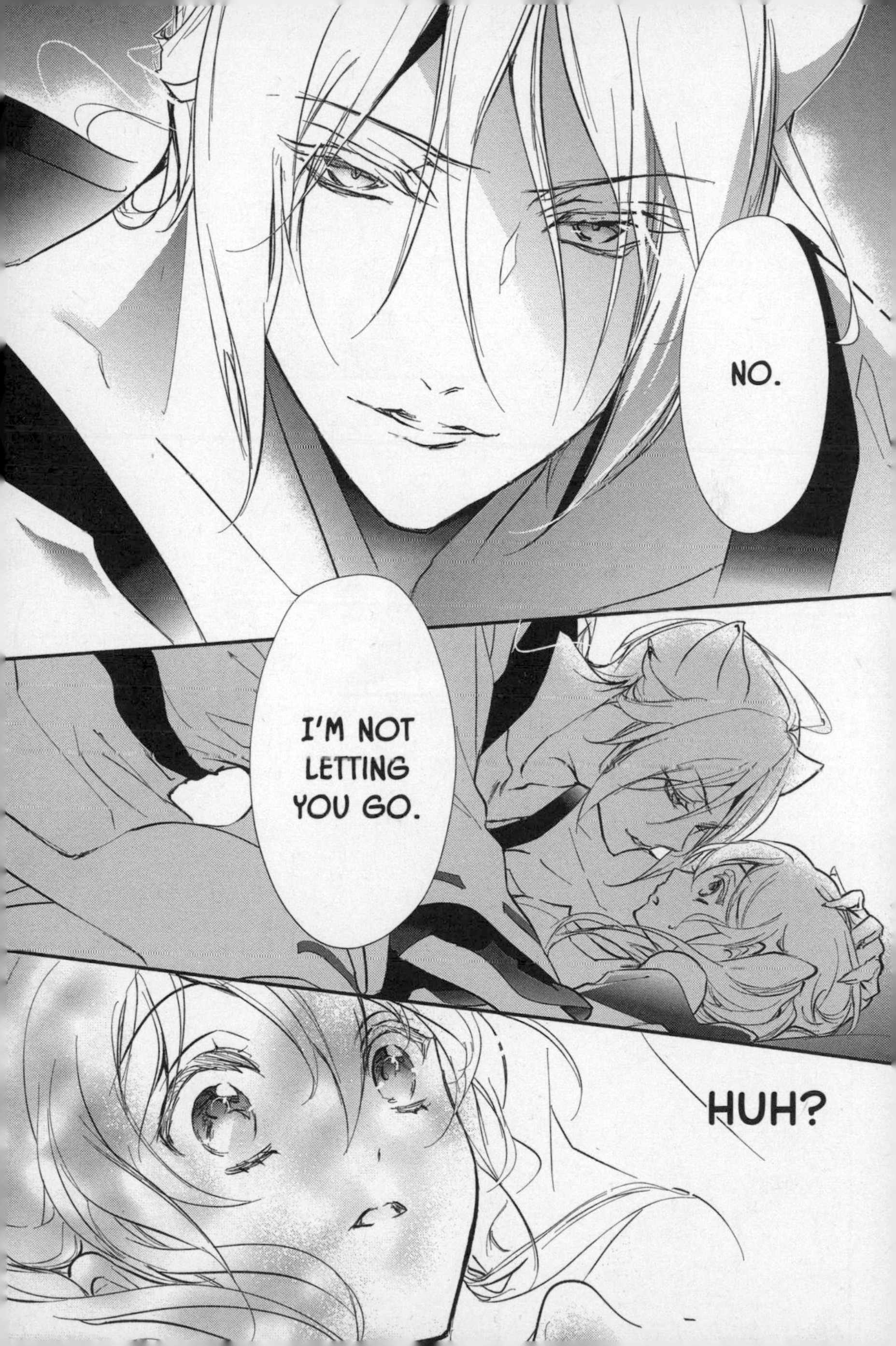
NO.
I'M NOT LETTING YOU GO.
HUH?

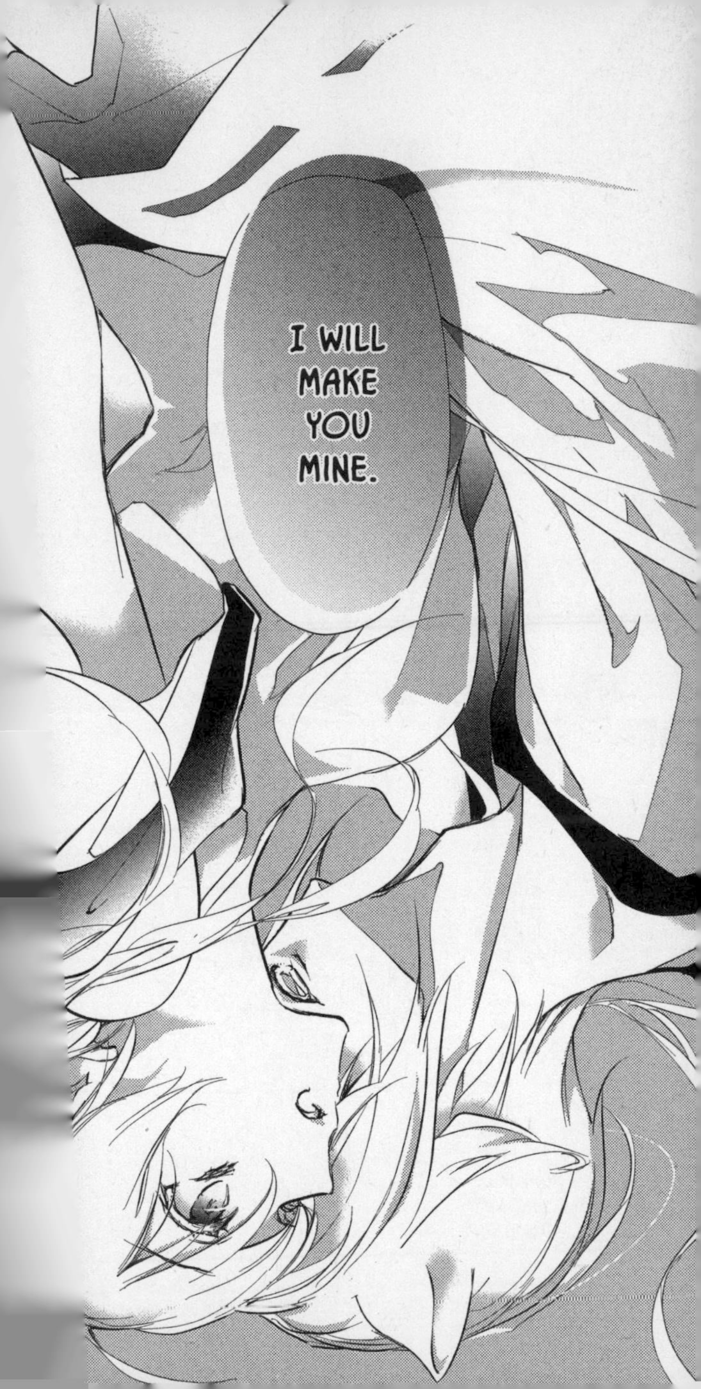
I WILL MAKE YOU MINE.

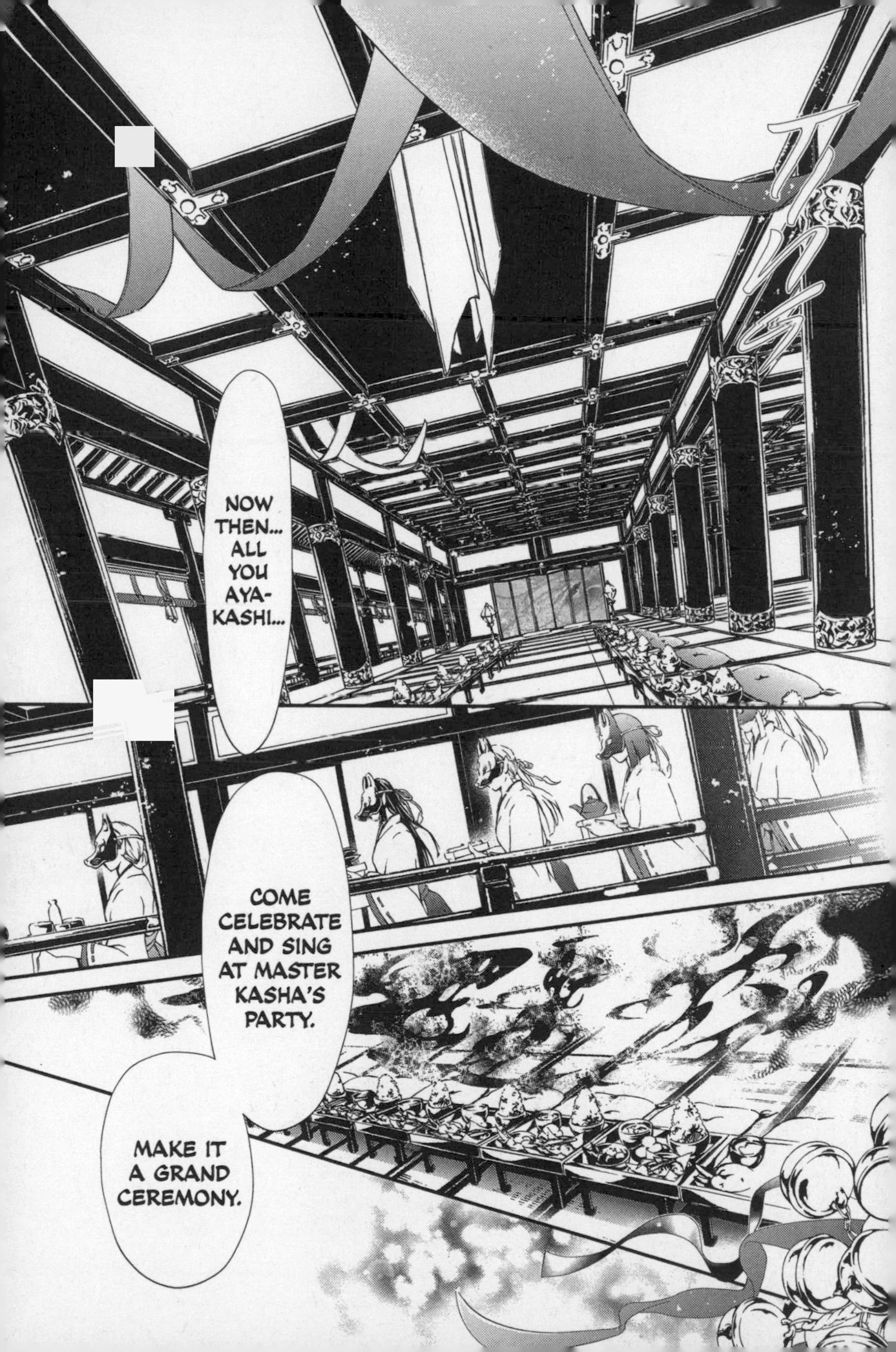
NOW THEN... ALL YOU AYA-KASHI...
COME CELEBRATE AND SING AT MASTER KASHA'S PARTY.
MAKE IT A GRAND CEREMONY.

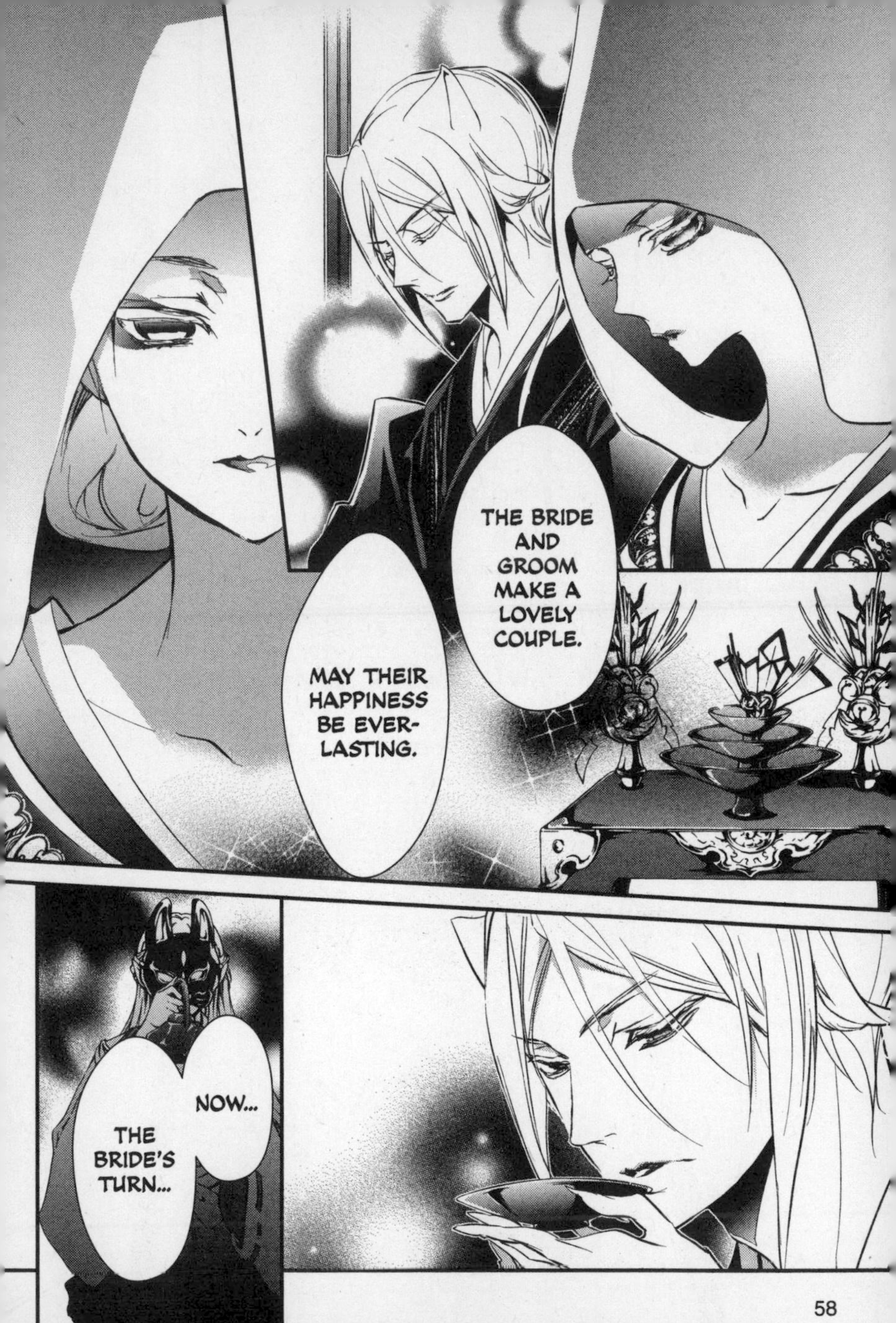
THE BRIDE AND GROOM MAKE A LOVELY COUPLE.
MAY THEIR HAPPINESS BE EVER-LASTING.
NOW...
THE BRIDE'S TURN...

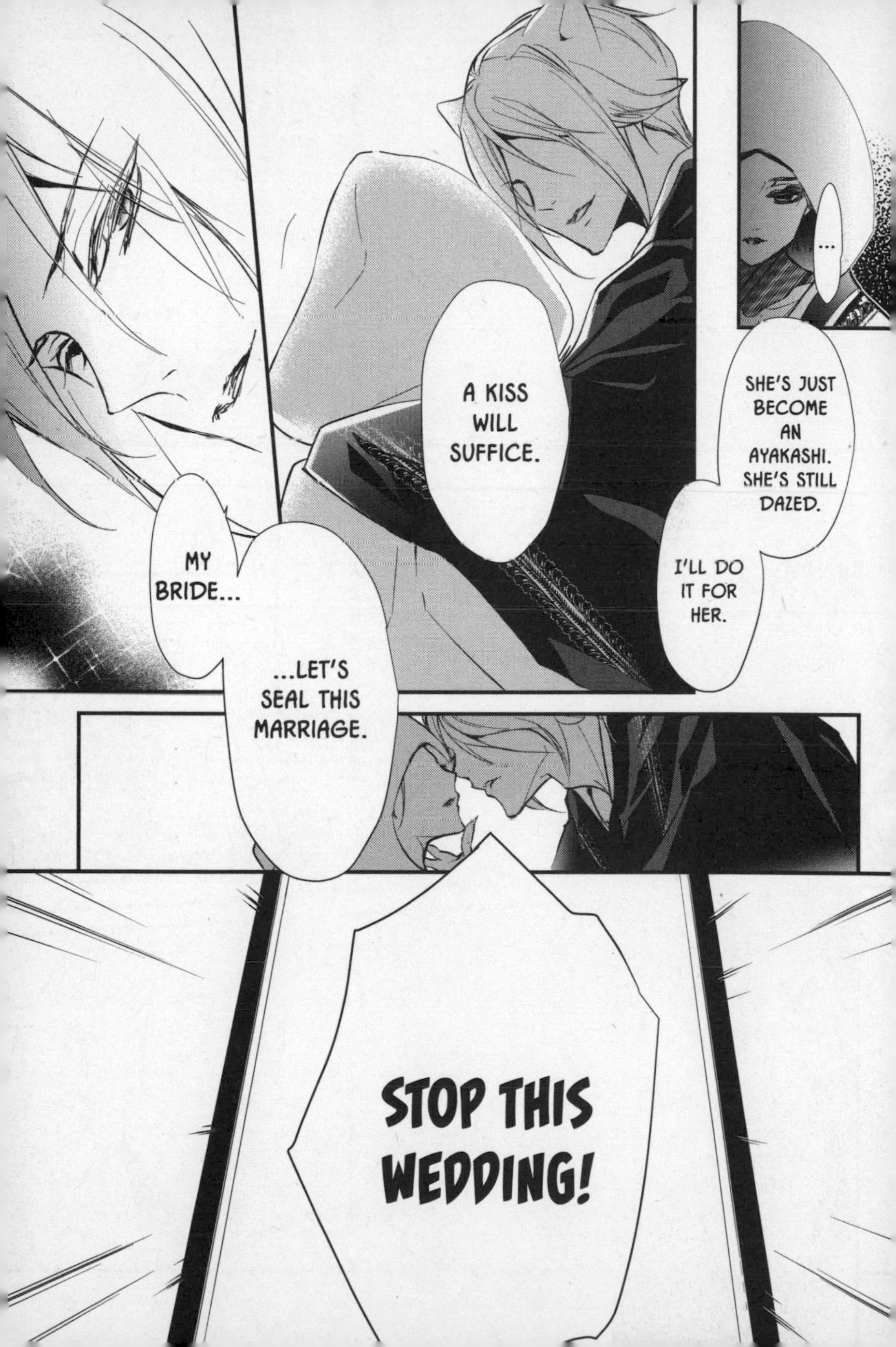
...
SHE'S JUST BECOME AN AYAKASHI. SHE'S STILL DAZED.
I'LL DO IT FOR HER.
A KISS WILL SUFFICE.
MY BRIDE...
...LET'S SEAL THIS MARRIAGE.
STOP THIS WEDDING!

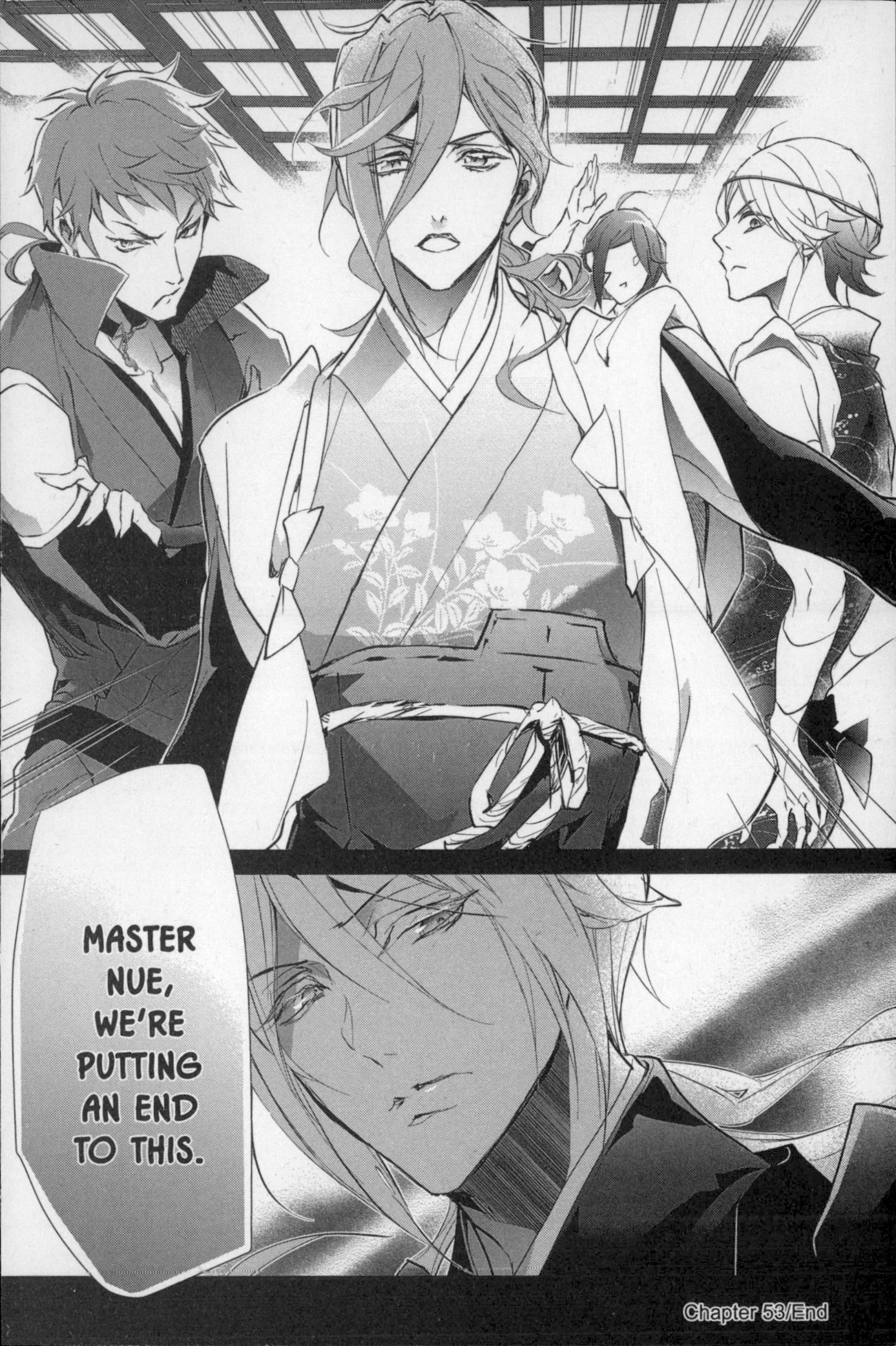
MASTER NUE, WE'RE PUTTING AN END TO THIS.

Chapter 53/End

CHAPTER 54
Defy the Social Order! The Shikigami Revolt

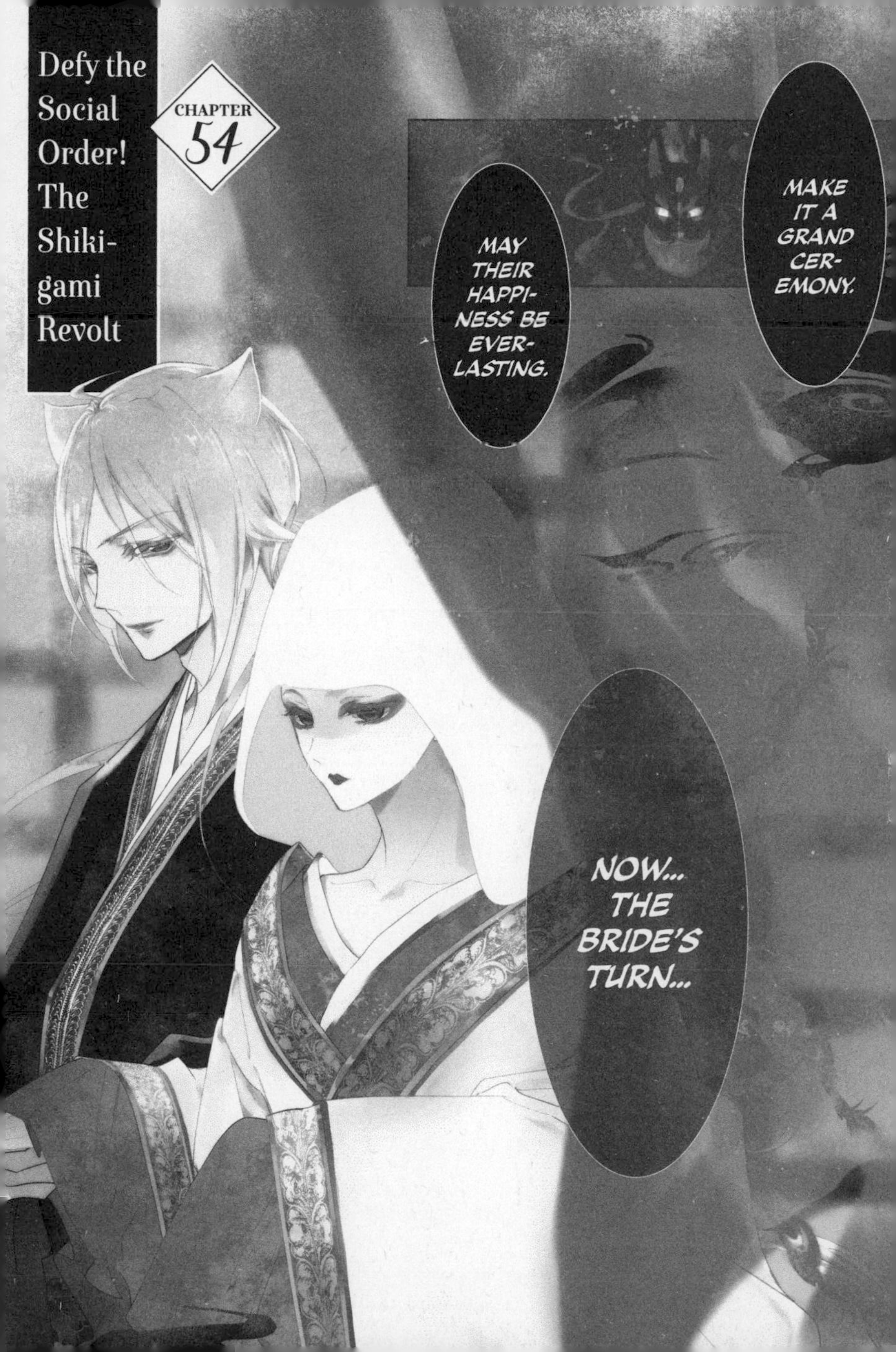
MAKE IT A GRAND CEREMONY.
MAY THEIR HAPPINESS BE EVERLASTING.
NOW... THE BRIDE'S TURN...

The
DEMON
PRINCE
of MOMOCHI
HOUSE

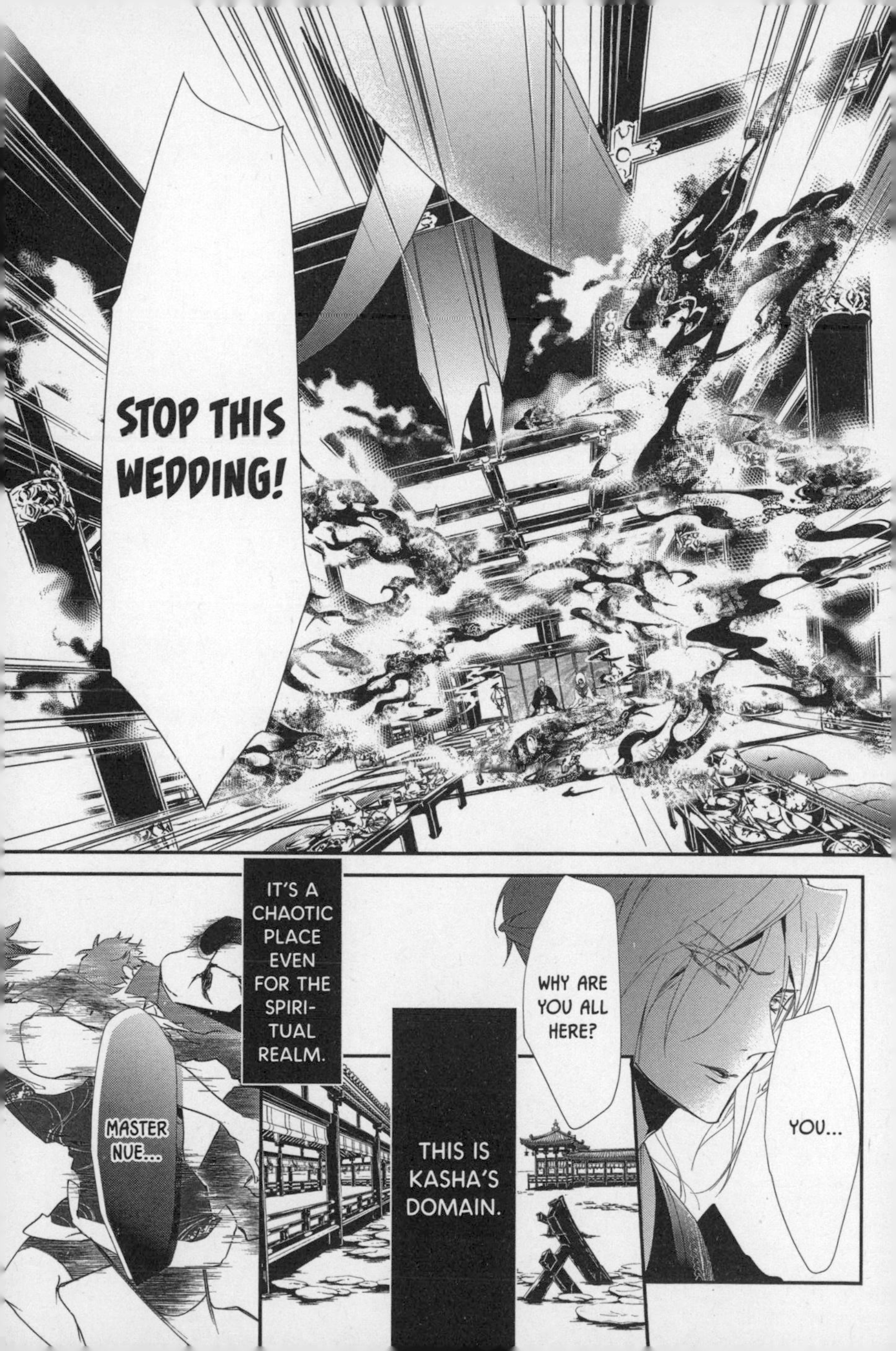
STOP THIS WEDDING!
YOU...
WHY ARE YOU ALL HERE?
THIS IS KASHA'S DOMAIN.
IT'S A CHAOTIC PLACE EVEN FOR THE SPIRITUAL REALM.
MASTER NUE...

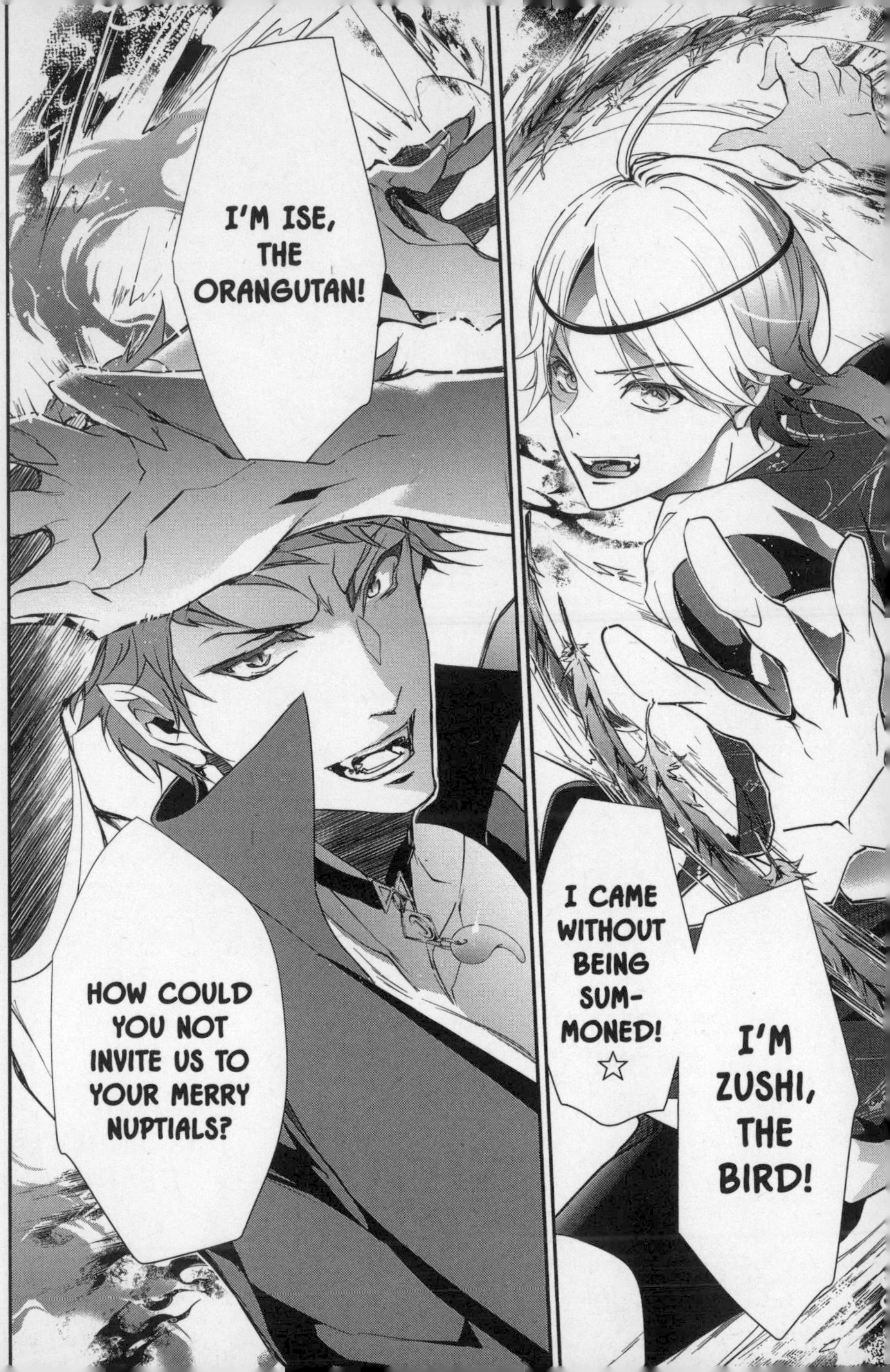
I'M ZUSHI, THE BIRD!
I CAME WITHOUT BEING SUM-MONED! ☆
I'M ISE, THE ORANGUTAN!
HOW COULD YOU NOT INVITE US TO YOUR MERRY NUPTIALS?

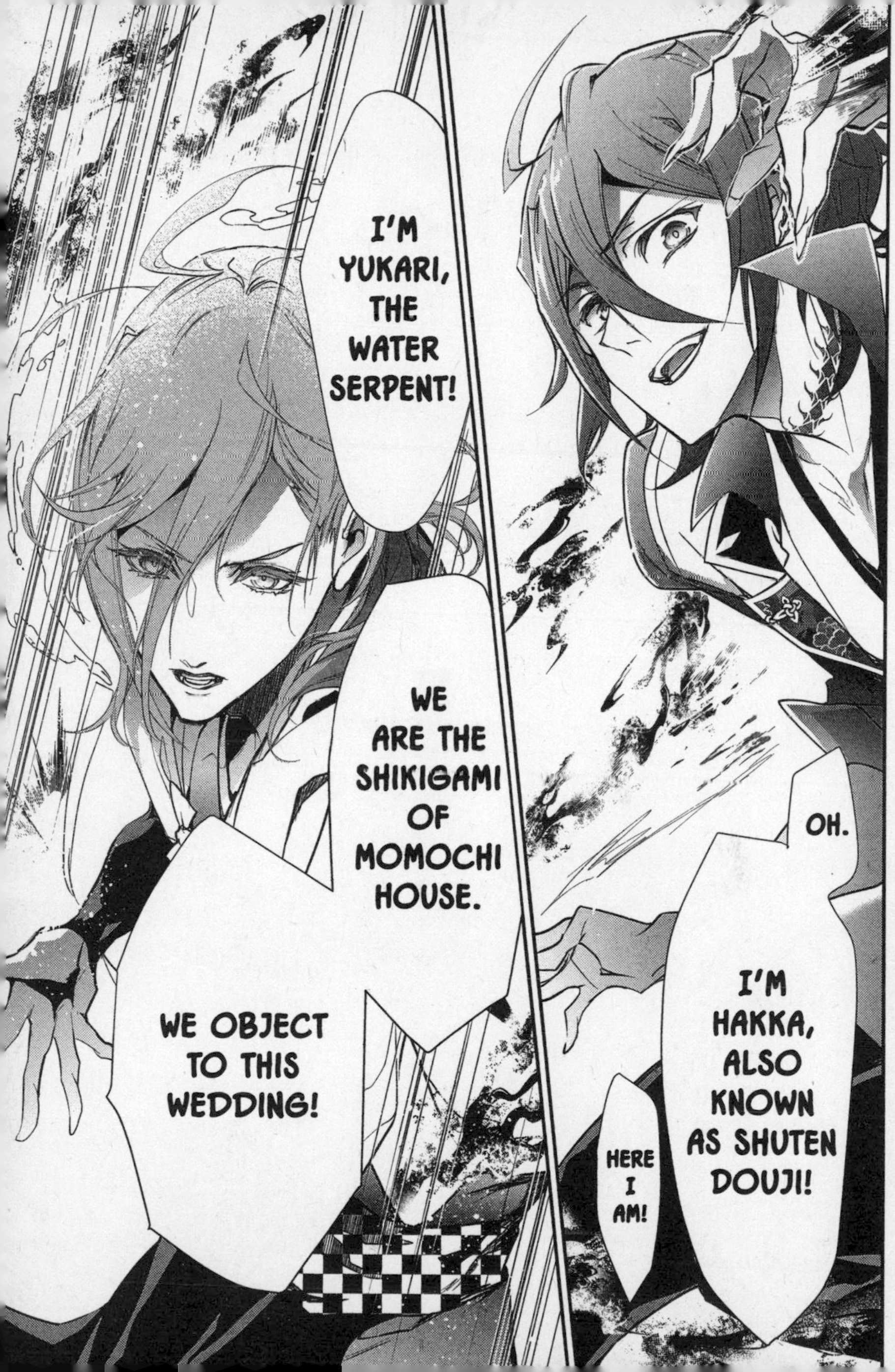
OH.
I'M HAKKA, ALSO KNOWN AS SHUTEN DOUJI!
HERE I AM!
I'M YUKARI, THE WATER SERPENT!
WE ARE THE SHIKIGAMI OF MOMOCHI HOUSE.
WE OBJECT TO THIS WEDDING!

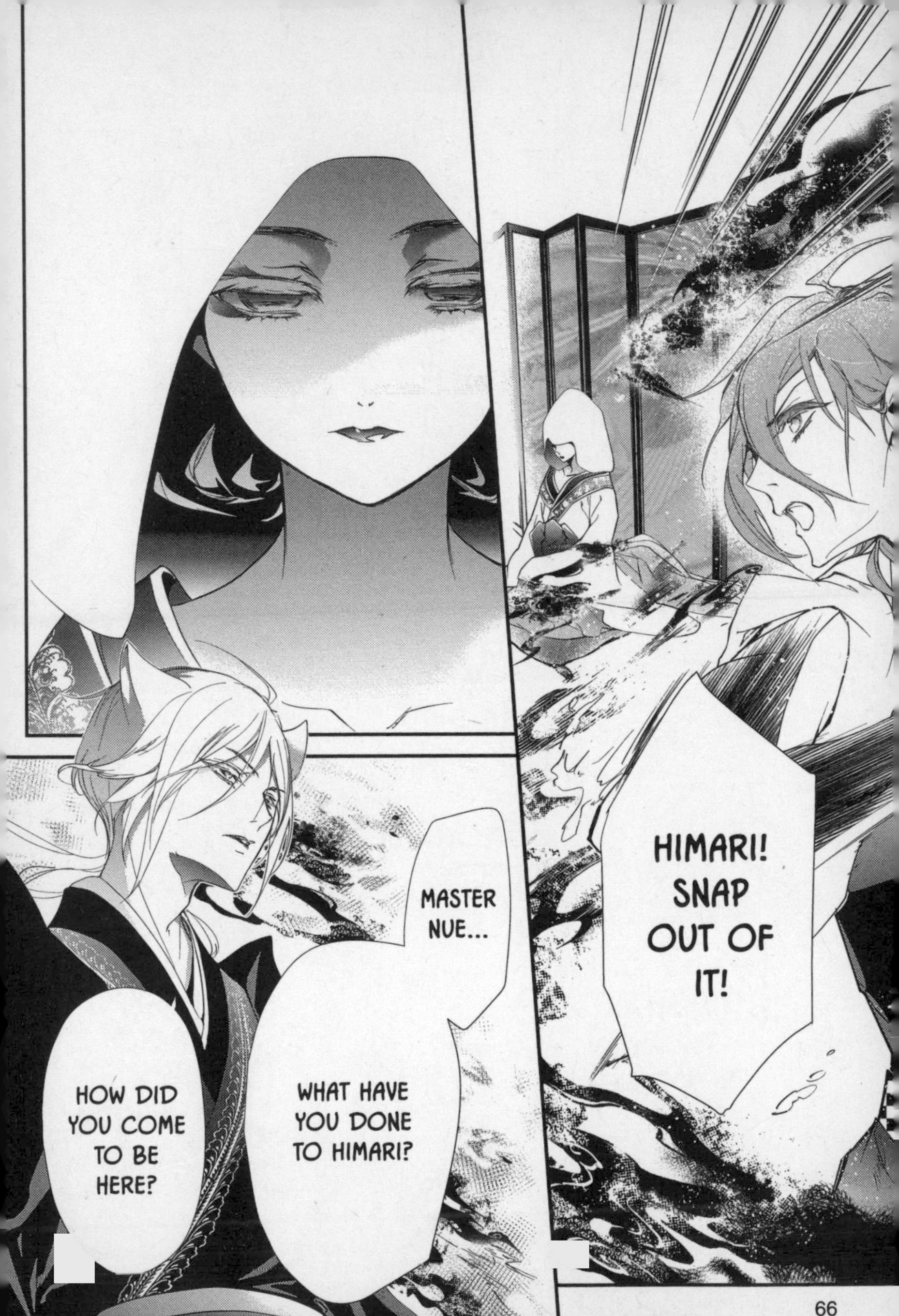
HIMARI! SNAP OUT OF IT!
MASTER NUE...
WHAT HAVE YOU DONE TO HIMARI?
HOW DID YOU COME TO BE HERE?

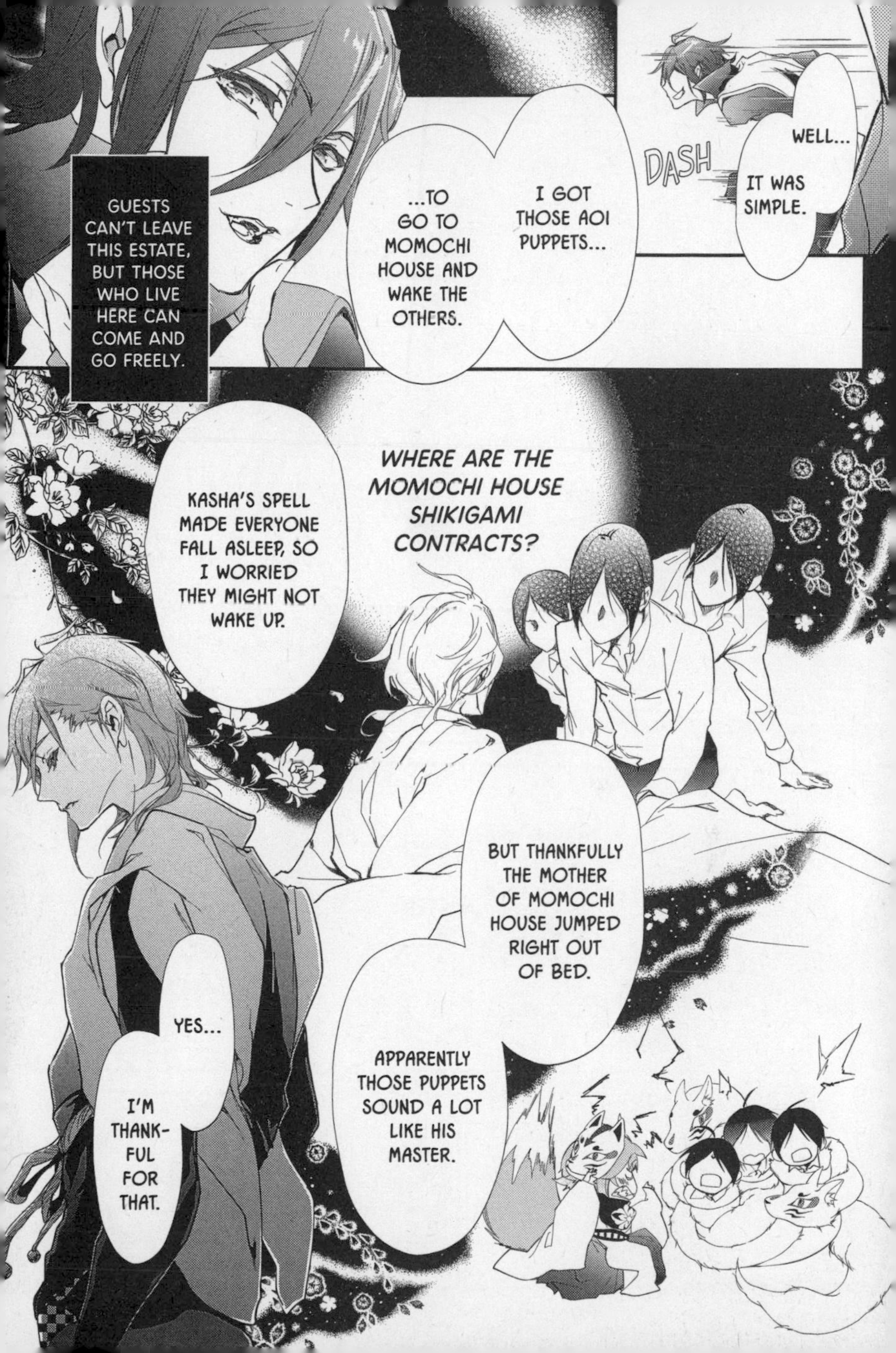
DASH
WELL...
IT WAS SIMPLE.
I GOT THOSE AOI PUPPETS...
...TO GO TO MOMOCHI HOUSE AND WAKE THE OTHERS.
GUESTS CAN'T LEAVE THIS ESTATE, BUT THOSE WHO LIVE HERE CAN COME AND GO FREELY.
WHERE ARE THE MOMOCHI HOUSE SHIKIGAMI CONTRACTS?
KASHA'S SPELL MADE EVERYONE FALL ASLEEP, SO I WORRIED THEY MIGHT NOT WAKE UP.
BUT THANKFULLY THE MOTHER OF MOMOCHI HOUSE JUMPED RIGHT OUT OF BED.
APPARENTLY THOSE PUPPETS SOUND A LOT LIKE HIS MASTER.
YES...
I'M THANK-FUL FOR THAT.

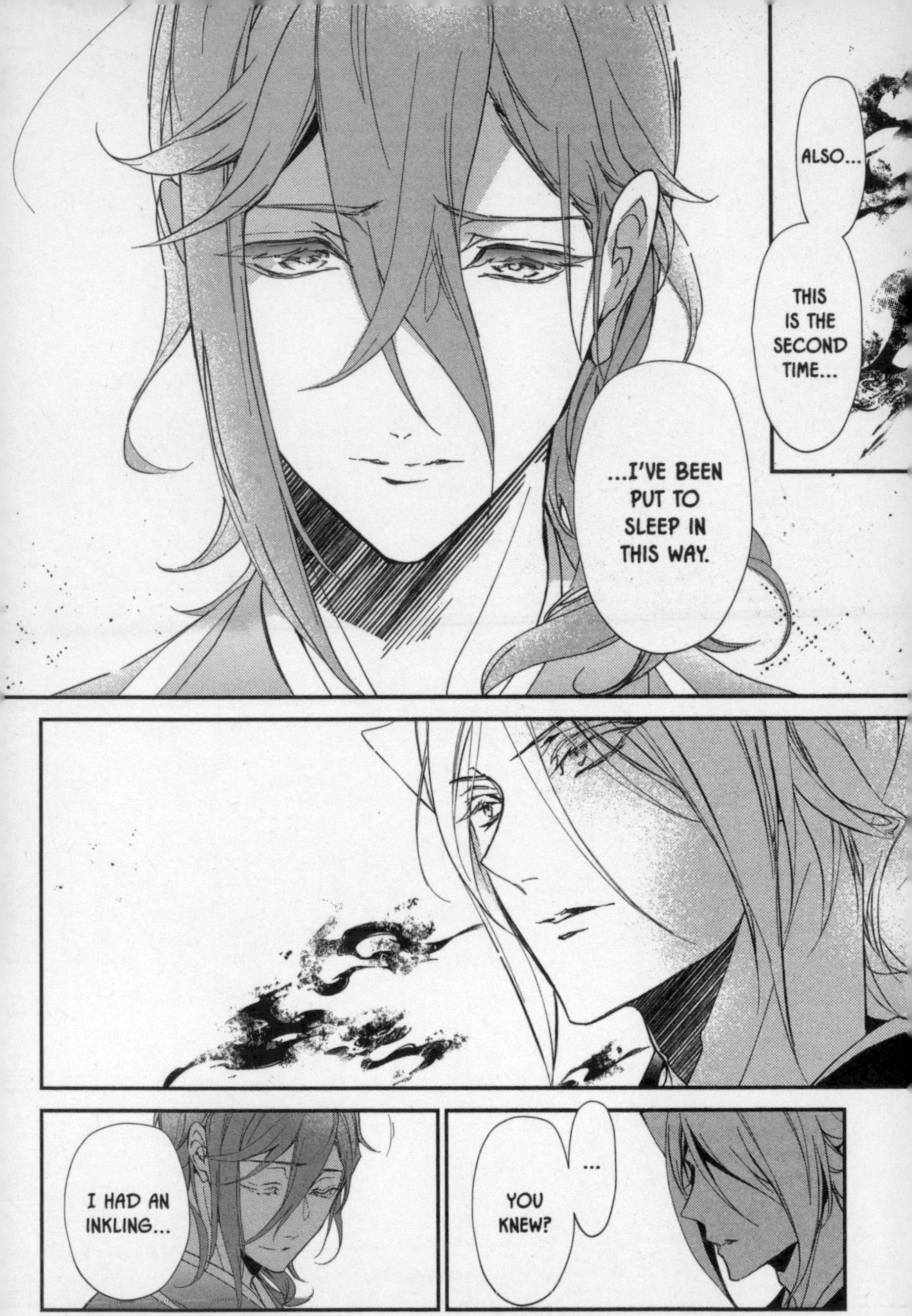
ALSO...
THIS IS THE SECOND TIME...
...I'VE BEEN PUT TO SLEEP IN THIS WAY.
...
YOU KNEW?
I HAD AN INKLING...

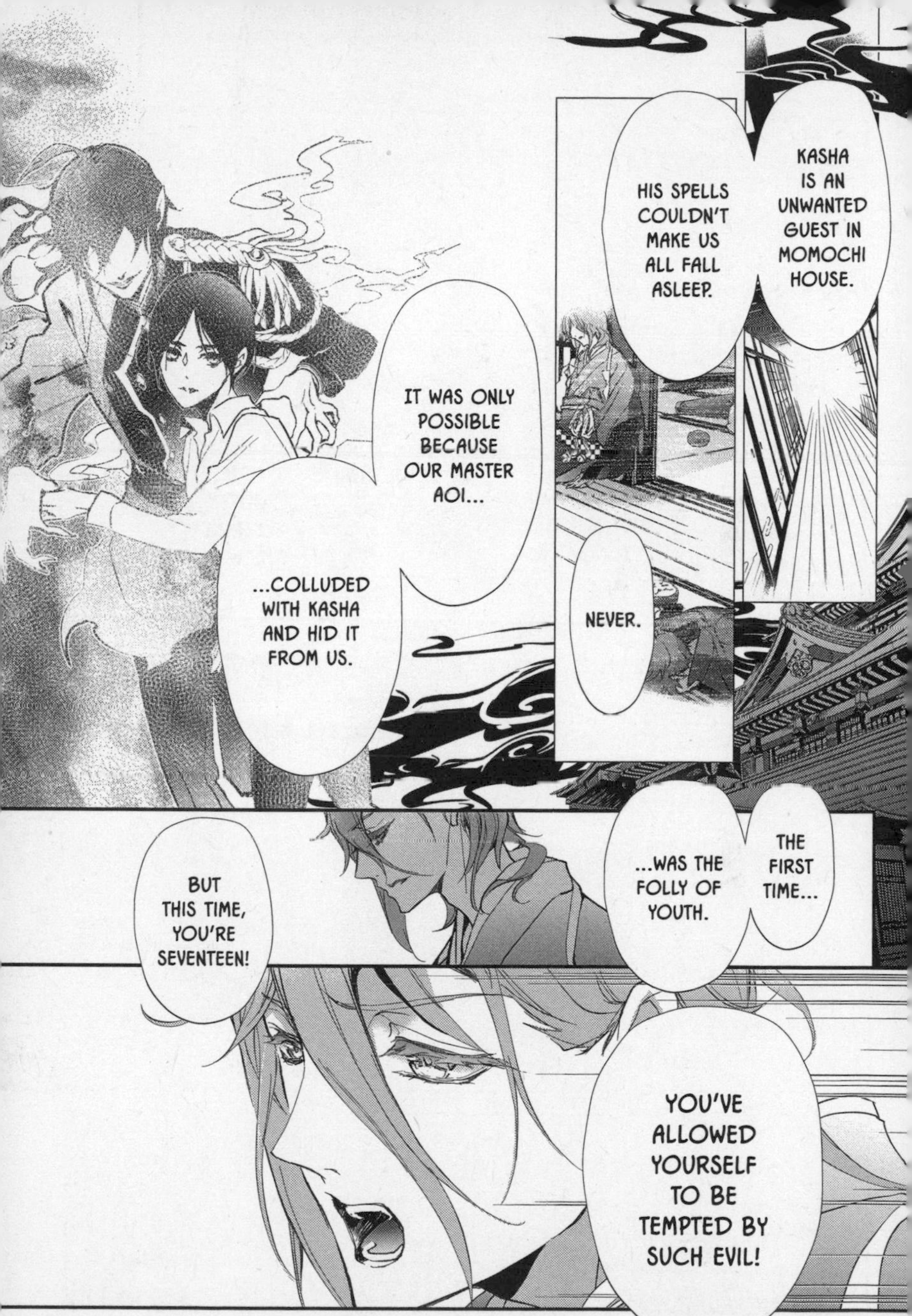
KASHA IS AN UNWANTED GUEST IN MOMOCHI HOUSE.
HIS SPELLS COULDN'T MAKE US ALL FALL ASLEEP.
NEVER.
IT WAS ONLY POSSIBLE BECAUSE OUR MASTER AOI...
...COLLUDED WITH KASHA AND HID IT FROM US.
THE FIRST TIME...
...WAS THE FOLLY OF YOUTH.
BUT THIS TIME, YOU'RE SEVENTEEN!
YOU'VE ALLOWED YOURSELF TO BE TEMPTED BY SUCH EVIL!

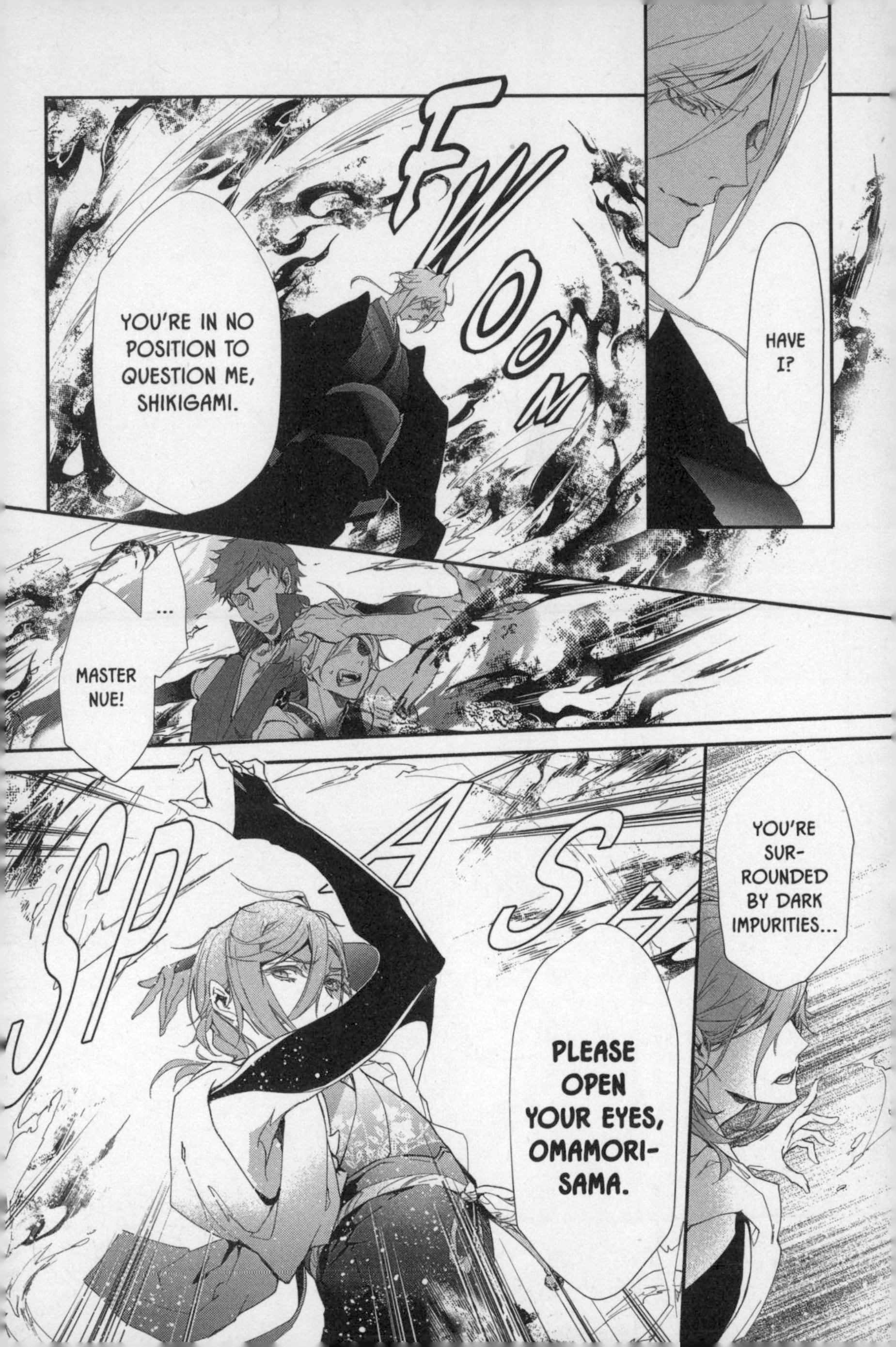
HAVE I?
FWOOOM
YOU'RE IN NO POSITION TO QUESTION ME, SHIKIGAMI.
...
MASTER NUE!
YOU'RE SUR-ROUNDED BY DARK IMPURITIES...
SPASH
PLEASE OPEN YOUR EYES, OMAMORI-SAMA.

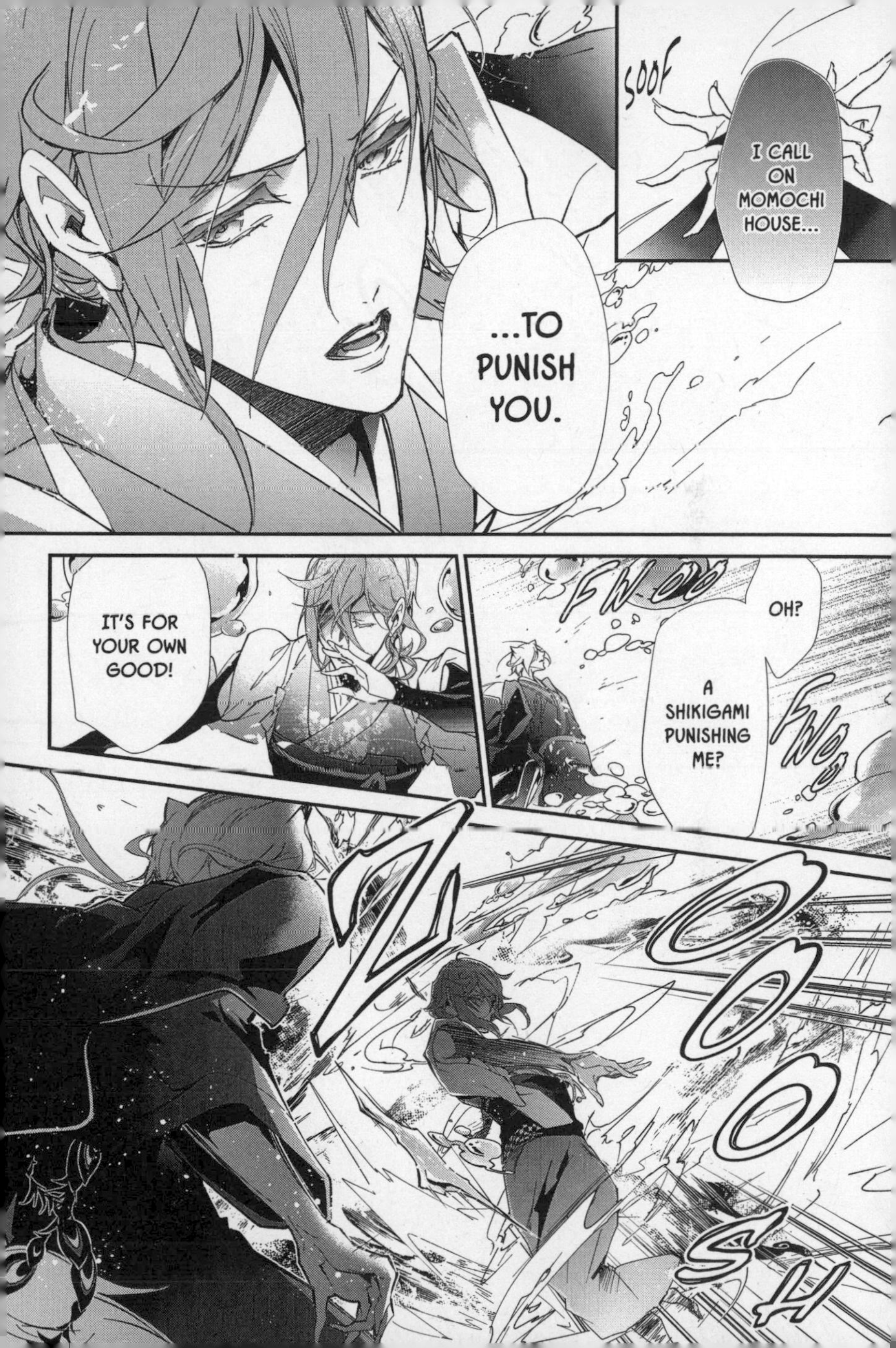
SOOF
I CALL ON MOMOCHI HOUSE...
...TO PUNISH YOU.
FWOO
OH?
A SHIKIGAMI PUNISHING ME?
FWOO
IT'S FOR YOUR OWN GOOD!
ZOOOOSH

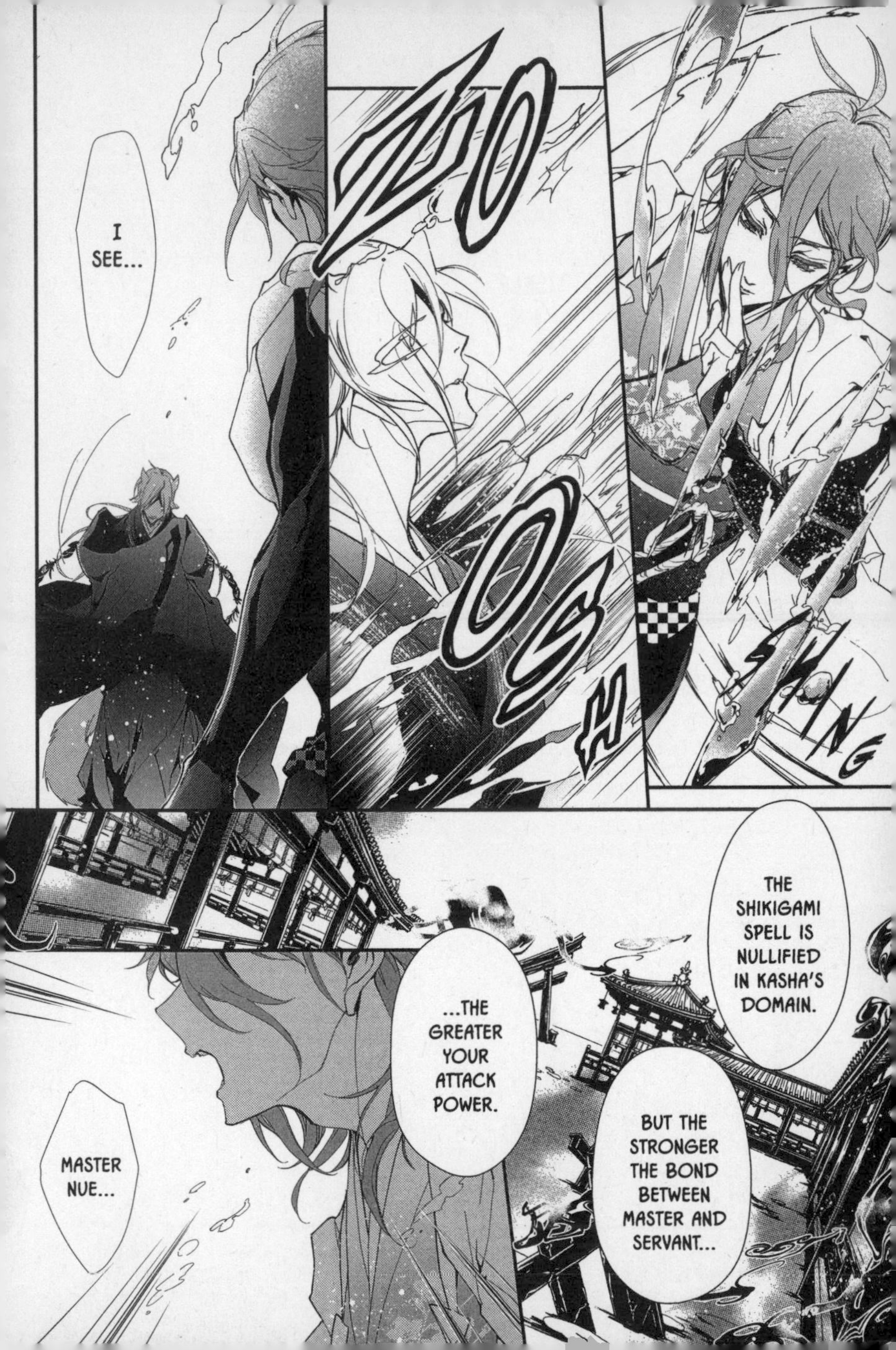
SHING
WHOOSH
I SEE...
THE SHIKIGAMI SPELL IS NULLIFIED IN KASHA'S DOMAIN.
BUT THE STRONGER THE BOND BETWEEN MASTER AND SERVANT...
...THE GREATER YOUR ATTACK POWER.
MASTER NUE...

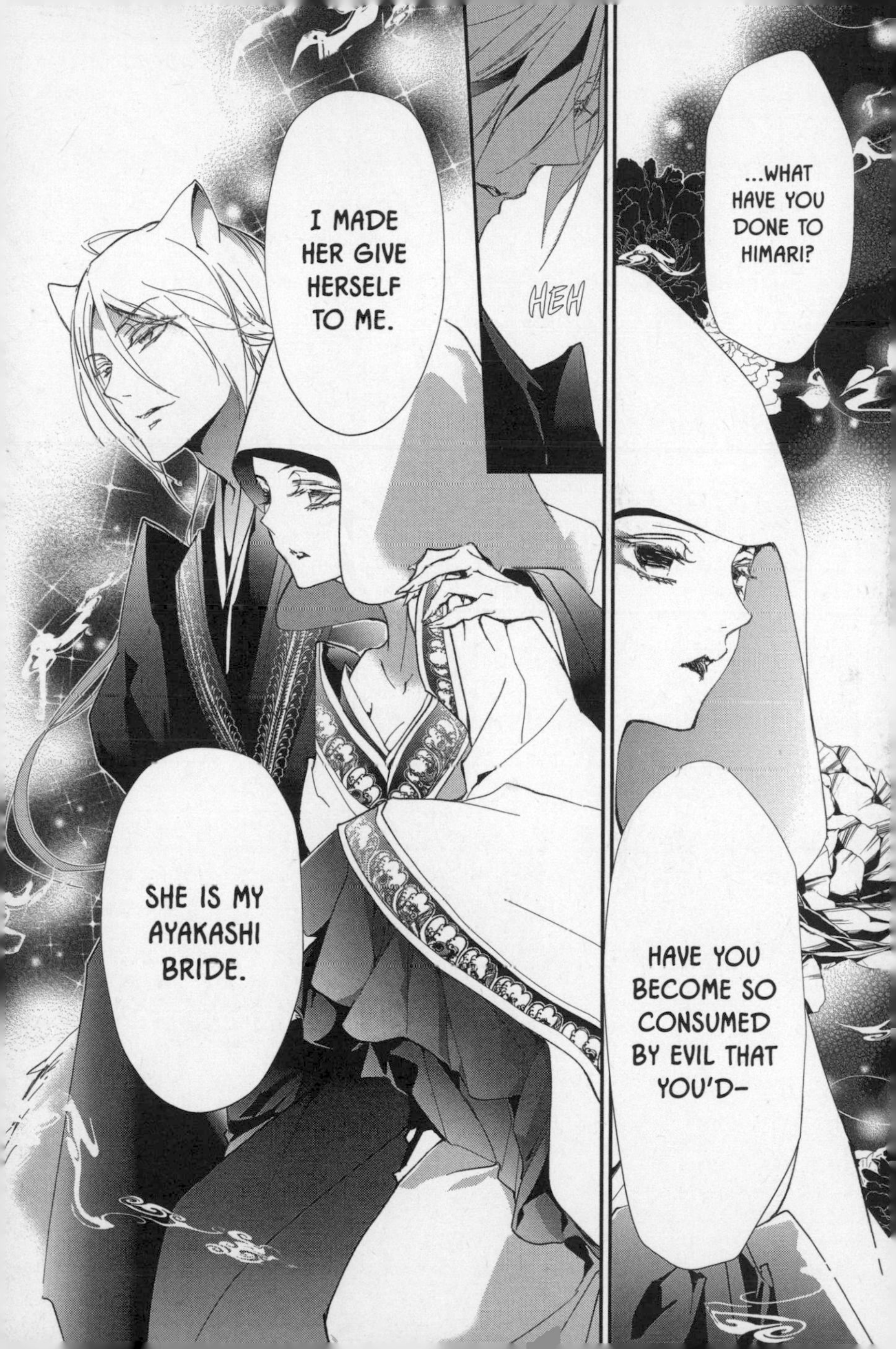
...WHAT HAVE YOU DONE TO HIMARI?
HAVE YOU BECOME SO CONSUMED BY EVIL THAT YOU'D–
HEH
I MADE HER GIVE HERSELF TO ME.
SHE IS MY AYAKASHI BRIDE.

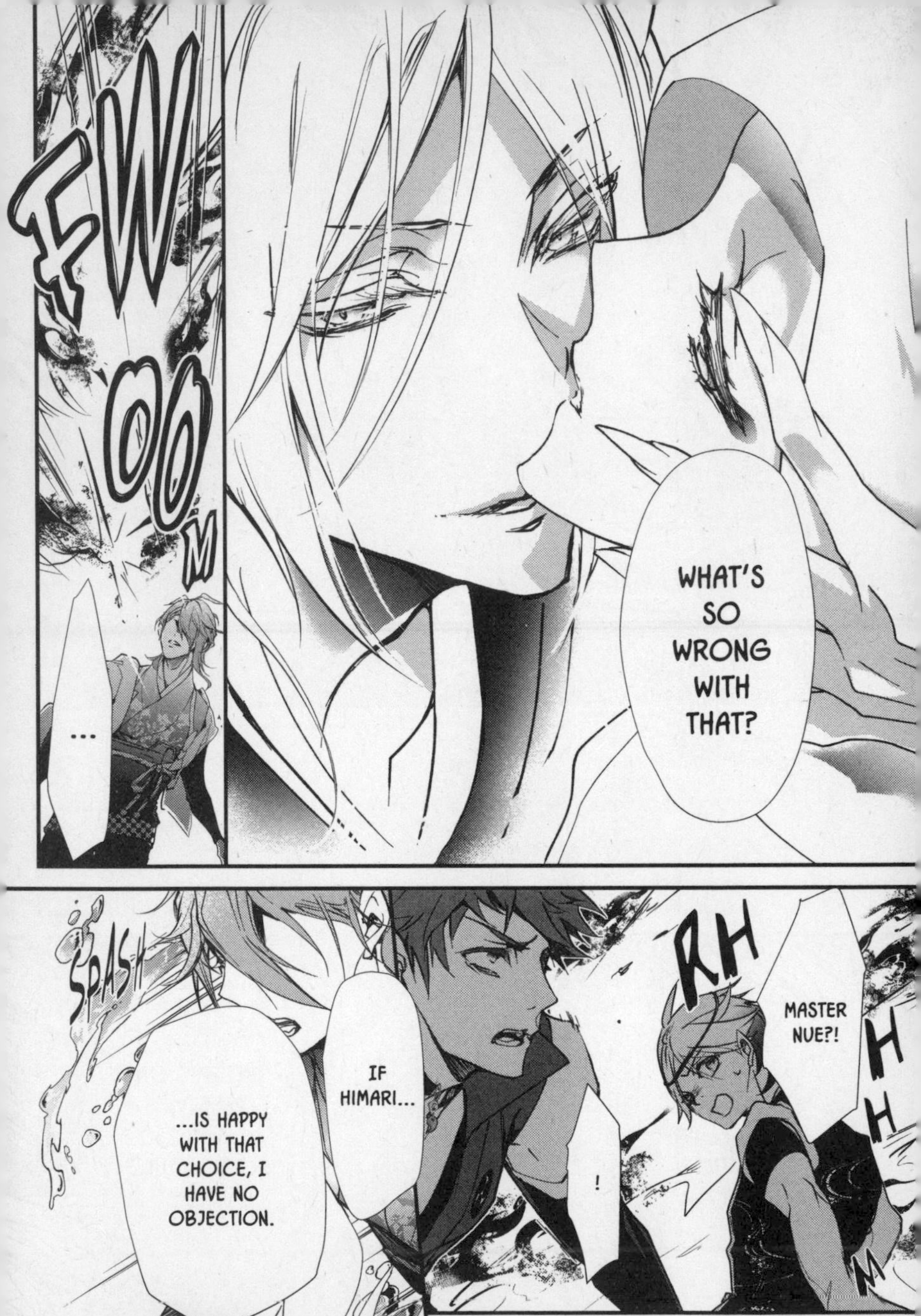
WHAT'S SO WRONG WITH THAT?
FWOOM
...
RHHHM
MASTER NUE?!
!
IF HIMARI...
...IS HAPPY WITH THAT CHOICE, I HAVE NO OBJECTION.
SPASH

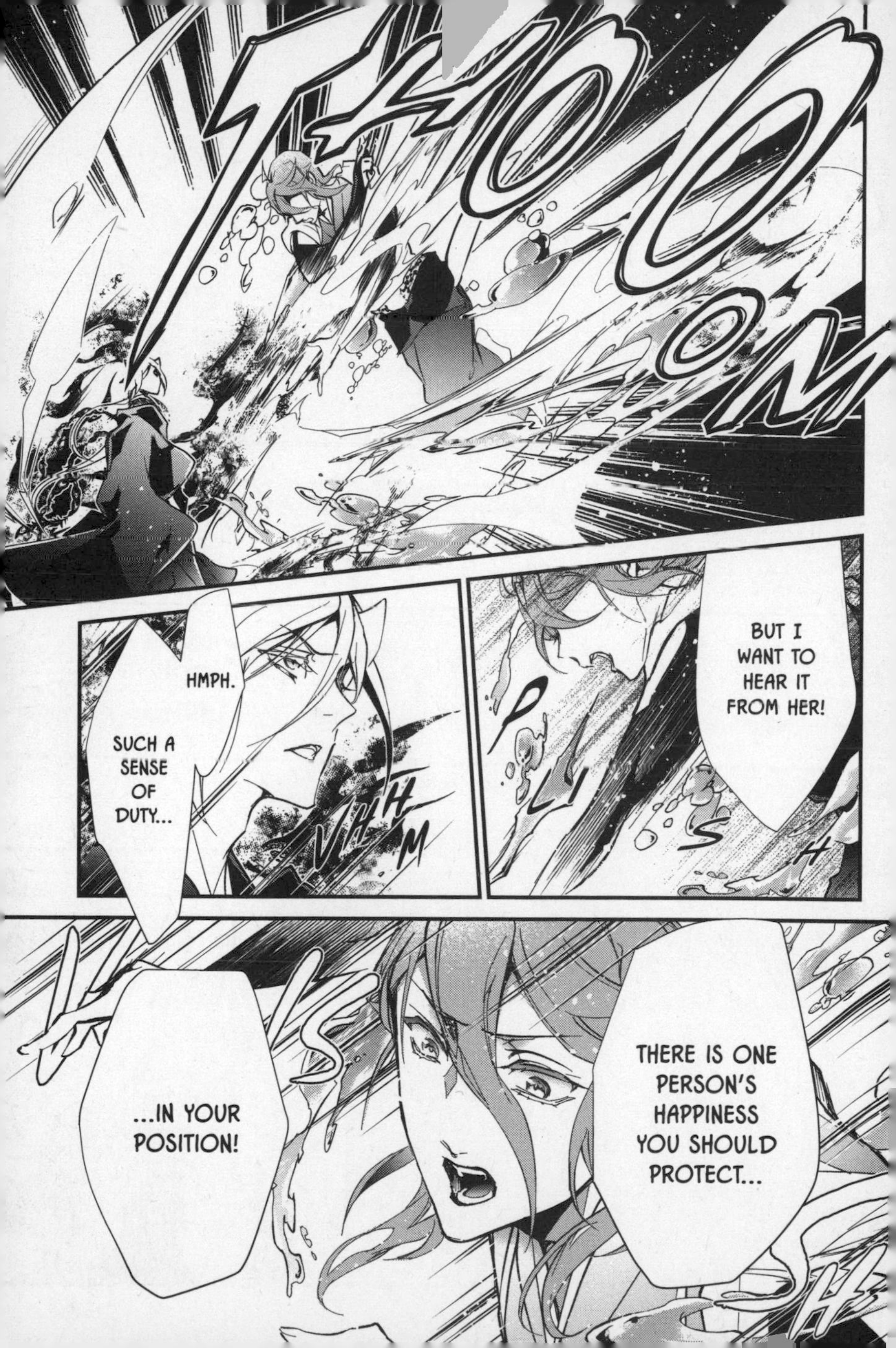
BUT I WANT TO HEAR IT FROM HER!
HMPH.
SUCH A SENSE OF DUTY...
THERE IS ONE PERSON'S HAPPINESS YOU SHOULD PROTECT...
...IN YOUR POSITION!

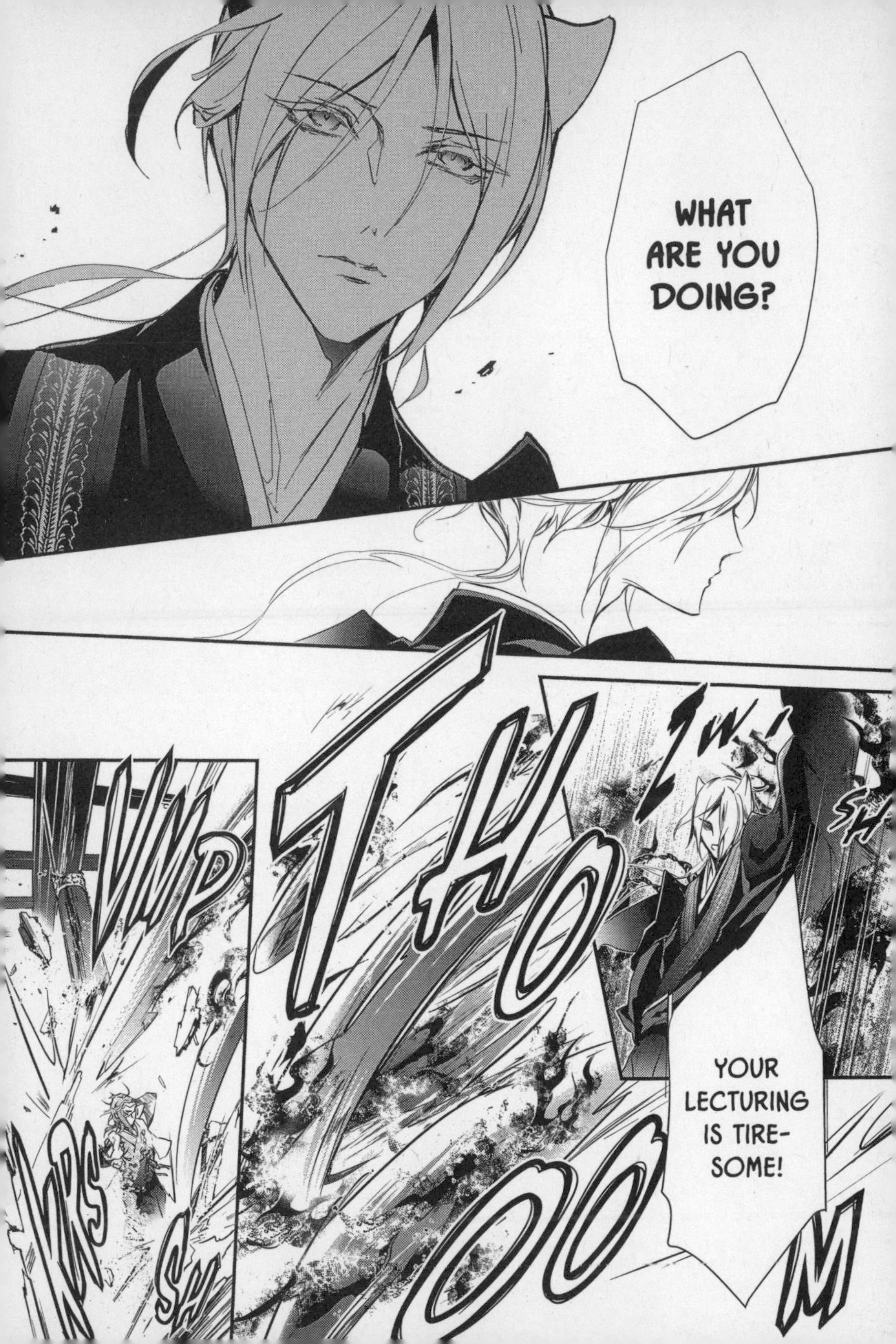
WHAT ARE YOU DOING?
YOUR LECTURING IS TIRE-SOME!

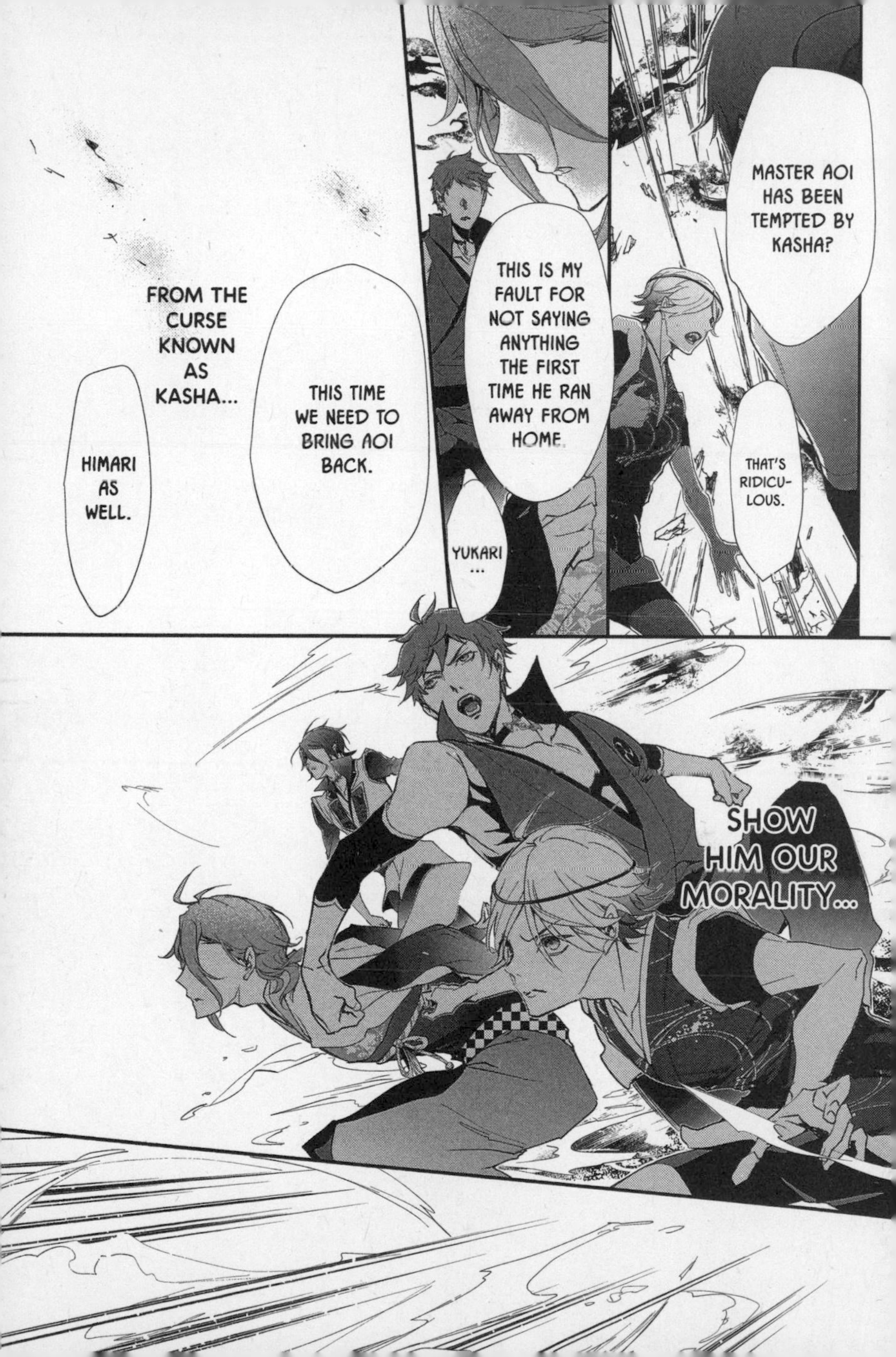
MASTER AOI HAS BEEN TEMPTED BY KASHA?
THAT'S RIDICU-LOUS.
THIS IS MY FAULT FOR NOT SAYING ANYTHING THE FIRST TIME HE RAN AWAY FROM HOME.
YUKARI ...
THIS TIME WE NEED TO BRING AOI BACK.
FROM THE CURSE KNOWN AS KASHA...
HIMARI AS WELL.
SHOW HIM OUR MORALITY...

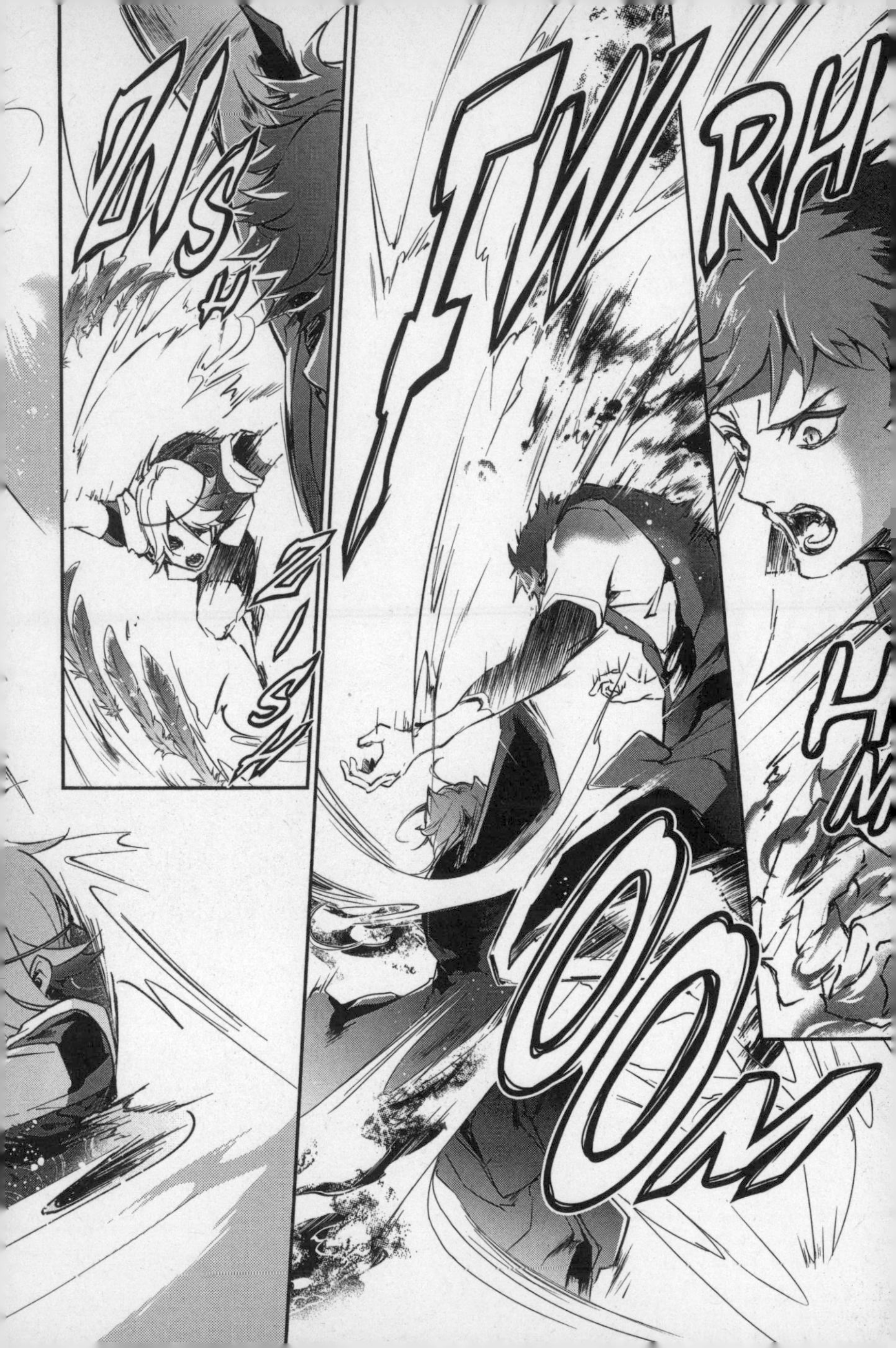
WSH
FW
RH
OOM

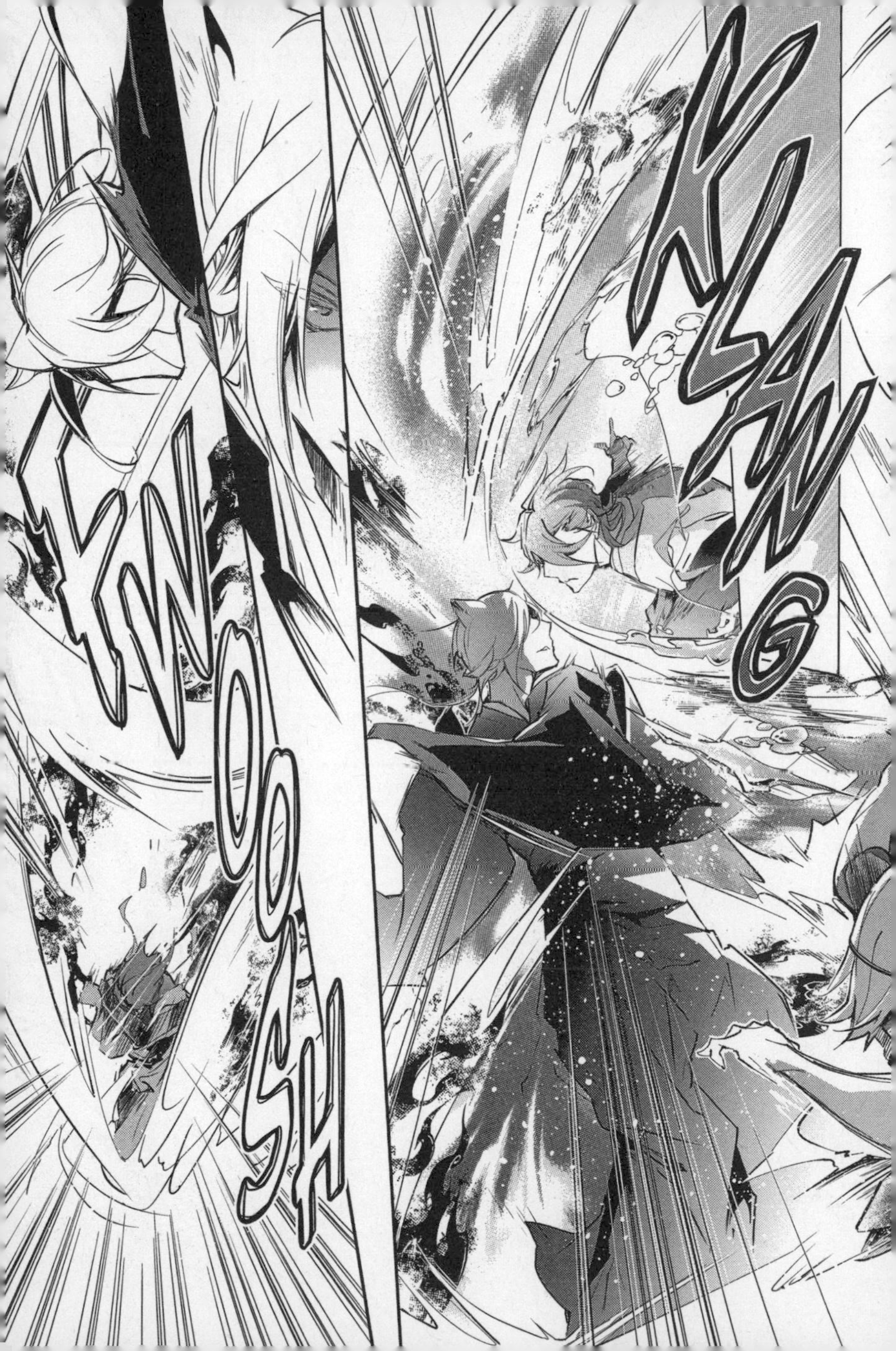
KLANG
FWOOSH

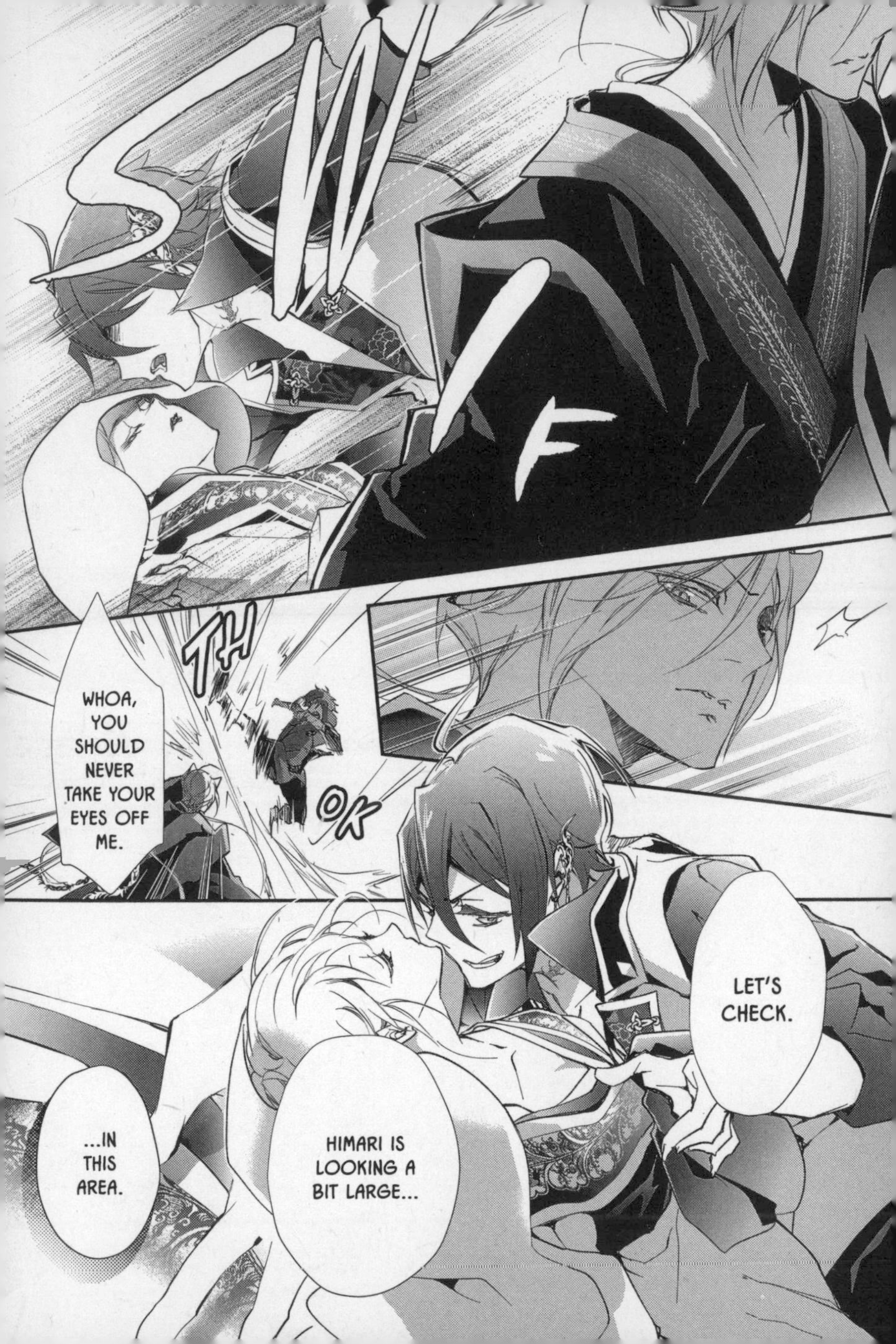
THOK
WHOA, YOU SHOULD NEVER TAKE YOUR EYES OFF ME.
LET'S CHECK.
HIMARI IS LOOKING A BIT LARGE...
...IN THIS AREA.

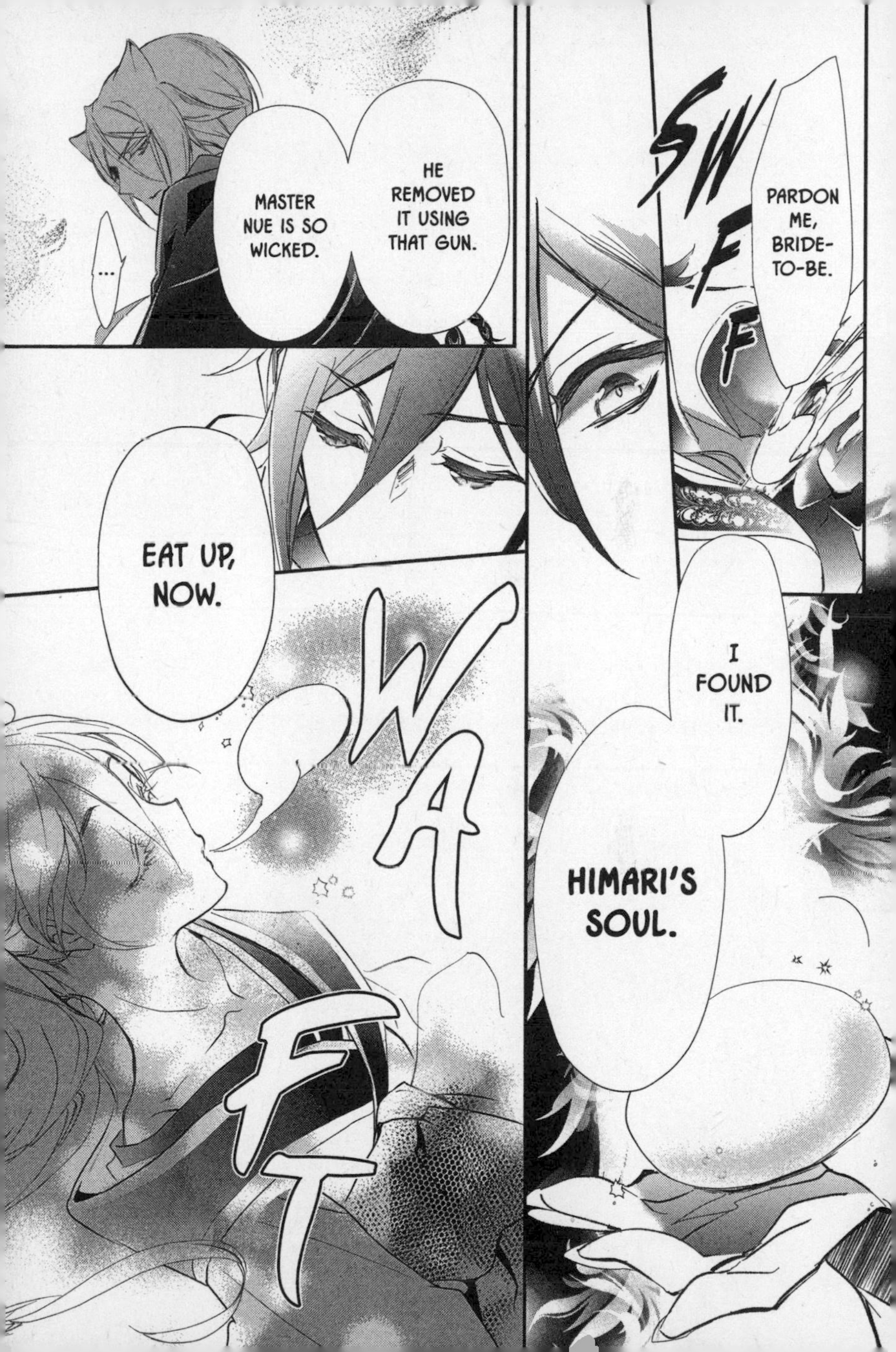
SWFF
PARDON ME, BRIDE-TO-BE.
I FOUND IT.
HIMARI'S SOUL.
HE REMOVED IT USING THAT GUN.
MASTER NUE IS SO WICKED.
...
EAT UP, NOW.
WA
FFT

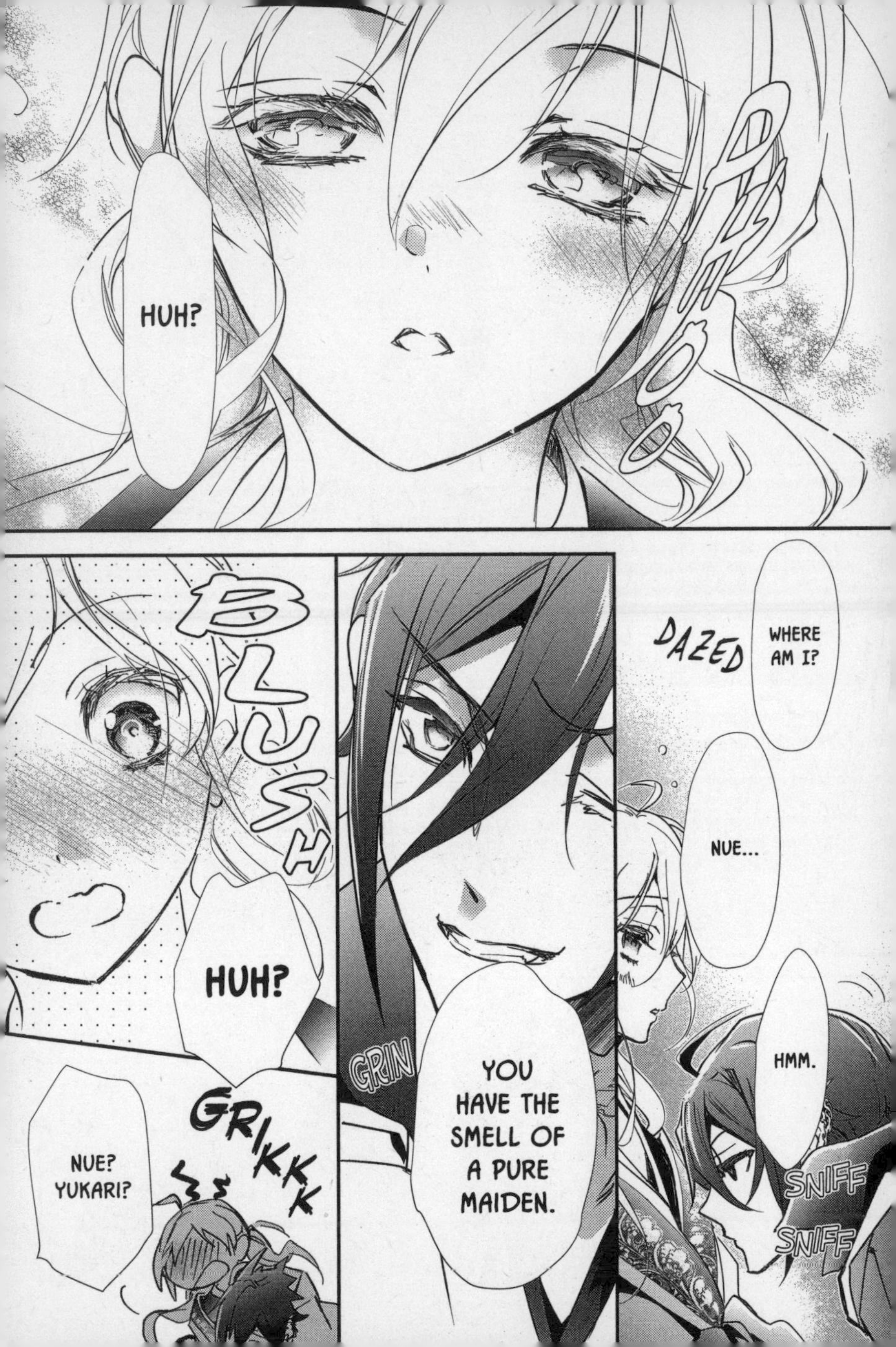
HUH?
WHERE AM I?
DAZED
NUE...
HMM.
SNIFF
SNIFF
YOU HAVE THE SMELL OF A PURE MAIDEN.
GRIN
BLUSH
HUH?
GRIKKK
NUE? YUKARI?

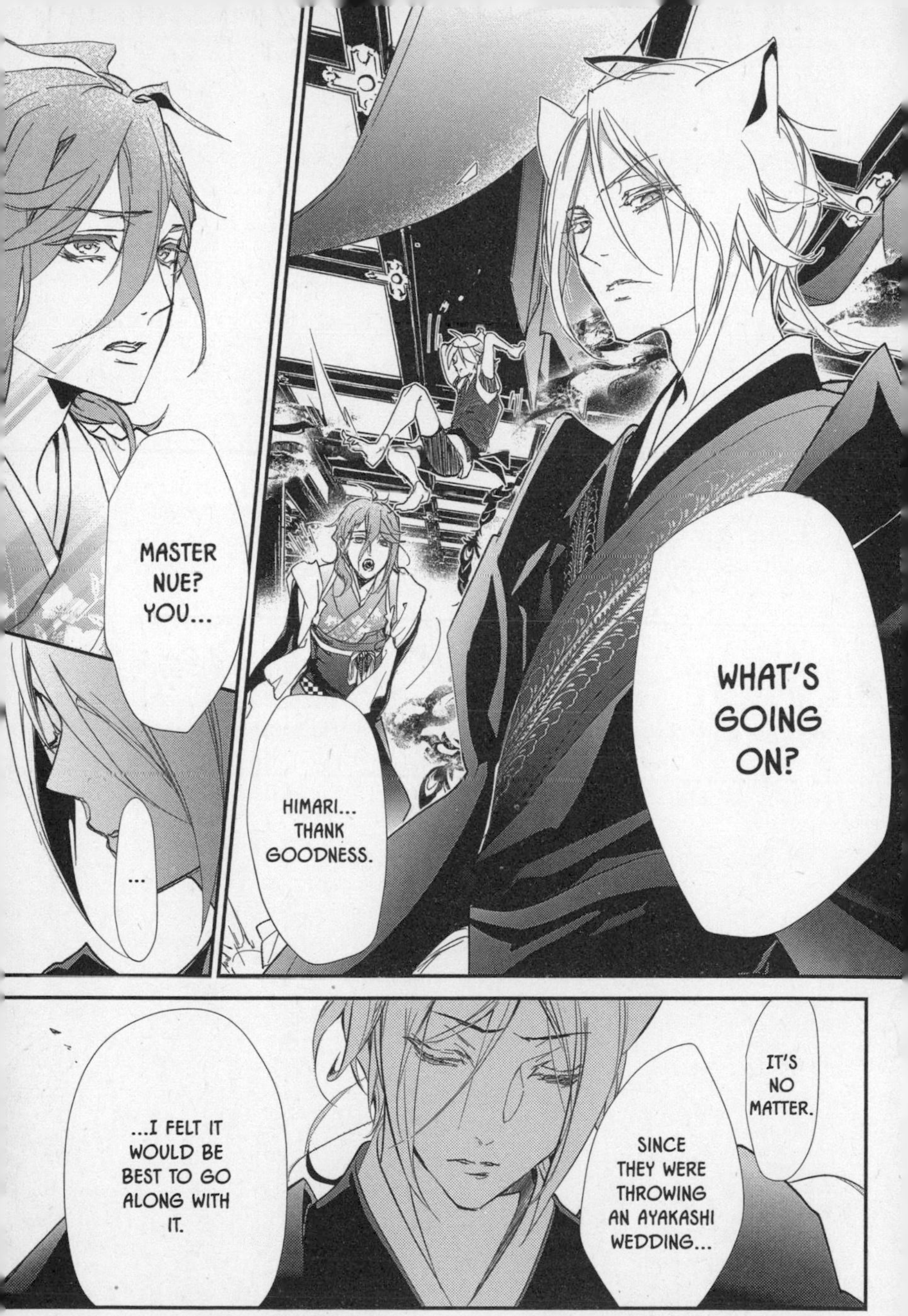
WHAT'S GOING ON?
HIMARI... THANK GOODNESS.
MASTER NUE? YOU...
...
IT'S NO MATTER.
SINCE THEY WERE THROWING AN AYAKASHI WEDDING...
...I FELT IT WOULD BE BEST TO GO ALONG WITH IT.

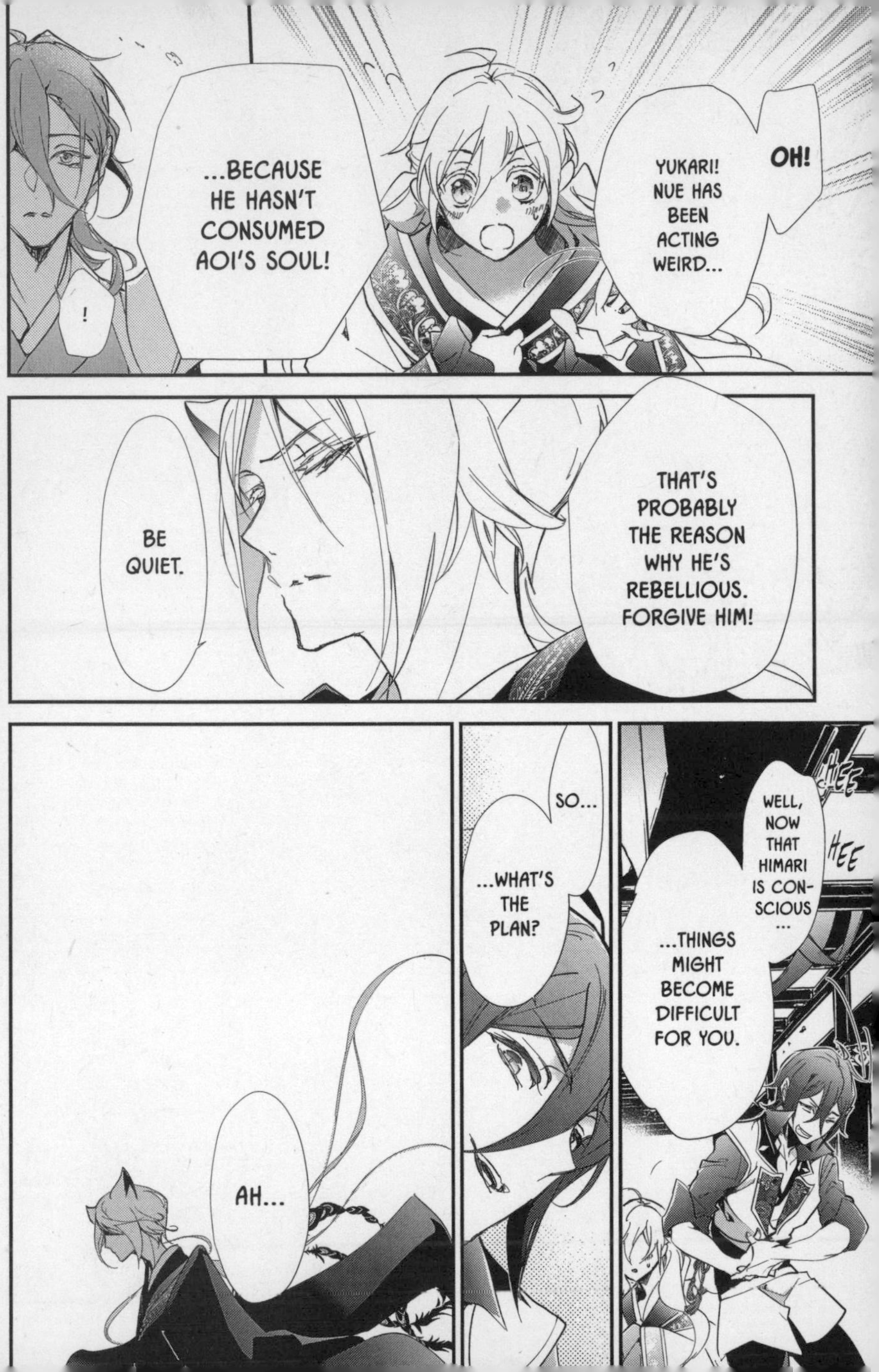
OH!
YUKARI! NUE HAS BEEN ACTING WEIRD...
...BECAUSE HE HASN'T CONSUMED AOI'S SOUL!
!
THAT'S PROBABLY THE REASON WHY HE'S REBELLIOUS. FORGIVE HIM!
BE QUIET.
HEE
HEE
WELL, NOW THAT HIMARI IS CON-SCIOUS...
...THINGS MIGHT BECOME DIFFICULT FOR YOU.
SO...
...WHAT'S THE PLAN?
AH...

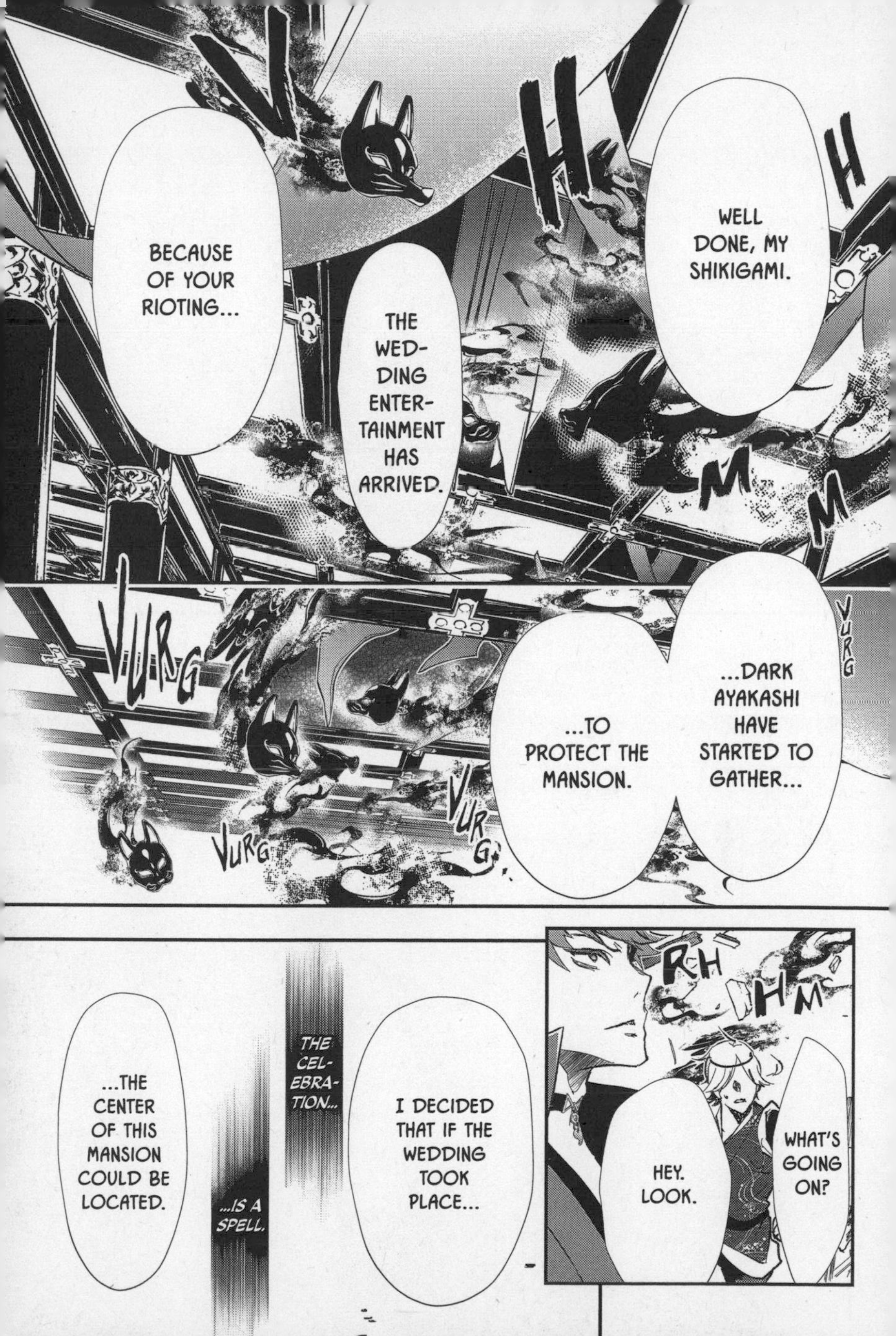
WELL DONE, MY SHIKIGAMI.
THE WEDDING ENTERTAINMENT HAS ARRIVED.
BECAUSE OF YOUR RIOTING...
VURG
...DARK AYAKASHI HAVE STARTED TO GATHER...
...TO PROTECT THE MANSION.
VURG
VURG
VURG
RHHM
WHAT'S GOING ON?
HEY. LOOK.
I DECIDED THAT IF THE WEDDING TOOK PLACE...
THE CELEBRATION...
...IS A SPELL.
...THE CENTER OF THIS MANSION COULD BE LOCATED.

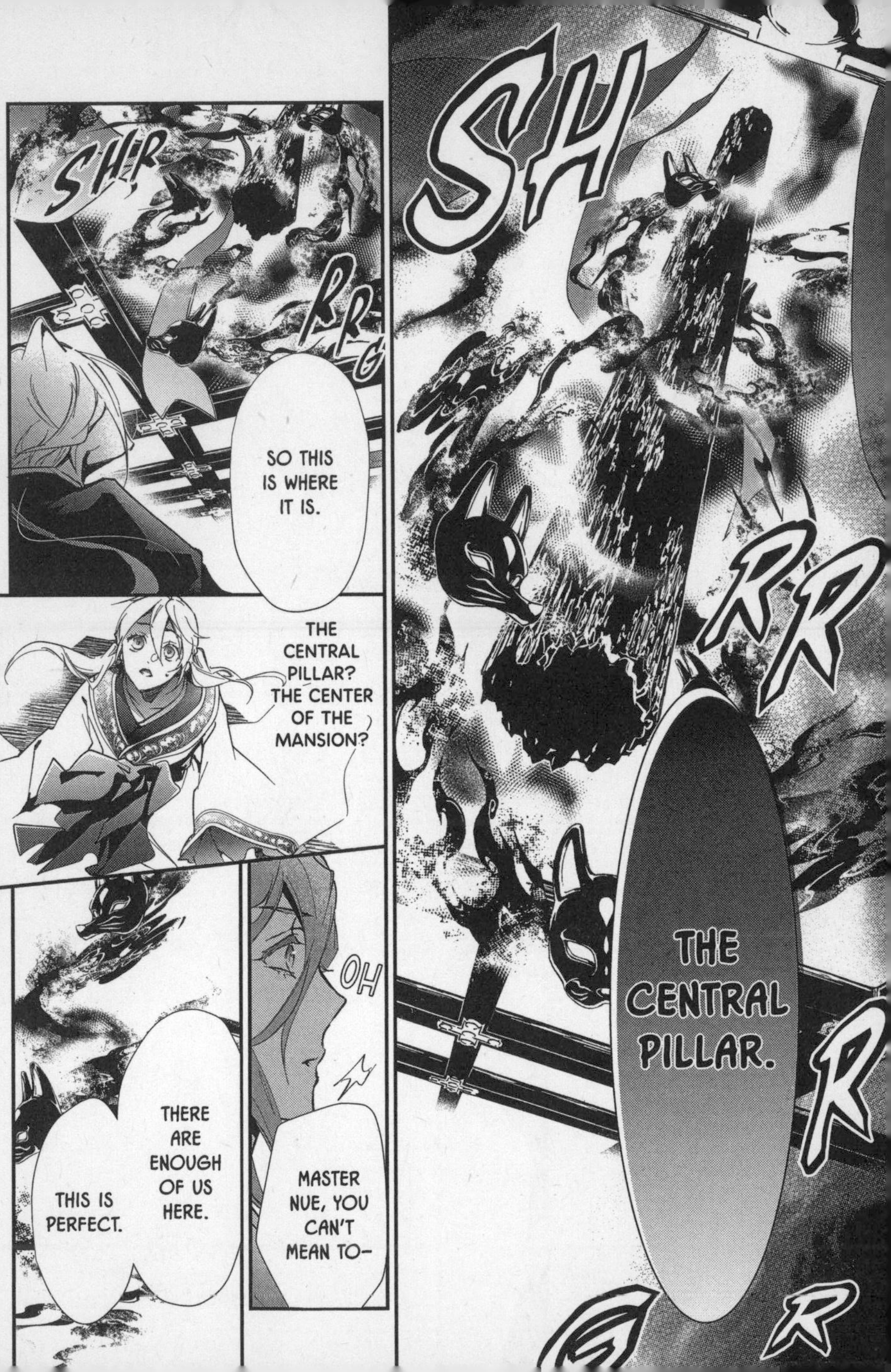
SH
RR
R
R
THE CENTRAL PILLAR.
SHR
RRG
SO THIS IS WHERE IT IS.
THE CENTRAL PILLAR? THE CENTER OF THE MANSION?
OH
MASTER NUE, YOU CAN'T MEAN TO—
THERE ARE ENOUGH OF US HERE.
THIS IS PERFECT.

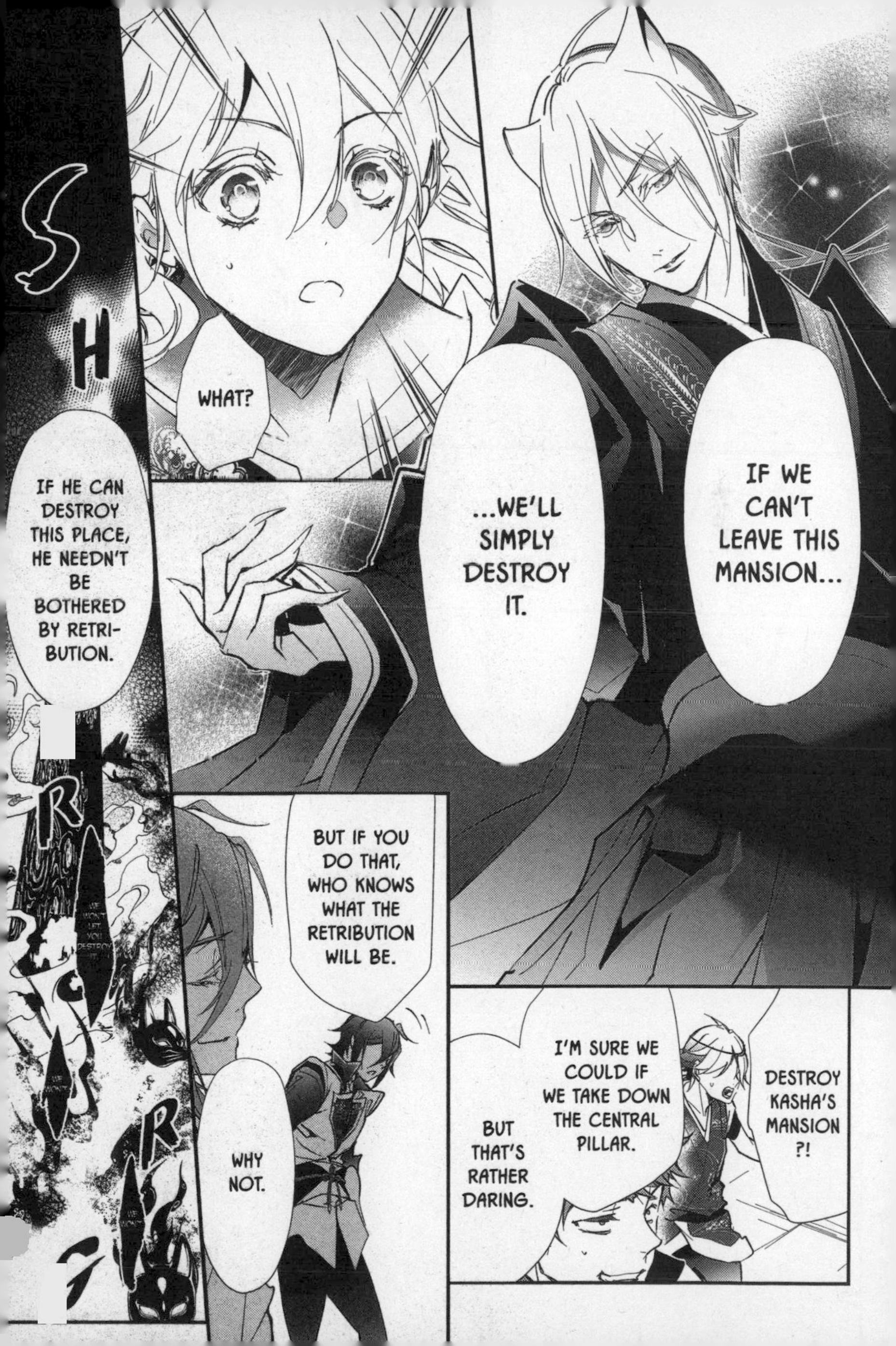
IF WE CAN'T LEAVE THIS MANSION...
...WE'LL SIMPLY DESTROY IT.
WHAT?
DESTROY KASHA'S MANSION?!
I'M SURE WE COULD IF WE TAKE DOWN THE CENTRAL PILLAR.
BUT THAT'S RATHER DARING.
BUT IF YOU DO THAT, WHO KNOWS WHAT THE RETRIBUTION WILL BE.
WHY NOT.
IF HE CAN DESTROY THIS PLACE, HE NEEDN'T BE BOTHERED BY RETRIBUTION.
SHRRRG
WE WON'T LET YOU DESTROY IT.

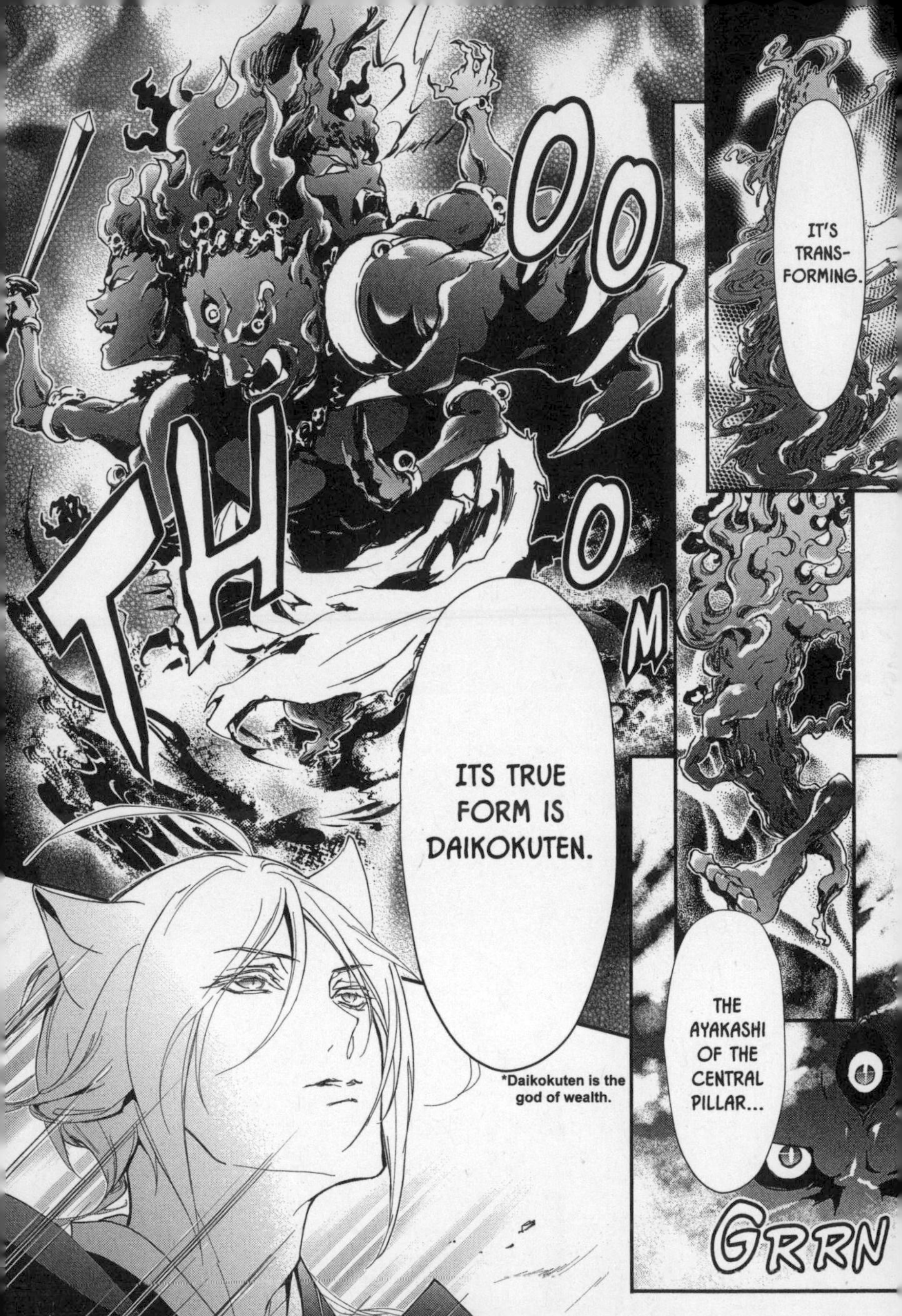
IT'S TRANS-FORMING.
THE AYAKASHI OF THE CENTRAL PILLAR...
GRRN
THOOOM
ITS TRUE FORM IS DAIKOKUTEN.
*Daikokuten is the god of wealth.

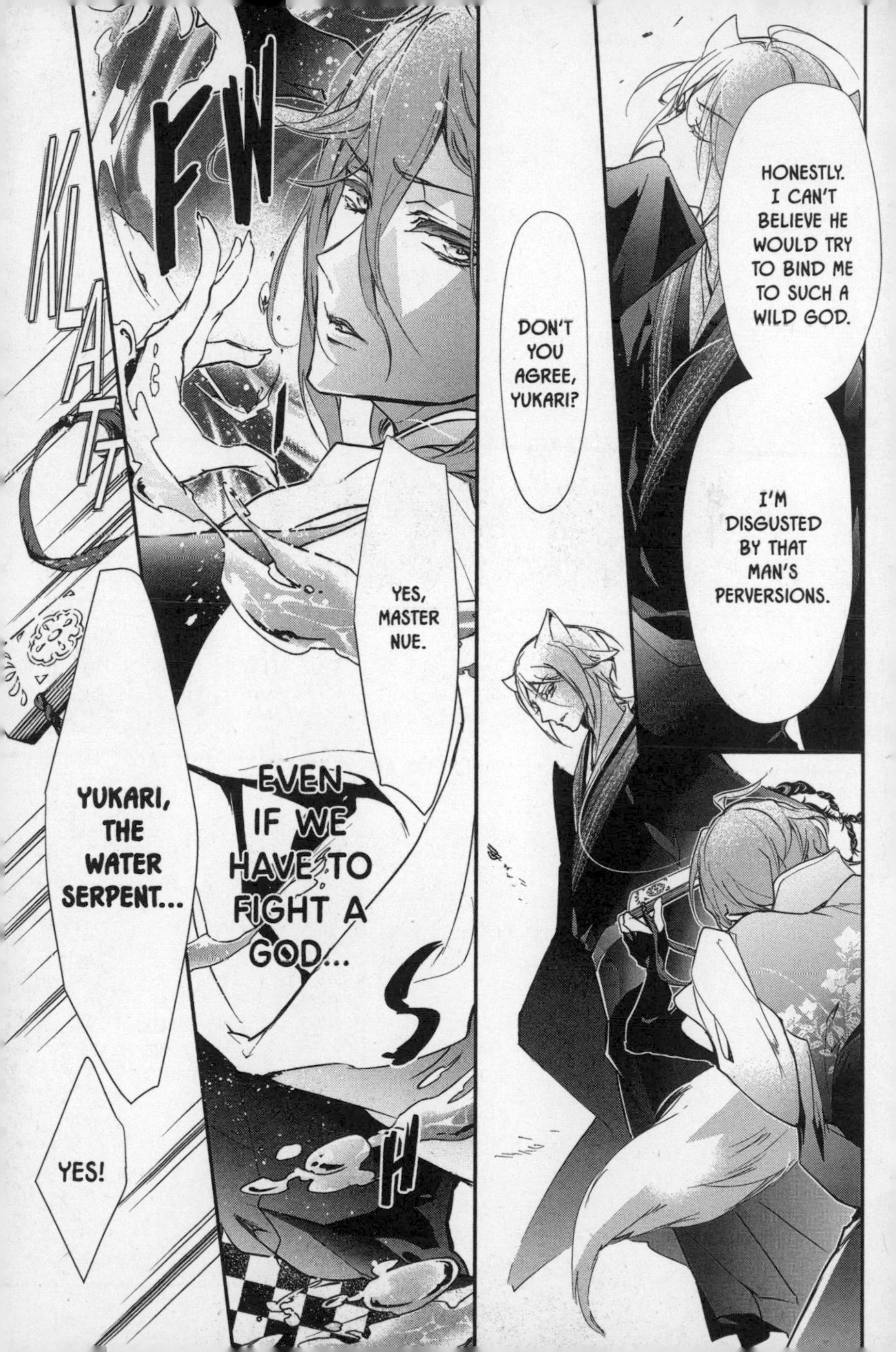
HONESTLY. I CAN'T BELIEVE HE WOULD TRY TO BIND ME TO SUCH A WILD GOD.
I'M DISGUSTED BY THAT MAN'S PERVERSIONS.
DON'T YOU AGREE, YUKARI?
FW
YES, MASTER NUE.
EVEN IF WE HAVE TO FIGHT A GOD...
SH
KLATT
YUKARI, THE WATER SERPENT...
YES!

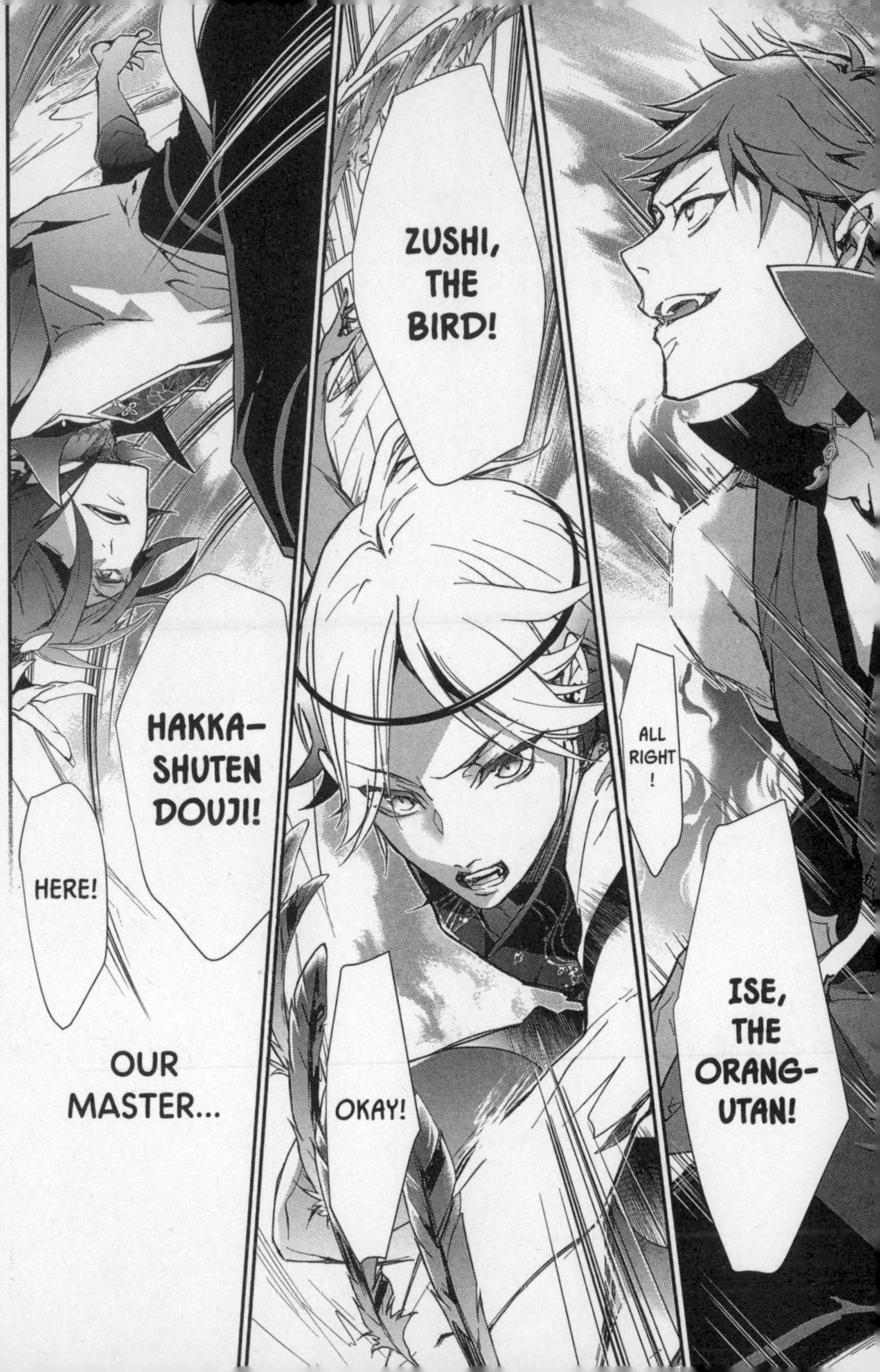
ISE, THE ORANGUTAN!
ALL RIGHT!
ZUSHI, THE BIRD!
OKAY!
HAKKA-SHUTEN DOUJI!
HERE!
OUR MASTER...

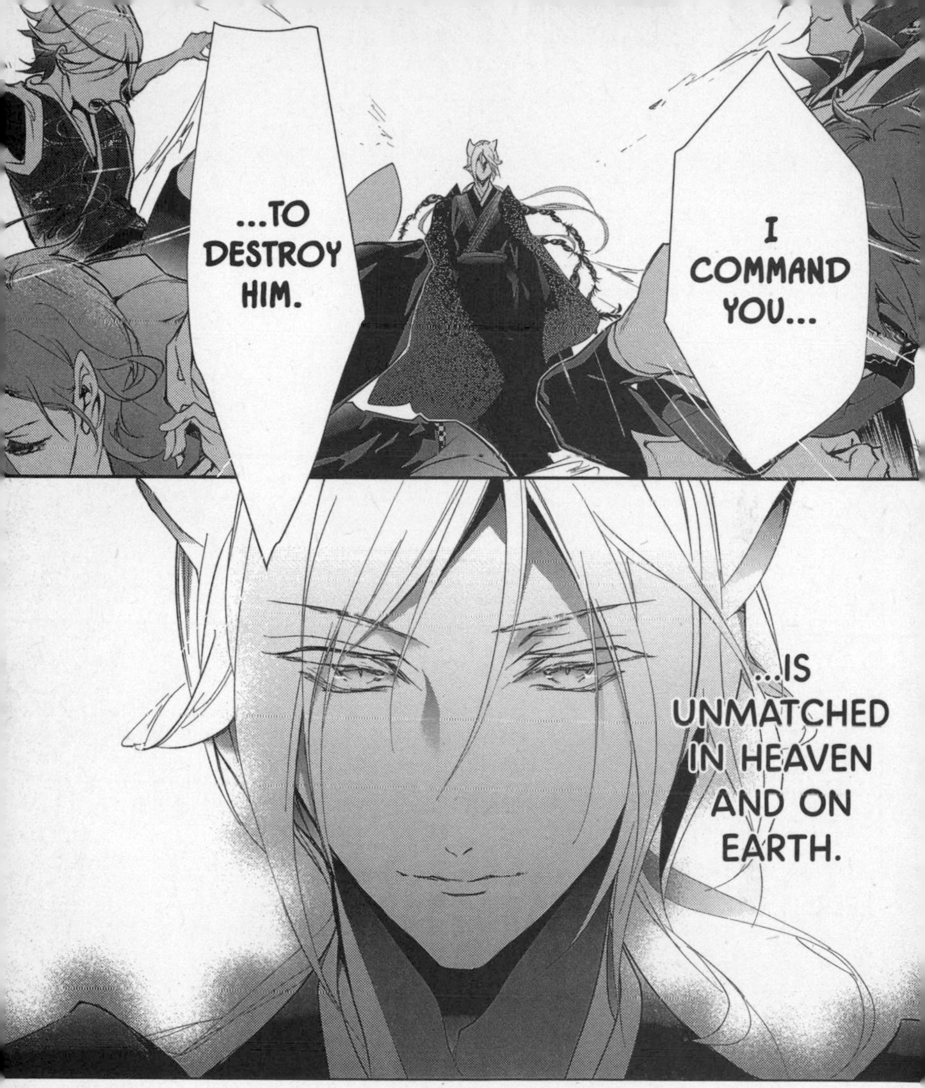
I COMMAND YOU...
...TO DESTROY HIM.
...IS UNMATCHED IN HEAVEN AND ON EARTH.

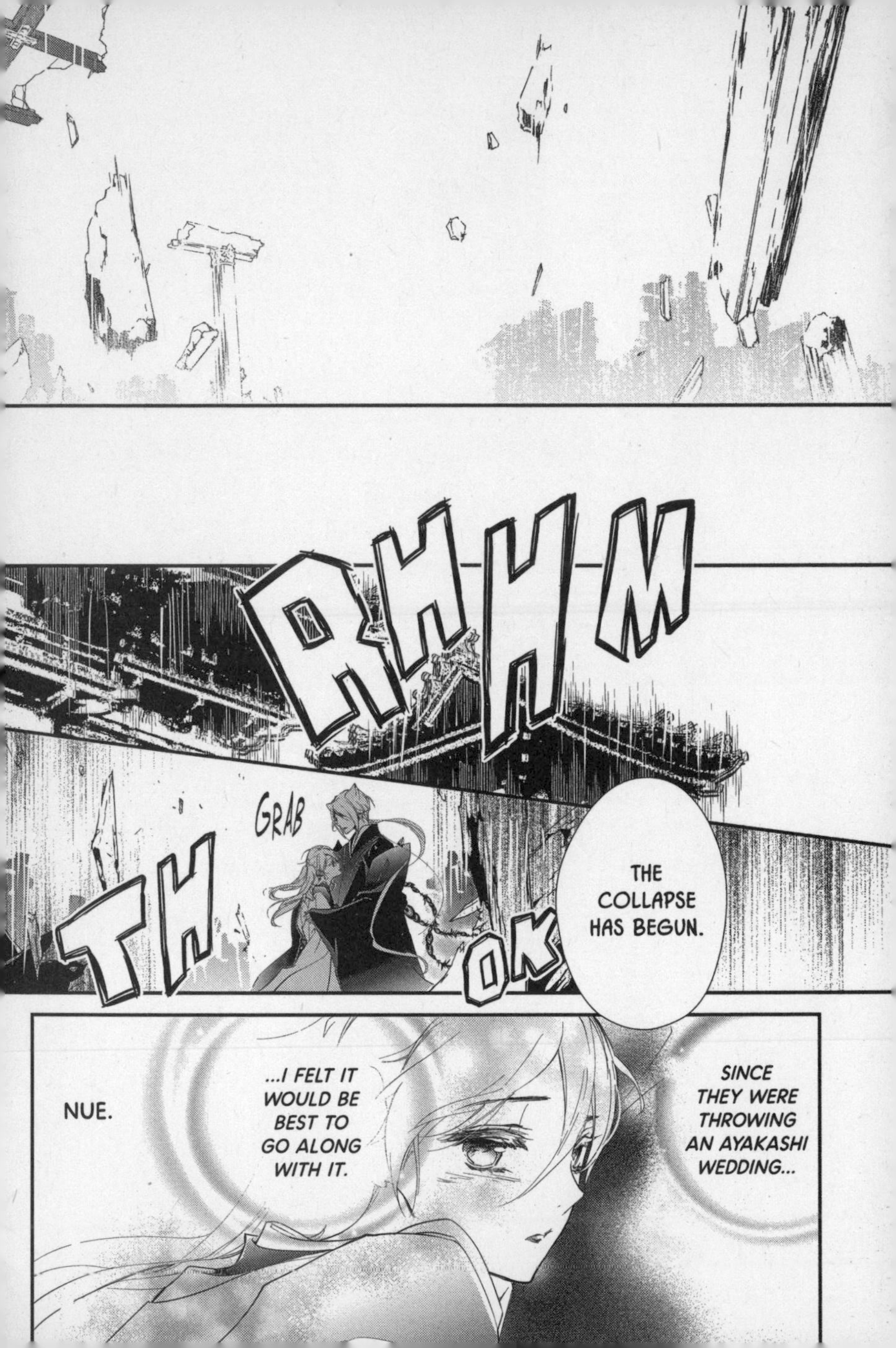
RHHM
THE COLLAPSE HAS BEGUN.
THOK
GRAB
SINCE THEY WERE THROWING AN AYAKASHI WEDDING...
...I FELT IT WOULD BE BEST TO GO ALONG WITH IT.
NUE.

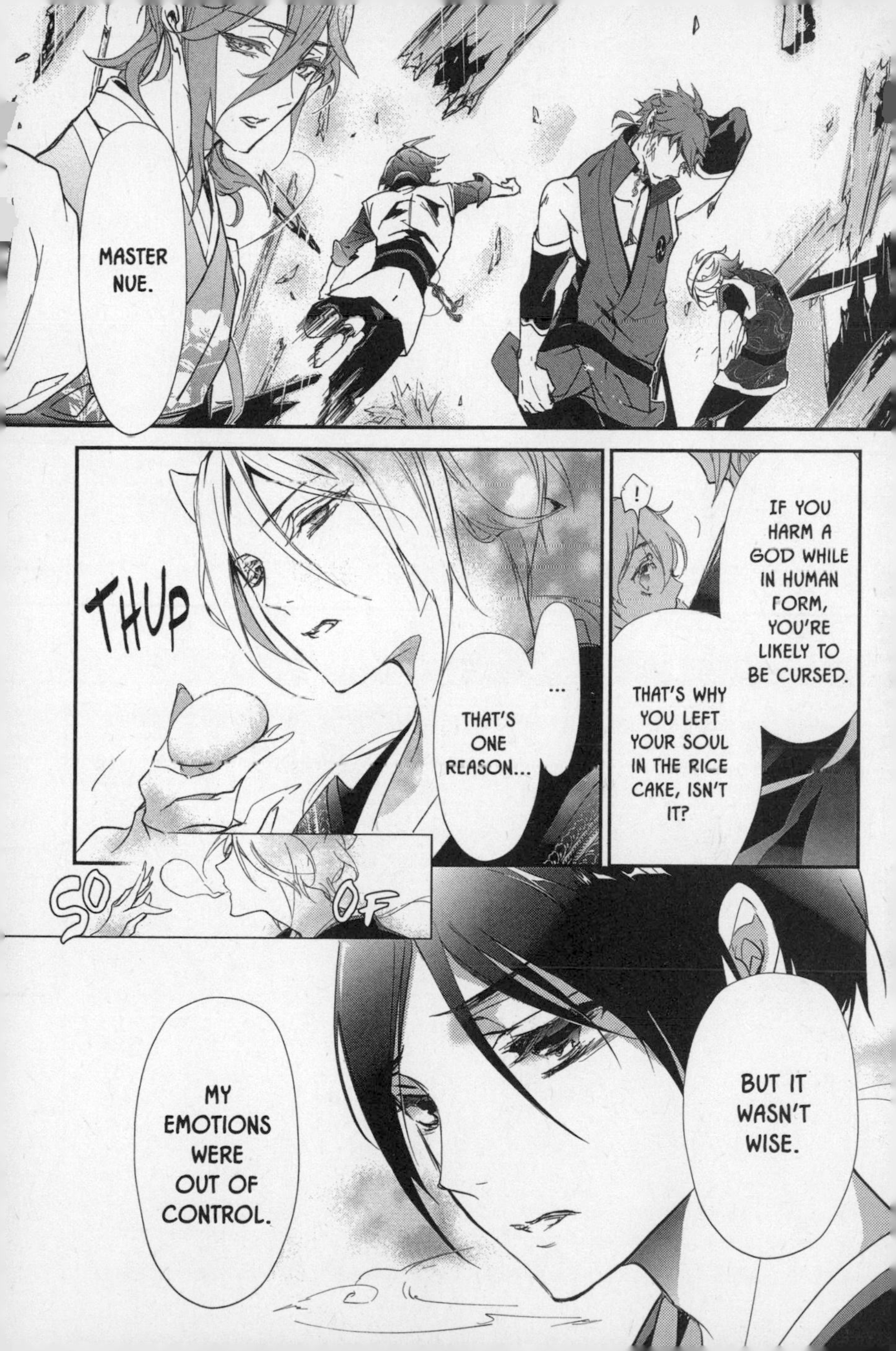
MASTER NUE.
IF YOU HARM A GOD WHILE IN HUMAN FORM, YOU'RE LIKELY TO BE CURSED.
!
THAT'S WHY YOU LEFT YOUR SOUL IN THE RICE CAKE, ISN'T IT?
... THAT'S ONE REASON...
THUP
SO OF
BUT IT WASN'T WISE.
MY EMOTIONS WERE OUT OF CONTROL.

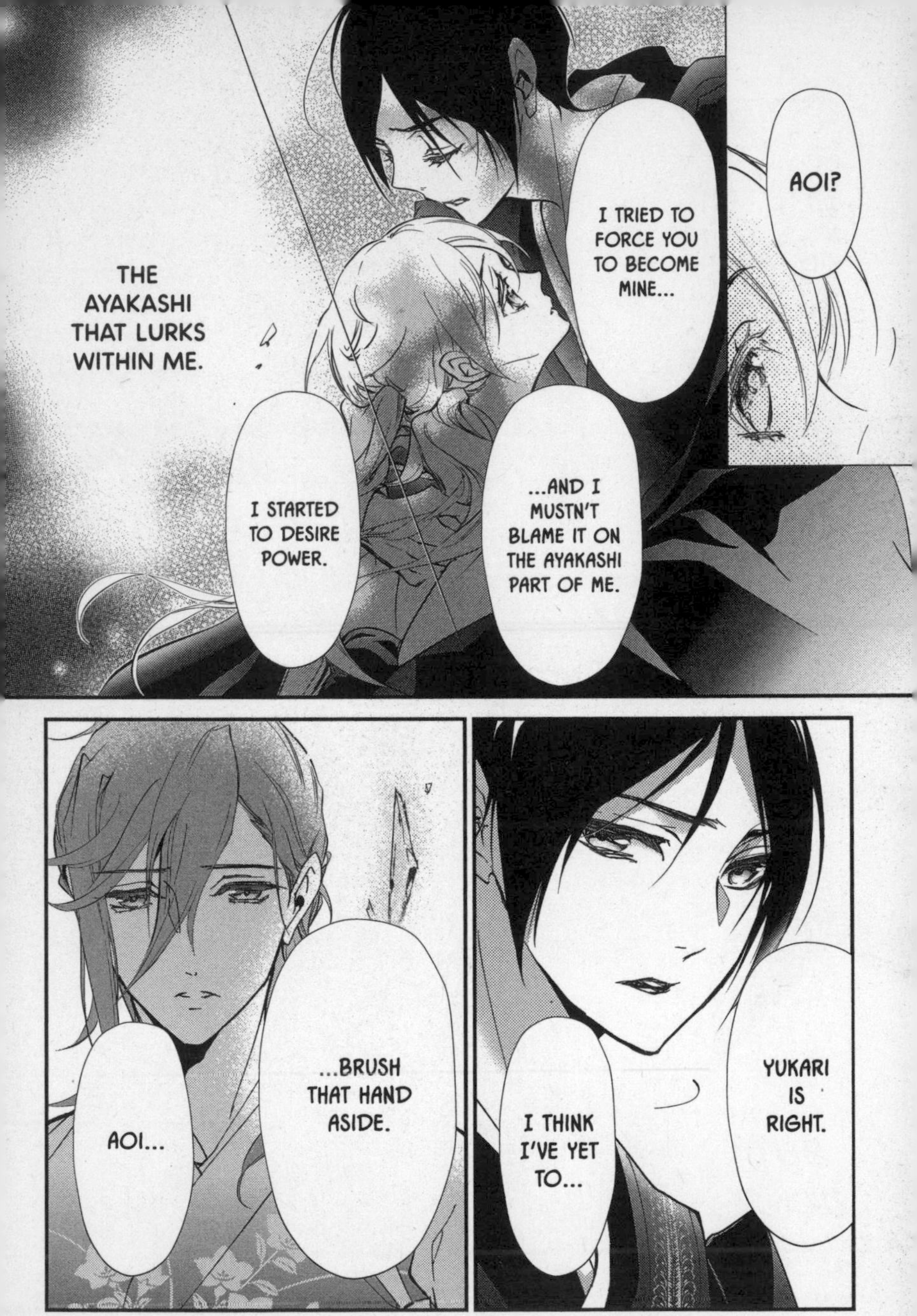
AOI?
I TRIED TO FORCE YOU TO BECOME MINE...
...AND I MUSTN'T BLAME IT ON THE AYAKASHI PART OF ME.
I STARTED TO DESIRE POWER.
THE AYAKASHI THAT LURKS WITHIN ME.
YUKARI IS RIGHT.
I THINK I'VE YET TO...
...BRUSH THAT HAND ASIDE.
AOI...

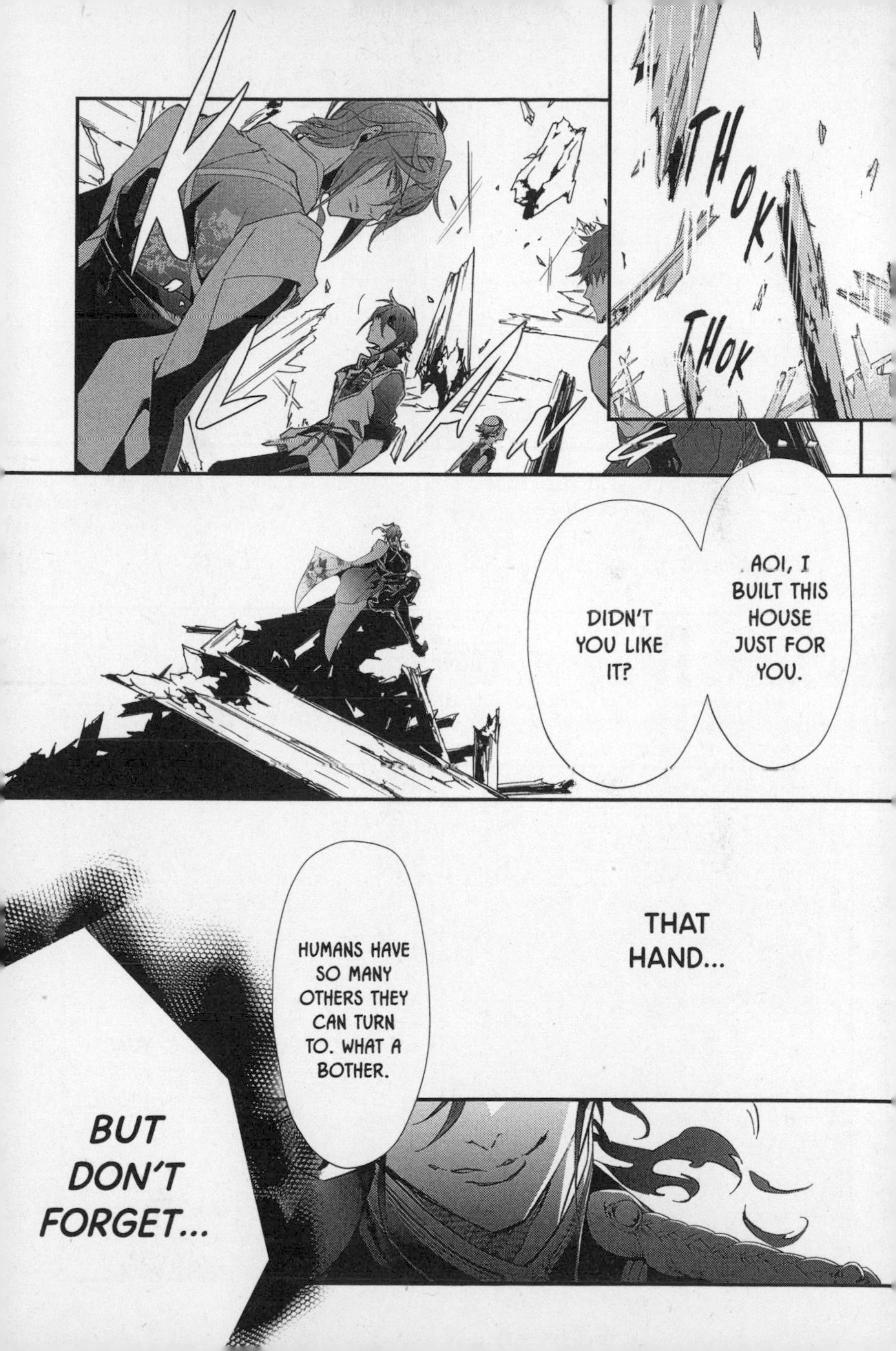
THOK
THOK
AOI, I BUILT THIS HOUSE JUST FOR YOU.
DIDN'T YOU LIKE IT?
THAT HAND...
HUMANS HAVE SO MANY OTHERS THEY CAN TURN TO. WHAT A BOTHER.
BUT DON'T FORGET...

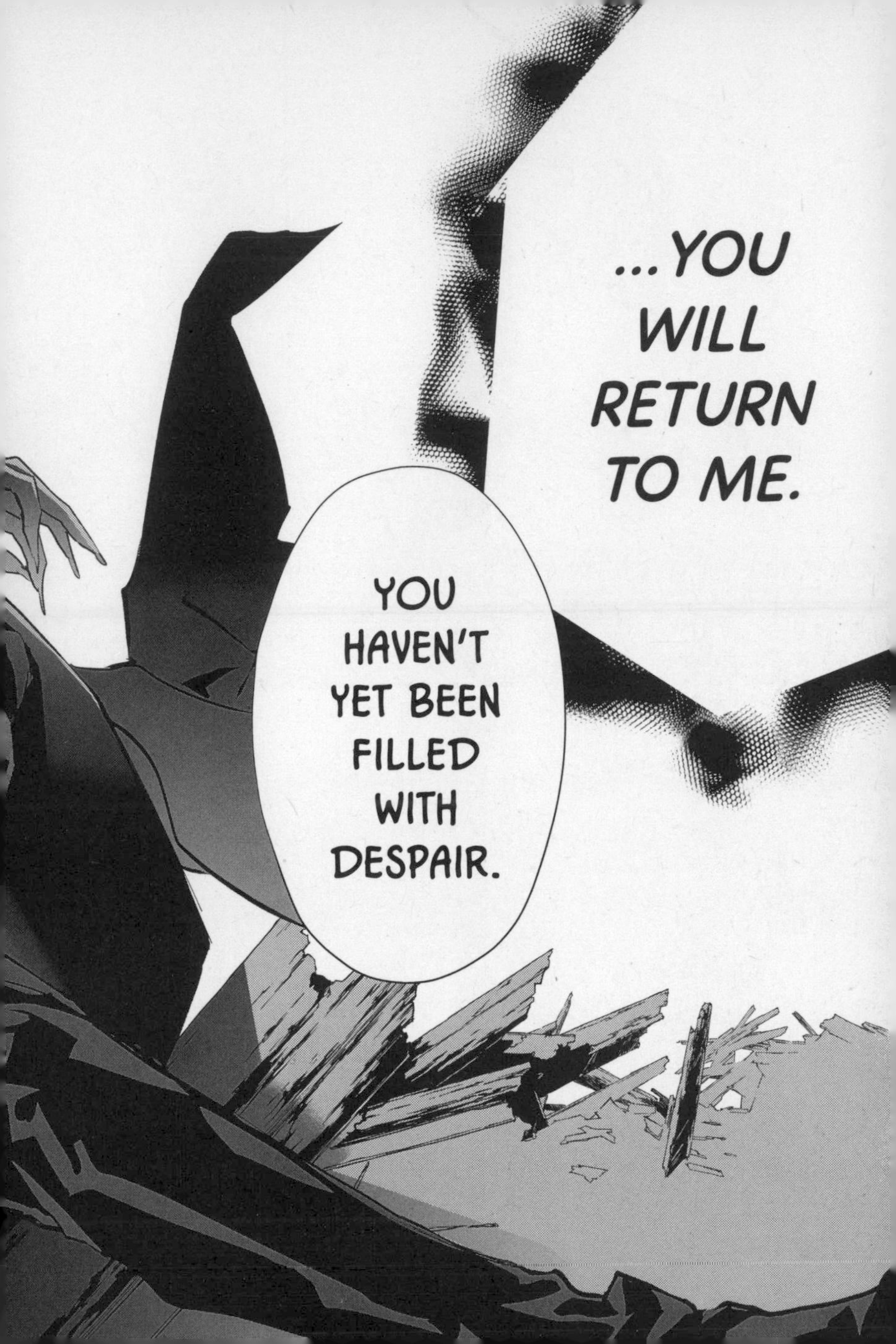
...YOU WILL RETURN TO ME.
YOU HAVEN'T YET BEEN FILLED WITH DESPAIR.

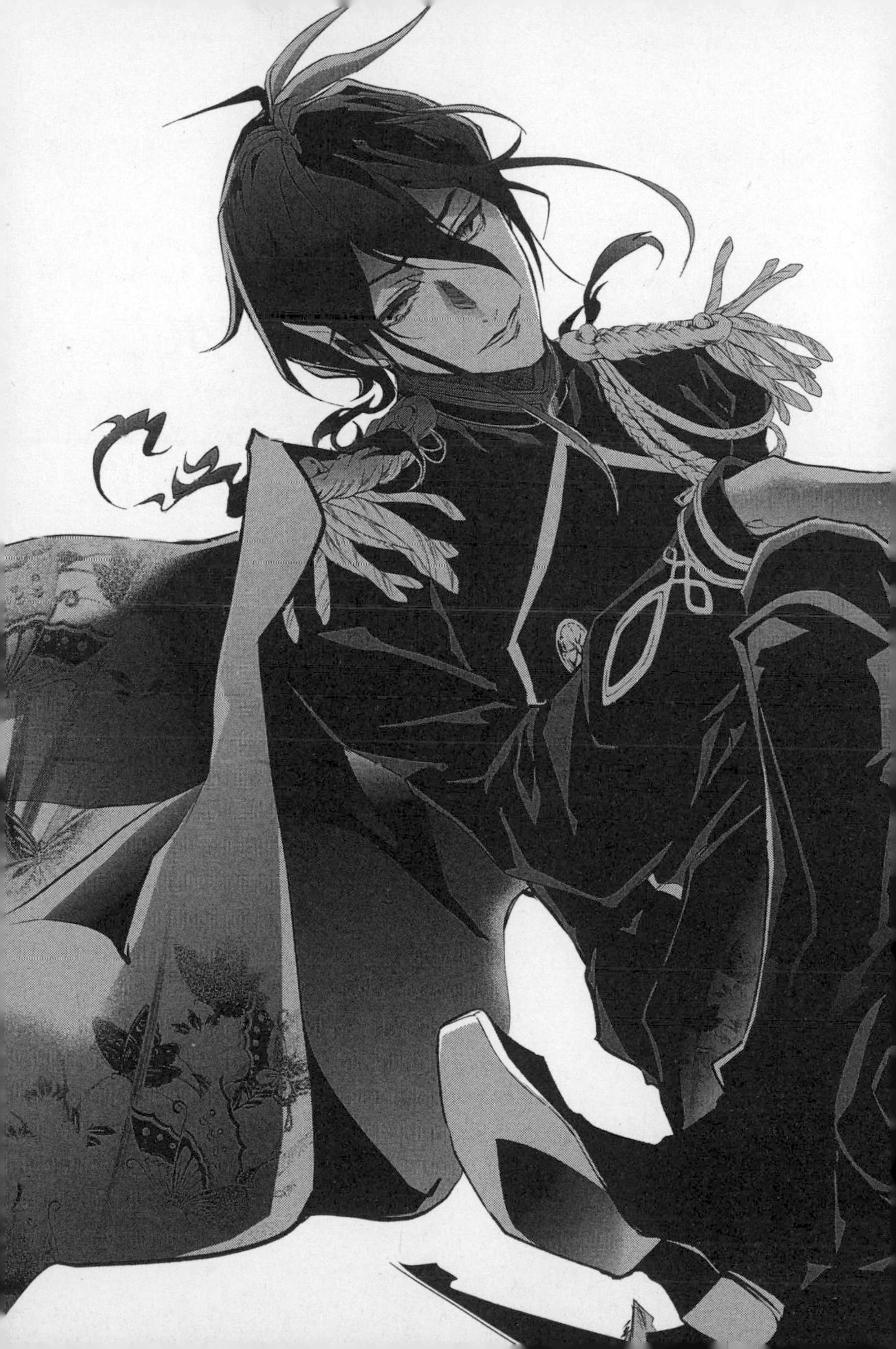

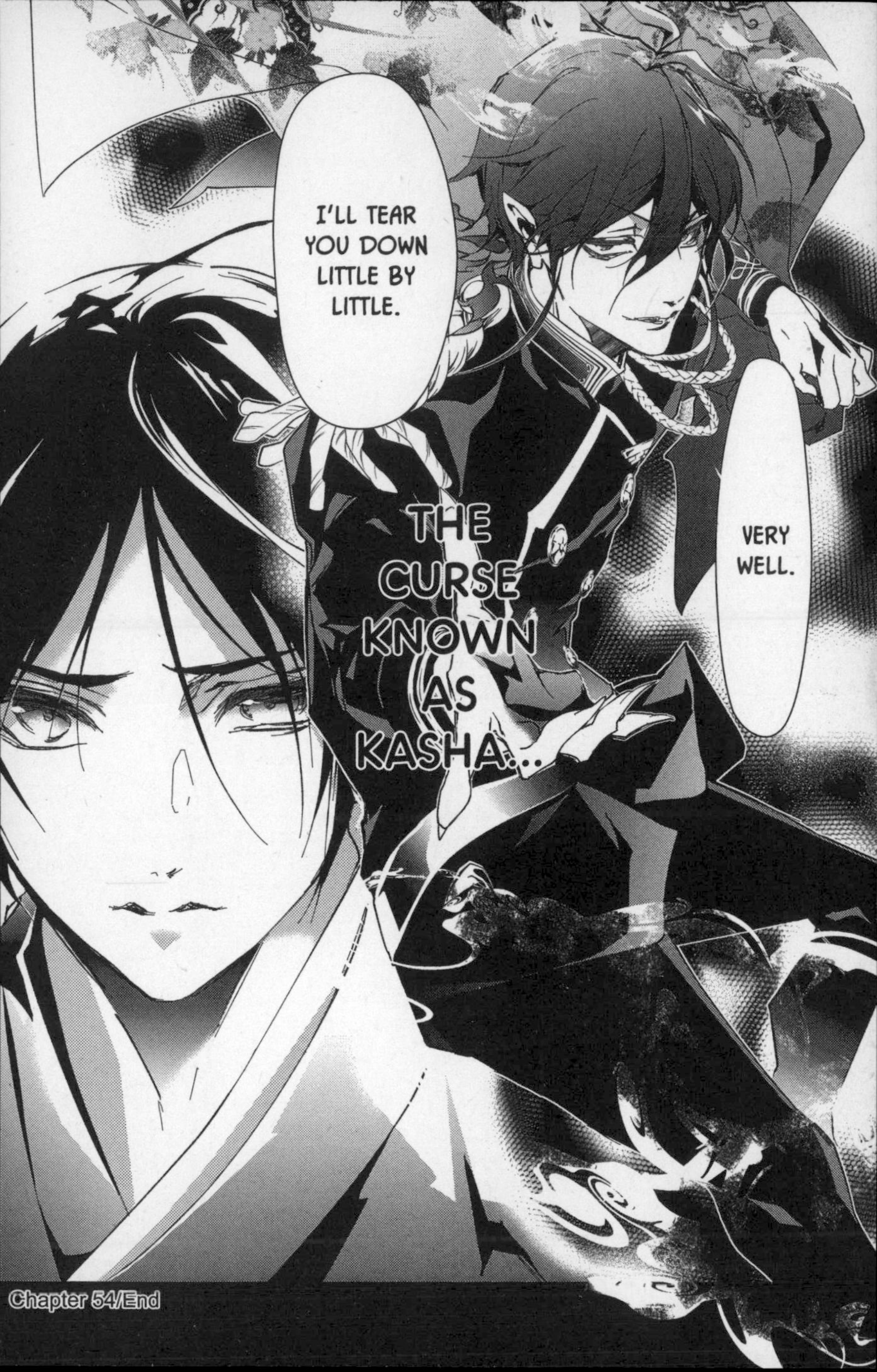
I'LL TEAR YOU DOWN LITTLE BY LITTLE.
VERY WELL.
THE CURSE KNOWN AS KASHA...

Chapter 54/End

The DEMON PRINCE of MOMOCHI HOUSE

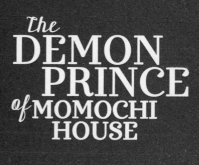

The
DEMON
PRINCE
of MOMOCHI
HOUSE

CHAPTER 55

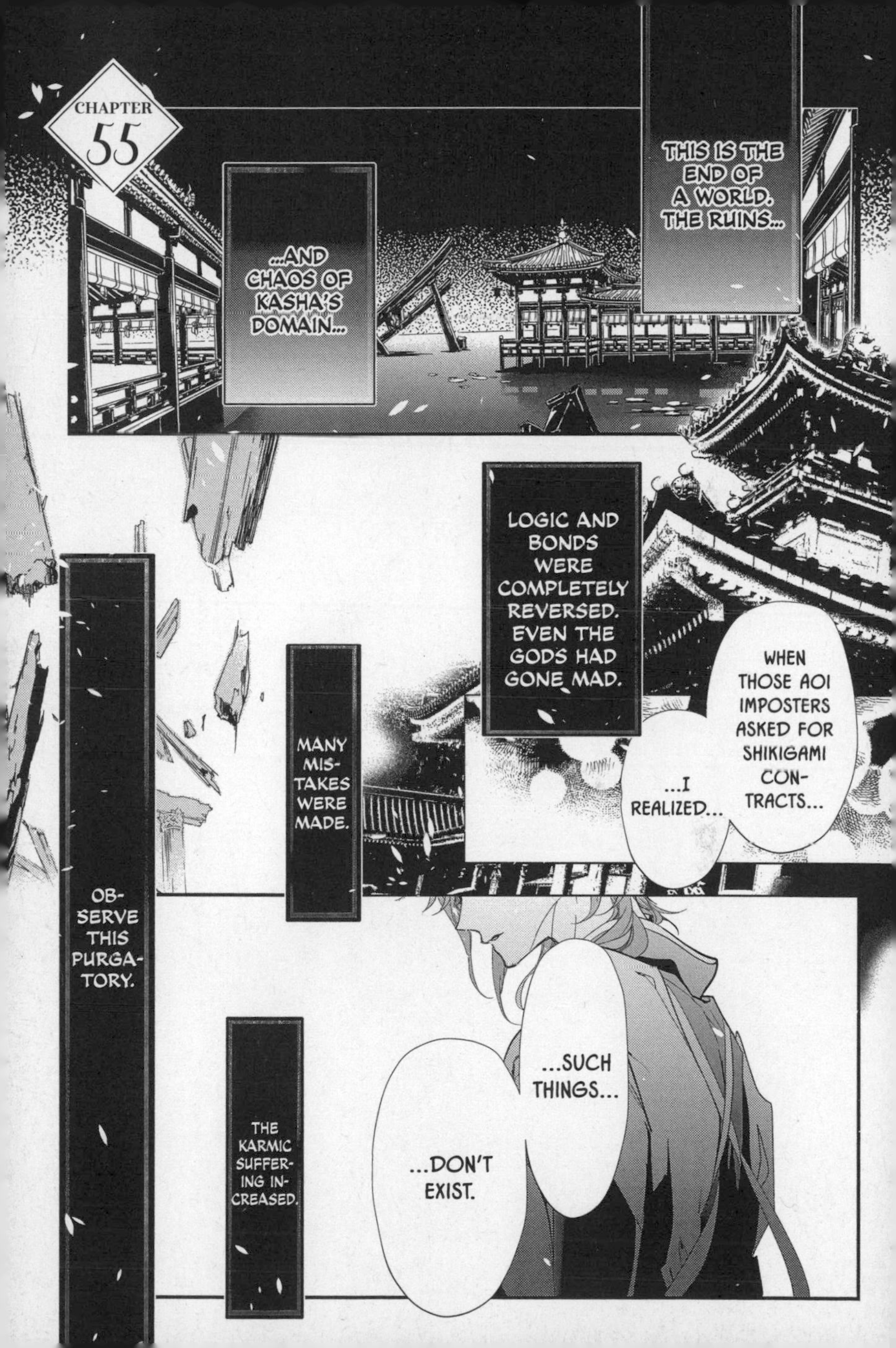
THIS IS THE END OF A WORLD. THE RUINS...
...AND CHAOS OF KASHA'S DOMAIN...
LOGIC AND BONDS WERE COMPLETELY REVERSED. EVEN THE GODS HAD GONE MAD.
WHEN THOSE AOI IMPOSTERS ASKED FOR SHIKIGAMI CONTRACTS...
...I REALIZED...
MANY MISTAKES WERE MADE.
...SUCH THINGS...
...DON'T EXIST.
THE KARMIC SUFFERING INCREASED.
OBSERVE THIS PURGATORY.

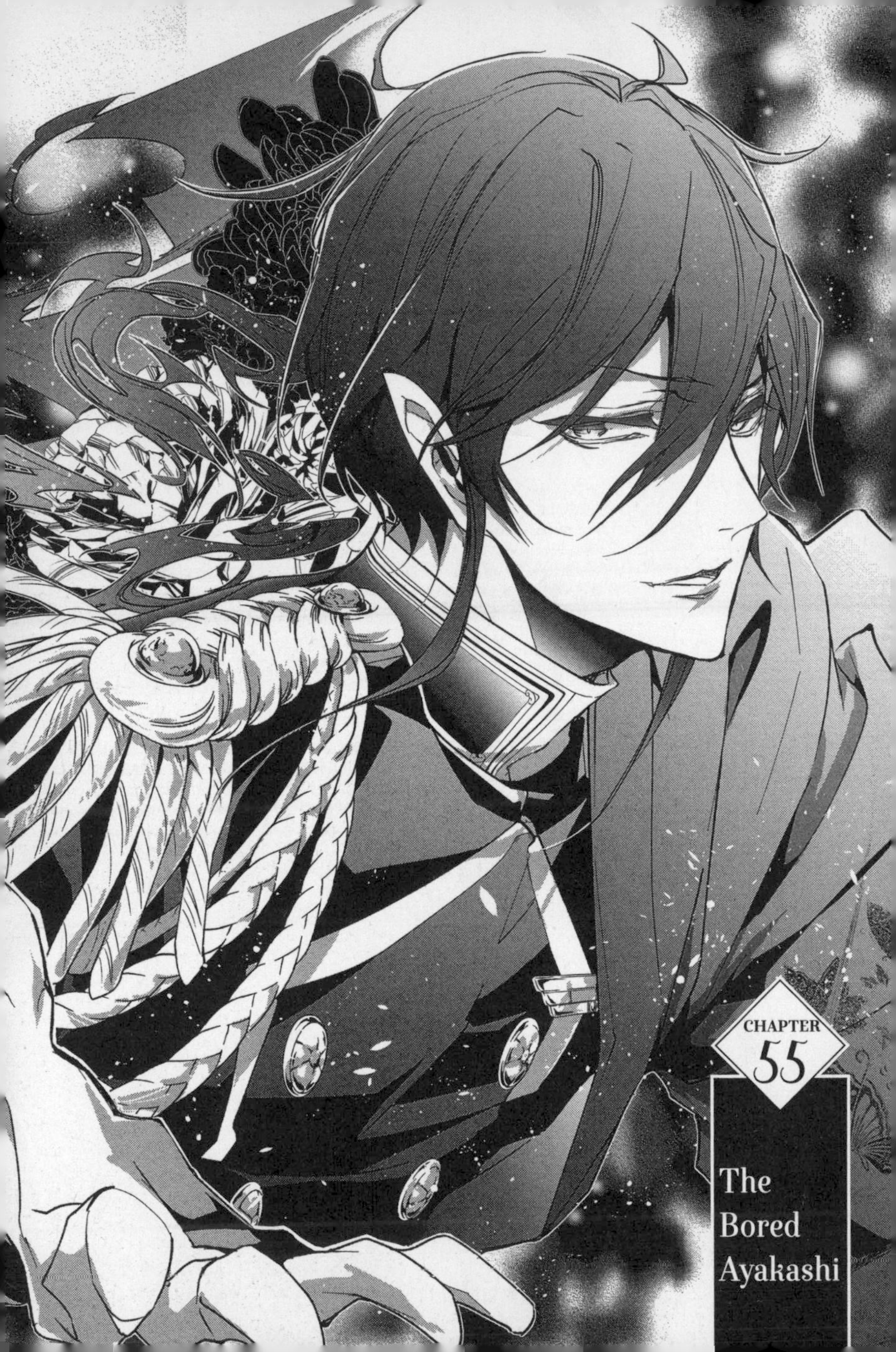
CHAPTER
55
The Bored Ayakashi

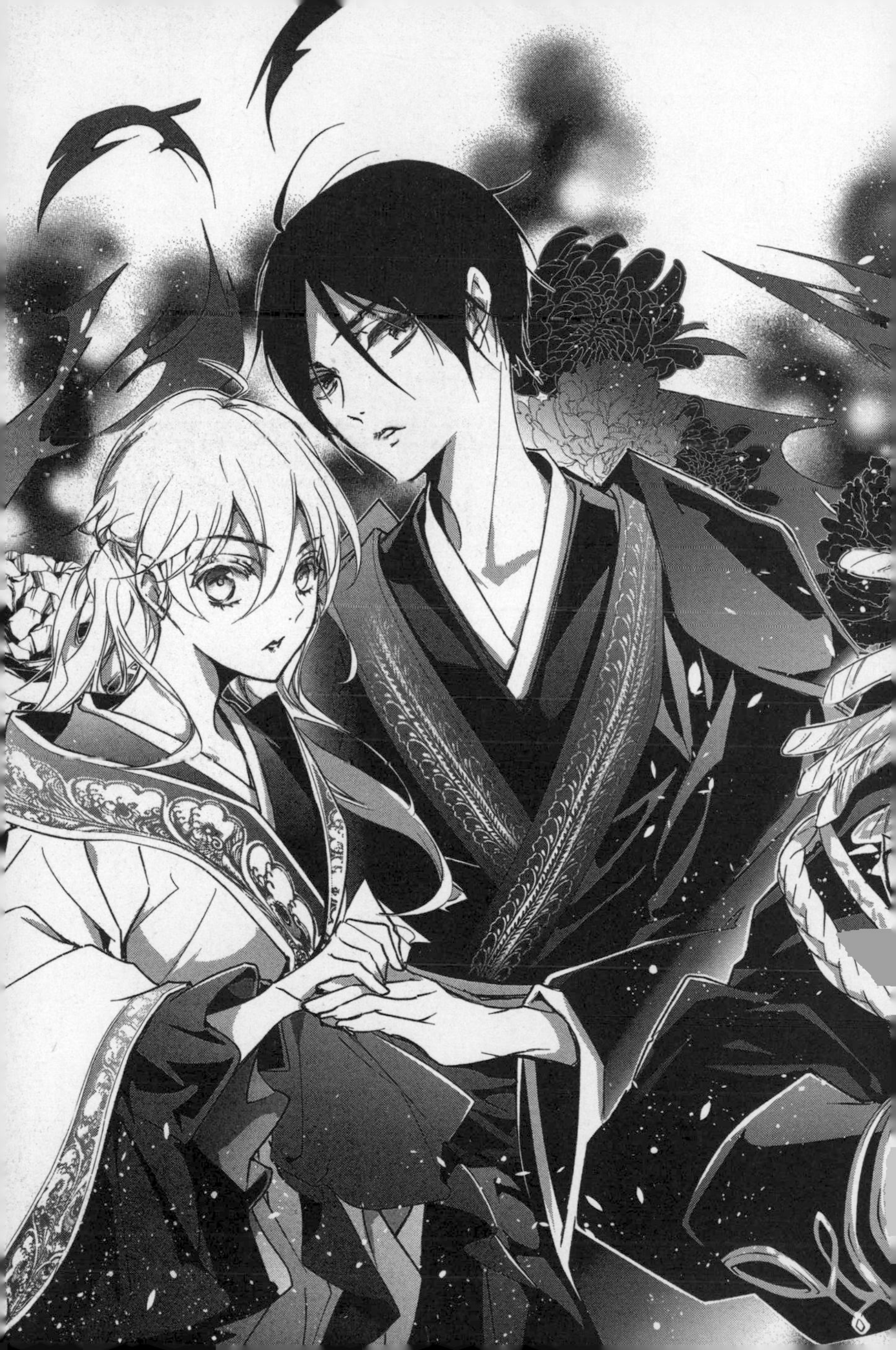

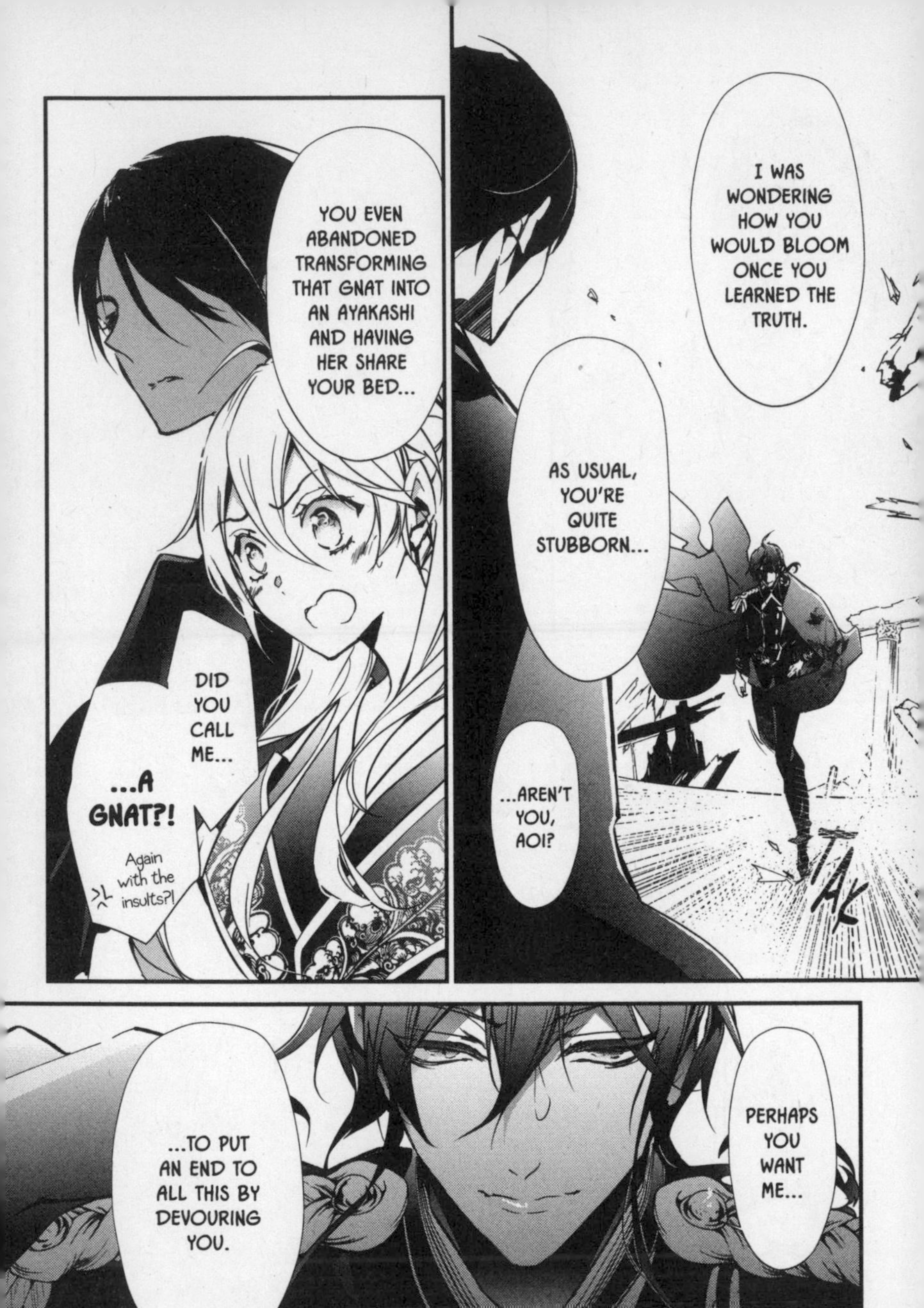
I WAS WONDERING HOW YOU WOULD BLOOM ONCE YOU LEARNED THE TRUTH.
AS USUAL, YOU'RE QUITE STUBBORN...
...AREN'T YOU, AOI?
TAK
YOU EVEN ABANDONED TRANSFORMING THAT GNAT INTO AN AYAKASHI AND HAVING HER SHARE YOUR BED...
DID YOU CALL ME...
...A GNAT?!
Again with the insults?!
PERHAPS YOU WANT ME...
...TO PUT AN END TO ALL THIS BY DEVOURING YOU.

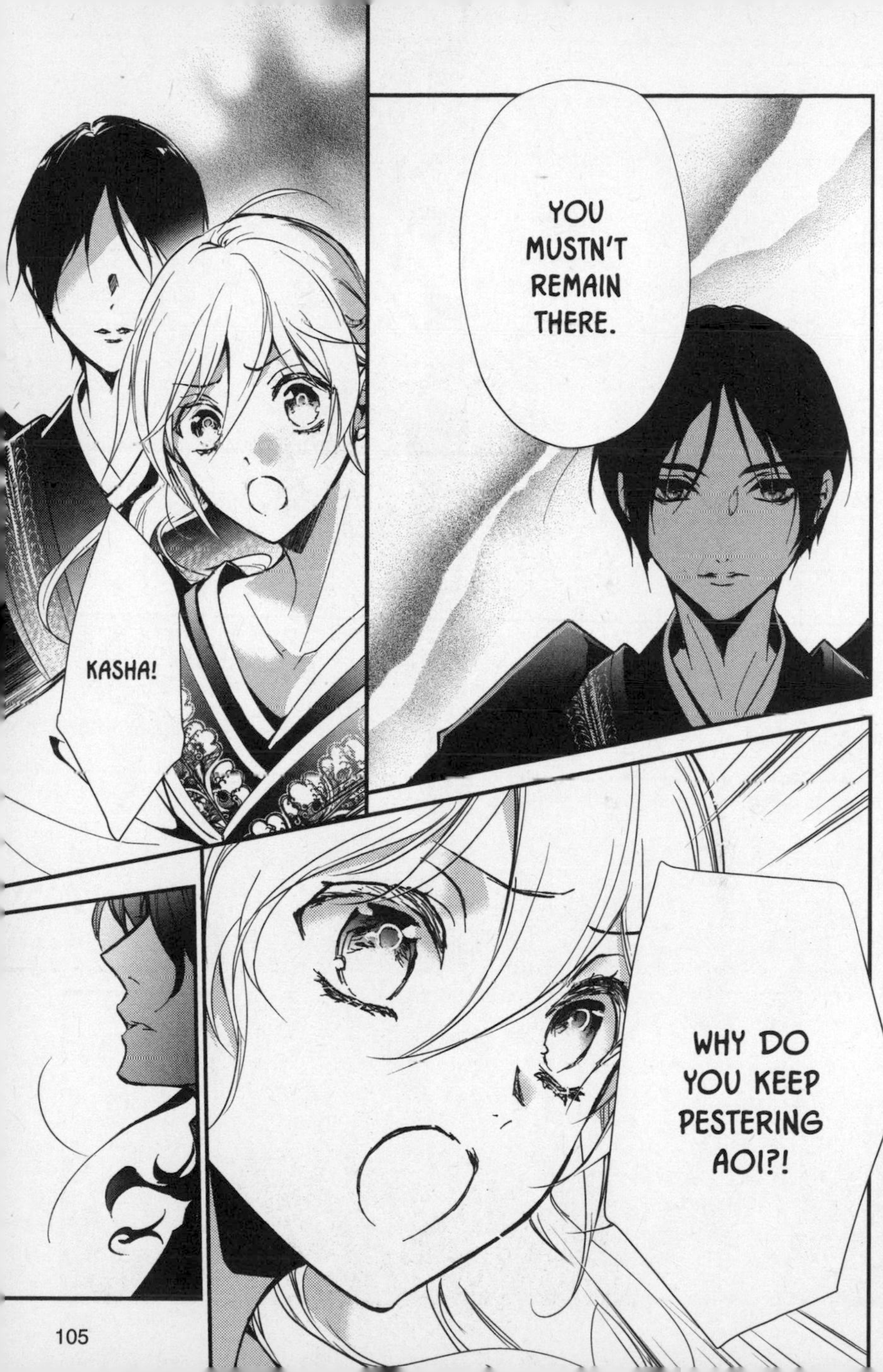
YOU MUSTN'T REMAIN THERE.
KASHA!
WHY DO YOU KEEP PESTERING AOI?!

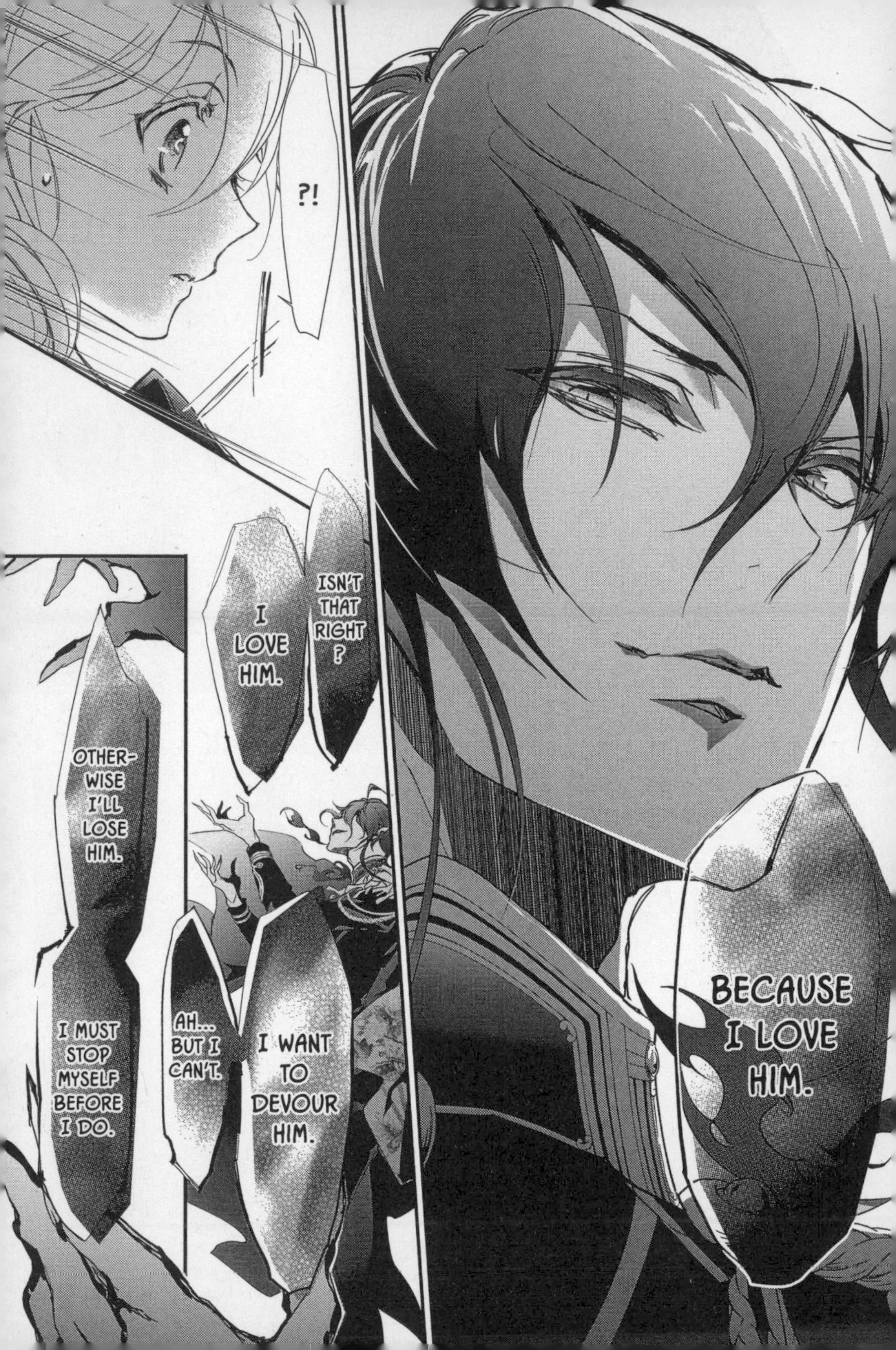
BECAUSE I LOVE HIM.
?!
ISN'T THAT RIGHT?
I LOVE HIM.
I WANT TO DEVOUR HIM.
AH... BUT I CAN'T.
OTHER-WISE I'LL LOSE HIM.
I MUST STOP MYSELF BEFORE I DO.

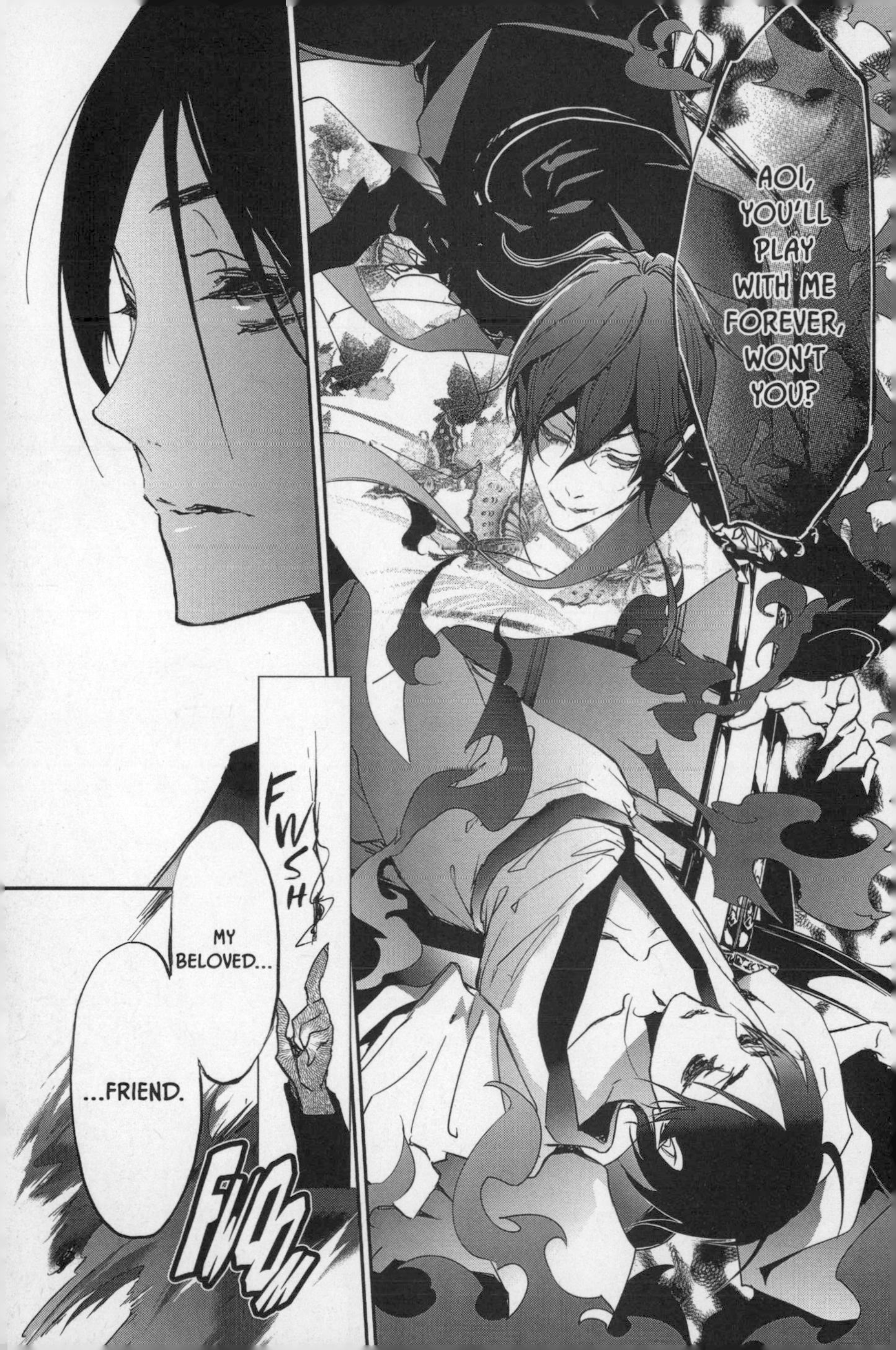
AOI, YOU'LL PLAY WITH ME FOREVER, WON'T YOU?
FWSH
MY BELOVED...
...FRIEND.

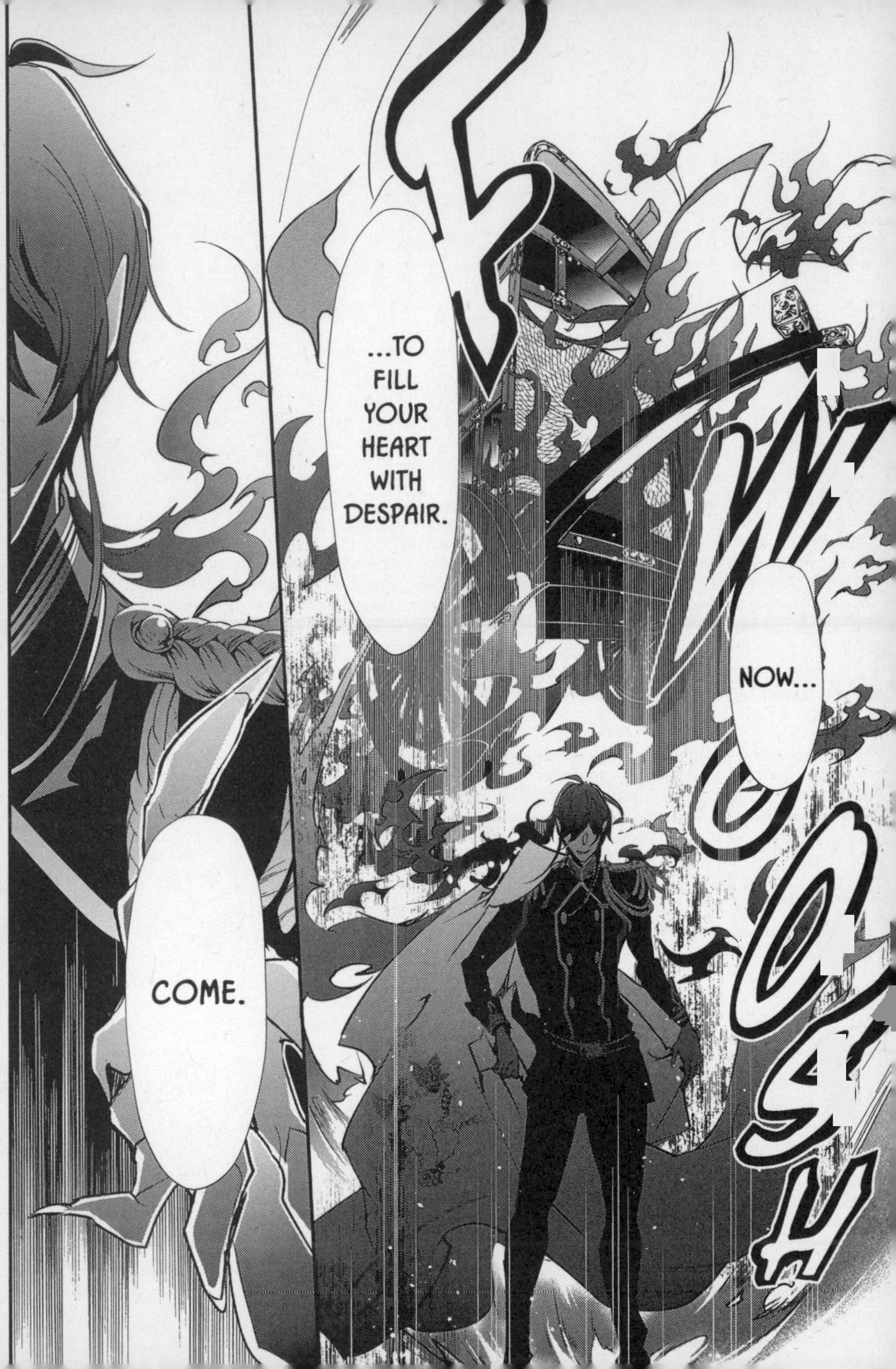
WOOSH
NOW...
...TO FILL YOUR HEART WITH DESPAIR.
COME.

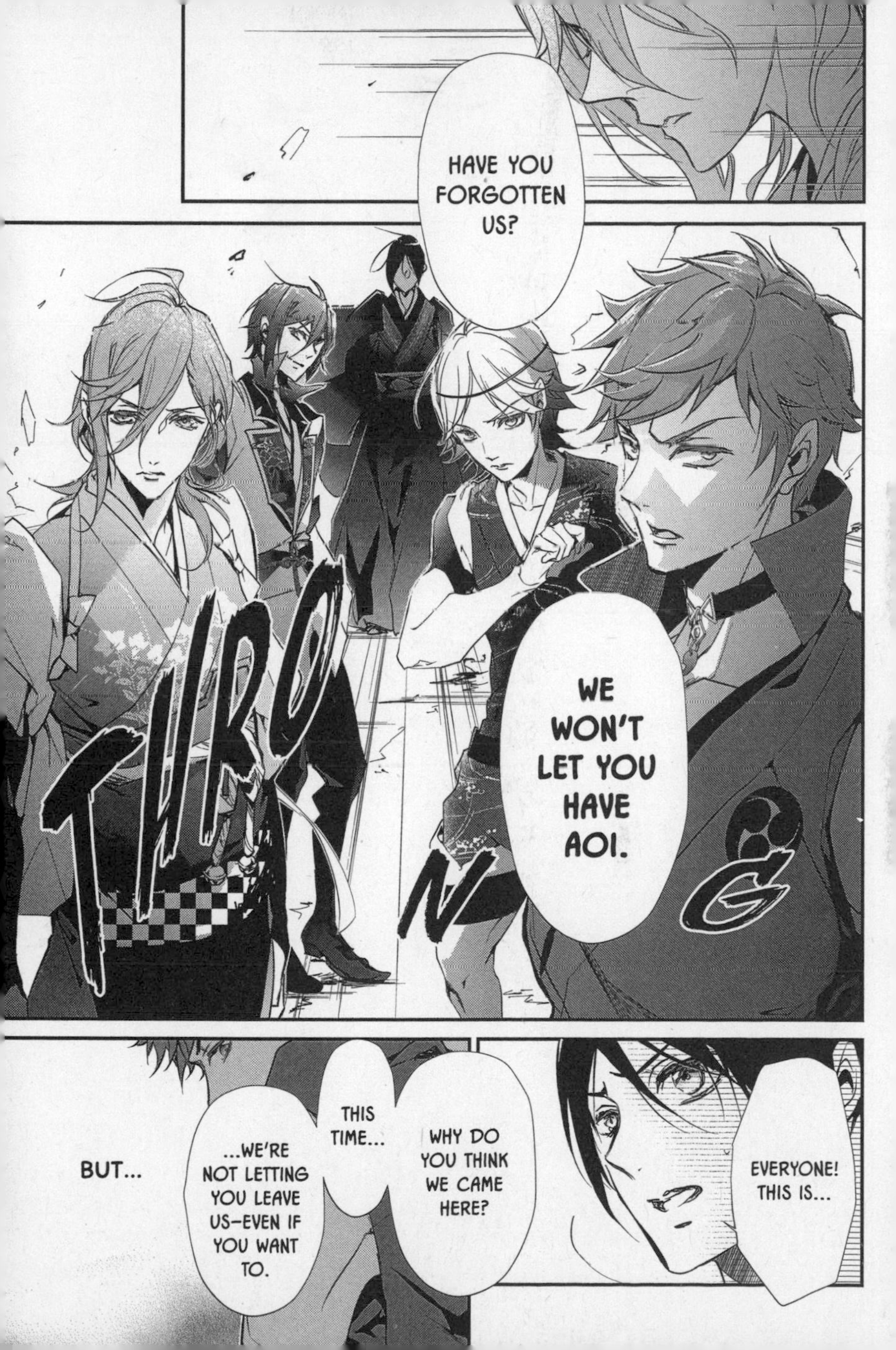
HAVE YOU FORGOTTEN US?
WE WON'T LET YOU HAVE AOI.
THRONG
EVERYONE! THIS IS...
WHY DO YOU THINK WE CAME HERE?
THIS TIME...
...WE'RE NOT LETTING YOU LEAVE US—EVEN IF YOU WANT TO.
BUT...

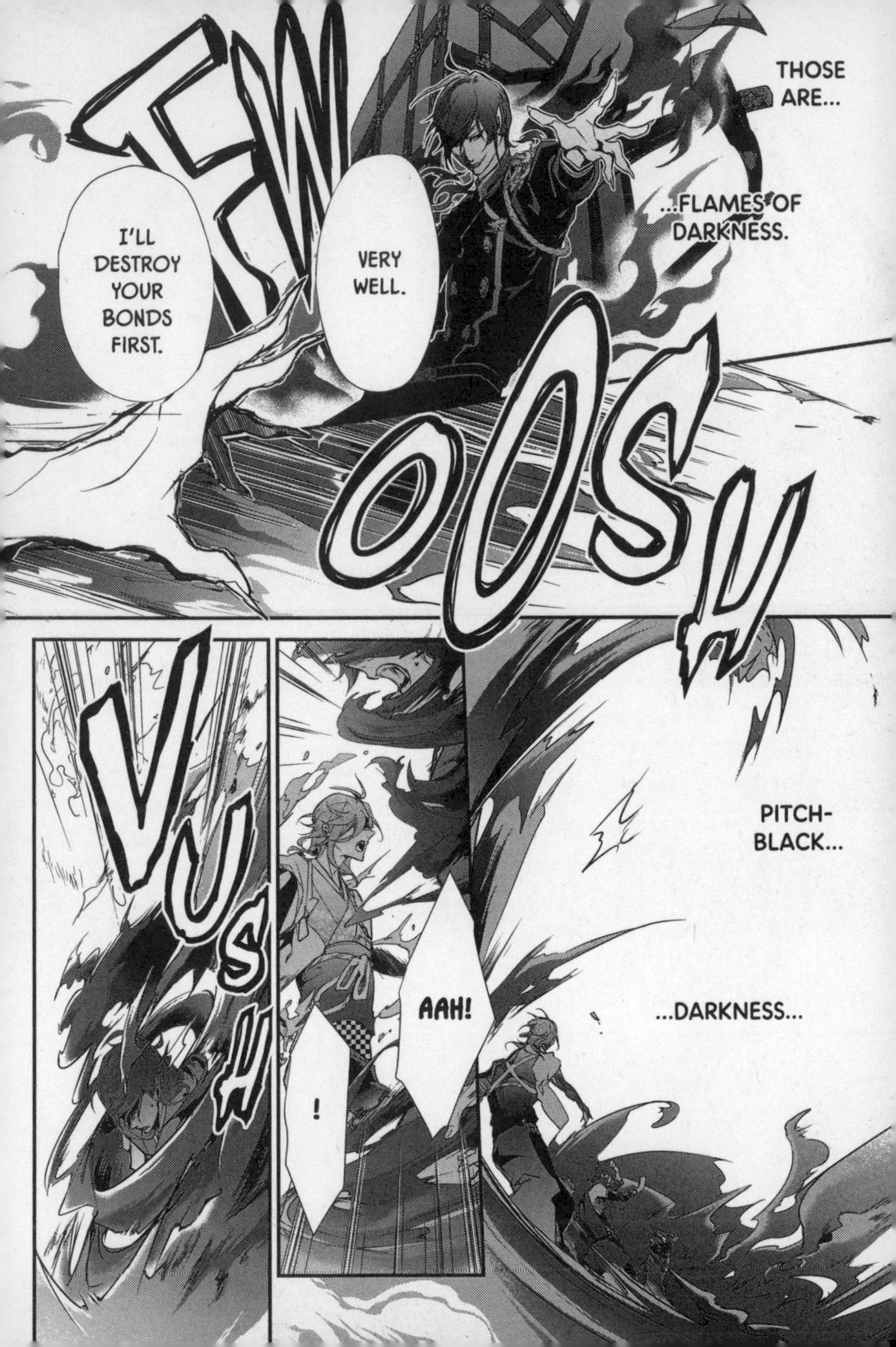
THOSE ARE...
...FLAMES OF DARKNESS.
VERY WELL.
I'LL DESTROY YOUR BONDS FIRST.
PITCH-BLACK...
...DARKNESS...
AAH!
!
VUSH!

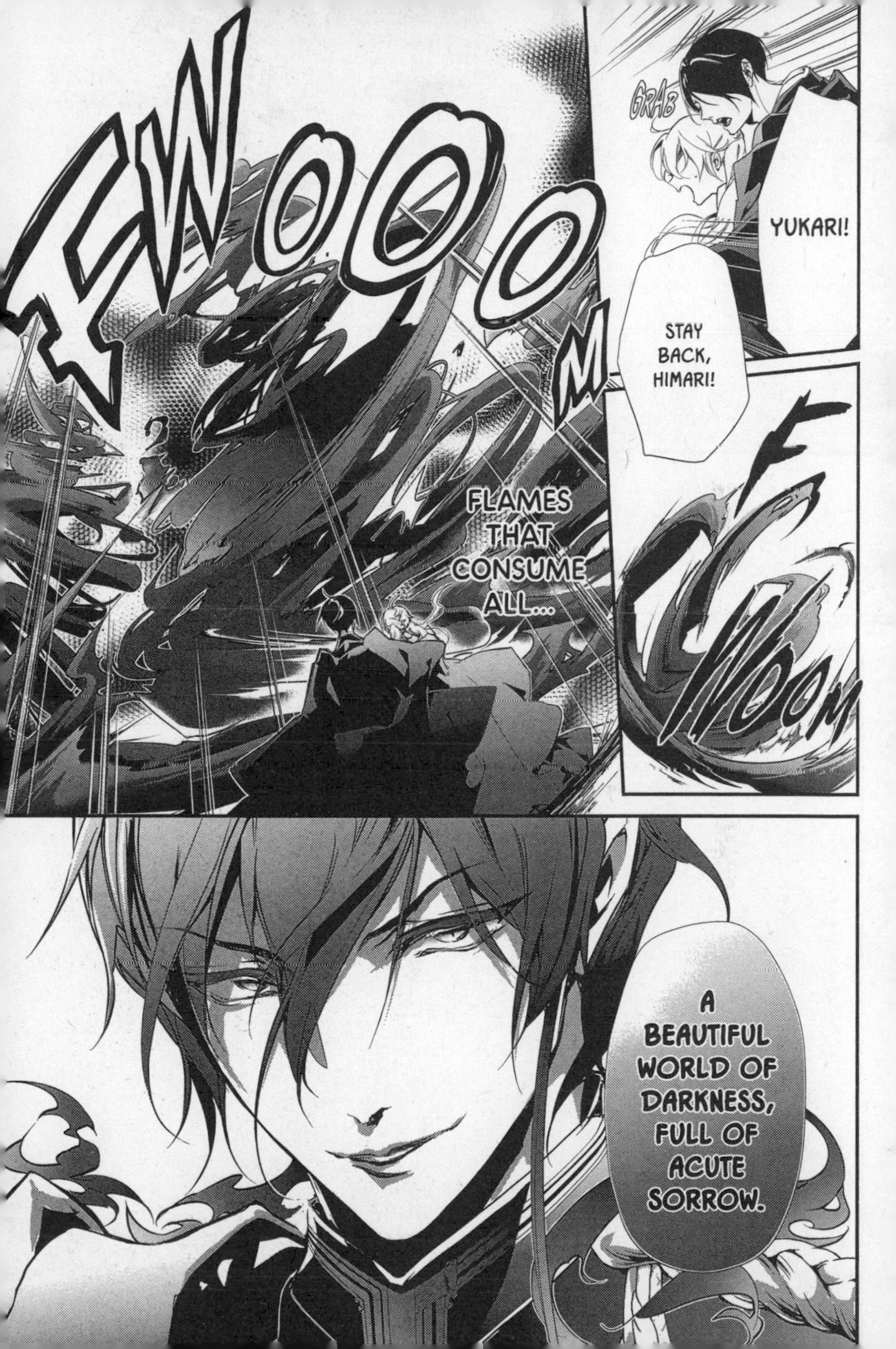
GRAB
YUKARI!
STAY BACK, HIMARI!
FWOOM
FWOOOOM
FLAMES THAT CONSUME ALL...
A BEAUTIFUL WORLD OF DARKNESS, FULL OF ACUTE SORROW.

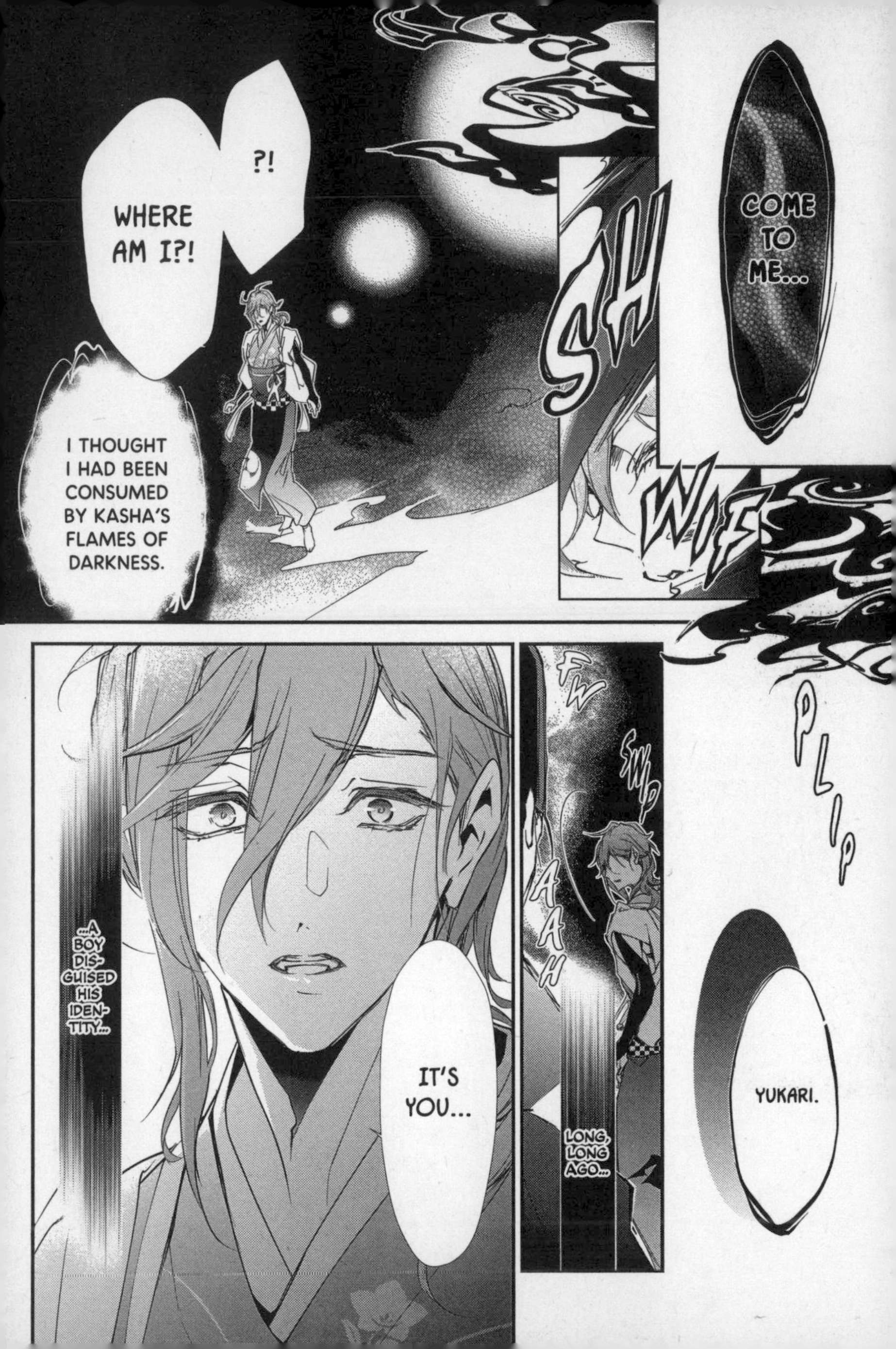
COME TO ME...
SHWF
?!
WHERE AM I?!
I THOUGHT I HAD BEEN CONSUMED BY KASHA'S FLAMES OF DARKNESS.
PLIP
YUKARI.
FW
LONG, LONG AGO...
IT'S YOU...
...A BOY DISGUISED HIS IDENTITY...

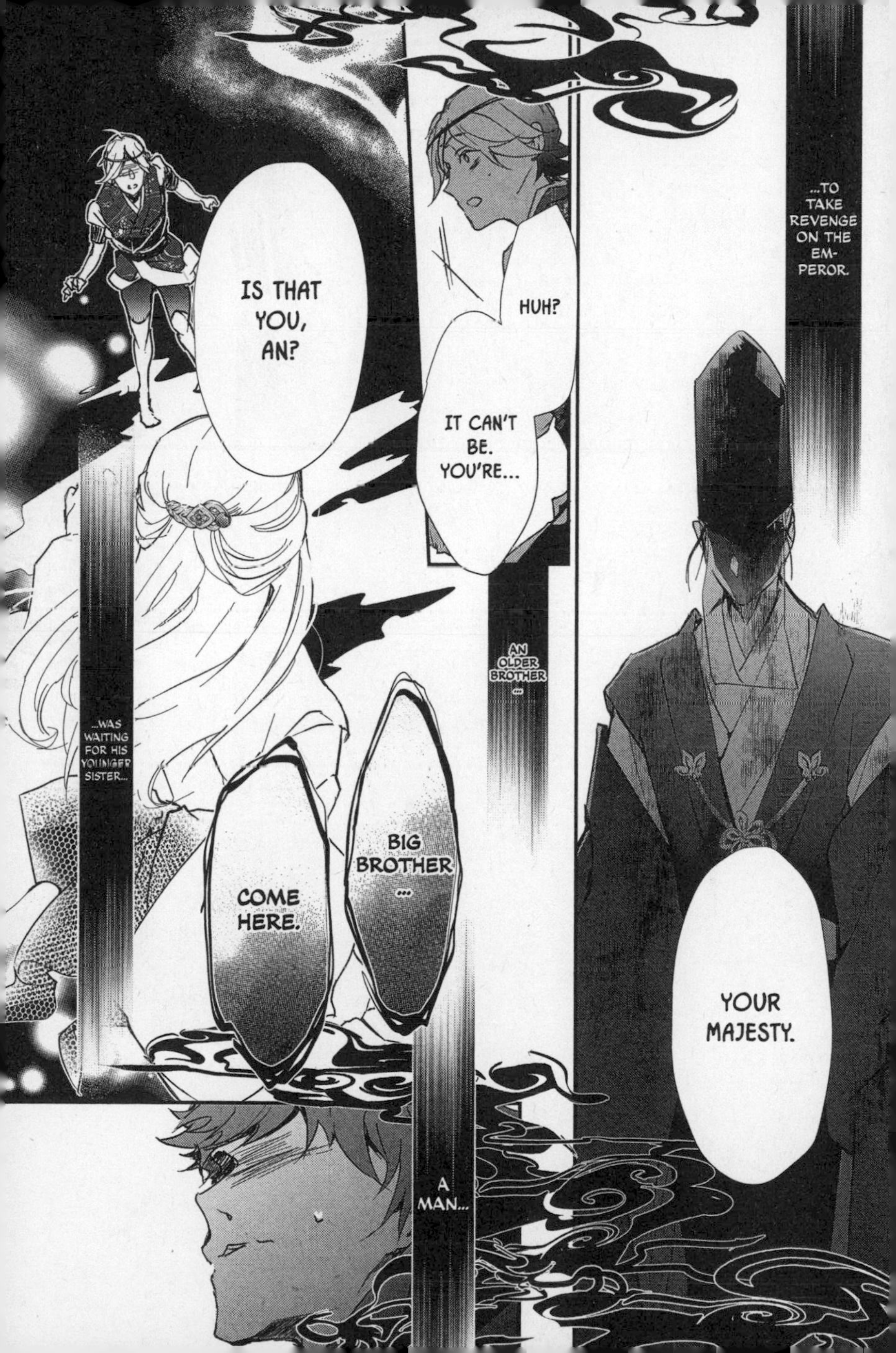
...TO TAKE REVENGE ON THE EM-PEROR.
YOUR MAJESTY.
HUH?
IT CAN'T BE. YOU'RE...
AN OLDER BROTHER...
A MAN...
IS THAT YOU, AN?
BIG BROTHER...
COME HERE.
...WAS WAITING FOR HIS YOUNGER SISTER...

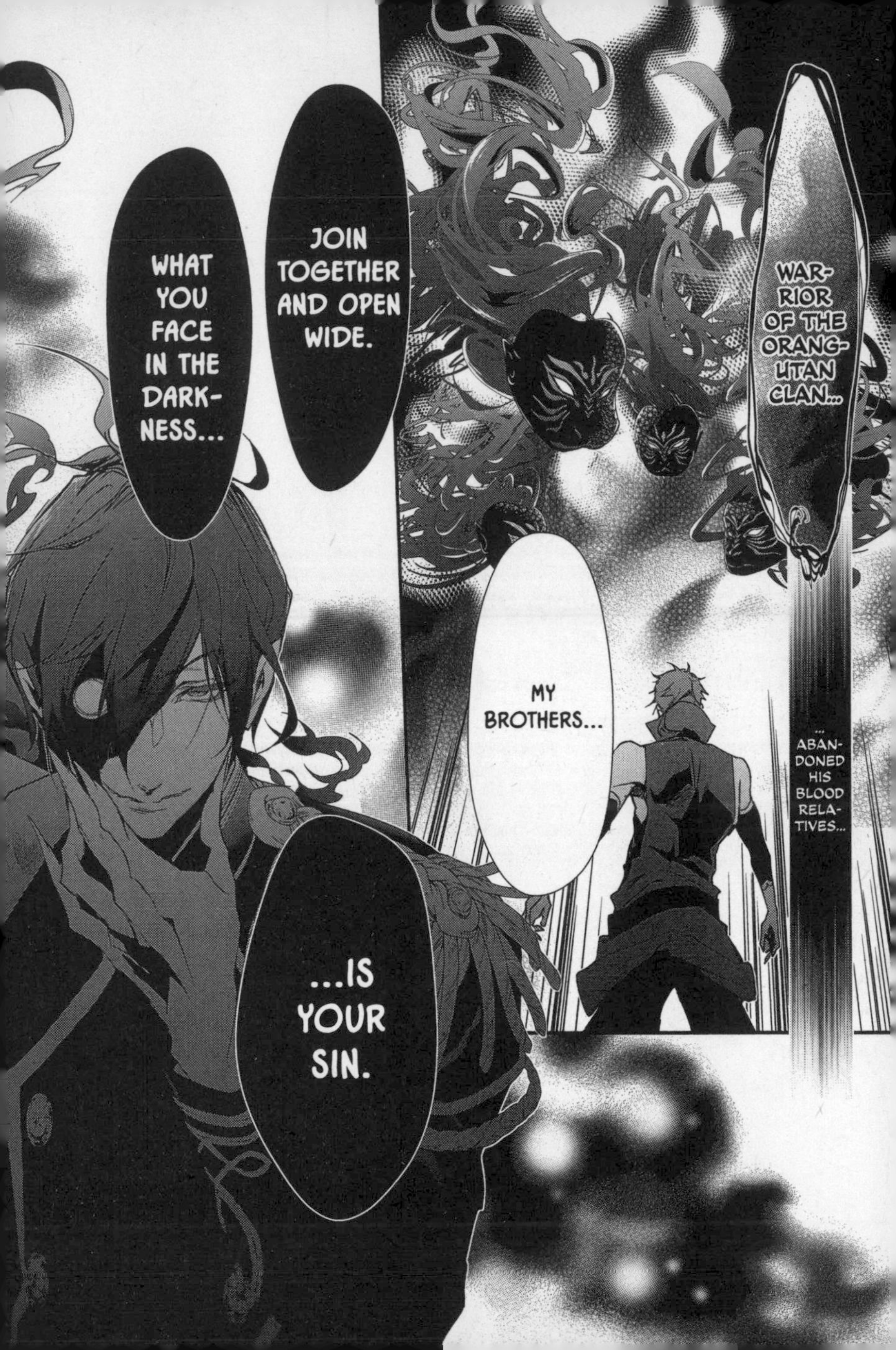
WAR-RIOR OF THE ORANG-UTAN CLAN...
...ABAN-DONED HIS BLOOD RELA-TIVES...
MY BROTHERS...
JOIN TOGETHER AND OPEN WIDE.
WHAT YOU FACE IN THE DARK-NESS...
...IS YOUR SIN.

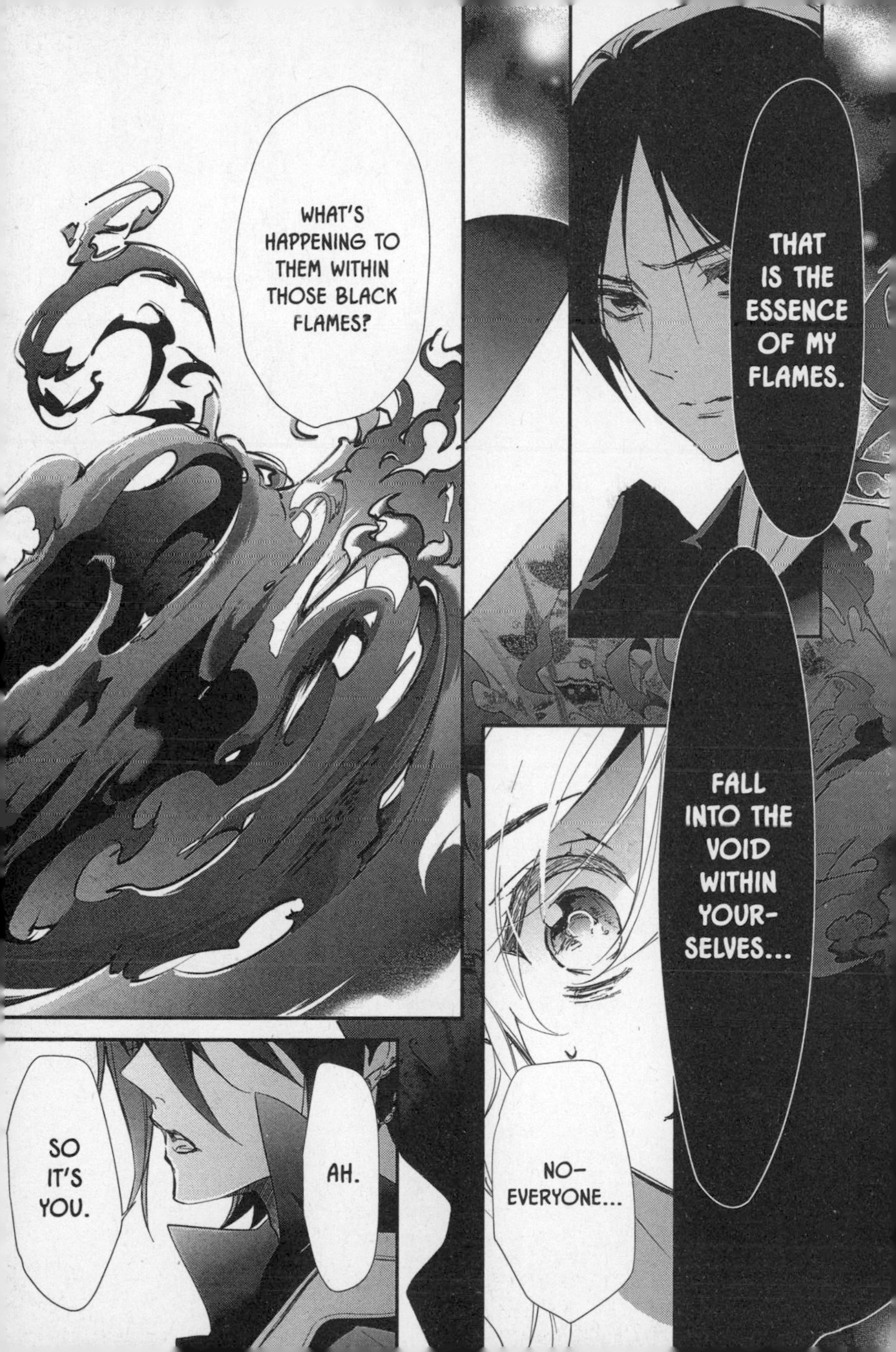
THAT IS THE ESSENCE OF MY FLAMES.
WHAT'S HAPPENING TO THEM WITHIN THOSE BLACK FLAMES?
FALL INTO THE VOID WITHIN YOUR-SELVES...
NO— EVERYONE...
AH.
SO IT'S YOU.

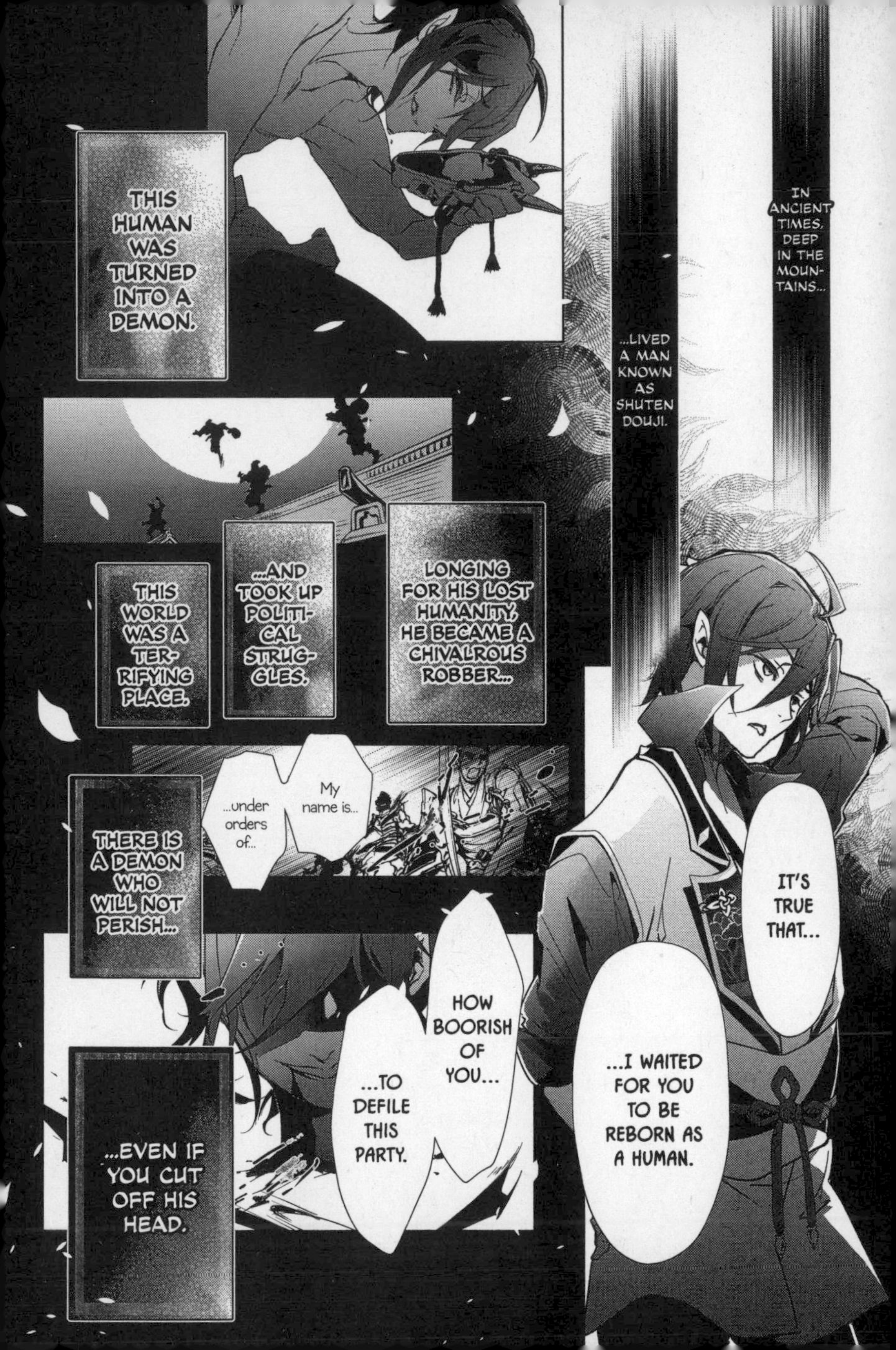
IN ANCIENT TIMES, DEEP IN THE MOUNTAINS...
...LIVED A MAN KNOWN AS SHUTEN DOUJI.
THIS HUMAN WAS TURNED INTO A DEMON.
LONGING FOR HIS LOST HUMANITY, HE BECAME A CHIVALROUS ROBBER...
...AND TOOK UP POLITICAL STRUGGLES.
THIS WORLD WAS A TERRIFYING PLACE.
My name is...
...under orders of...
THERE IS A DEMON WHO WILL NOT PERISH...
HOW BOORISH OF YOU...
...TO DEFILE THIS PARTY.
...EVEN IF YOU CUT OFF HIS HEAD.
IT'S TRUE THAT...
...I WAITED FOR YOU TO BE REBORN AS A HUMAN.

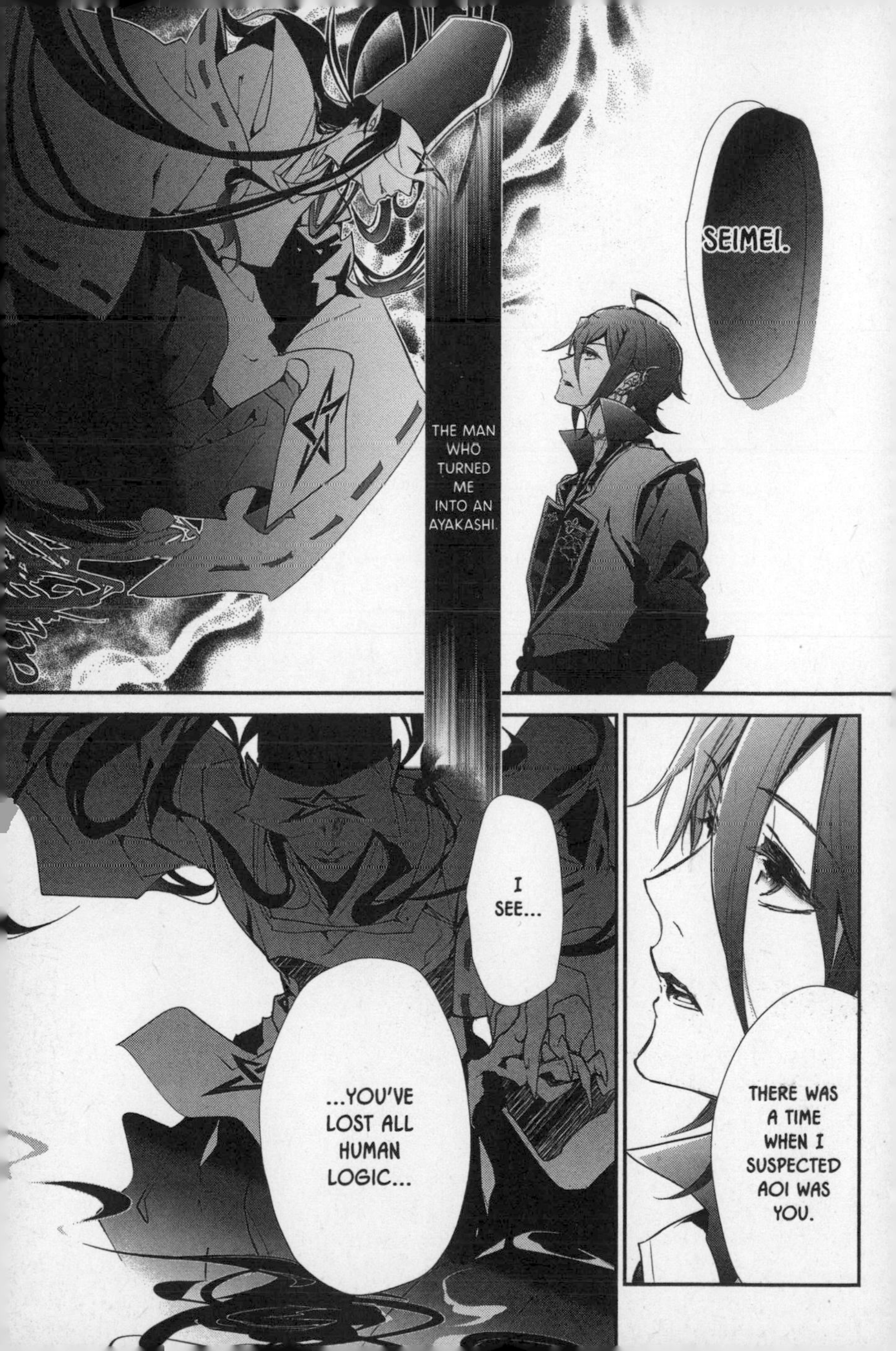
SEIMEI.
THE MAN WHO TURNED ME INTO AN AYAKASHI.
THERE WAS A TIME WHEN I SUSPECTED AOI WAS YOU.
I SEE...
...YOU'VE LOST ALL HUMAN LOGIC...

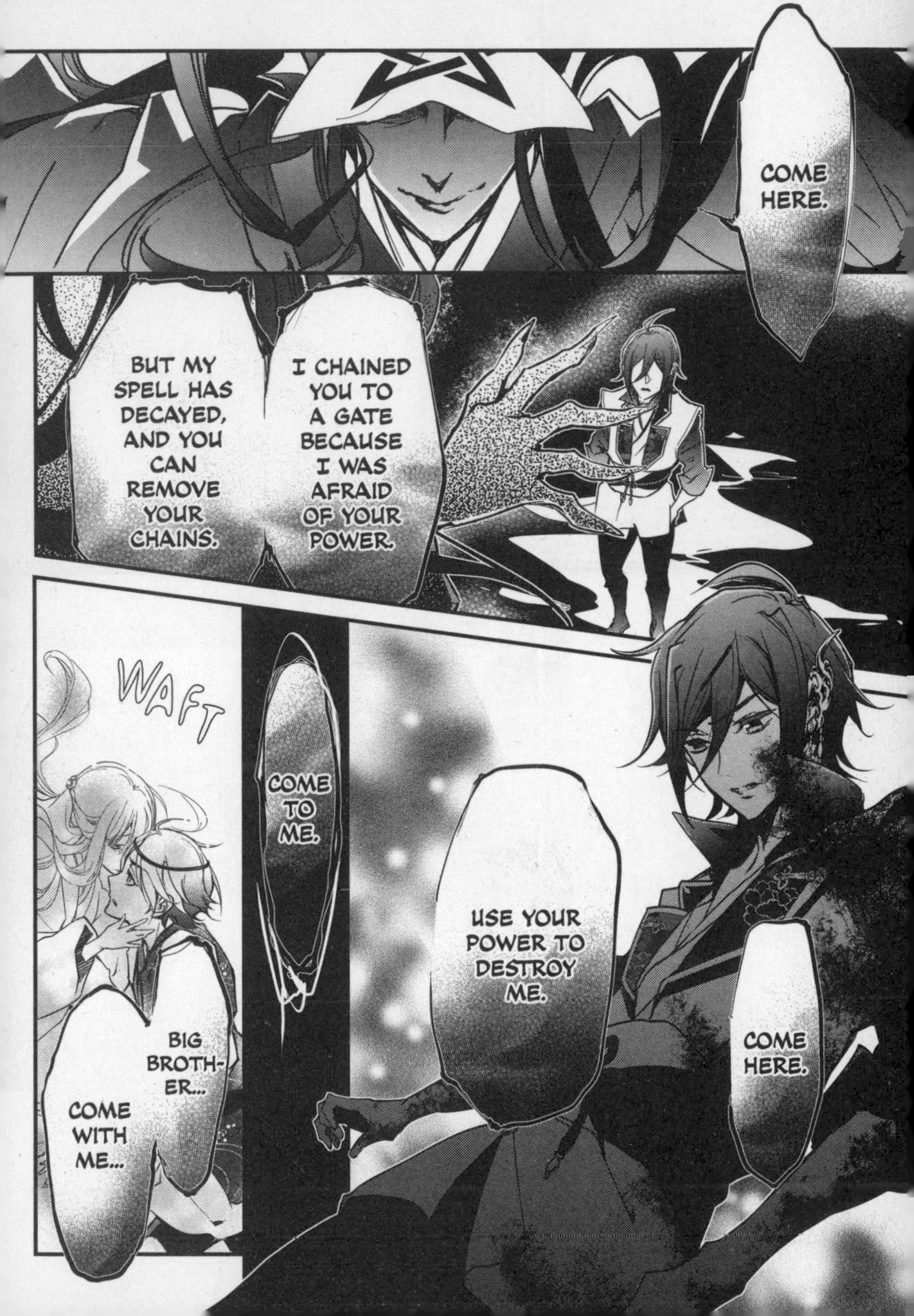
COME HERE.
I CHAINED YOU TO A GATE BECAUSE I WAS AFRAID OF YOUR POWER.
BUT MY SPELL HAS DECAYED, AND YOU CAN REMOVE YOUR CHAINS.
USE YOUR POWER TO DESTROY ME.
COME HERE.
COME TO ME.
WAFT
BIG BROTH-ER...
COME WITH ME...

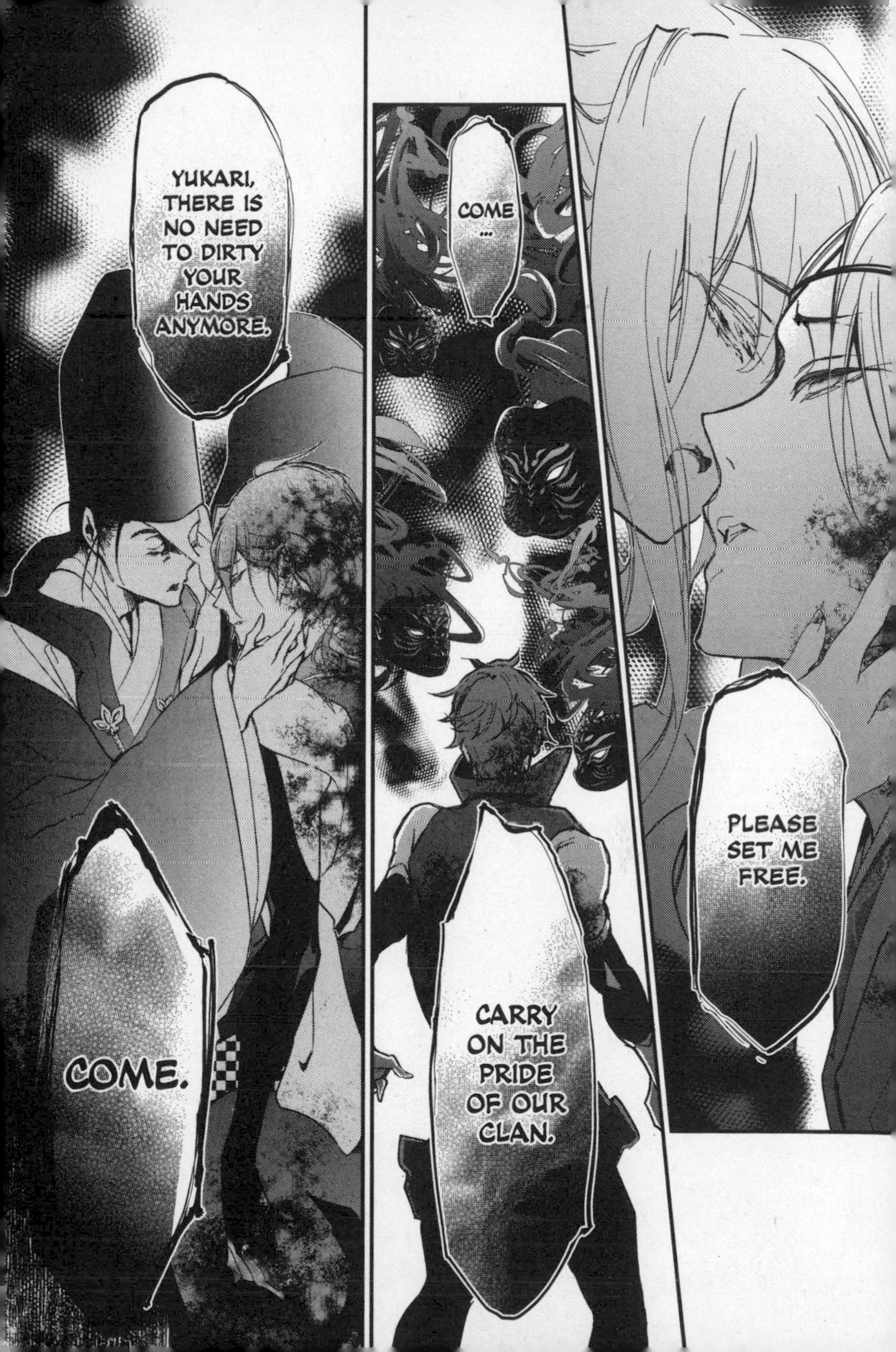
PLEASE SET ME FREE.
COME ...
CARRY ON THE PRIDE OF OUR CLAN.
YUKARI, THERE IS NO NEED TO DIRTY YOUR HANDS ANYMORE.
COME.

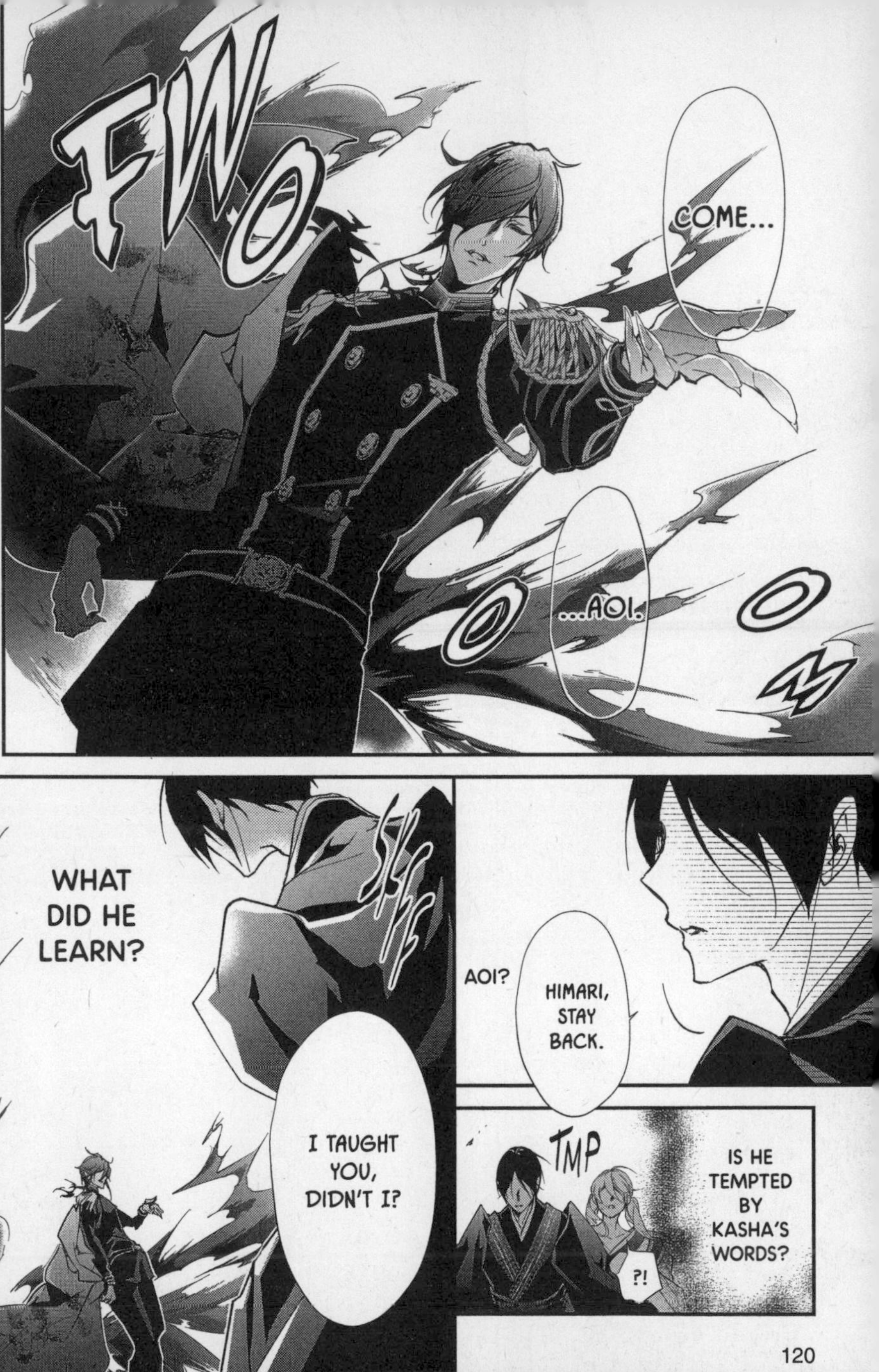
COME...
FWOOOM
...AOI.
HIMARI, STAY BACK.
AOI?
IS HE TEMPTED BY KASHA'S WORDS?
TMP
?!
WHAT DID HE LEARN?
I TAUGHT YOU, DIDN'T I?

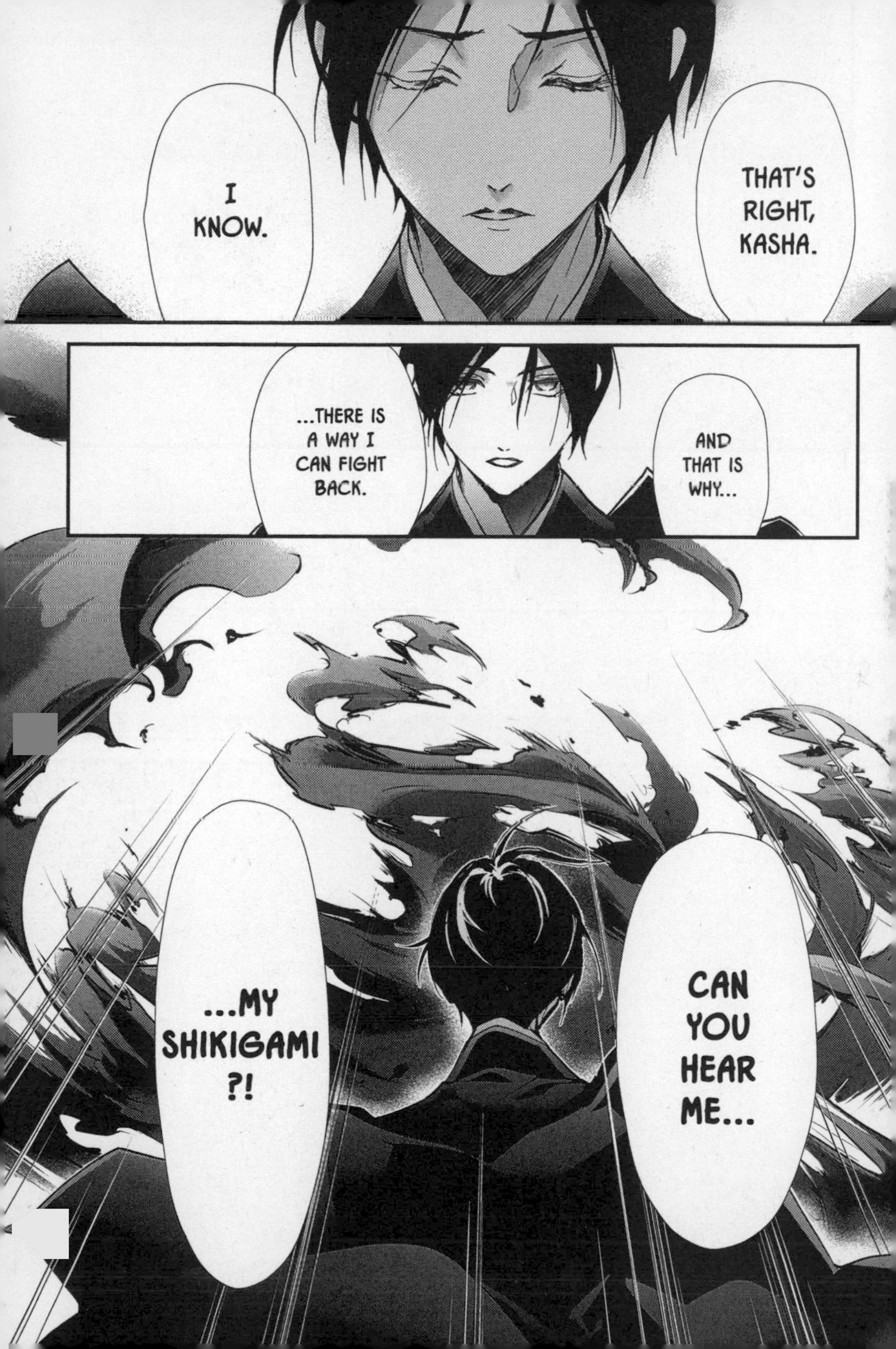
THAT'S RIGHT, KASHA.
I KNOW.
AND THAT IS WHY...
...THERE IS A WAY I CAN FIGHT BACK.
CAN YOU HEAR ME...
...MY SHIKIGAMI ?!

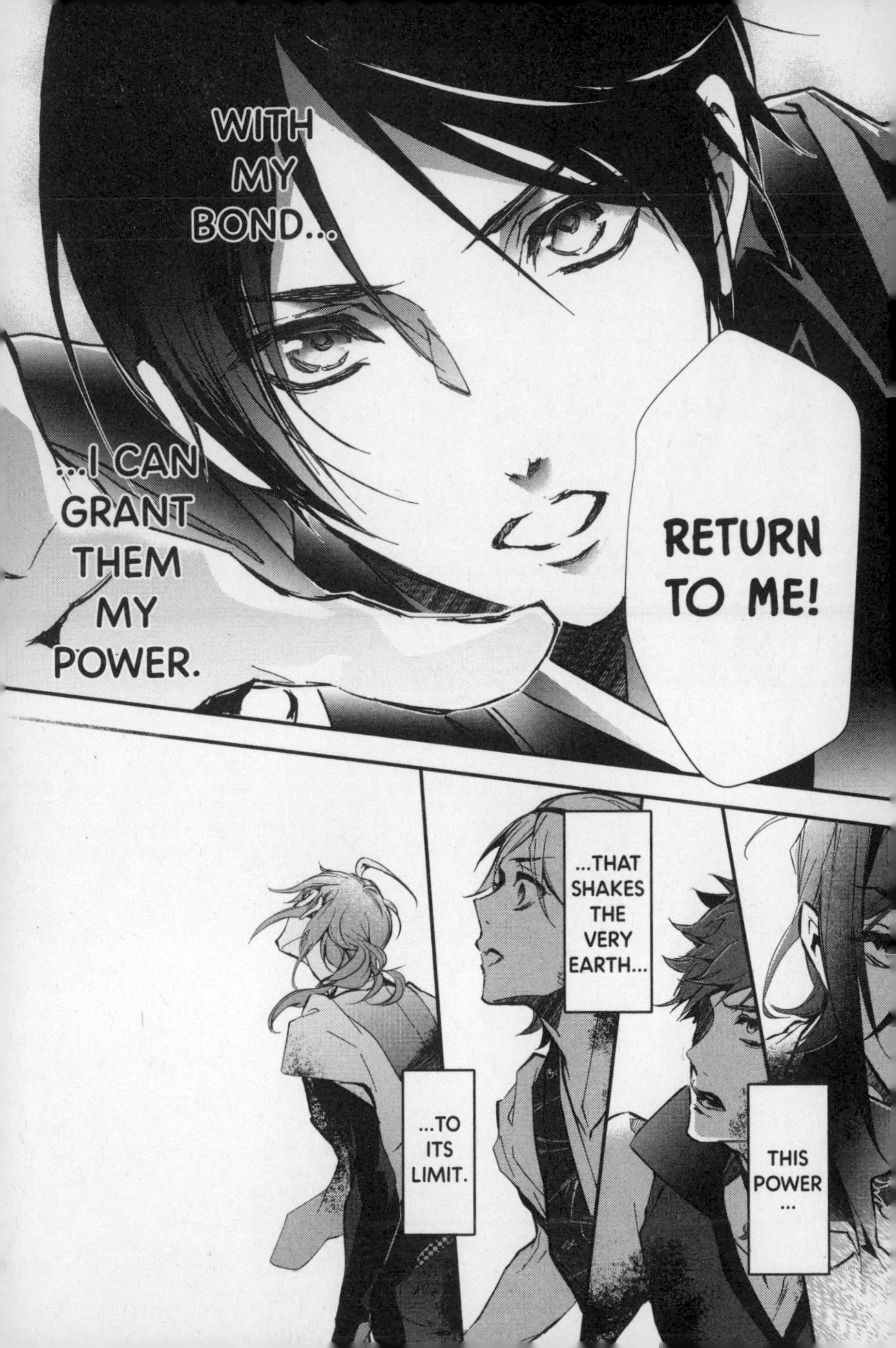
RETURN TO ME!
WITH MY BOND...
...I CAN GRANT THEM MY POWER.
THIS POWER...
...THAT SHAKES THE VERY EARTH...
...TO ITS LIMIT.

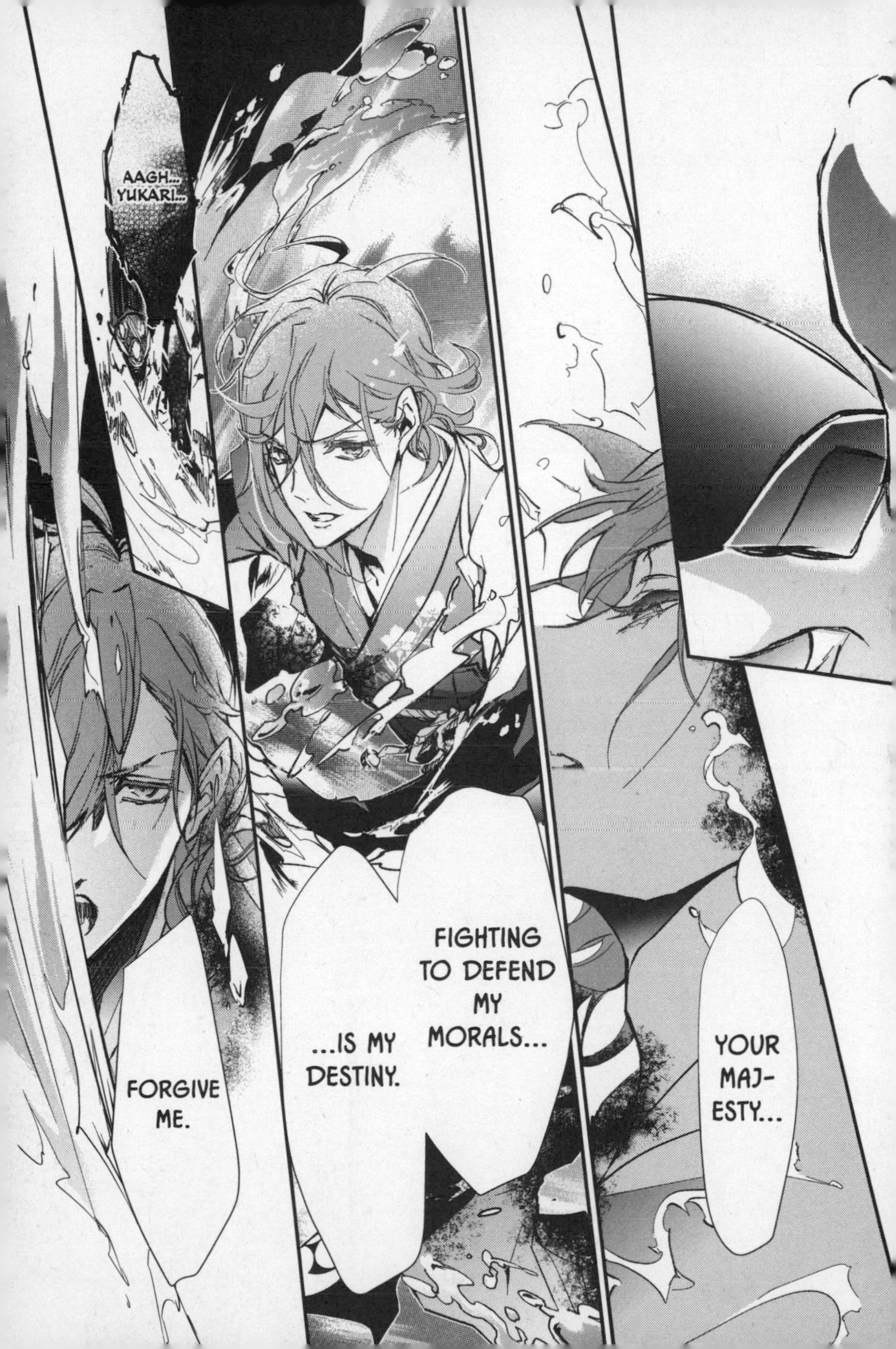
YOUR MAJ-ESTY...
FIGHTING TO DEFEND MY MORALS...
...IS MY DESTINY.
AAGH... YUKARI...
FORGIVE ME.

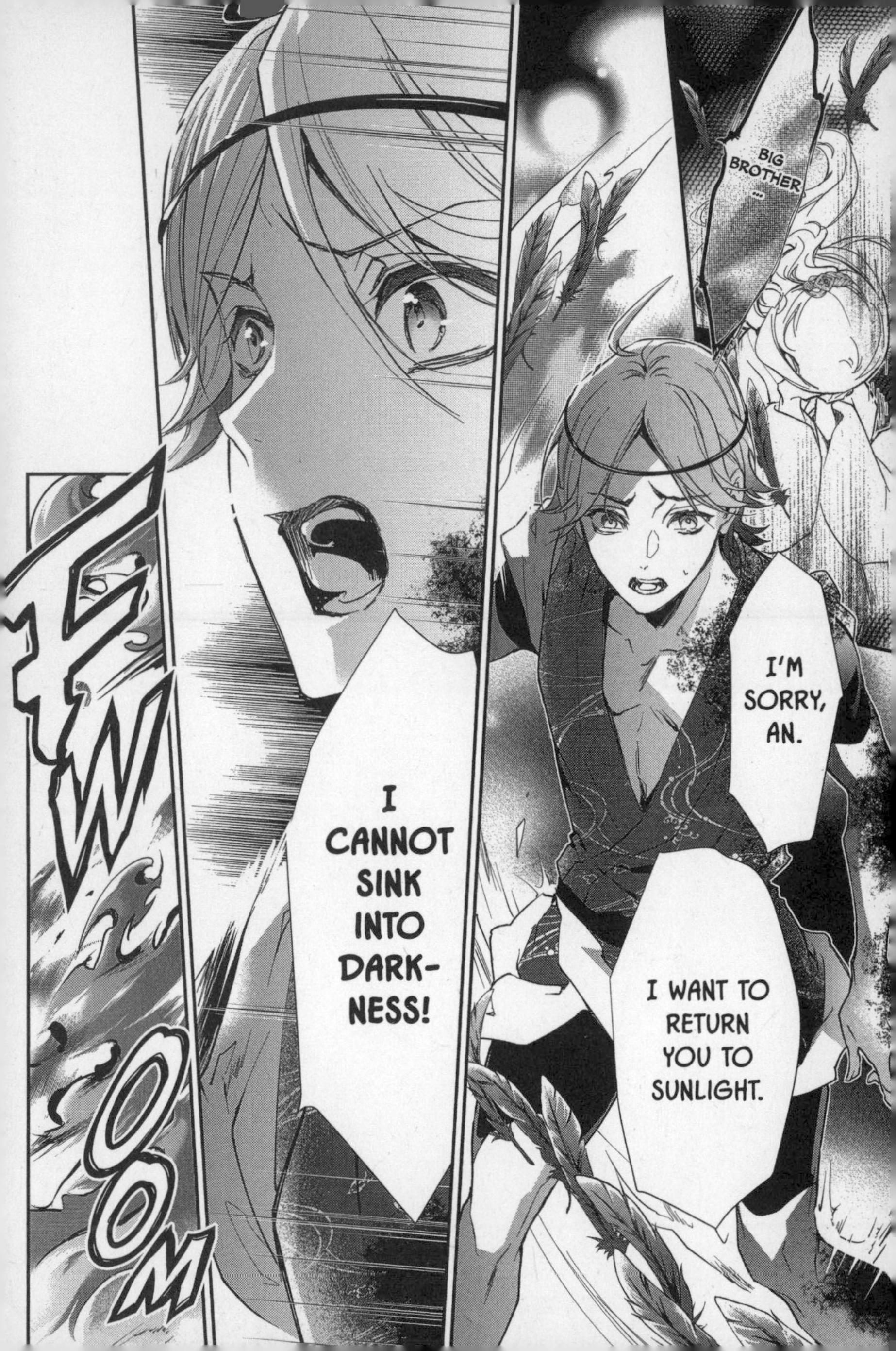
BIG BROTHER...
I'M SORRY, AN.
I WANT TO RETURN YOU TO SUNLIGHT.
I CANNOT SINK INTO DARK-NESS!
FWOOM

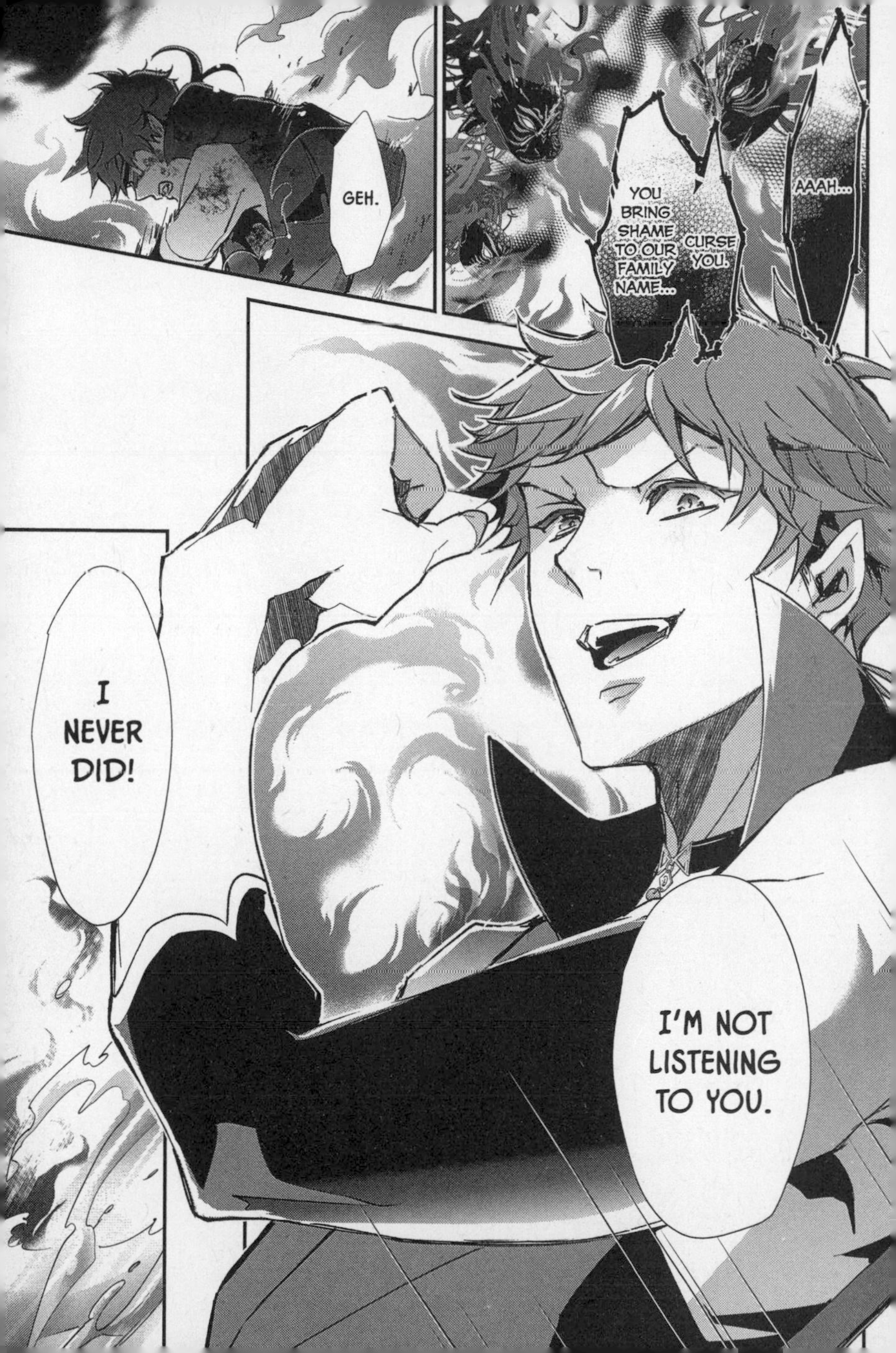
AAAH...
CURSE YOU.
YOU BRING SHAME TO OUR FAMILY NAME...
GEH.
I'M NOT LISTENING TO YOU.
I NEVER DID!

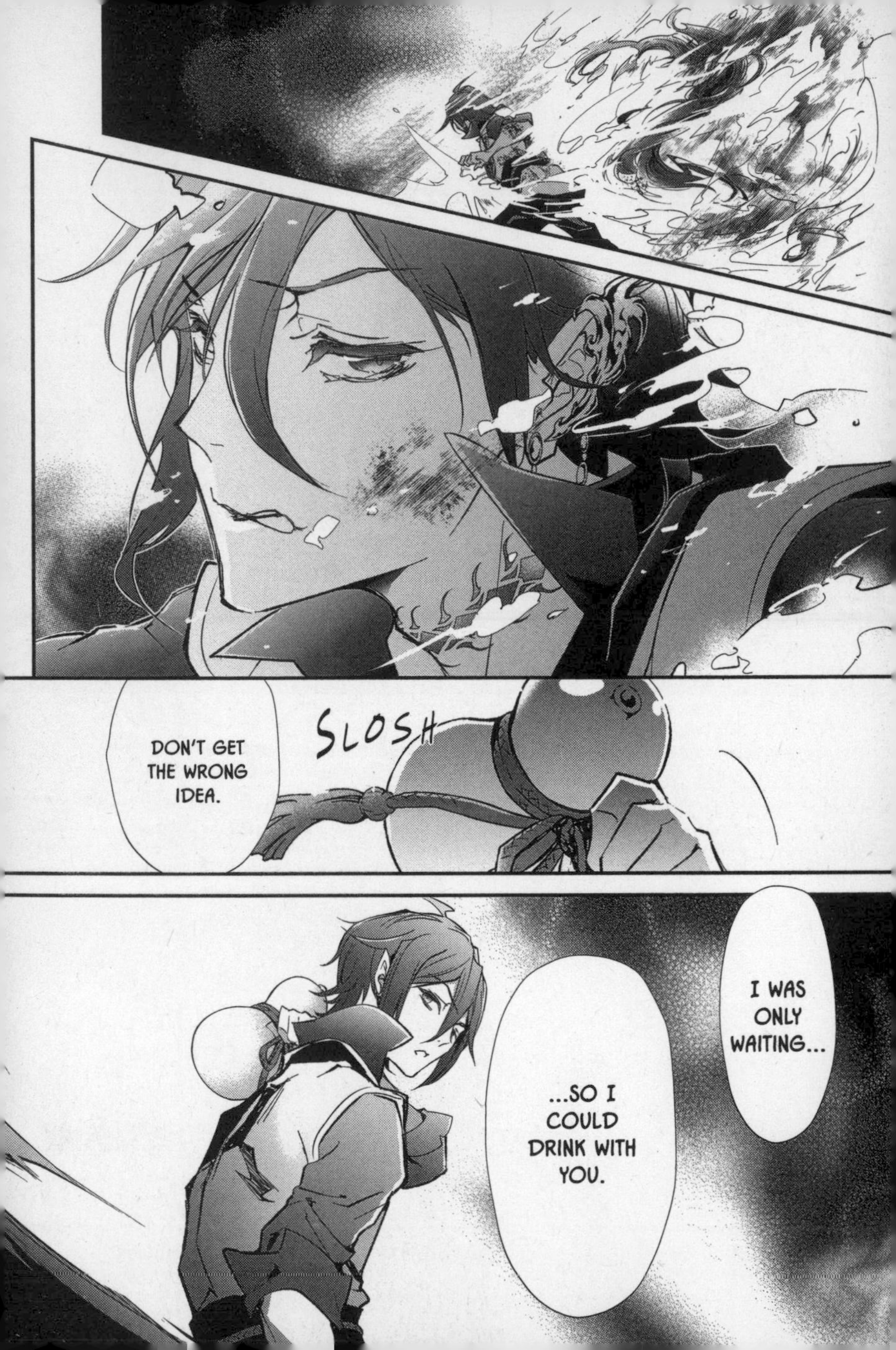
SLOSH
DON'T GET THE WRONG IDEA.
I WAS ONLY WAITING...
...SO I COULD DRINK WITH YOU.

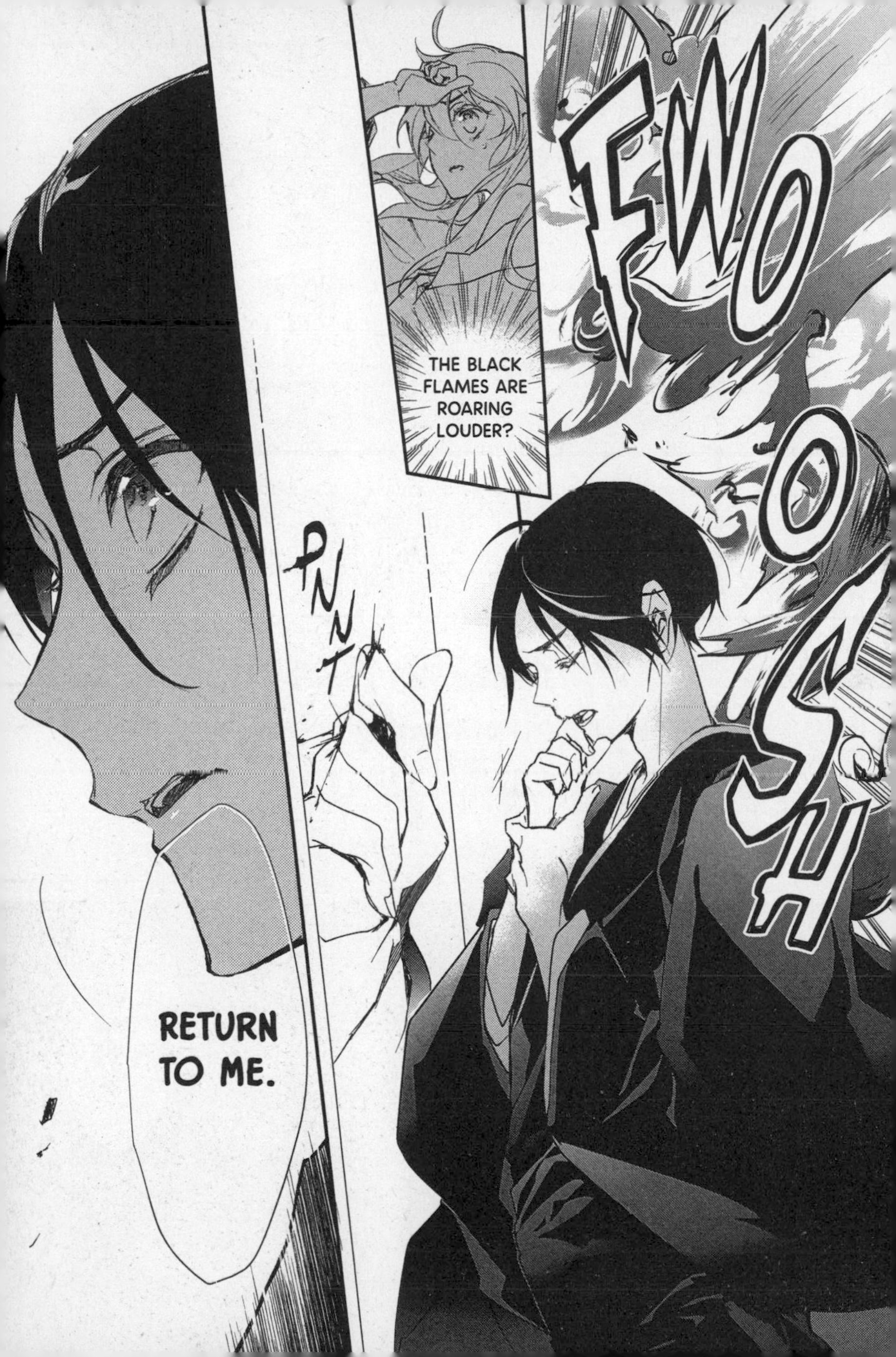
FWOOSH
THE BLACK FLAMES ARE ROARING LOUDER?
PNNT
RETURN TO ME.

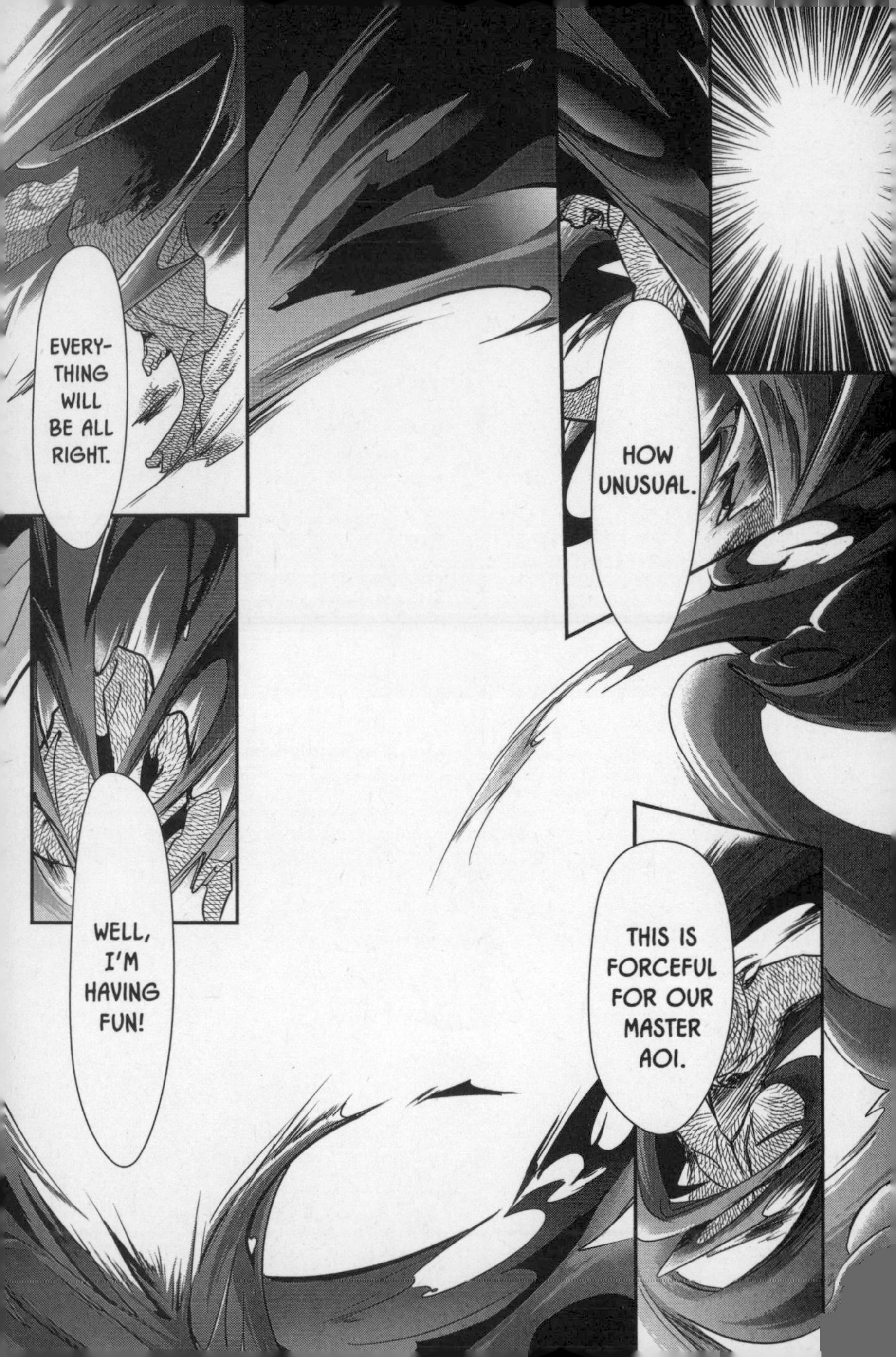
HOW UNUSUAL.
EVERY-THING WILL BE ALL RIGHT.
THIS IS FORCEFUL FOR OUR MASTER AOI.
WELL, I'M HAVING FUN!

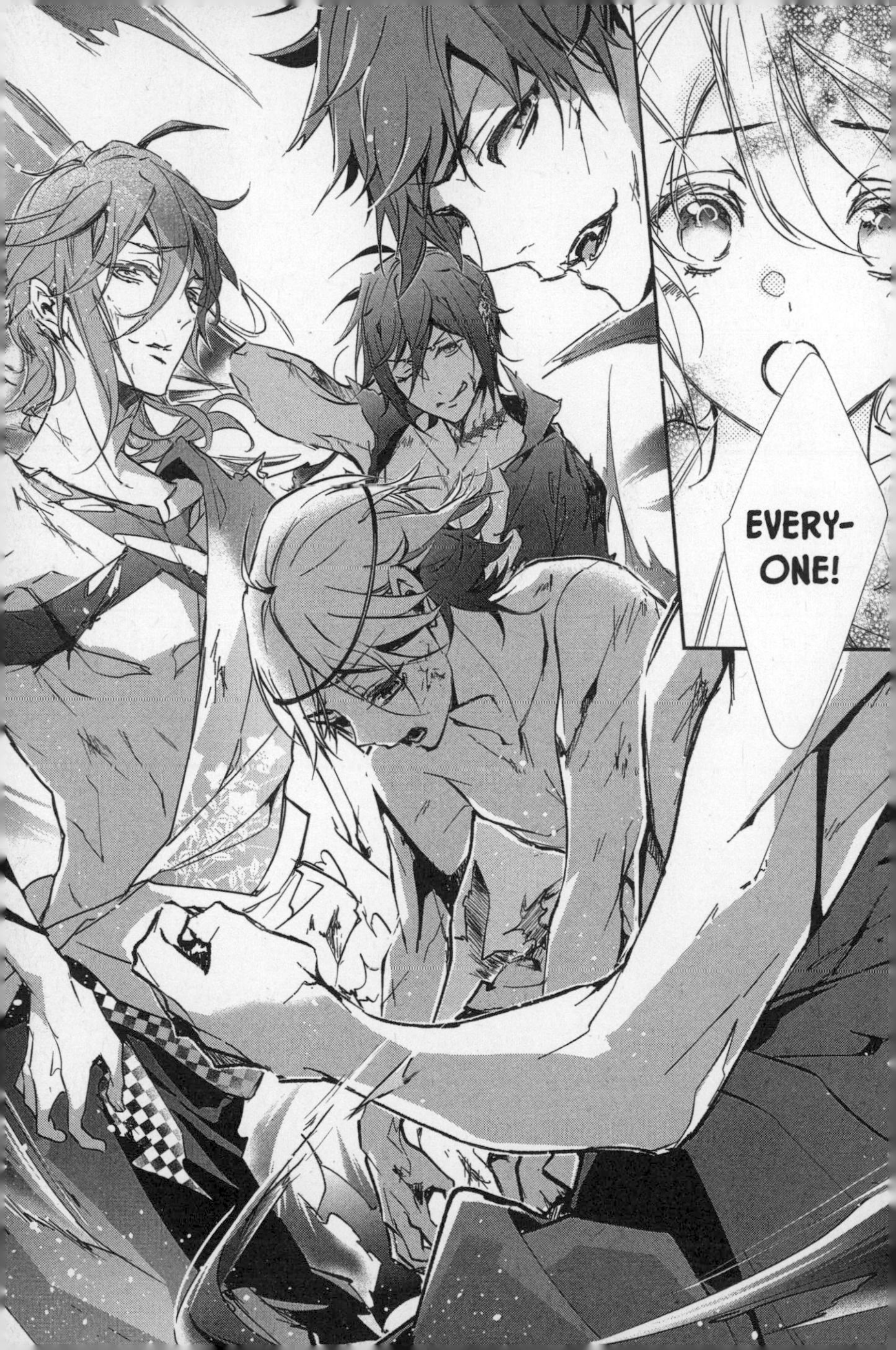
EVERY-
ONE!

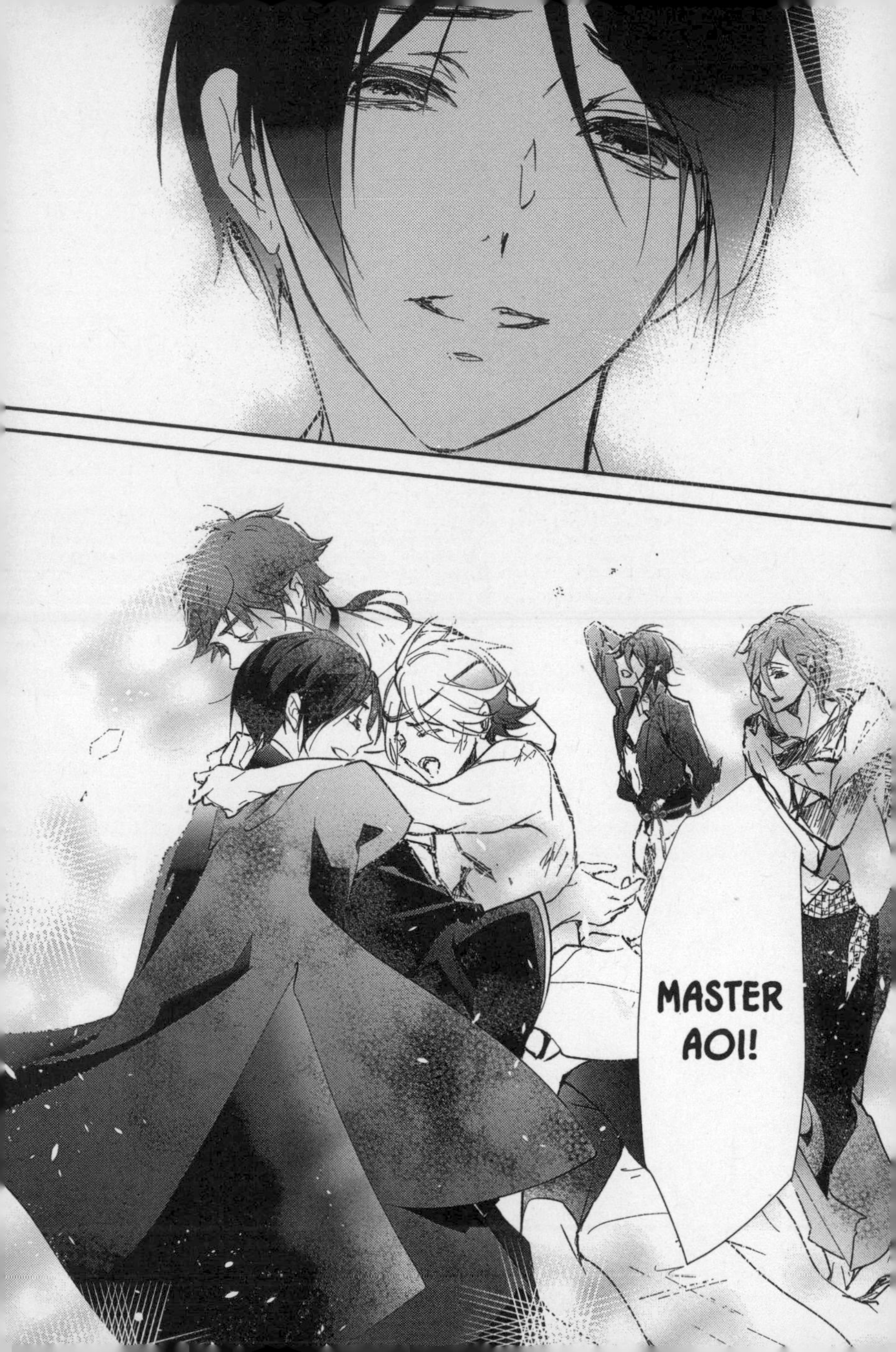
MASTER AOI!

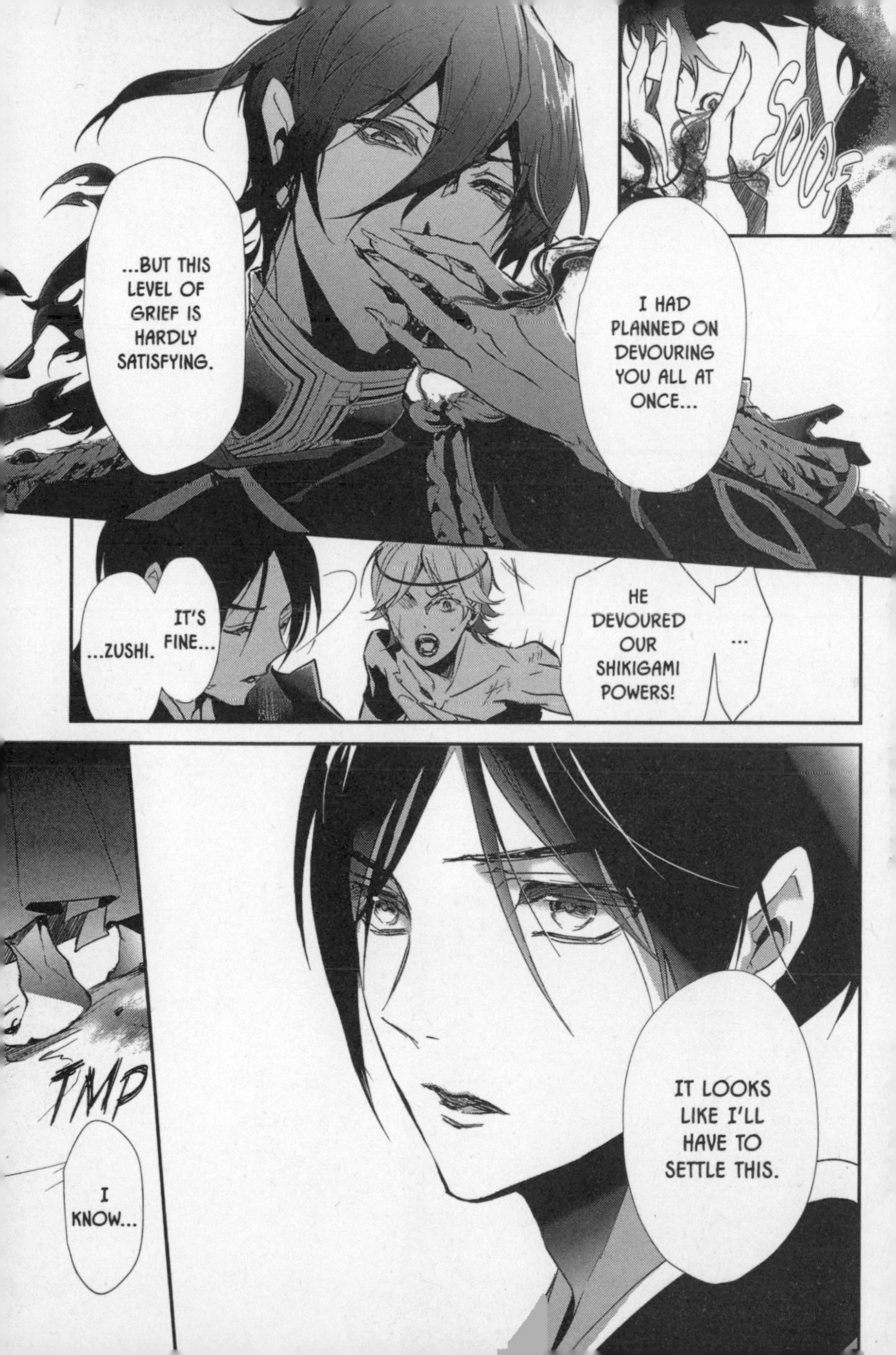
SOOF
I HAD PLANNED ON DEVOURING YOU ALL AT ONCE...
...BUT THIS LEVEL OF GRIEF IS HARDLY SATISFYING.
...
HE DEVOURED OUR SHIKIGAMI POWERS!
IT'S FINE...
...ZUSHI.
IT LOOKS LIKE I'LL HAVE TO SETTLE THIS.
TMP
I KNOW...

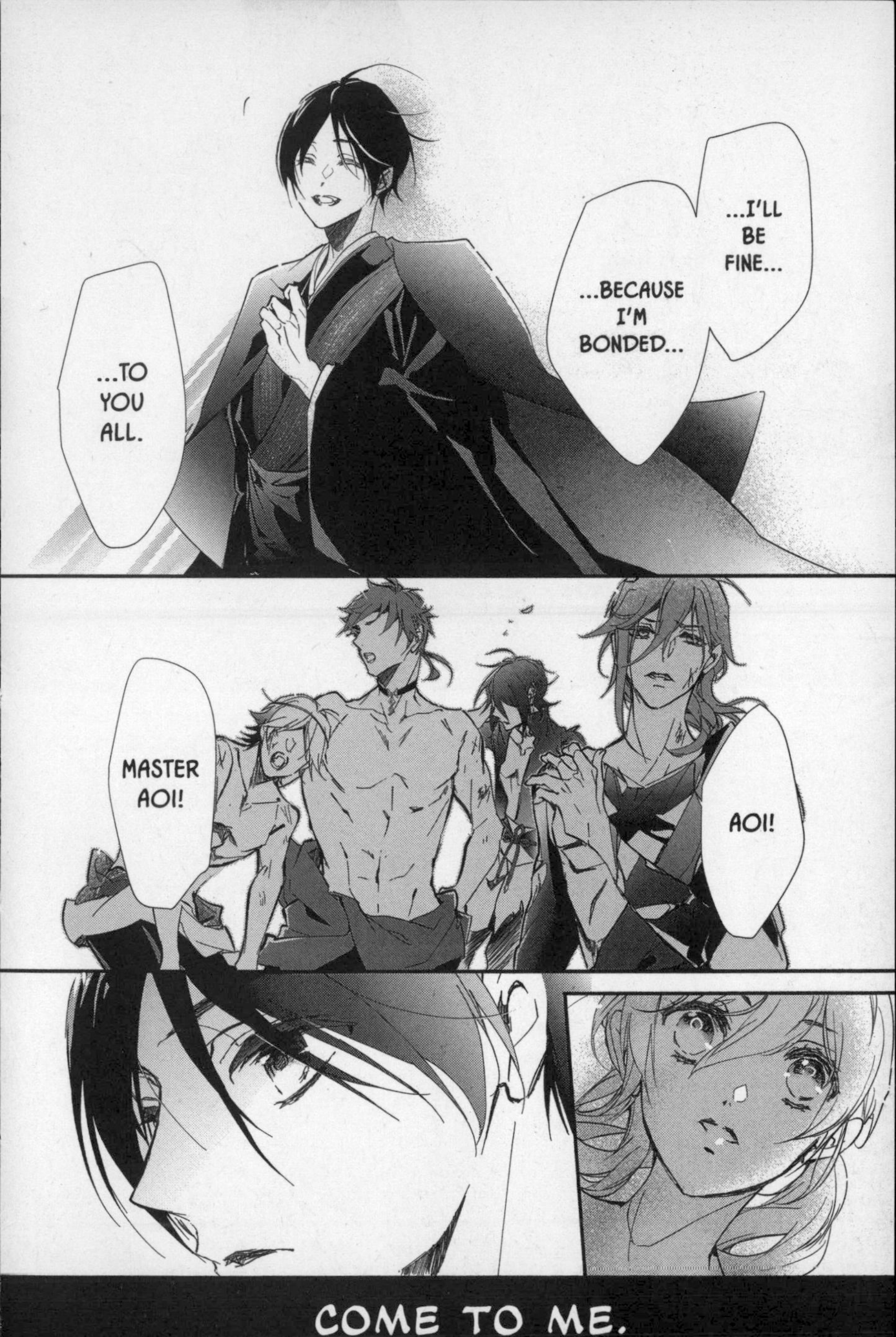
...I'LL BE FINE...
...BECAUSE I'M BONDED...
...TO YOU ALL.
AOI!
MASTER AOI!
COME TO ME.

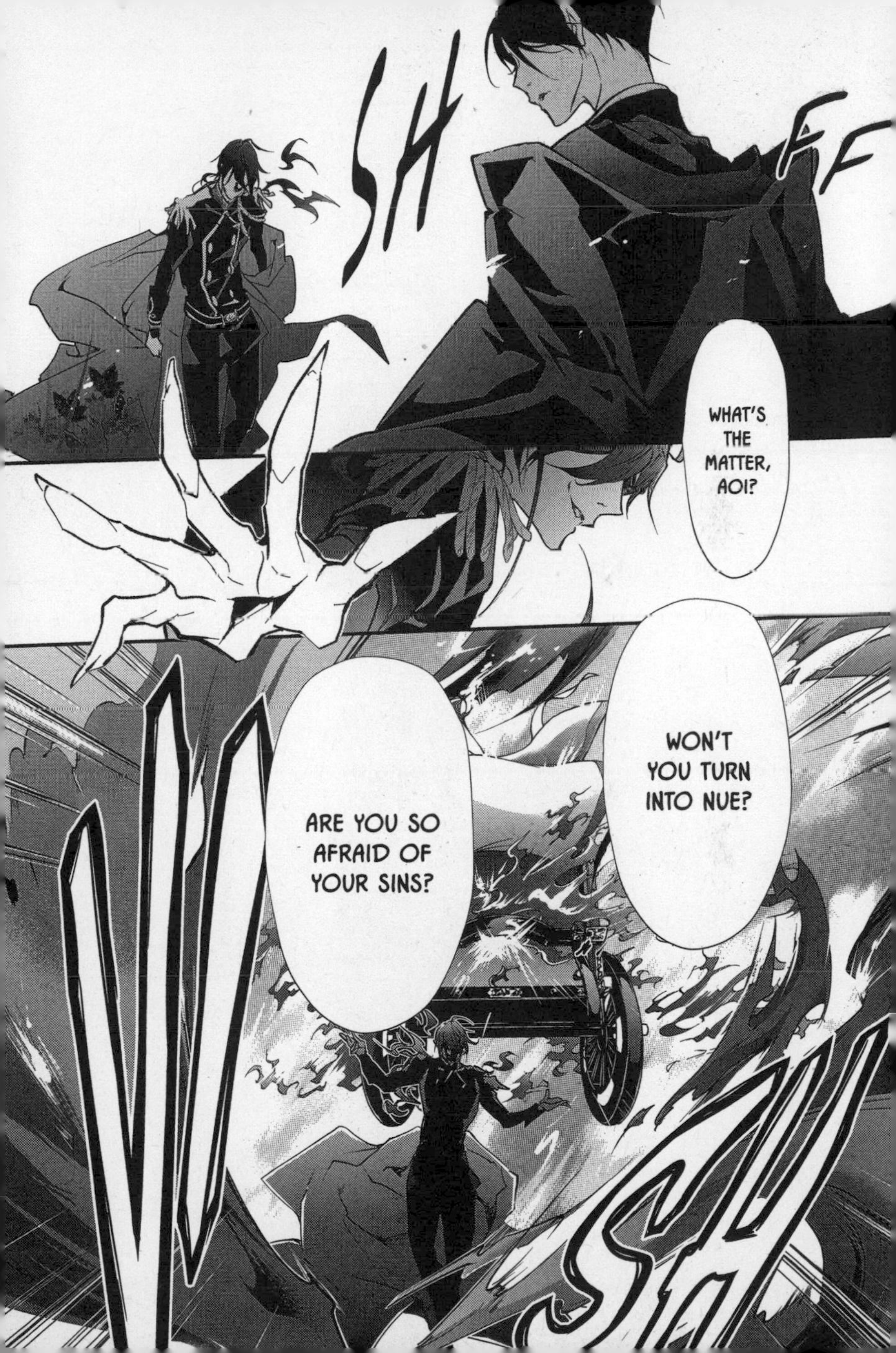
SH
FF
WHAT'S THE MATTER, AOI?
WON'T YOU TURN INTO NUE?
ARE YOU SO AFRAID OF YOUR SINS?
SH

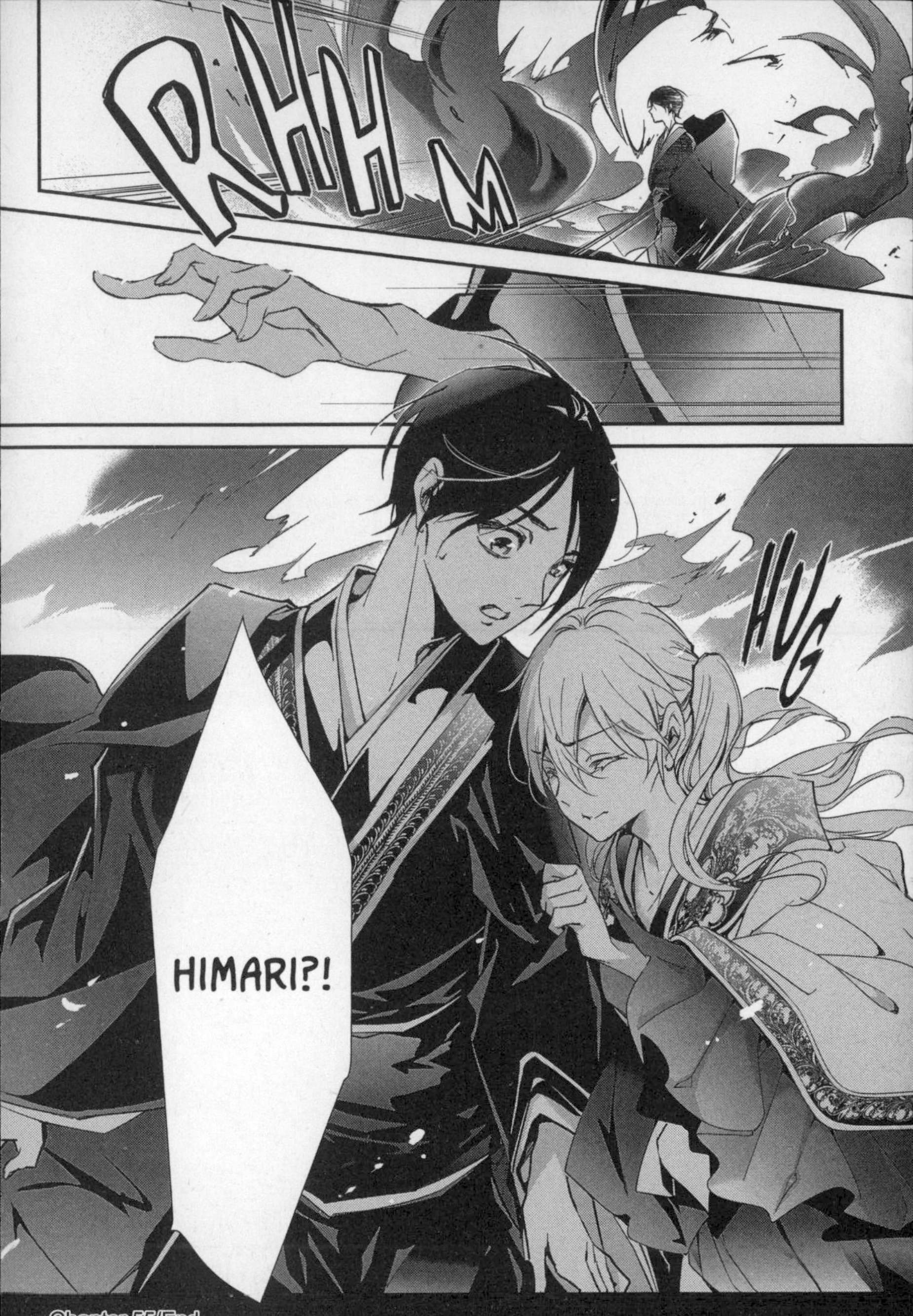
RHHM
HUG
HIMARI?!

Chapter 55/End

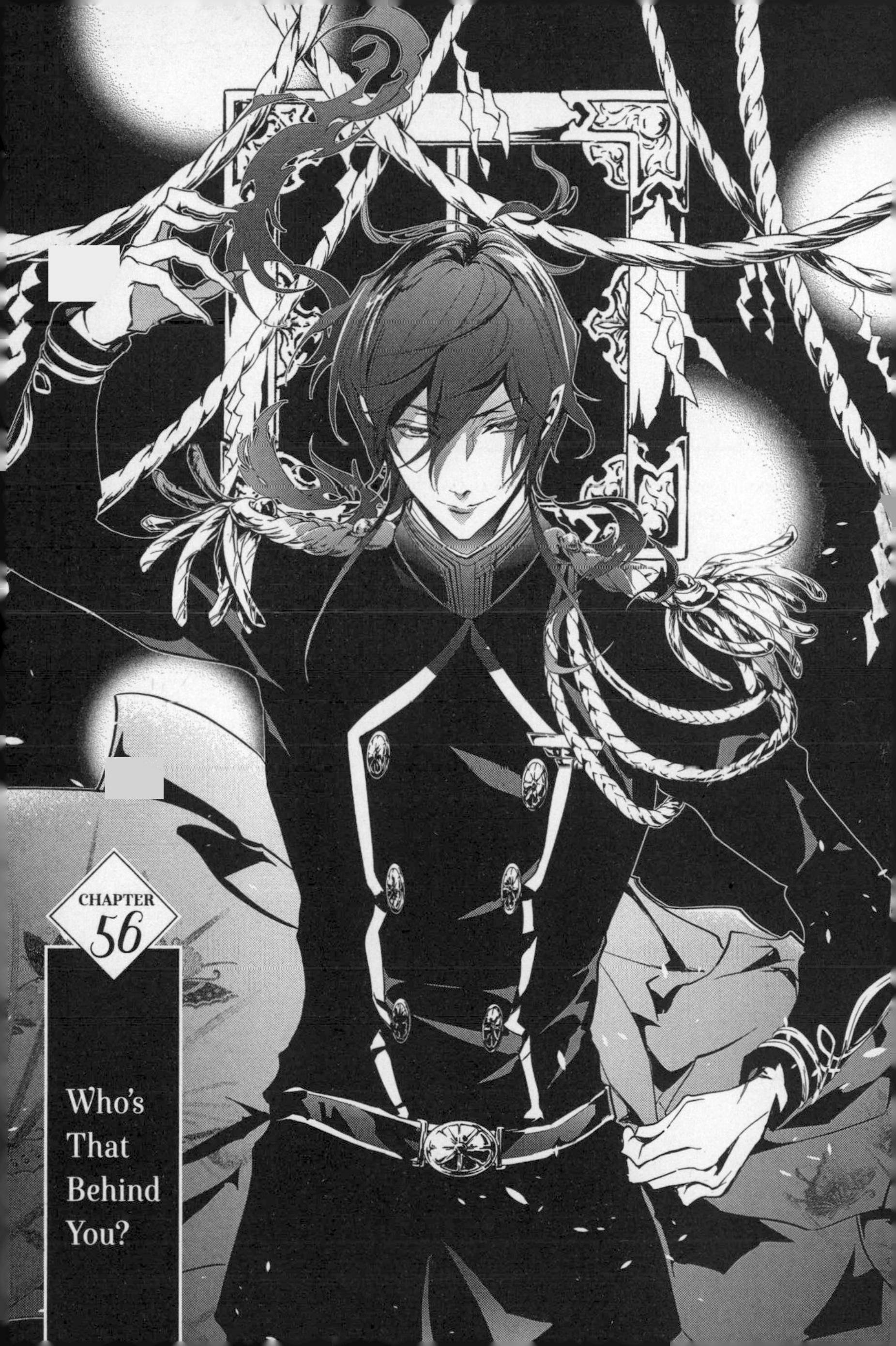
CHAPTER
56
Who's That Behind You?

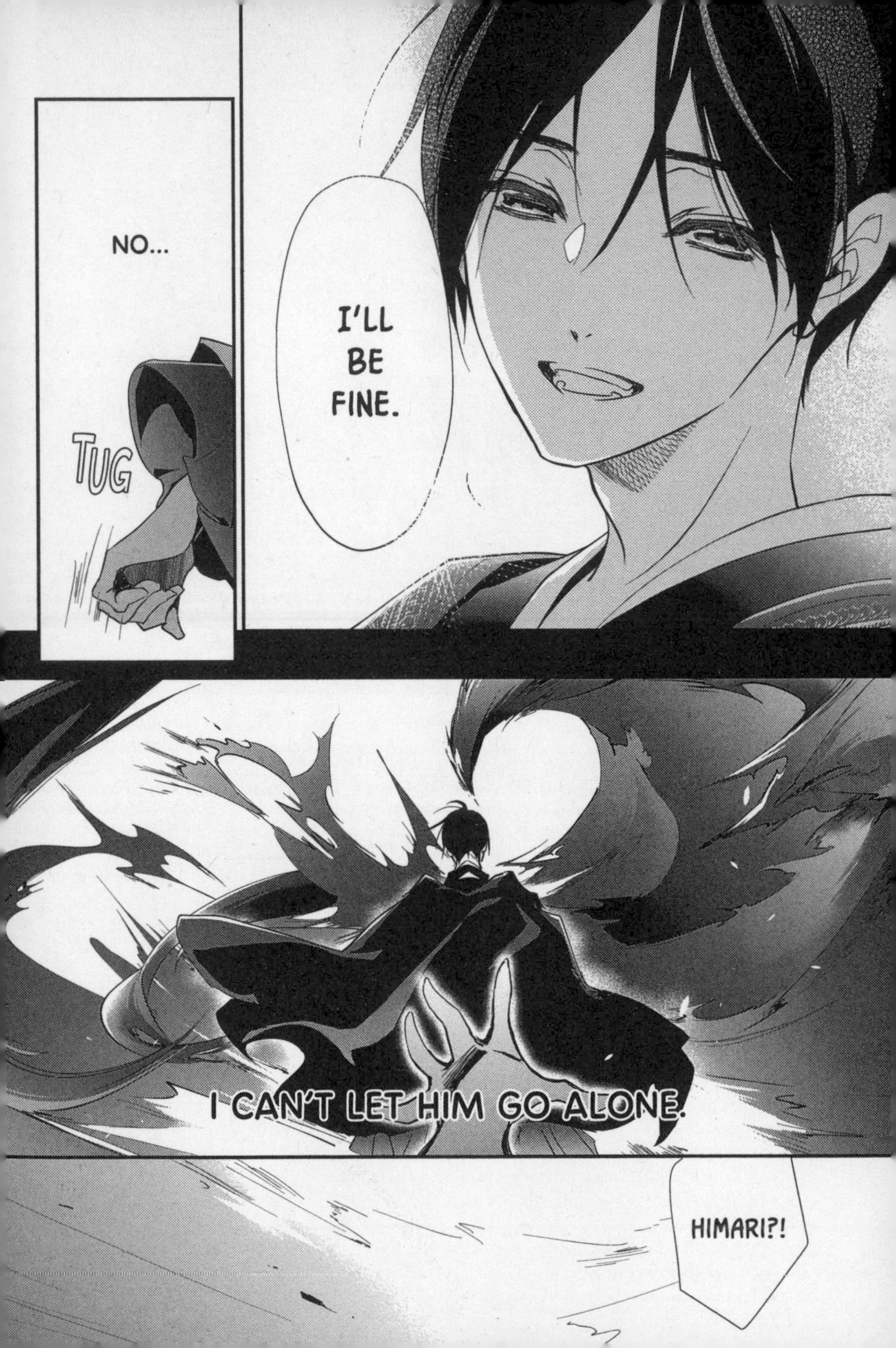
I'LL BE FINE.
NO...
TUG
I CAN'T LET HIM GO ALONE.
HIMARI?!

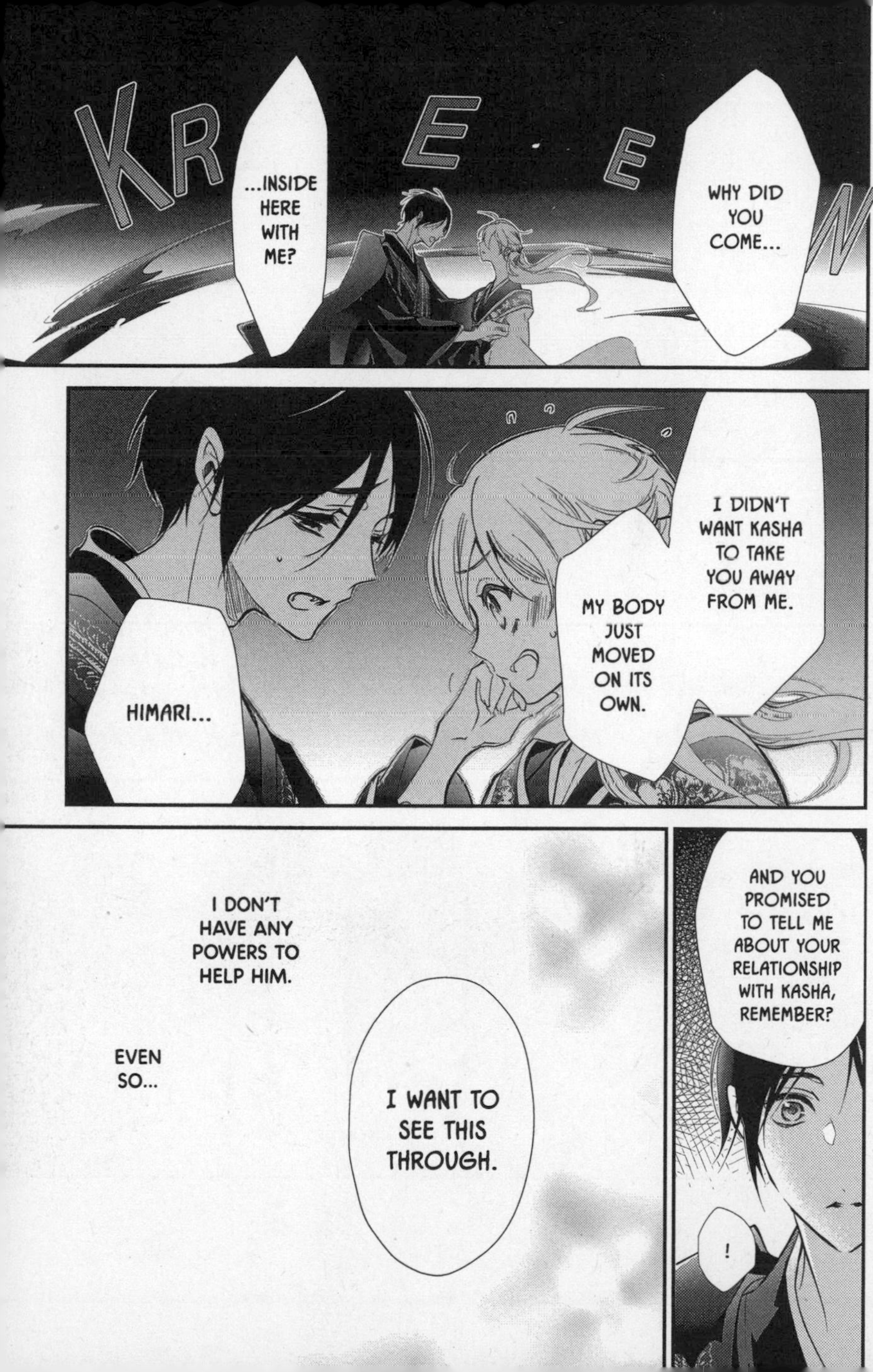
KREEN
WHY DID YOU COME...
...INSIDE HERE WITH ME?
I DIDN'T WANT KASHA TO TAKE YOU AWAY FROM ME.
MY BODY JUST MOVED ON ITS OWN.
HIMARI...
AND YOU PROMISED TO TELL ME ABOUT YOUR RELATIONSHIP WITH KASHA, REMEMBER?
!
I DON'T HAVE ANY POWERS TO HELP HIM.
EVEN SO...
I WANT TO SEE THIS THROUGH.

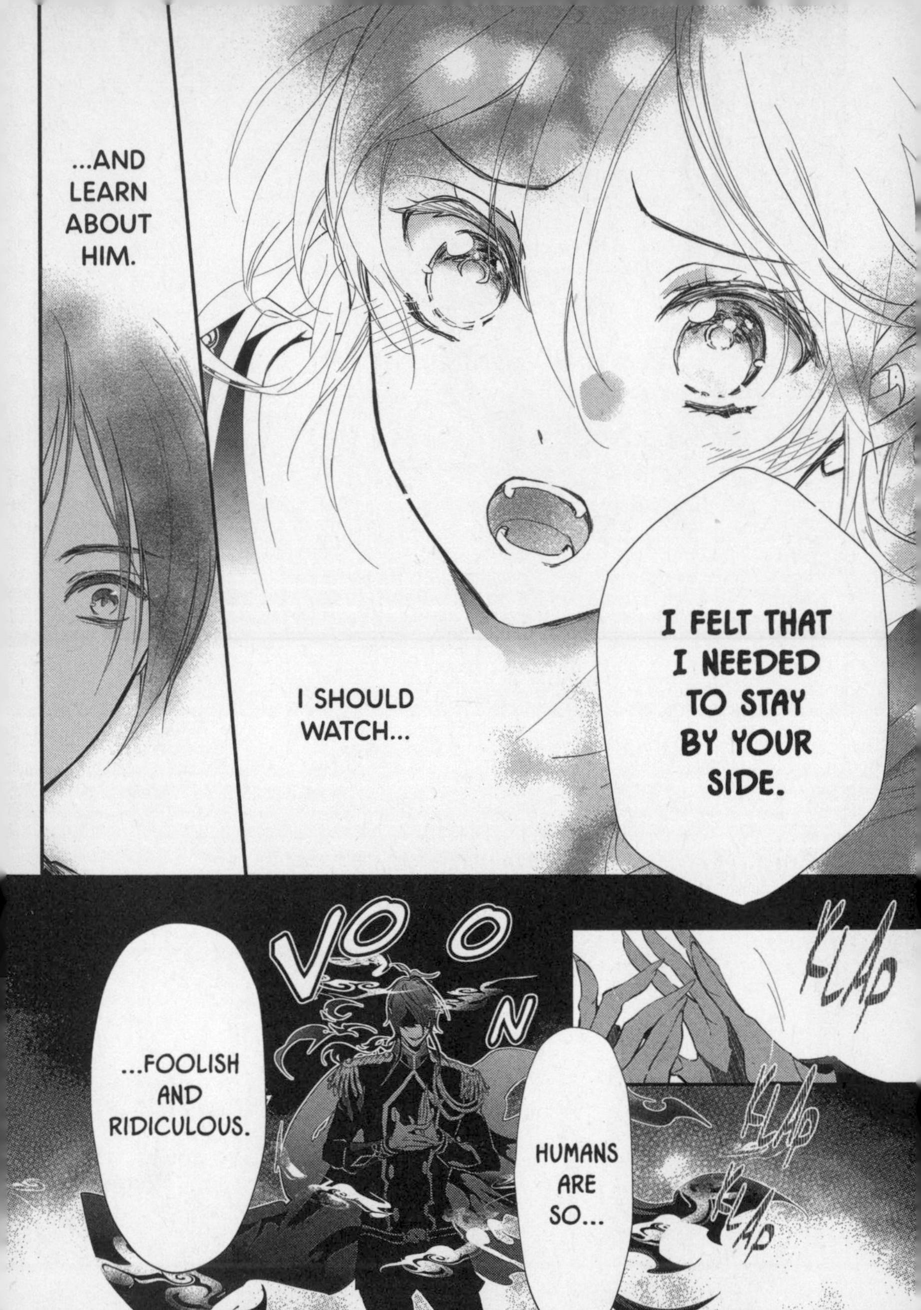
I FELT THAT I NEEDED TO STAY BY YOUR SIDE.
I SHOULD WATCH...
...AND LEARN ABOUT HIM.
KLAP
KLAP
KLAP
VOOON
HUMANS ARE SO...
...FOOLISH AND RIDICULOUS.

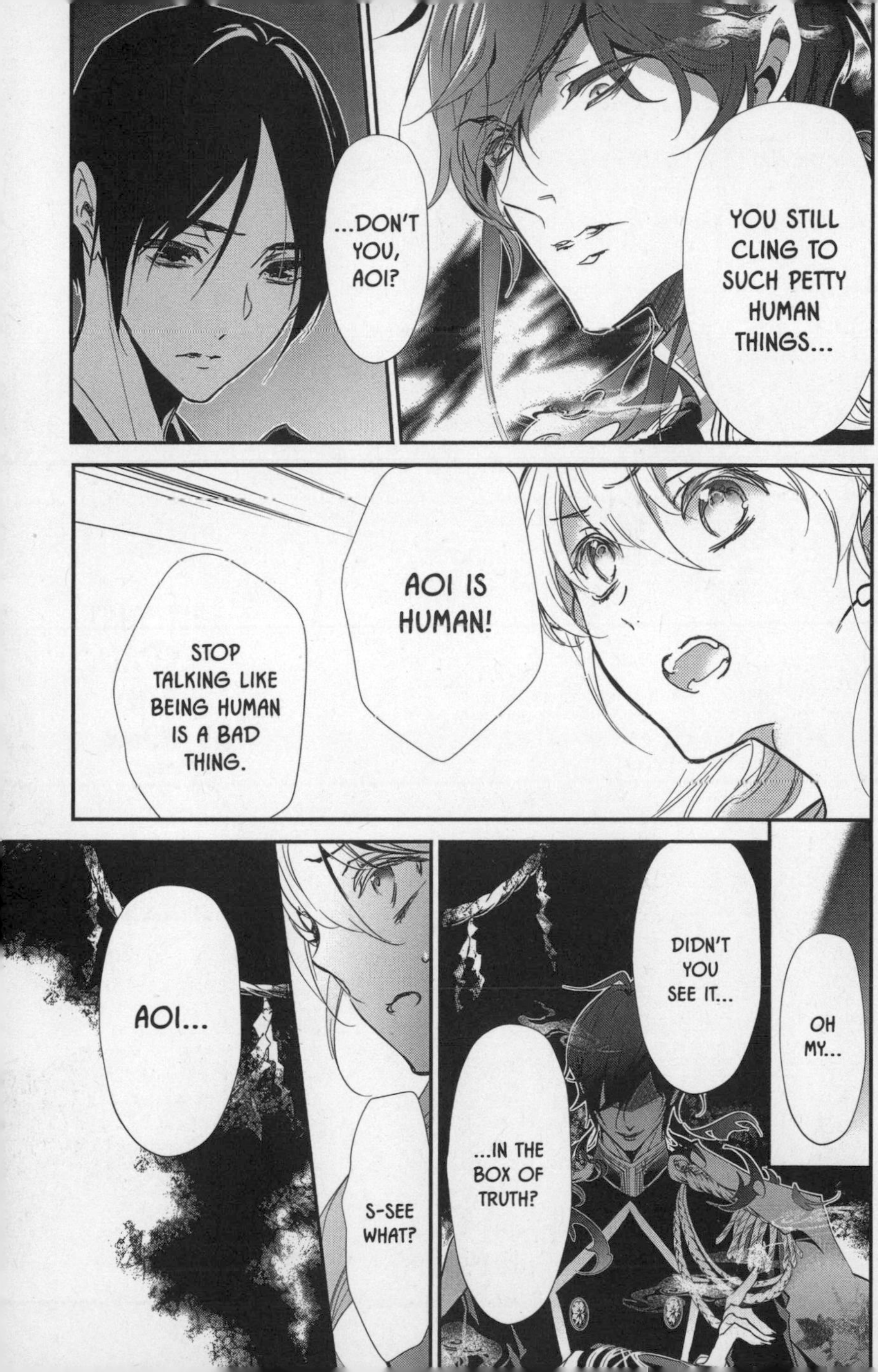
YOU STILL CLING TO SUCH PETTY HUMAN THINGS...
...DON'T YOU, AOI?
AOI IS HUMAN!
STOP TALKING LIKE BEING HUMAN IS A BAD THING.
OH MY...
DIDN'T YOU SEE IT...
...IN THE BOX OF TRUTH?
AOI...
S-SEE WHAT?

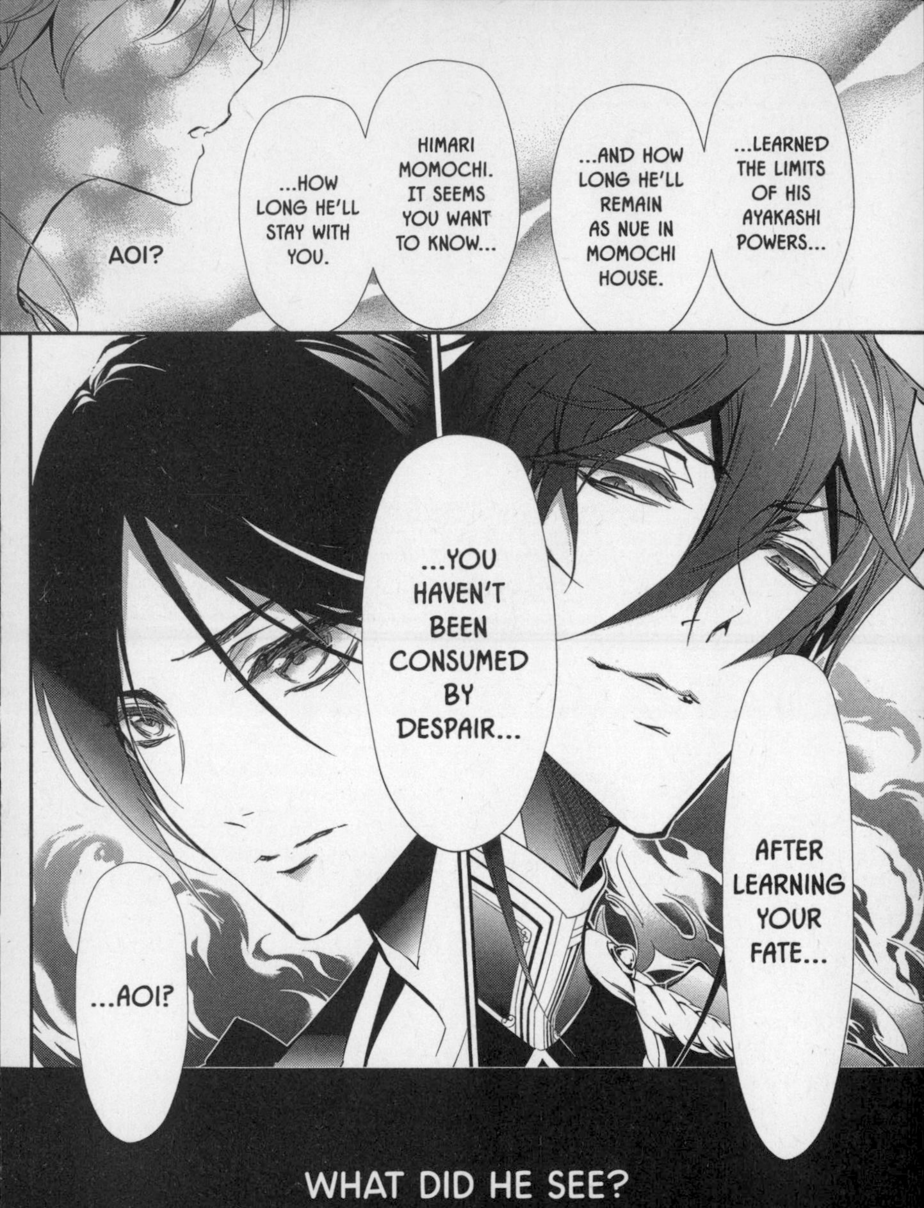

...LEARNED THE LIMITS OF HIS AYAKASHI POWERS...
...AND HOW LONG HE'LL REMAIN AS NUE IN MOMOCHI HOUSE.
HIMARI MOMOCHI. IT SEEMS YOU WANT TO KNOW...
...HOW LONG HE'LL STAY WITH YOU.
AOI?
AFTER LEARNING YOUR FATE...
...YOU HAVEN'T BEEN CONSUMED BY DESPAIR...
...AOI?
WHAT DID HE SEE?

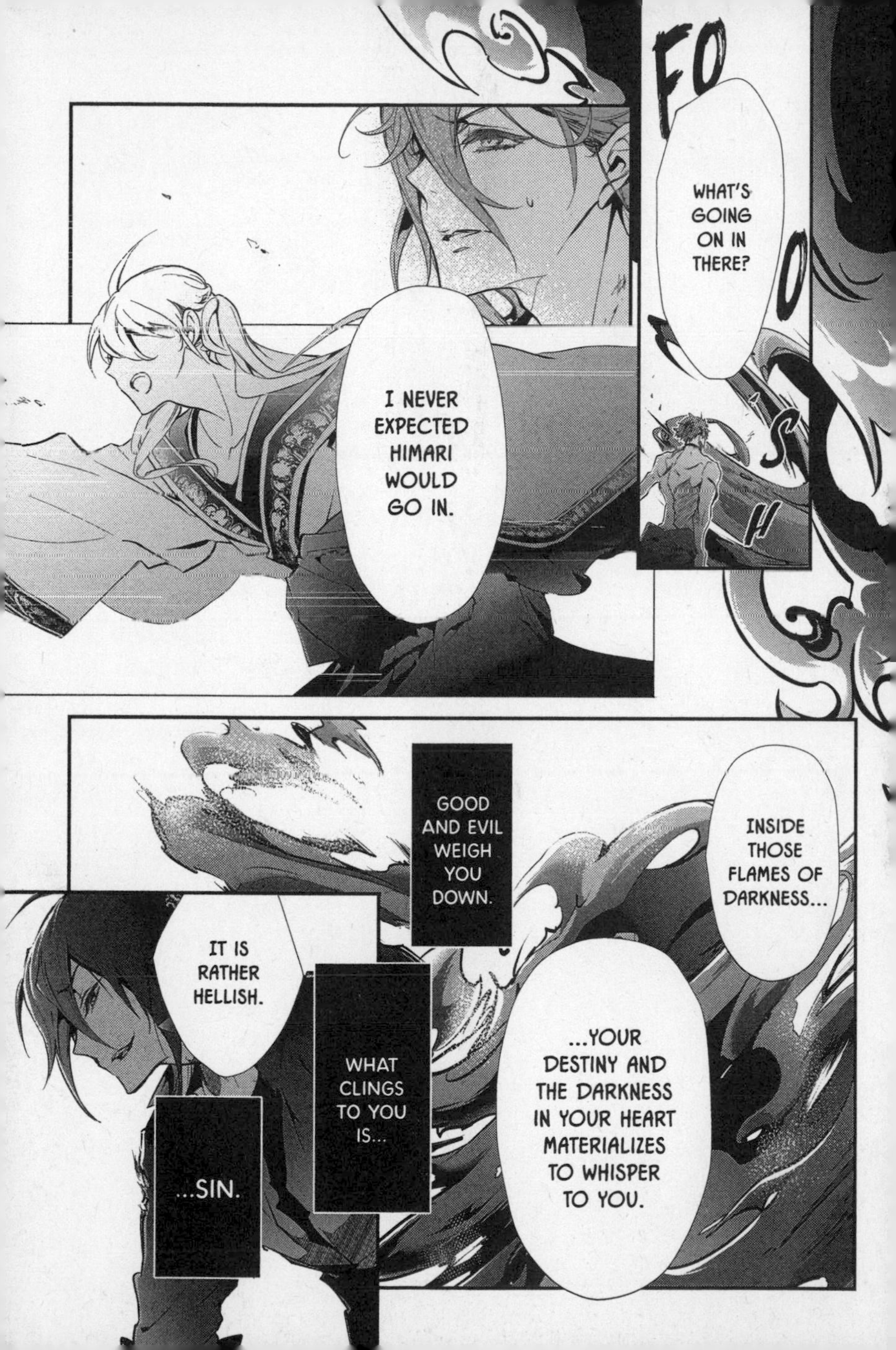
FOOSH
WHAT'S GOING ON IN THERE?
I NEVER EXPECTED HIMARI WOULD GO IN.
INSIDE THOSE FLAMES OF DARKNESS...
...YOUR DESTINY AND THE DARKNESS IN YOUR HEART MATERIALIZES TO WHISPER TO YOU.
GOOD AND EVIL WEIGH YOU DOWN.
IT IS RATHER HELLISH.
WHAT CLINGS TO YOU IS...
...SIN.

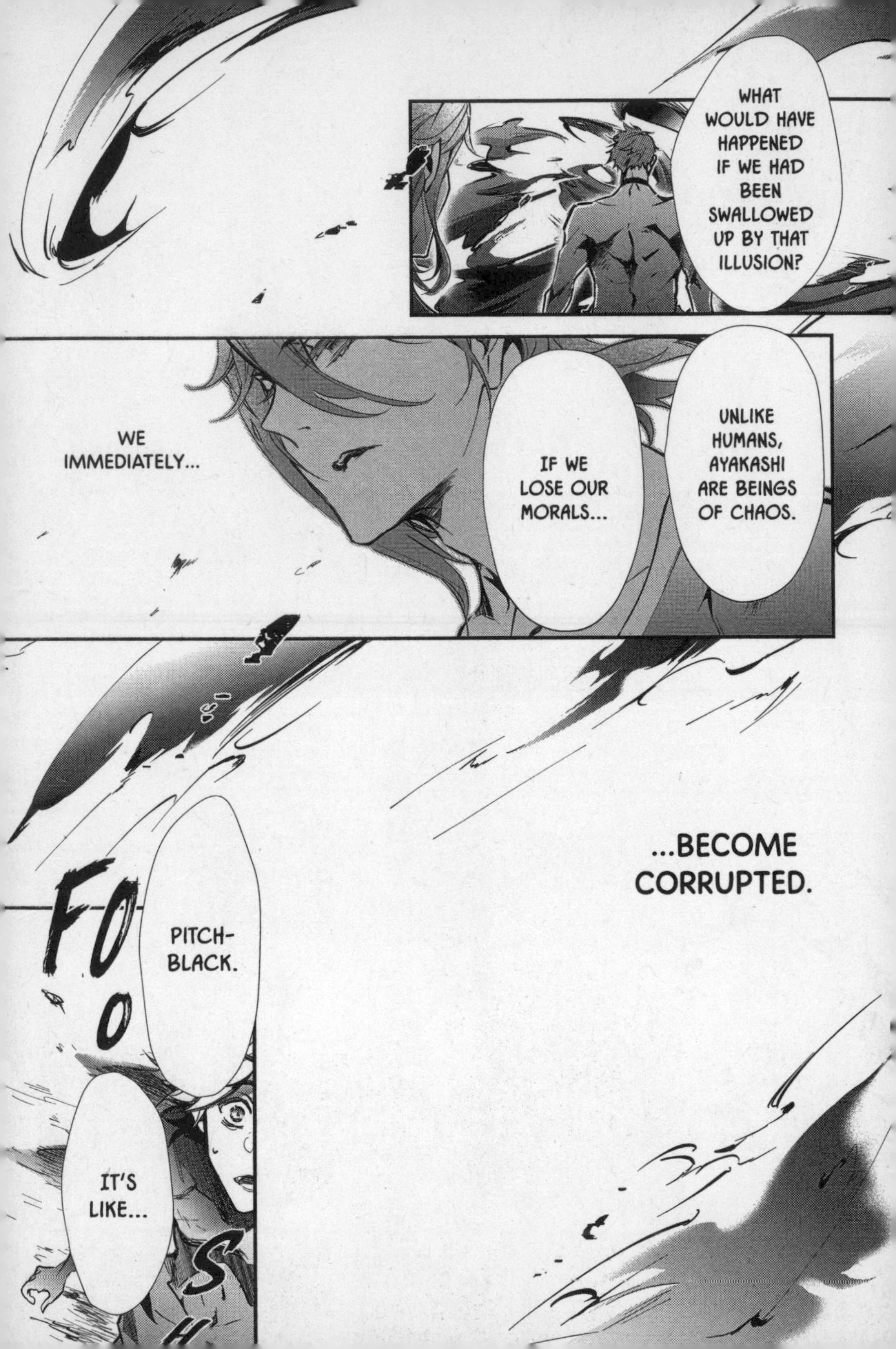
WHAT WOULD HAVE HAPPENED IF WE HAD BEEN SWALLOWED UP BY THAT ILLUSION?
UNLIKE HUMANS, AYAKASHI ARE BEINGS OF CHAOS.
IF WE LOSE OUR MORALS...
WE IMMEDIATELY...
...BECOME CORRUPTED.
FOOSH
PITCH-BLACK.
IT'S LIKE...

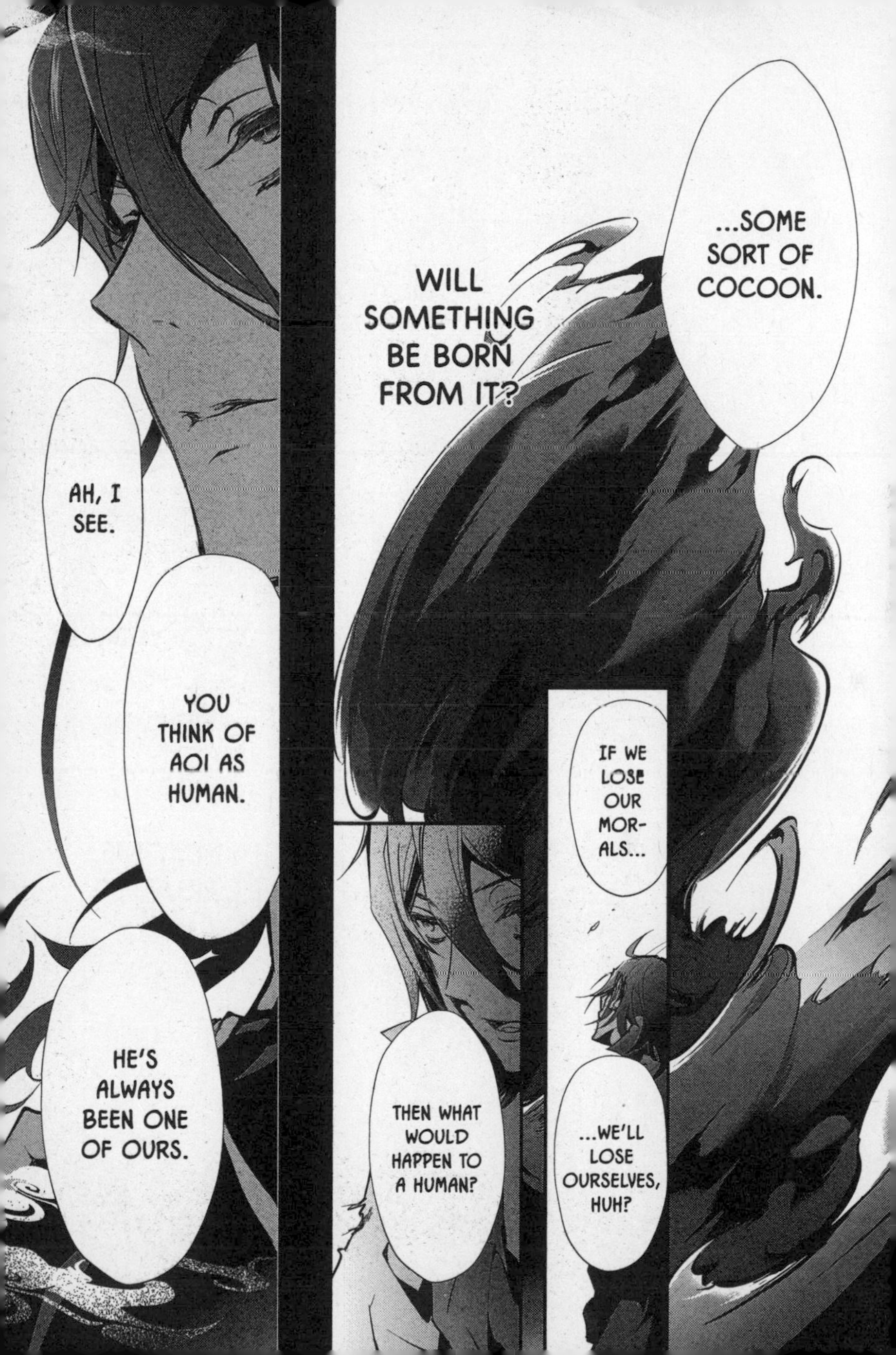

...SOME SORT OF COCOON.
WILL SOMETHING BE BORN FROM IT?
IF WE LOSE OUR MOR-ALS...
...WE'LL LOSE OURSELVES, HUH?
THEN WHAT WOULD HAPPEN TO A HUMAN?
AH, I SEE.
YOU THINK OF AOI AS HUMAN.
HE'S ALWAYS BEEN ONE OF OURS.

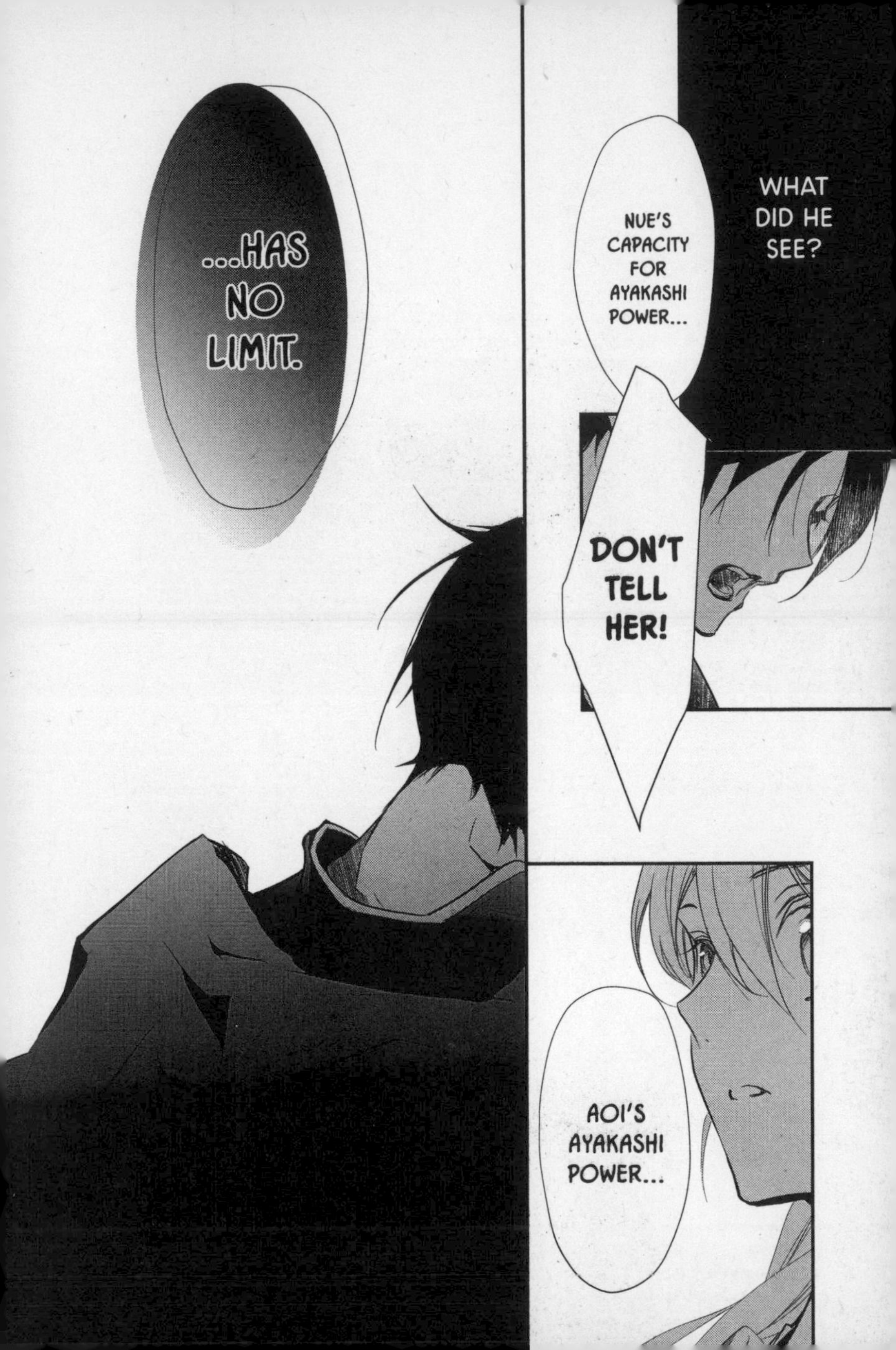
WHAT DID HE SEE?
NUE'S CAPACITY FOR AYAKASHI POWER...
DON'T TELL HER!
AOI'S AYAKASHI POWER...
...HAS NO LIMIT.

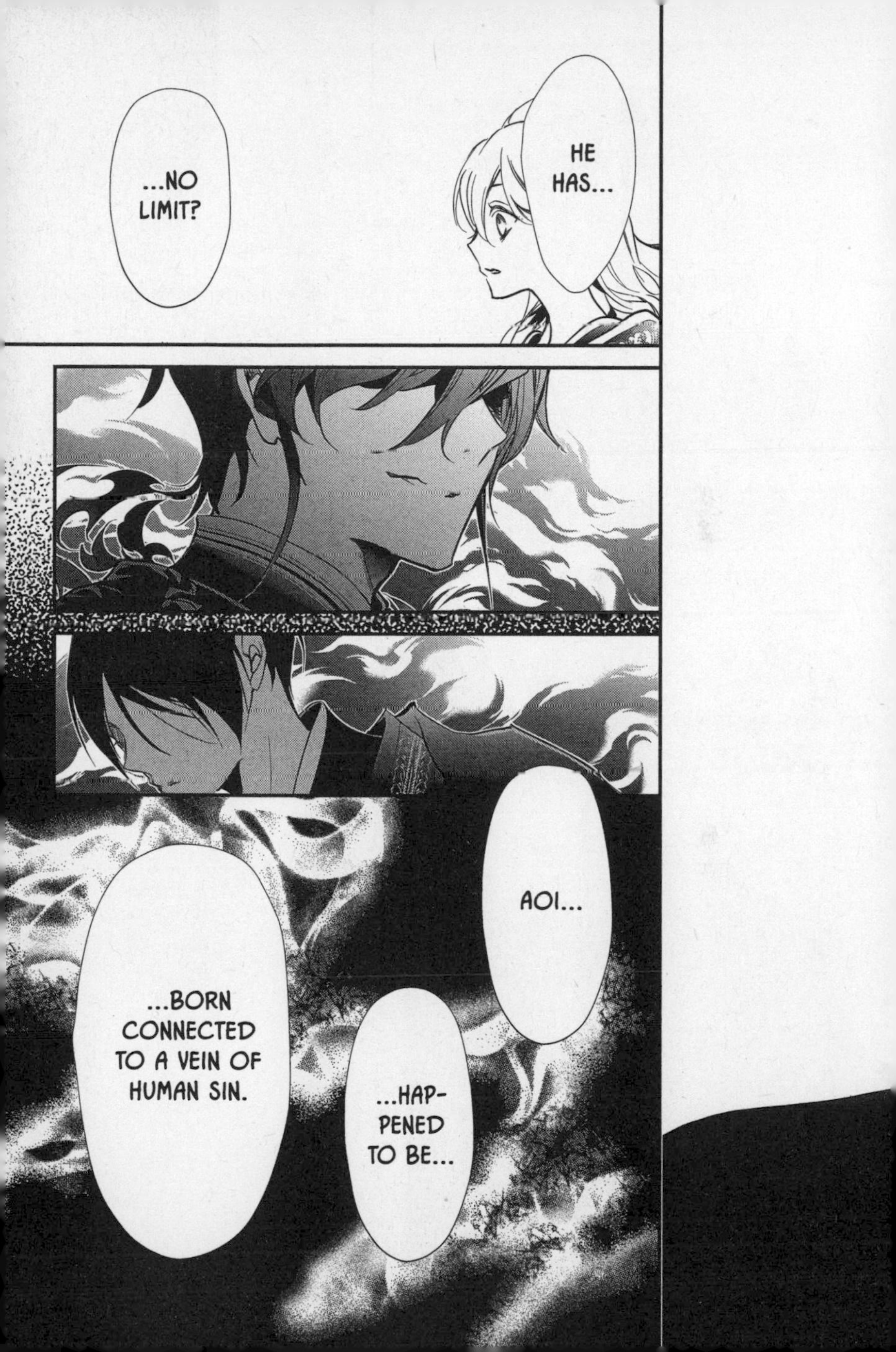
HE HAS...
...NO LIMIT?
AOI...
...HAP-PENED TO BE...
...BORN CONNECTED TO A VEIN OF HUMAN SIN.

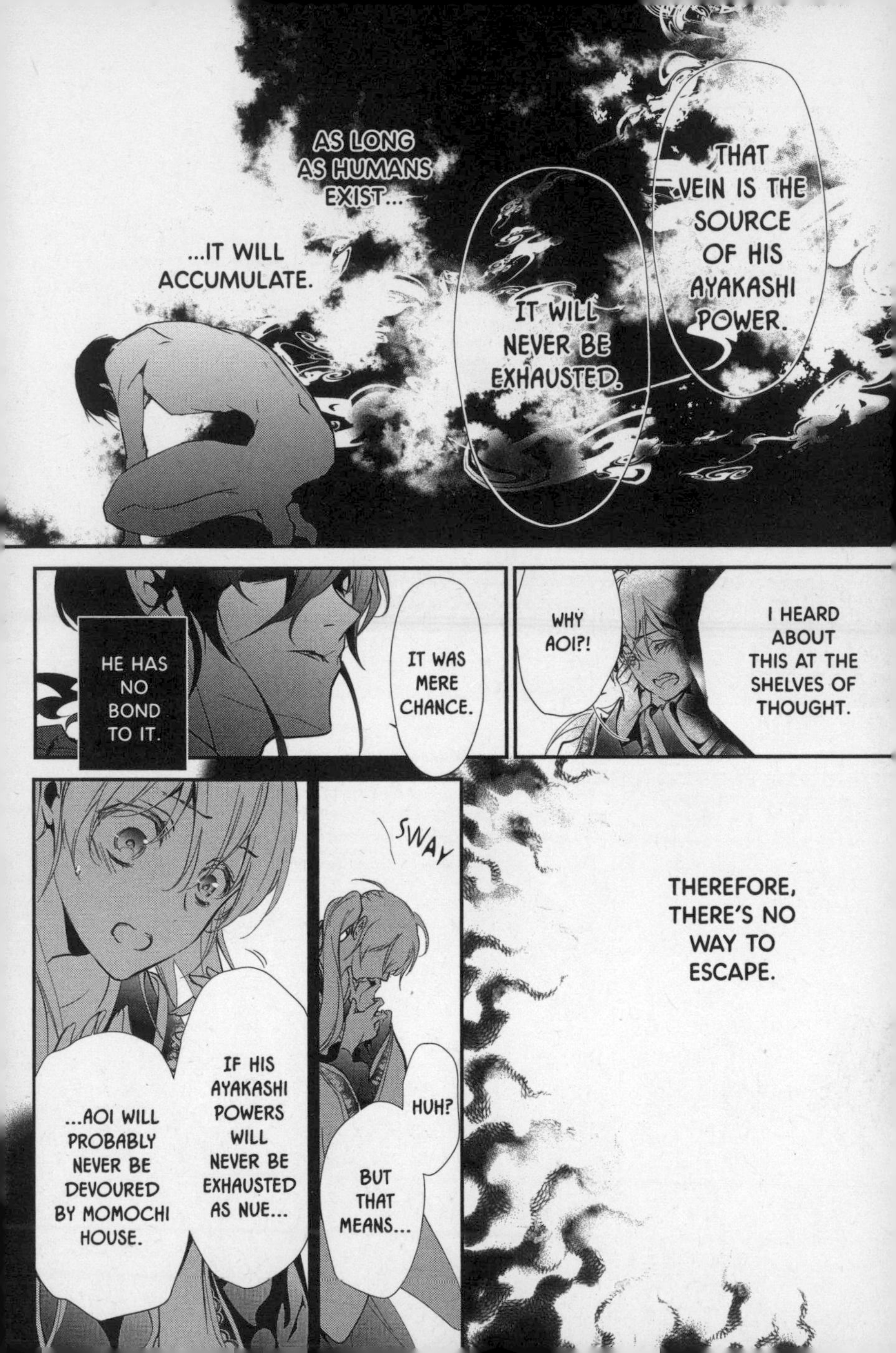
THAT VEIN IS THE SOURCE OF HIS AYAKASHI POWER.
IT WILL NEVER BE EXHAUSTED.
AS LONG AS HUMANS EXIST...
...IT WILL ACCUMULATE.
I HEARD ABOUT THIS AT THE SHELVES OF THOUGHT.
WHY AOI?!
IT WAS MERE CHANCE.
HE HAS NO BOND TO IT.
THEREFORE, THERE'S NO WAY TO ESCAPE.
SWAY
HUH?
BUT THAT MEANS...
IF HIS AYAKASHI POWERS WILL NEVER BE EXHAUSTED AS NUE...
...AOI WILL PROBABLY NEVER BE DEVOURED BY MOMOCHI HOUSE.

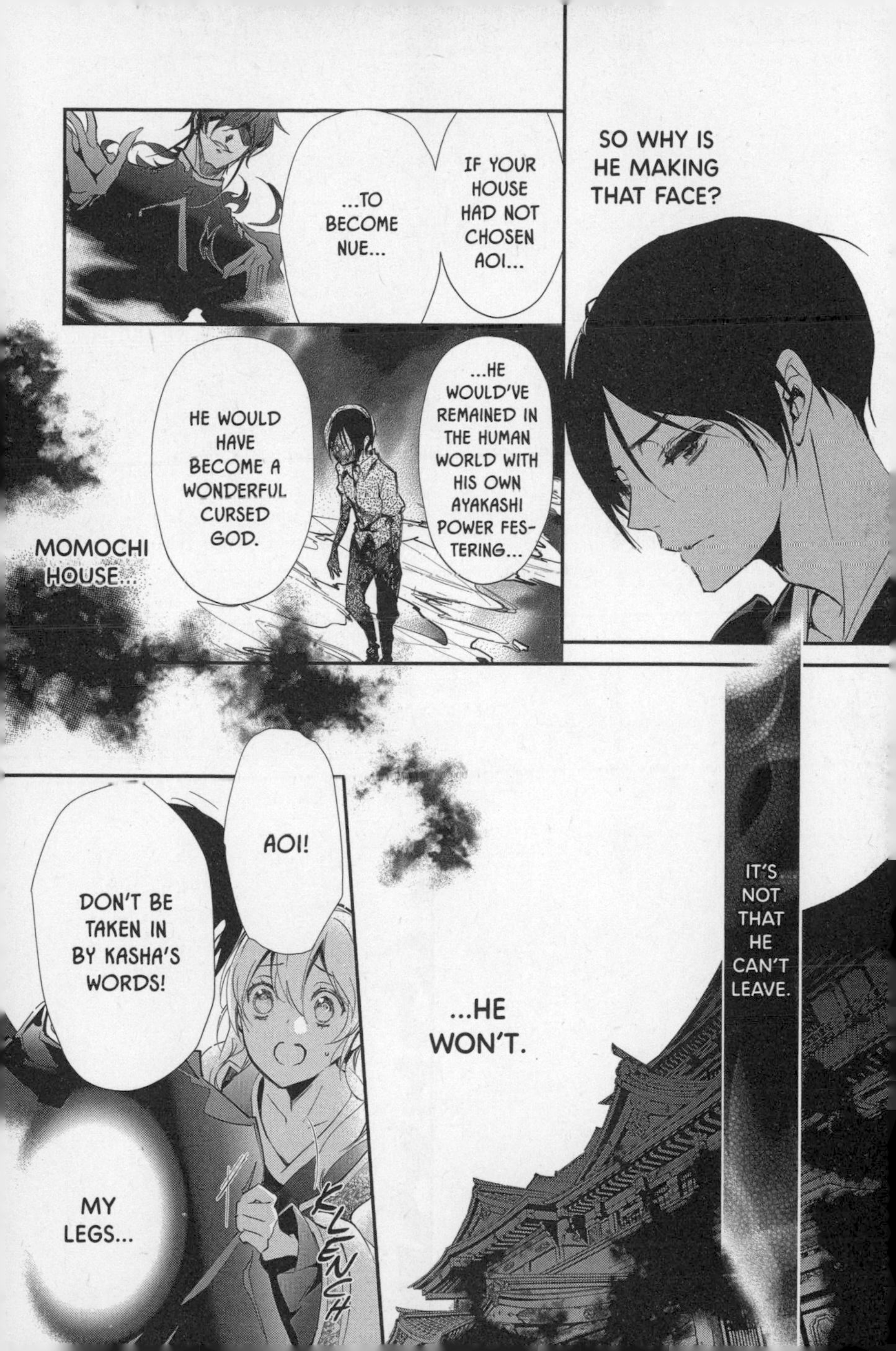
SO WHY IS HE MAKING THAT FACE?
IF YOUR HOUSE HAD NOT CHOSEN AOI...
...TO BECOME NUE...
...HE WOULD'VE REMAINED IN THE HUMAN WORLD WITH HIS OWN AYAKASHI POWER FES-TERING...
HE WOULD HAVE BECOME A WONDERFUL CURSED GOD.
MOMOCHI HOUSE...
IT'S NOT THAT HE CAN'T LEAVE.
...HE WON'T.
AOI!
DON'T BE TAKEN IN BY KASHA'S WORDS!
KLENCH
MY LEGS...

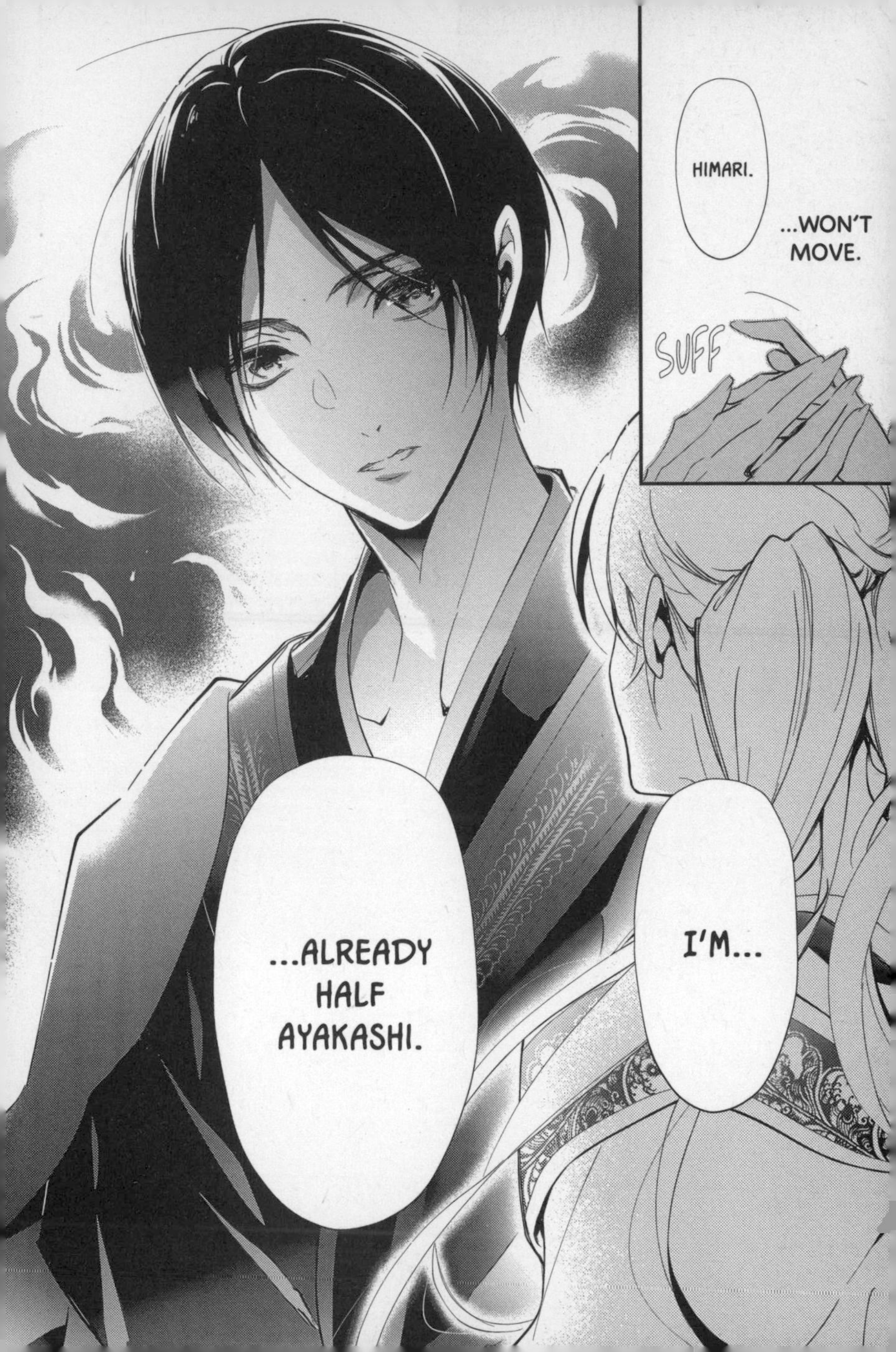
HIMARI.
...WON'T MOVE.
SUFF
I'M...
...ALREADY HALF AYAKASHI.

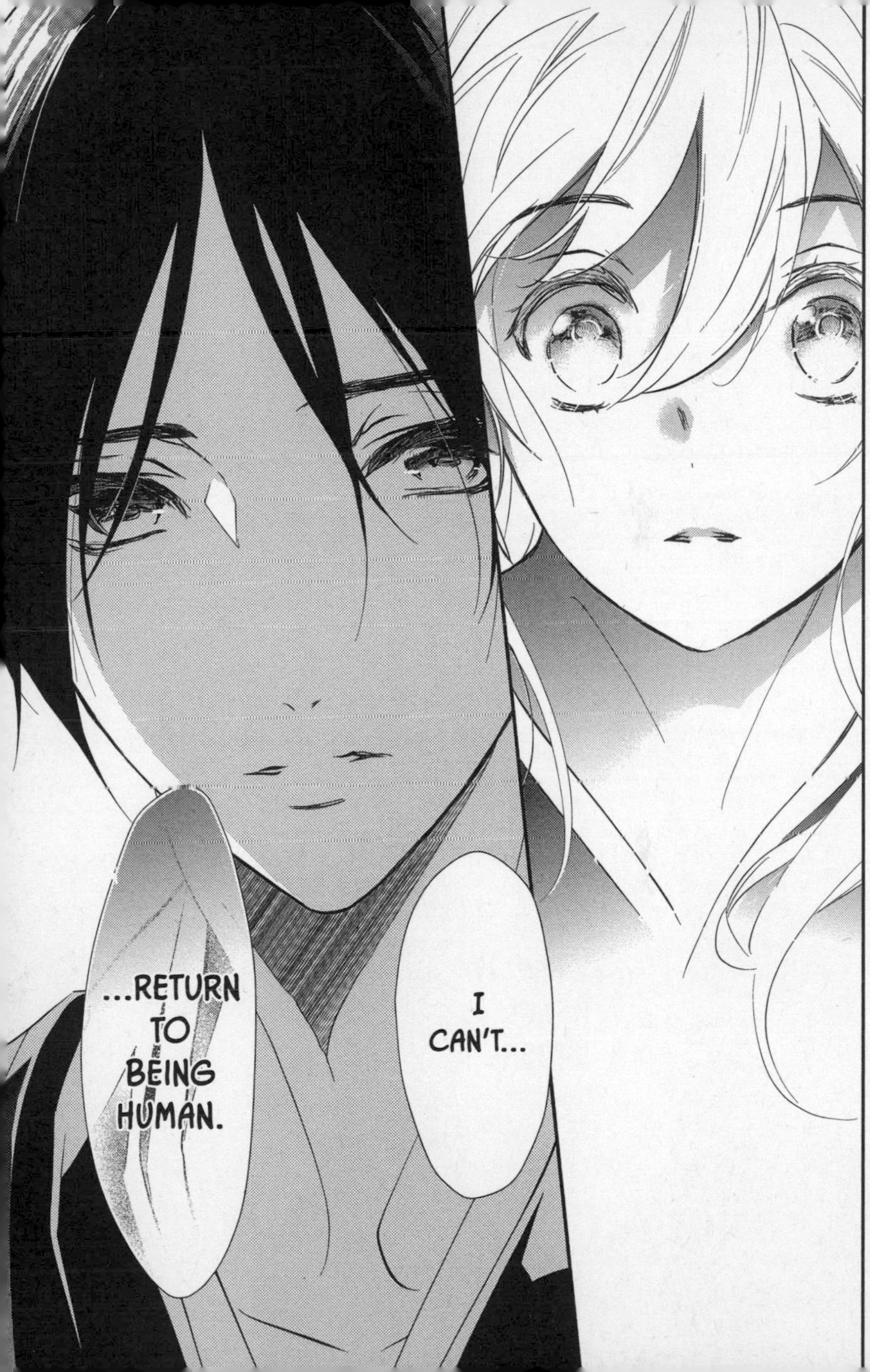
I CAN'T...
...RETURN TO BEING HUMAN.

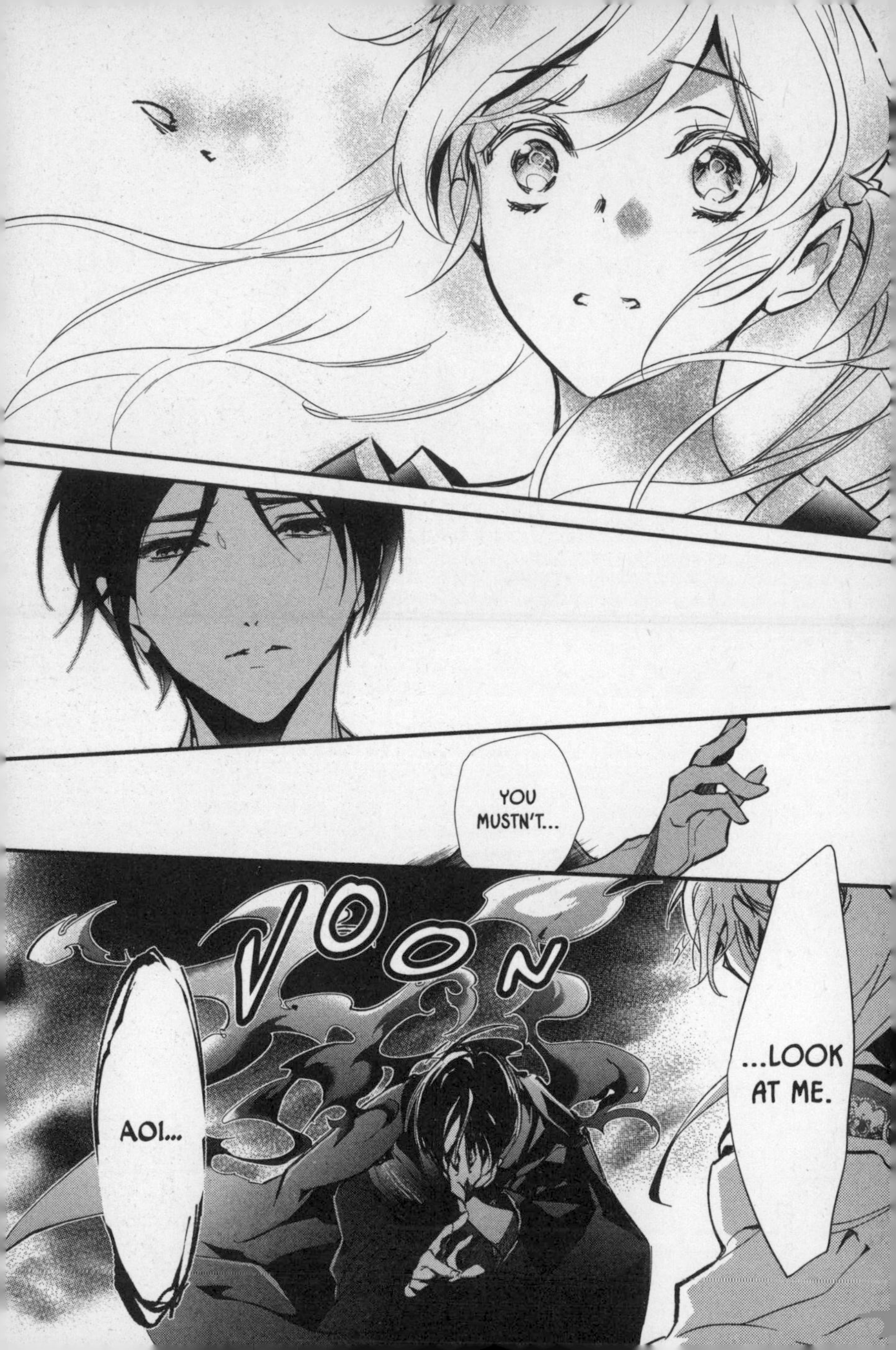
YOU MUSTN'T...
...LOOK AT ME.
VOOON
AOI...

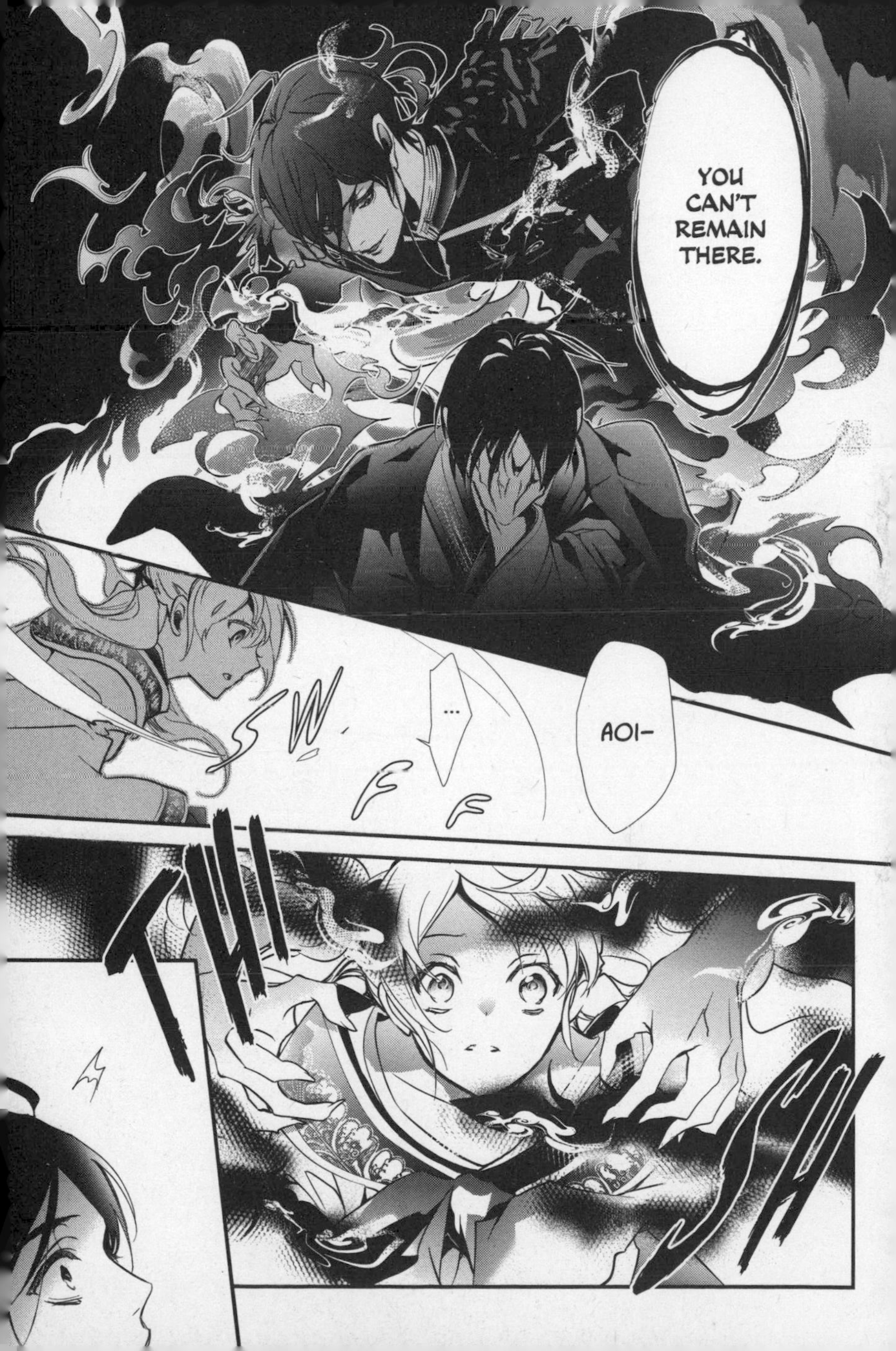
YOU CAN'T REMAIN THERE.
AOI-
...

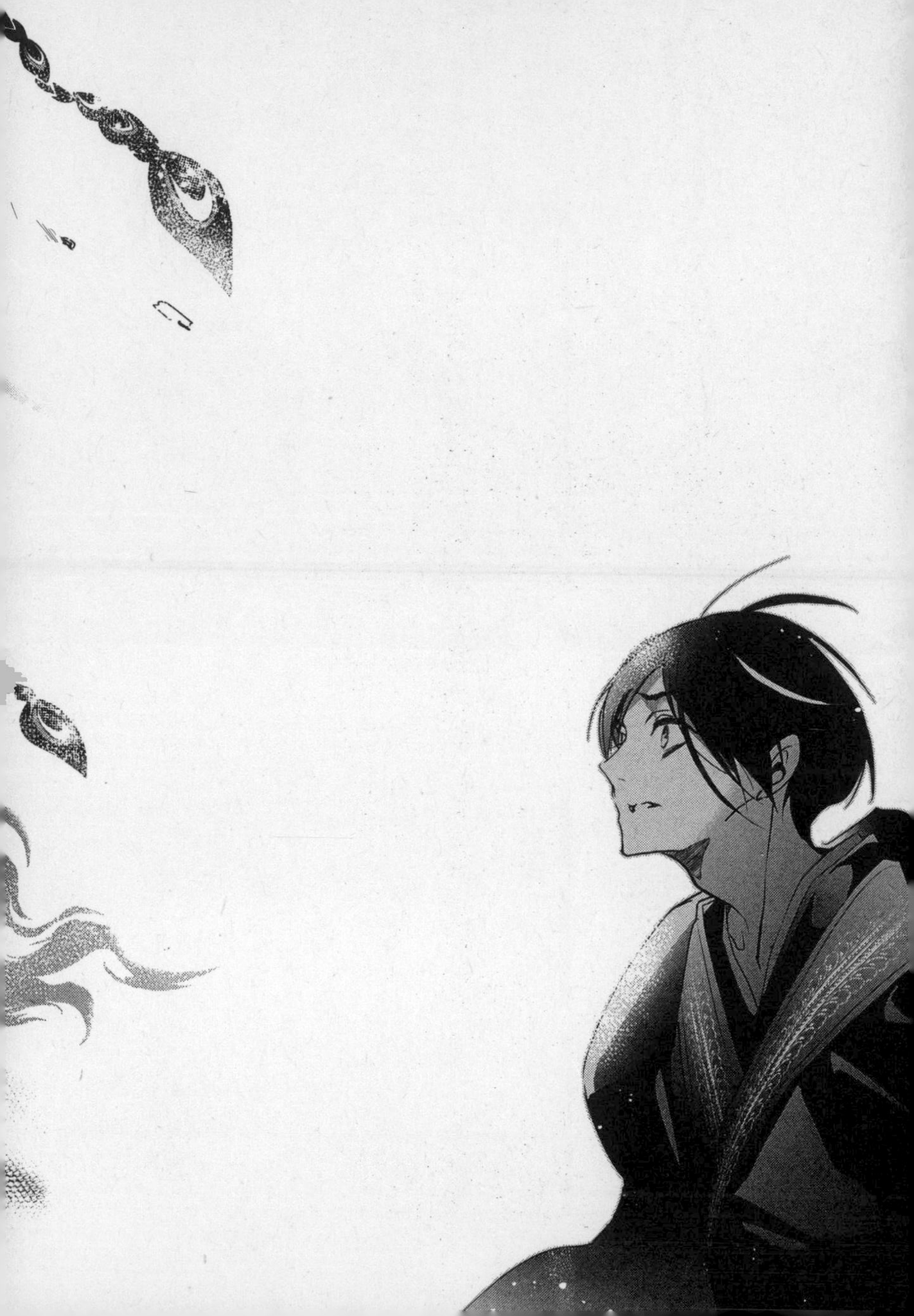

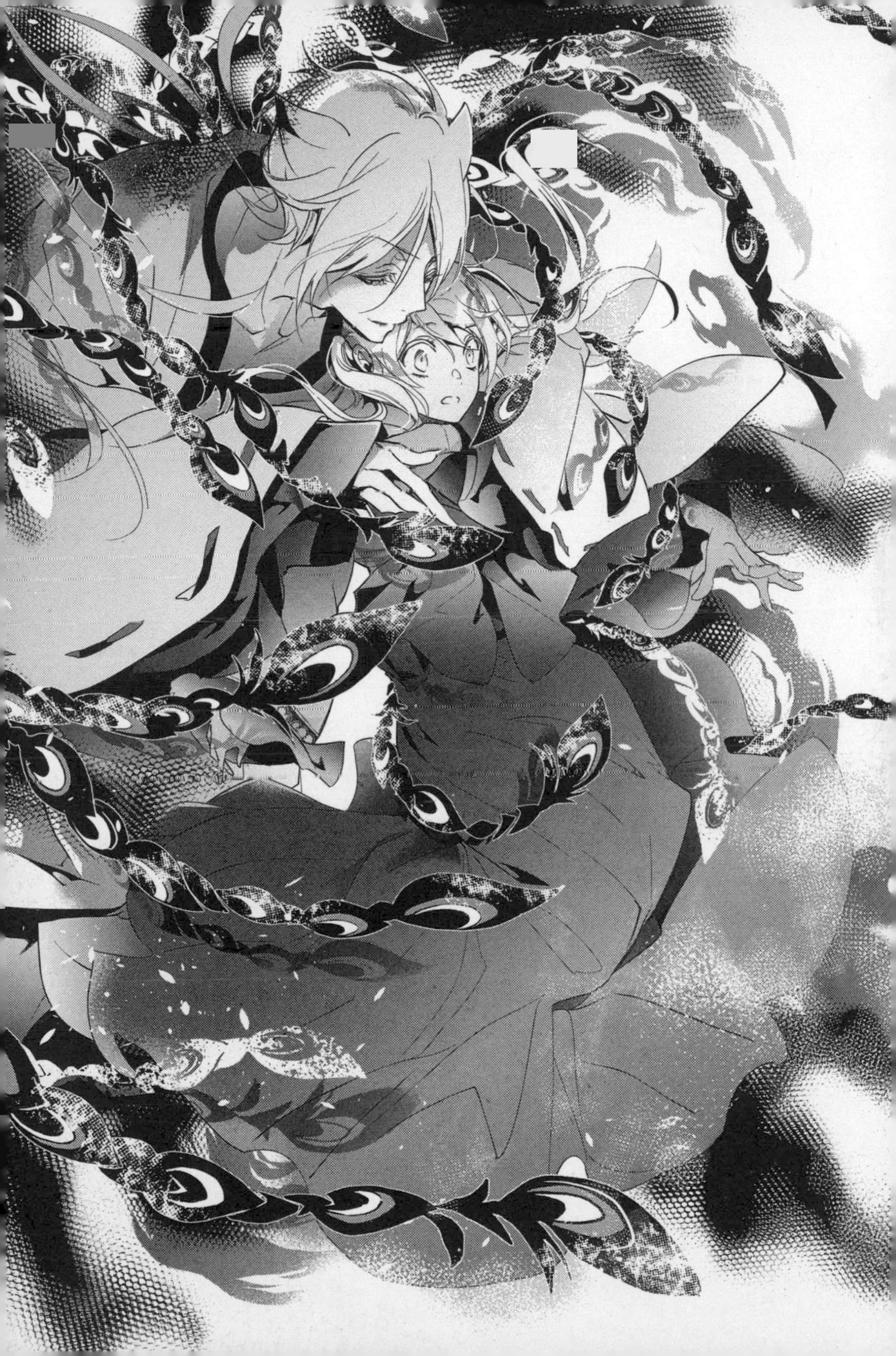

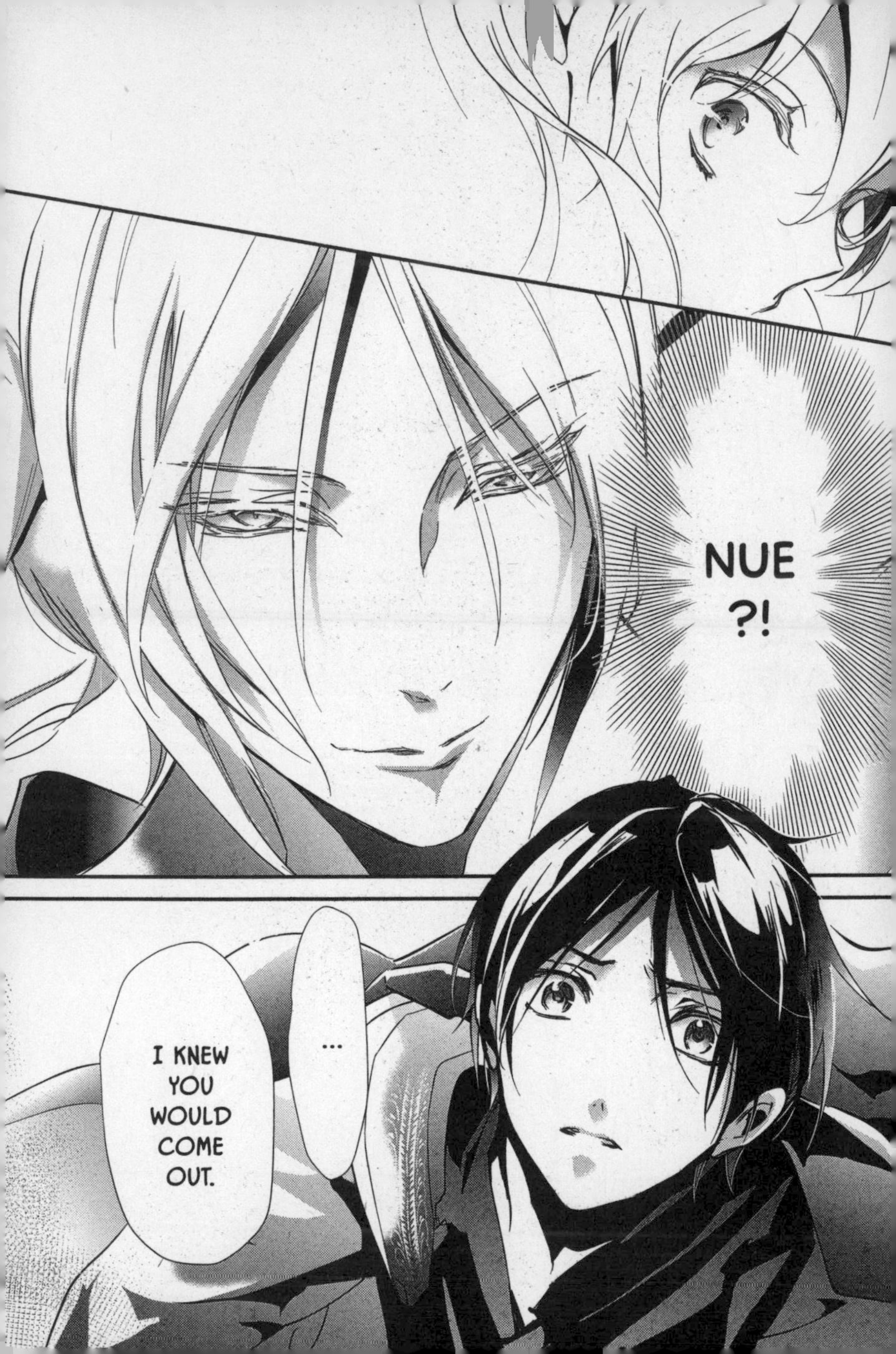
NUE ?!
...
I KNEW YOU WOULD COME OUT.

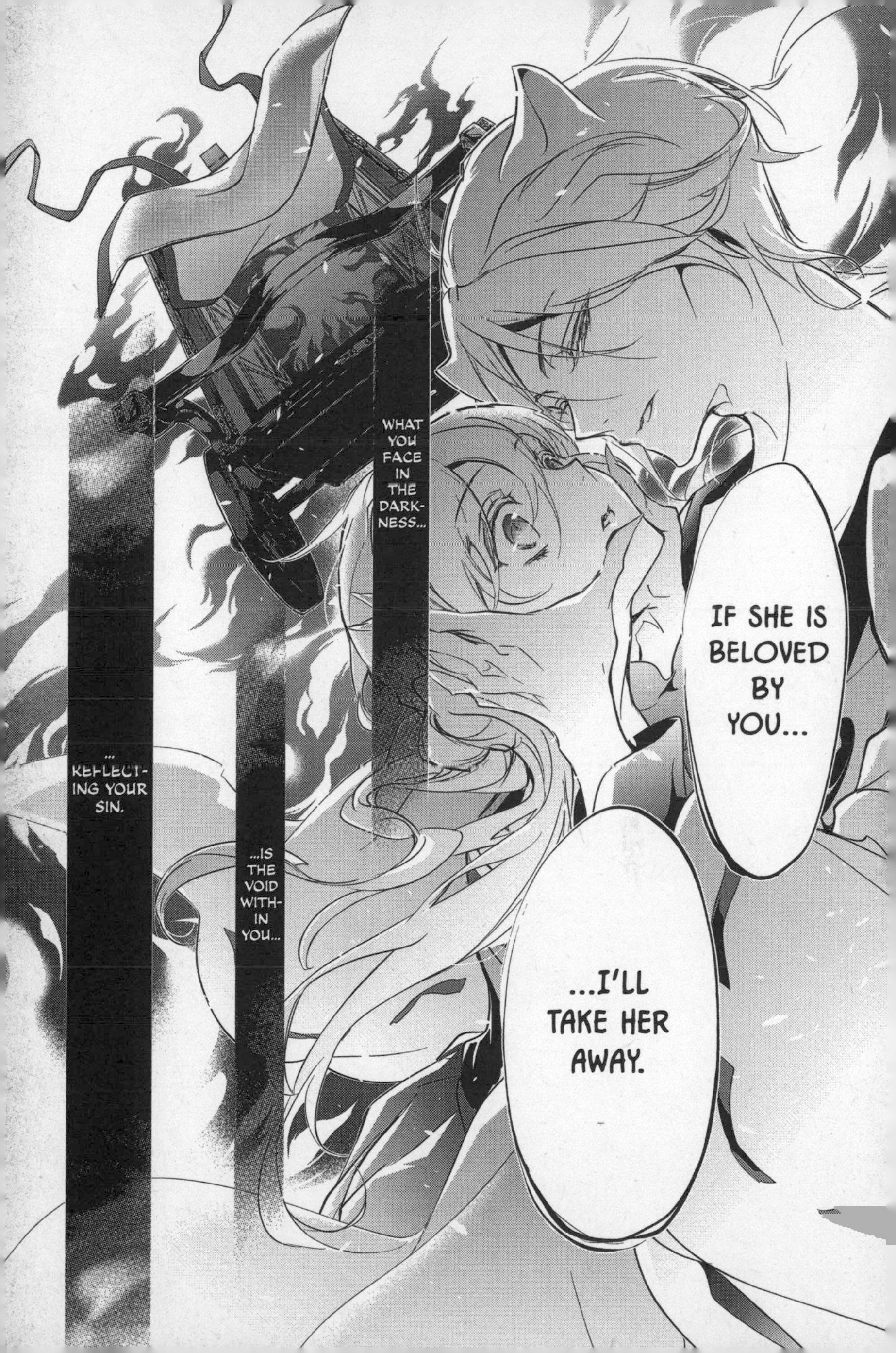
IF SHE IS BELOVED BY YOU...
...I'LL TAKE HER AWAY.
WHAT YOU FACE IN THE DARK-NESS...
...IS THE VOID WITH-IN YOU...
...REFLECT-ING YOUR SIN.

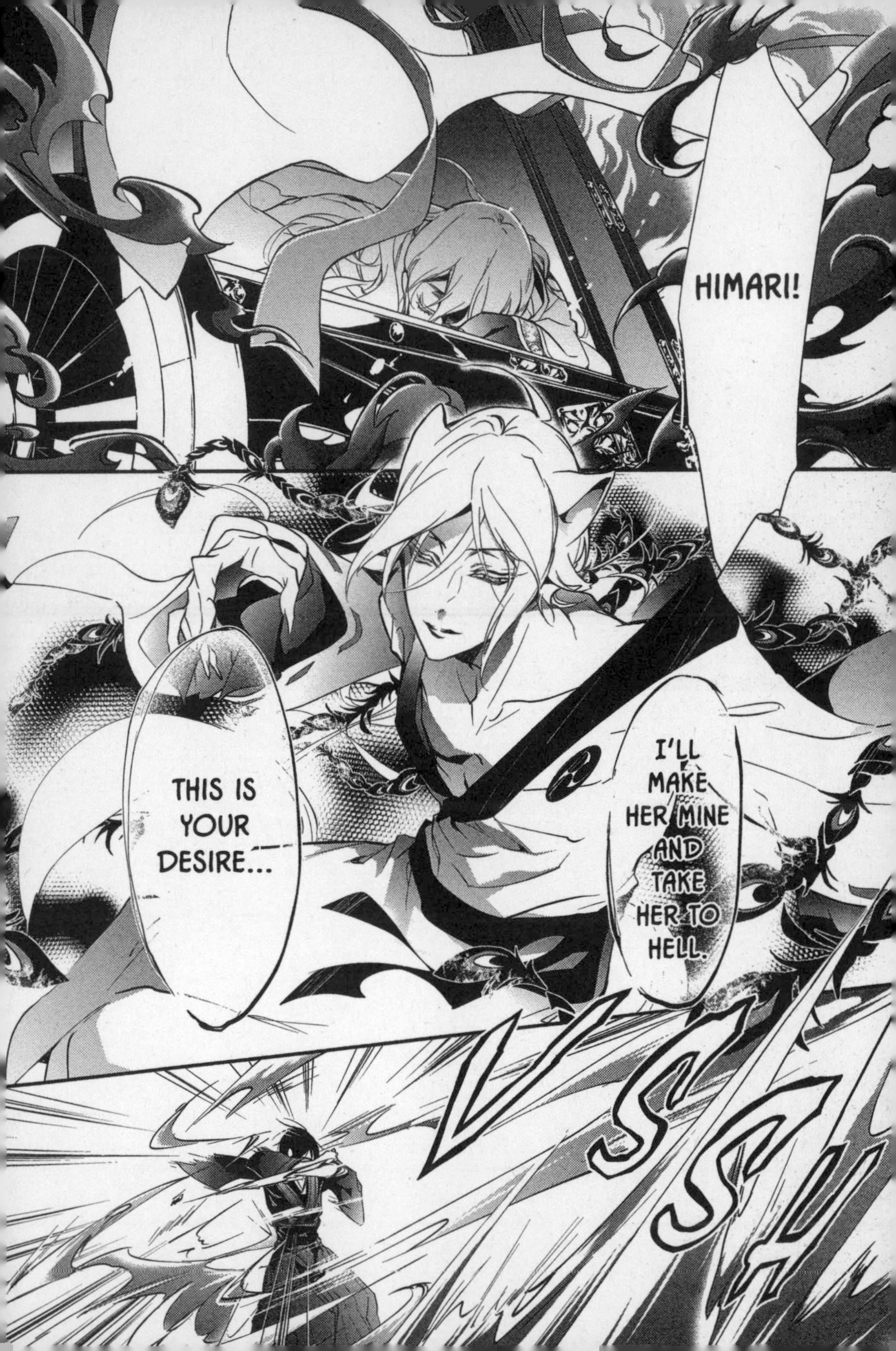
HIMARI!
I'LL MAKE HER MINE AND TAKE HER TO HELL.
THIS IS YOUR DESIRE...
VSSH

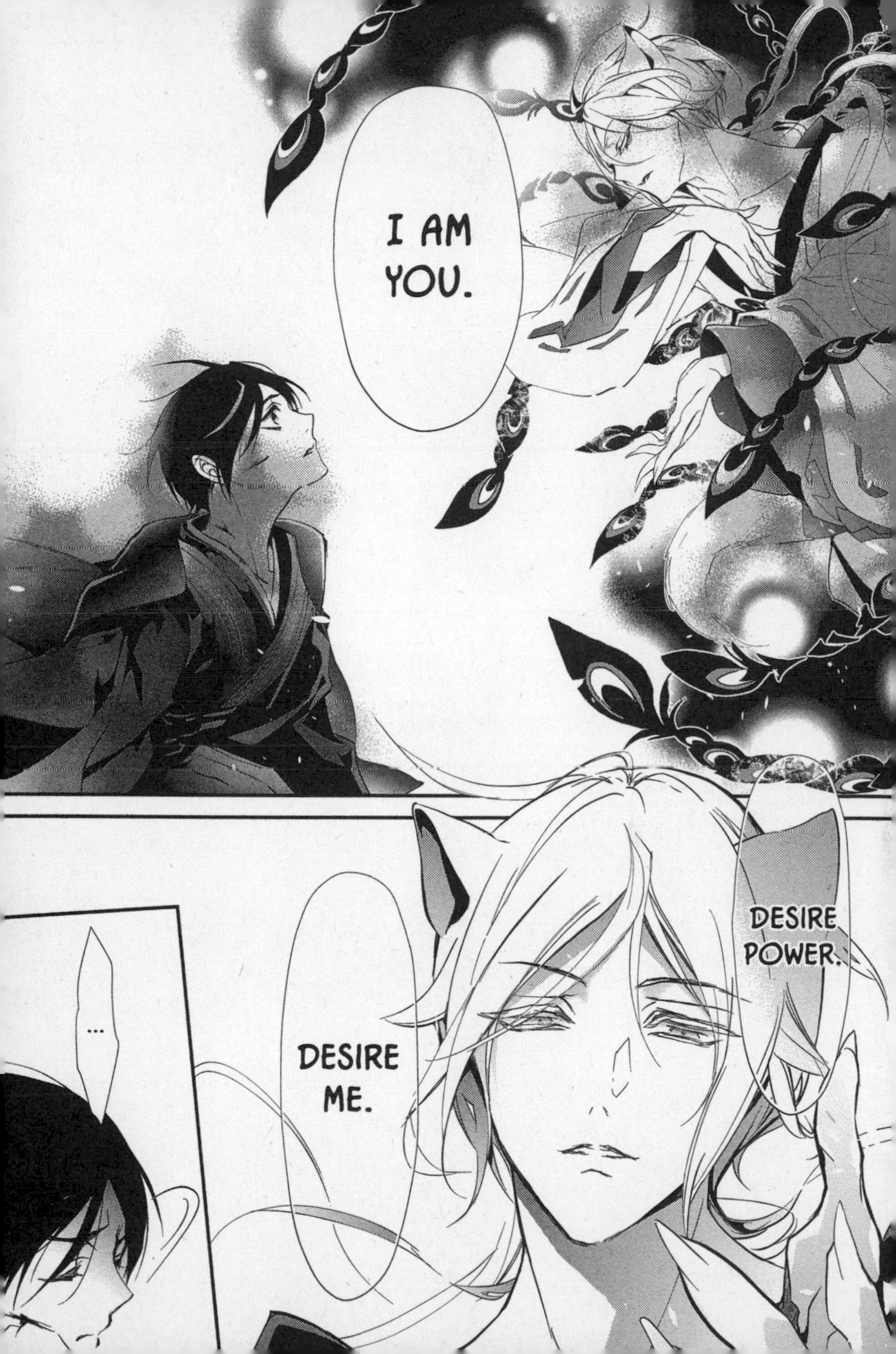
I AM YOU.
DESIRE POWER.
DESIRE ME.
...

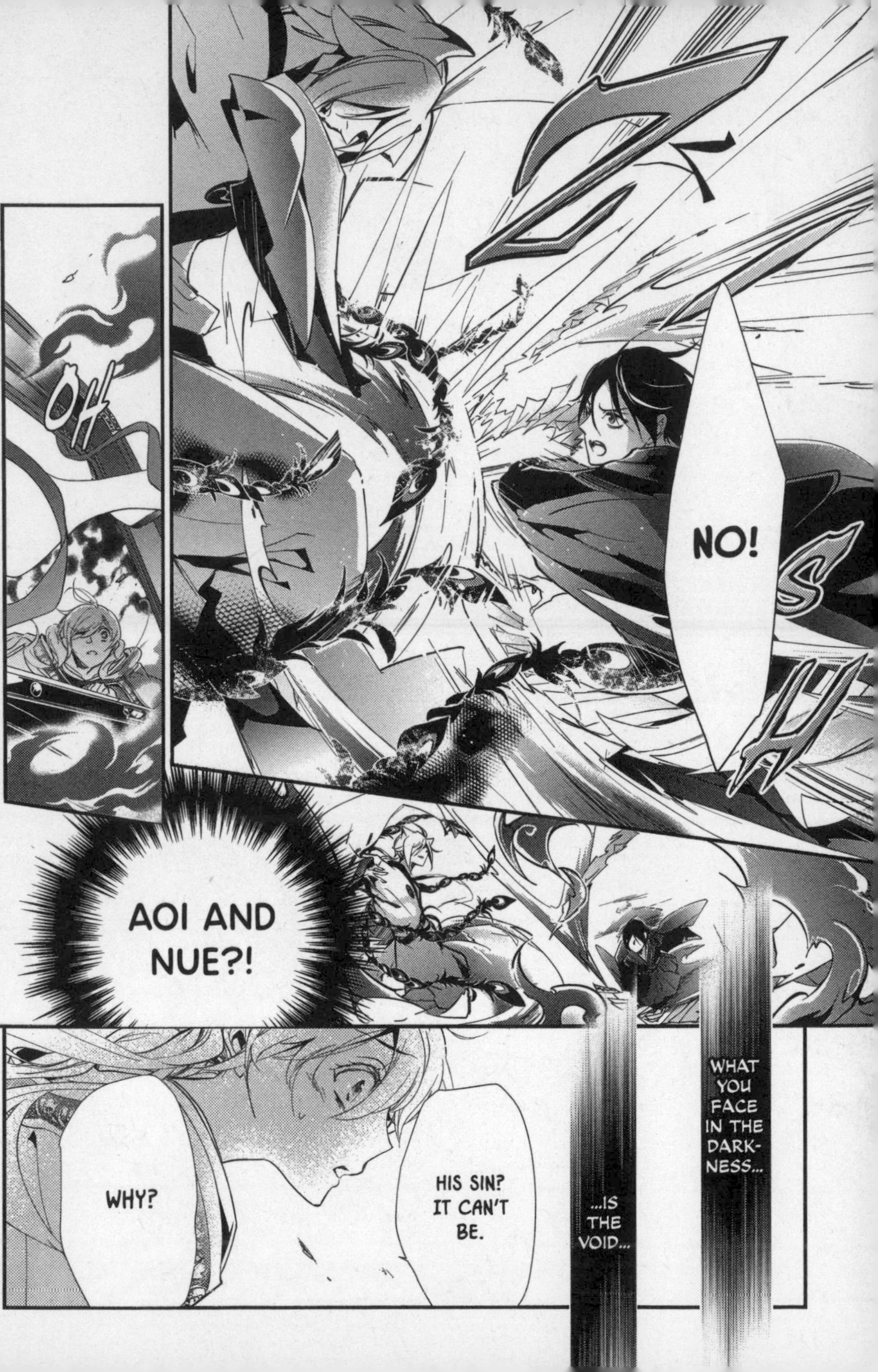
NO!
OH
WHAT YOU FACE IN THE DARKNESS...
...IS THE VOID...
AOI AND NUE?!
HIS SIN? IT CAN'T BE.
WHY?

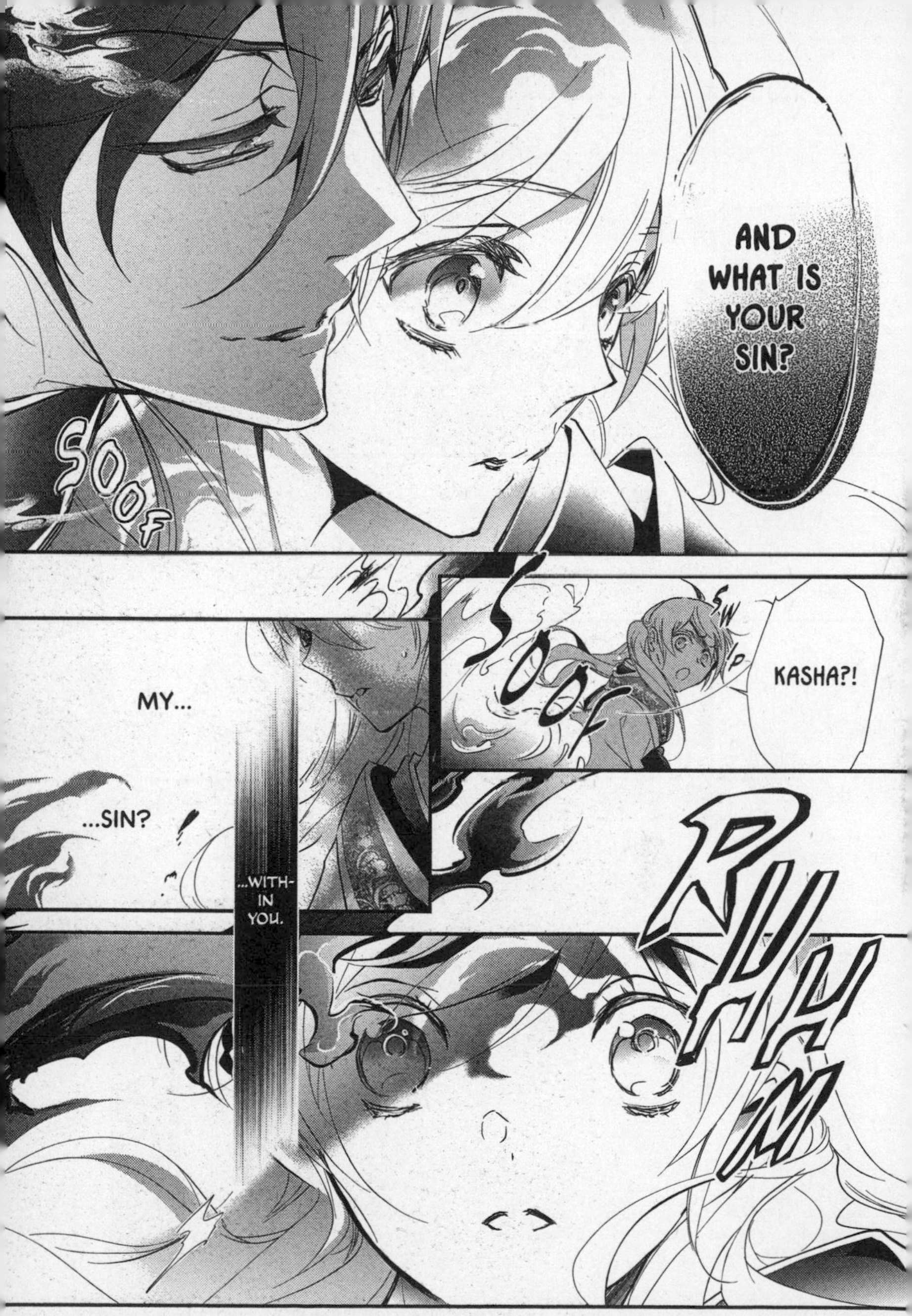
AND WHAT IS YOUR SIN?
SOOF
SWIP
KASHA?!
SOOF
MY...
...SIN?
...WITH-IN YOU.
RUHHM

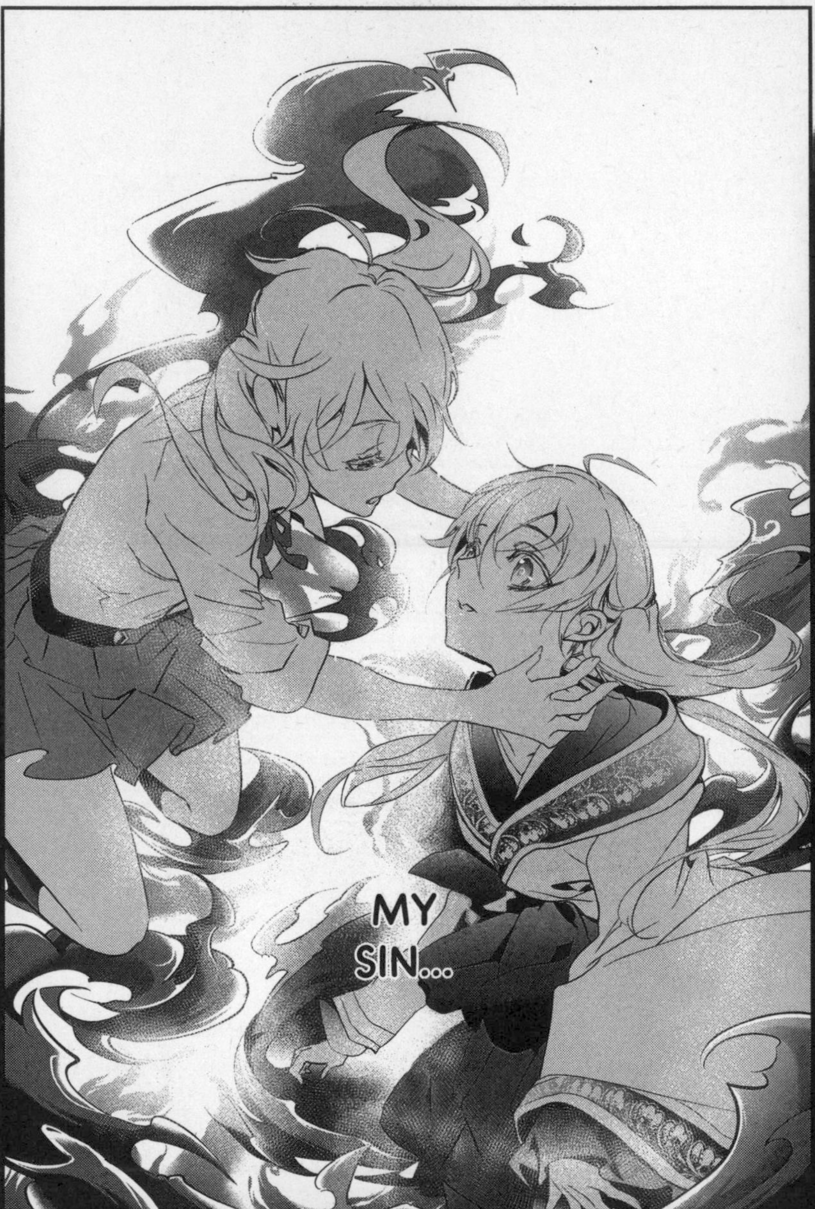
MY SIN...

Chapter 56/End

The
DEMON
PRINCE
of MOMOCHI
HOUSE

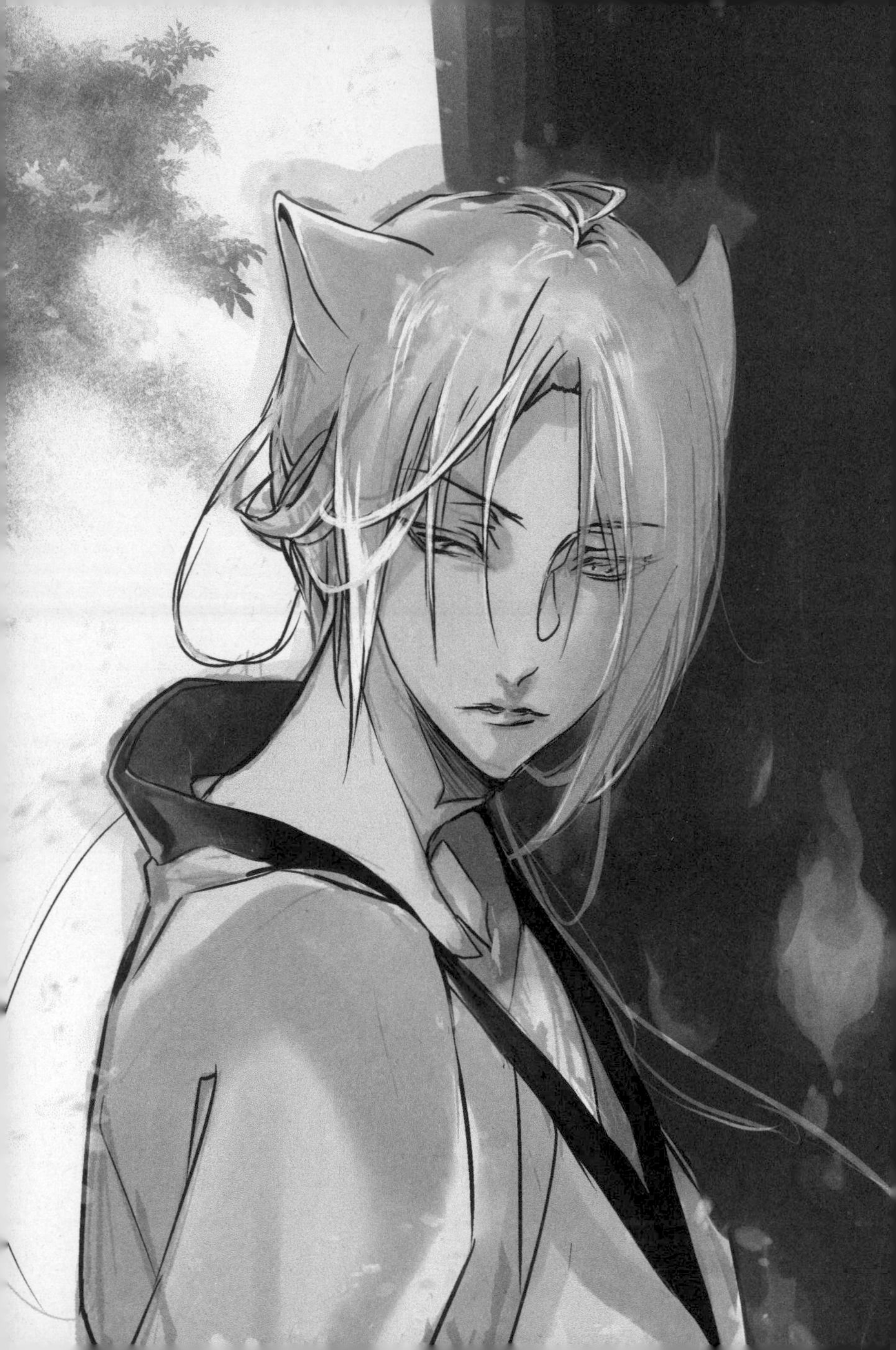

Thank you very much for sticking with
me through volume 14. In the next
book, we will be entering the final arc
of *The Demon Prince of Momochi
House.* I hope you'll read this story until
the end. It will take place in summer.

Aya Shouoto xxx

Aya Shouoto

We've reached volume 14.
Just the other day I determined
that Aoi Nanamori's birthday
is May 9. I chose it because the
birth flower for that day is
the Chinese clematis.

-Aya Shouoto

Aya Shouoto was born on December 25.
Her hobbies are traveling, staying at hotels,
sewing and daydreaming. She currently
lives in Tokyo and enjoys listening to J-pop
anime theme songs while she works.

The Demon Prince of Momochi House

Volume 14
Shojo Beat Edition

Story and Art by **Aya Shouoto**

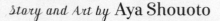

Translation JN Productions
Touch-Up Art & Lettering Inori Fukuda Trant
Design J. Shikuma
Editor Nancy Thistlethwaite

MOMOCHISANCHI NO AYAKASHI OUJI Volume 14
© Aya SHOUOTO 2018
First published in Japan in 2018 by KADOKAWA CORPORATION, Tokyo.
English translation rights arranged with KADOKAWA CORPORATION, Tokyo.

The stories, characters and incidents mentioned
in this publication are entirely fictional.

No portion of this book may be reproduced or transmitted in any form or
by any means without written permission from the copyright holders.

Printed in the U.S.A.

Published by VIZ Media, LLC
P.O. Box 77010
San Francisco, CA 94107

10 9 8 7 6 5 4 3 2 1
First printing, September 2019

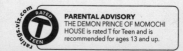

PARENTAL ADVISORY
THE DEMON PRINCE OF MOMOCHI
HOUSE is rated T for Teen and is
recommended for ages 13 and up.

viz.com

shojobeat.com

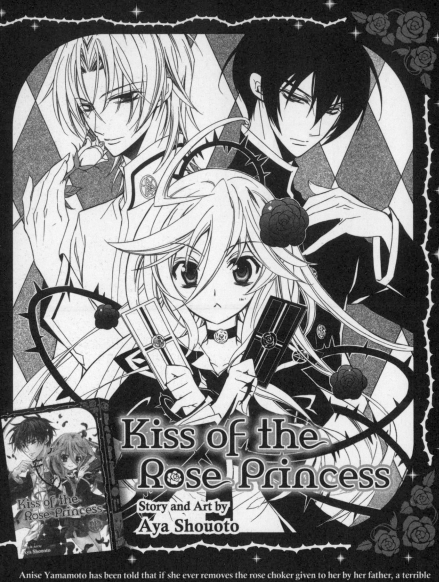

Kiss of the Rose Princess

Story and Art by Aya Shouoto

Anise Yamamoto has been told that if she ever removes the rose choker given to her by her father, a terrible punishment will befall her. Unfortunately she loses that choker when a bat-like being named Ninufa falls from the sky and hits her. Ninufa gives Anise four cards representing four knights whom she can summon with a kiss. But now that she has these gorgeous men at her beck and call, what exactly is her quest?!

KISS OF ROSE PRINCESS Volume 1 ©Aya SHOUOTO 2009

"**Bloody**" **Mary**, a vampire with a death wish, has spent the past 400 years chasing down a modern-day exorcist named Maria who is thought to have inherited "The Blood of Maria" and is the only one who can kill Mary. To Mary's dismay, Maria doesn't know how to kill vampires. Desperate to die, Mary agrees to become Maria's bodyguard until Maria can find a way to kill him.

Bloody✝Mary

Story and Art by

akaza samamiya

VIZ MEDIA

Shojo Beat

www.viz.com

BLOODY MARY Volume 1 © Akaza SAMAMIYA 2014

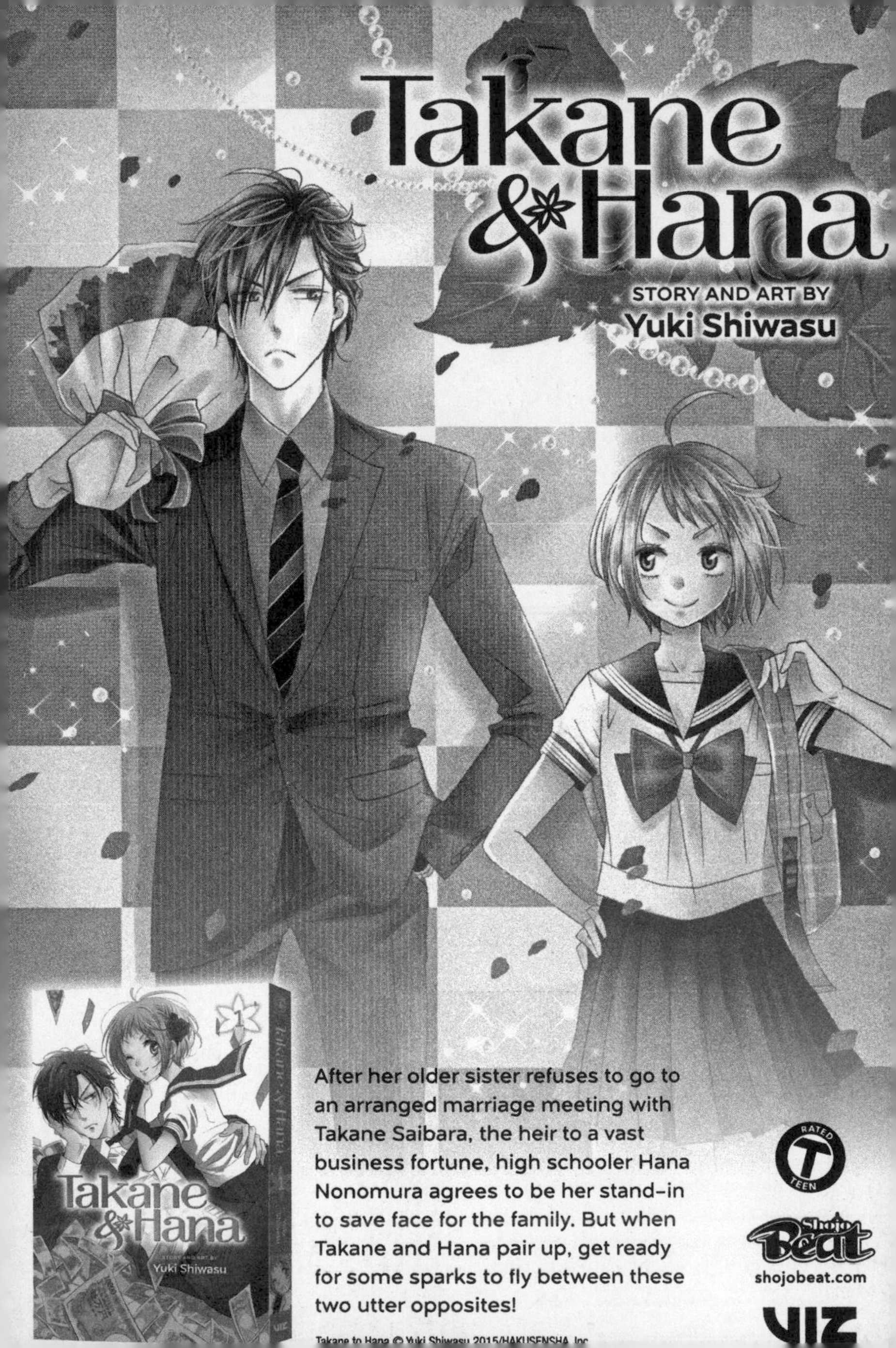
Takane & Hana
STORY AND ART BY
Yuki Shiwasu
Takane & Hana
STORY AND ART BY
Yuki Shiwasu
After her older sister refuses to go to an arranged marriage meeting with Takane Saibara, the heir to a vast business fortune, high schooler Hana Nonomura agrees to be her stand-in to save face for the family. But when Takane and Hana pair up, get ready for some sparks to fly between these two utter opposites!
RATED T TEEN
Shojo Beat
shojobeat.com
VIZ
Takane to Hana © Yuki Shiwasu 2015/HAKUSENSHA, Inc.

THE INSPIRATION FOR THE ANIME

yona
of the
Dawn

Story & Art by
Mizuho Kusanagi

*Princess Yona lives an ideal life as
the only princess of her kingdom.*
Doted on by her father, the king, and
protected by her faithful guard Hak,
she cherishes the time spent with the
man she loves, Su-won. But everything
changes on her 16th birthday when
tragedy strikes her family!

shojo
Beat
shojobeat.com

viz media
viz.com

RATED
T
FOR
TEEN

Akatsuki no Yona © Mizuho Kusanagi 2010/ HAKUSENSHA, Inc.

Queen's Quality

Story & Art by
Kyousuke Motomi

Fumi Nishioka lives with Kyutaro Horikita and his family of "Sweepers," people who specialize in cleaning the minds of those overcome by negative energy and harmful spirits. Fumi has always displayed mysterious abilities, but will those powers be used for evil when she begins to truly awaken as a Queen?

Shojo Beat
shojobeat.com

viz media
viz.com

RATED
T
FOR TEEN